International and Comparative Law in the Asia Pacific

International and Comparative Law in the Asia Pacific is an ambitious and timely series dedicated to exploring the dynamic and multifaceted landscape of legal systems across the Asia Pacific. The series aims to provide a comprehensive and scholarly examination of the legal traditions, contemporary practices, challenges, and law reforms in jurisdictions across the Asia Pacific, offering valuable insights into their convergence and divergence within the broader context of international and comparative law. This series will also delve into specific areas of law, offering in-depth analyses and comparative perspectives that highlight the unique legal landscapes of individual countries while also identifying common trends and regional patterns.

The primary objectives of this series are multifaceted and aim to:

1. Bridge the Gap Between International and Domestic Law: Enhance understanding and foster dialogue among legal scholars, practitioners, and policymakers by exploring the interaction between international law and the diverse legal systems of the Asia Pacific.
2. Advance Comparative Legal Research: Develop the field of comparative law by conducting in-depth analyses that highlight the similarities and differences among legal systems in the Asia Pacific. This will provide a foundation for understanding how various countries address similar legal issues.
3. Promote Harmonisation of Laws: Facilitate the harmonisation of laws across the Asia Pacific by identifying common legal principles and encouraging the adoption of best practices. This objective aims to support regional integration and cooperation.
4. Examine Dispute Resolution and Propose Law Reforms: Assess various dispute resolution mechanisms, including arbitration, mediation, and judicial reforms. The objective is to evaluate the effectiveness of these mechanisms in providing justice and resolving conflicts in diverse legal contexts.
5. Foster Legal Scholarship and Education: Promote the development of legal scholarship and education in the Asia Pacific by providing a platform for high-quality research and discussion. This will support the academic and professional growth of legal experts in the region.

Kailiang Ma

Shareholder Rights Protection Mechanisms for Chinese Financial Holding Companies

A Comparative Law Perspective

Springer

Kailiang Ma
HSBC Business School
Peking University
Shenzhen, Guangdong, China

Qianhai Financial Holdings
Shenzhen, Guangdong, China

ISSN 3059-2178 ISSN 3059-2186 (electronic)
International and Comparative Law in the Asia Pacific
ISBN 978-981-97-9730-1 ISBN 978-981-97-9731-8 (eBook)
https://doi.org/10.1007/978-981-97-9731-8

This Springer imprint is published by the registered company Springer Nature Singapore Pte Ltd.
The registered company address is: 152 Beach Road, #21-01/04 Gateway East, Singapore 189721, Singapore

Acknowledgements

The writing of this book stems from the experience of doing doctoral research in Paris, France, and those years together explored the commonalities and differences between China and Europe. This book looks at the differences in legal and regulatory cultures between China and other countries on the basis of a particular form of business, the financial holding company, and hopes to provide a novel perspective on understanding the East and West society from both a business and a legal point of view. Formally benefiting from that invaluable experience, I finally completed this book; therefore, I would like to express my gratitude for the lost years.

Research is a gradual process. From a junior to a senior researcher, an open-mindedness approach is needed to listen to different voices from all over the world, which can help correct the faults of the research to a certain extent. Therefore, I would like to thank those professors, teachers, and business people who have given me advice on my research to express my sincere gratitude.

Finally, I would like to thank the editors of the publisher and all the people involved who put in all the work and effort to make this book possible. Without their support, the writing of this book would not have been able to achieve truly high-quality results.

Expert Notes

I had the pleasure of sitting on the jury for Mr. Kailiang Ma's defence of the great thesis that constitutes the book that readers have in the hands. The theme of the book aroused a keen interest in me as a researcher, given the major role played by financial holding companies in my fields of research. A comparative view of different legal systems (the Chinese, the Continental France, and the Anglo-Saxon) allows the jurist to extract himself from his own environment and assume a certain height, provided the work is carried out with rigour and open-mindedness.

This is the case of Mr. Kailiang Ma's monograph, which aims to address the shareholders protection issues in Chinese law for financial holding companies. These companies are holding companies whose main subsidiaries are regulated establishments in the banking, finance, or insurance sector, without necessarily having such a business themselves. There is therefore a risk of conflict of interest linked to this hybrid structure. The stakes are high, as these conglomerates carry with them a systemic risk that the failure of a single entity could have serious repercussions for the banking and financial system as a whole.

On reading the text, it becomes clear that most countries have an *ad hoc* statute regulating the parent company because of the systemic risk which poses to the system. The choice of subject for study is particularly pertinent, since this status has only existed in China since 2020, making it a novelty with a potential imperfection and fully justifying a comparative study.

The work accomplished is edifying. The subject is dealt with rigorously, bringing together the challenges of corporate governance and those of financial regulation. The author's thinking is particularly structured and demonstrates a clarity of mind that benefits the readers, in the mass of rules and rights mobilised. He doesn't just stop at the surface: like a guide, he takes the readers into new areas, such as the regulation of blockchain technology, which is taking up the attention of many legislators. It also takes a fresh look at the role of the Chinese Communist Party in business law.

The research objectives have been fully achieved. We can only wish Mr. Kailiang Ma a very successful career and hope that he will continue to take up the pen to pursue the fascinating work on corporate governance in financial law.

Patrick Barban
Professor of Law
CY Cergy Paris Université
Paris, France
September 2024

This book uses a comparative research approach to sort out the special kind of financial enterprise that is a financial holding company, focusing on relevant aspects of Chinese, French, U.S. and English law. It provides readers a clear understanding of what a financial holding company is and how to protect the shareholders rights of such an enterprise in the global context. It provides a complete analytical framework on corporate, financial, and comparative law, making a valuable contribution to existing legal research findings. In addition, the People's Bank of China issued the first regulation framework on Chinese financial holding companies in 2020, and this book will be quite valuable to those readers who are interested in Chinese law.

Jieche Su
Professor of Law
School of Law
Zhejiang GongShang University
Hangzhou, China
September 2024

Contents

About the Author

Dr. Kailiang Ma is a Postdoc in finance at Peking University HSBC Business School and Qianhai Financial Holdings in China now. He holds a Ph.D. in Law from Paris-Saclay University (France), a Master in Economic Law from China University of Political Science and Law. Also, he was visiting a scholar/researcher in many universities like University of Copenhagen (Denmark) and Norwegian School of Economics (Norway). To date, he has published some original research papers in renowned academic journals and participated high level research programmes. He was also invited to attend and speak in many international conferences organised in U.S., UK, Denmark, Belgium, and Luxembourg. Further information about his work and previous publications can be found here: https://orcid.org/0000-0002-7796-4129

List of Tables

Chapter 1
Introduction

Abstract Financial holding companies (FHCs) are a type of business widely found in countries around the world that share some common features across jurisdictions, such as an emphasis on control and the special requirements of subsidiaries. The history of FHCs can be traced back to approximately the 1970s, while the legislation and development of FHCs in China emerged gradually after the twentieth century. Using classic methods of legal research such as doctrinal, comparative, and historical analyses, this book draws on the experiences of major countries in the world in the regulation and governance of FHCs and endeavours to provide lessons for the future development of financial holding companies in China.

Keywords Financial holding companies · Financial market regulation · Corporate governance · Research methodology · Shareholder rights

The "financial holding company (FHC)" is a legal term. It was developed mainly after the 1970s. European law, for example, can be traced back to the Directive of 1978.[1] Japanese regulators permitted the establishment of FHCs in 1998 [12]. It was also the first Asian country to establish an FHC. In U.S. law, it was born out of the enactment of the Gramm-Leach-Bliley Act (GLBA) in 1999 [14]. However, before this, a "bank holding company (BHC)" already existed in America; in fact, there was a large difference between the two items.[2] After 2000, this form of company gradually gained acceptance in other jurisdictions, with Asian countries being the most active. For example, South Korea enacted the regulation of FHCs in 2000.[3]

[1] See Article 5, Fourth Council Directive of 25 July 1978 Based on Article 54 (3) (g) of the Treaty on the Annual Accounts of Certain Types of Companies. This provision defines the FHC. FHCs are only those companies whose sole objective is to acquire shares in other undertakings, manage them, and convert them into profits, without participating directly or indirectly in the management of those undertakings, and the above does not affect their rights as shareholders. However, it is important to note that this definition is also being updated.

[2] After GLBA, bank holding company is one type of FHCs in U.S.

[3] See Financial Holding Companies Act (금융지주회사법/金融持株會社).

K. Ma, *Shareholder Rights Protection Mechanisms for Chinese Financial Holding Companies*, International and Comparative Law in the Asia Pacific,
https://doi.org/10.1007/978-981-97-9731-8_1

Singapore enacted the FHC Regulation Act in 2013.[4] On the other hand, in mainland China, regulatory requirements were issued only by the People's Bank of China (PBOC) in 2020.[5]

The creation of FHCs has always been associated with financial crises and increased financial competition. Regardless of whether the shareholders of an FHC are governmental or private, the protection of their rights is always a central concern, and these rights are vividly demonstrated during financial crises and increased competitiveness. The case of the U.S. can be used as an example. Some U.S. politicians believe that the diversification of banking practices caused the Great Depression of 1930 in the United States [35]. This significantly undermines the interests of shareholders and the competitiveness of the market. Therefore, after that, the U.S. banned banks from engaging in nonbanking activities by enacting laws[6] when commercial and investment banks began to separate. The situation continued until 1999, when the U.S. passed legislation[7] that licenced banks to engage in nonbanking activities.[8] The subprime mortgage crisis[9] first occurred in the U.S. In 2008, scholars linked the enactment of the GLBA again [35]. The financial crisis has already created a significant threat to both shareholders and market stability. Indeed, other scholars disagree with this, and they believe that there is no evidence that the GLBA caused the 2008 crisis [4]. However, this controversy has also brought FHCs into the headlines regularly. In short, financial crises often lead to an expansion of government regulatory powers [34], and the creation of FHCs is a consequence of this trend.

By way of analysis, the FHC refers to a specific form of company defined by company law. It is a specific manifestation of a holding company. It usually exists as a parent company, which, together with its subsidiaries or other related entities, may form a financial group.[10] It exists primarily to gain and manage control. Its

---

[4] See Financial Holding Companies Act 2013 in Singapore.

[5] See Tentative Measures for Supervision and Administration of Financial Holding Companies (金融控股公司监督管理试行办法) (Hereinafter referred to as TMSAFHC).

[6] It refers to "the Banking Act of 1933", also known as "the Glass-Steagall Act".

[7] It is GLBA.

[8] The trend is also present in France. Specifically, the law that came into force on 24 January 1984 (La loi du 24 janvier 1984) allows French banks to engage in noncredit operations.

[9] It was a financial crisis in the United States that affected the nation and the rest of the world, triggered by the collapse of the housing bubble.

[10] Such as the relationship between financial groups and FHCs. It should be noted in particular that the relationship between the two concepts needs to be analysed in the specific legal context. However, few laws directly explain the relationship between the two in a clear manner. For the sake of clarity, the relationship is explained here using only French law as an example. Again, French law does not directly explain their relationship. However, it is possible to deduce this logically. The interpretation of this relationship by a French case law in 2018 is a validation of this relationship.

First, according to Article L511-20, Code monétaire et financier, a financial group is not a financial conglomerate. The latter is made up of subsidiaries of FHCs, credit institutions, investment companies or other companies that enjoy control over the financial sector. A financial conglomerate, on the other hand, is a special type of group of companies according to Article L517-3, Code monétaire et financier. Therefore, one can find that financial groups belong to a subconcept of the group concept, which is different from financial conglomerates.

subsidiaries are usually involved in banking, insurance, or securities market services, and so on. As a form of parent company, it is not necessarily necessary to engage in financial market activities, and it is possible for any form of company to become an FHC, subject to local regulatory requirements. However, the rules regarding parent and subsidiary companies vary depending on the specific rules of each jurisdiction. In addition, its shareholding structure can be fully public, private, or a mixture of public and private ownership [5]. In general, it is governed by a combination of company law, banking law, and other laws regulating financial markets.

Given that the regulation of FHCs in mainland China was promulgated in 2020 and is currently in a period of regulatory transition, many regulatory and governance issues of FHCs in the new era have gradually come to the forefront. Therefore, the Chinese FHCs discussed here refer mainly to the FHCs in mainland China. To lay the foundation for the argument in the main text, next, we detail the research background, research methodology, and basic facts of the book.

1.1 Research Background

The book aims to explore the mechanisms for the protection of shareholders' rights in Chinese FHCs in a global context so that it can present some basic information on the regulation and corporate governance of FHCs in China and in other jurisdictions beyond China. The current state of development of FHCs worldwide can be understood.

1.1.1 Chinese Financial Holding Companies

Compared with those in other jurisdictions, Chinese FHC regulations have come slowly, but research and exploration into the regulation of FHCs in China have gradually begun since 2000 [22]. Owing to the characteristics of the Chinese economic and political system, there are several special features in both the regulation and corporate governance of FHCs.

Second, according to Article L511-20, Code monétaire et financier, a group is composed of a parent company, subsidiaries and other entities together. Then, the structure of a financial group likewise follows these components of the group concept.

Third, according to Article L517-1, Code monétaire et financier, an FHC is a financial institution. Its subsidiaries are primarily or exclusively financial institutions or institutions, but at least one of them is an institution. Thus, the FHC itself exists as a form of parent company.

Finally, due to the broad nature of the concept on financial groups, it is possible, but not inevitable, that an FHC, as a parent company, and other subsidiaries may together constitute a financial group.

1.1.1.1 Features of Financial Market Regulation

In 2020, the PBOC enacted the TMSAFHC,[11] which was the first time that China formally regulated the various legal aspects of FHCs in law and was therefore a milestone event in the development of Chinese FHCs. It should be noted, however, that it is not the highest level of legal instrument in Chinese law, as it was not enacted by the Chinese People's Congress but was issued by the central bank of China. The content is divided into seven chapters. However, in terms of key issues, it answers questions in five main areas, including the definition of an FHC, establishment requirements, corporate governance, regulators, and legal responsibilities. To understand the content of this regulation instrument as a whole, several key aspects are presented.

In China, the regulation of FHCs was only promulgated by the PBOC in 2020, when FHCs were truly defined.[12] It refers to a limited liability company or company limited by shares established by law, which holds or effectively controls two or more financial institutions of different types and which itself only carries out equity investment management and does not directly engage in commercial business activities.[13] Since Chinese Company Law contains both limited liability companies and companies limited by shares,[14] a Chinese FHC is primarily a company under company law; thus, it has some characteristics that distinguish it from other types of companies: it controls more than two financial institutions; it is not directly involved in commercial operations; and it only carries out equity investment management activities. On the basis of this definition, the current direct regulation of Chinese FHCs is regulated mainly by Company Law and the TMSAFHC.[15] However, at a more specific level, various regulatory measures in the Chinese financial market, including banking law,

[11] It refers to the "Tentative Measures for Supervision and Administration of Financial Holding Companies (金融控股公司监督管理试行办法)".

[12] However, it is important to note that some of the governance requirements for FHCs can be found in a few scattered government documents in China over the past 20 years. For example, in 2005, the Financial Stability Bureau of the PBOC prepared a draft regulation on FHCs, through which regulators attempted to clarify the concept and market access conditions for FHCs. Nevertheless, the draft has not been promoted and enforced until now. In 2006, the Ningbo City Subbranch of the PBOC issued regulations on FHCs, in which FHCs is limited to two types. First, a financial institution holds a different kind of financial institution from its own, e.g. a commercial bank has a controlling interest in an insurance company, which can lead to the formation of an FHC. Second, nonfinancial enterprises hold financial institutions, which can also form a kind of FHC. It should be noted that it is an early example of the supervision of FHCs by local financial regulators in China. It is also only locally valid. Since then, in 2008, 2009, 2012, and 2016, a few central regulatory authorities and local governments have issued documents on FHCs. Therefore, the history of the regulation of FHCs in China can be divided into an exploration phase and a legalisation phase. In the exploration stage, it can be divided into two types of exploration by the central government and exploration by the local government.

[13] See Article 2, TMSAFHC.

[14] See Article 2, Company Law of the People's Republic of China (Amended in 2018).

[15] It refers to the "Tentative Measures for Supervision and Administration of Financial Holding Companies (金融控股公司监督管理试行办法)".

securities law, insurance law, and trust law, have had an impact on them. In addition, local government regulatory frameworks can also bind local FHCs.

According to the TMSAFHC,[16] natural persons, nonfinancial enterprises, and other legal persons approved by the regulator can apply to the PBOC to set up an FHC. Moreover, if these entities control more than two different financial institutions and meet the regulatory requirements in terms of capital size, then they must establish an FHC. Therefore, when an enterprise grows to a certain size, an FHC becomes a necessary option.

The TMSAFHC imposes high requirements on the governance of FHCs, which require that the FHC have a clear shareholding structure and that the beneficial owner and ultimate beneficiaries can be identified.[17] It cannot abuse its control to interfere with the operations of the controlled business. In addition, its directors, supervisors, and senior management are required to meet specific requirements and to file with the PBOC for review. In addition, it and the controlled enterprise must not infringe on the rights of users. Importantly, these are requirements for the governance of FHCs at the external regulation level, but there is no clear information on the internal governance mechanisms.

The TMSAFHC establishes the PBOC as the primary regulator of FHCs[18] but also expresses the need for a joint regulatory mechanism, which includes the central bank, banking and insurance supervision and administration authorities, securities supervision and administration authorities, foreign exchange authorities, finance departments, and state-owned asset management authorities.[19]

In terms of sanction mechanisms, the TMSAFHC focuses on penalties for the illegal operation of an FHC and the misconduct of its controlling shareholders, beneficial owners, and promoters, in the form of both administrative and criminal penalties.[20]

Prior to the enactment of the TMSAFHC by Chinese regulators in 2020, some regulatory pilots[21] for FHCs emerged in China. In total, these eight companies[22] can be divided into different categories. For example, the first classification is in terms of

[16] See Chapter II, TMSAFHC.

[17] See Chapter III, TMSAFHC.

[18] See Chapter VI, TMSAFHC.

[19] See Chapter V, TMSAFHC.

[20] See Chapter VI, TMSAFHC.

[21] In Chinese law, regulatory pilots can be understood as experimental regulatory objectives. Usually, the number of these targets is small. If these experimental targets ultimately prove to have positive effects, then the relevant regulatory policy will be considered for national implementation. If the effects of these experimental objectives are relatively negative, then regulatory measures applicable nationally may not be pursued.

[22] These include CITIC Group, China Everbright Group, and Ping An Insurance, announced by the Chinese government in 2002; and China Merchants Group, Shanghai International Group, Beijing Financial Holding Group, Ant Group and Suning.com, announced in 2018.

ownership structure, and they can be divided into state-owned FHCs and nonstate-owned FHCs[23]; the second classification is in terms of the company's development history, and they can be divided into traditional FHCs and internet FHCs; the third classification is in terms of whether they are listed, and they can be divided into listed companies and nonlisted companies.

When the TMSAFHC was enacted, the corresponding FHC approval process was given a legal basis. In 2022, the PBOC approved three companies[24] out of the previous eight to become definitive FHCs. Importantly, both FHCs are wholly state-owned companies in which the government is the sole shareholder. Nevertheless, some Chinese scholars believe that this represents two models [7] of FHCs in China. First, the Beijing Financial Holding Group was established in 2018 and is now approved as an FHC in its entirety; second, China CITIC Financial Holdings Limited is a subsidiary of the CITIC Group, and China Merchants Financial Holdings Limited is a subsidiary of the China Merchants Group. When these three newly approved FHCs are compared with the original eight FHC pilots, these three FHCs clearly represent two trends: pure FHCs (Beijing Financial Holding Group) and financial groups (CITIC Group and China Merchants Group) consisting of an FHC and its subsidiaries and other entities.

The regulation of Chinese FHCs has progressed from exploration to legalisation. This is indeed a major step forward in the regulation of Chinese FHC markets. In particular, prudential regulation by controlling shareholders[25] helps safeguard the interests of minority shareholders and manage chaos in the Chinese financial market. The shareholding structure, identity of controlling shareholders, and source of funds in Chinese FHCs are subject to very strict scrutiny. It is closely linked to the enormous influence of FHCs on financial markets, the governance of which revolves around multiple legal, economic, and political factors. However, the current regulatory measures are still imperfect, and there is still considerable room for progress in terms of the legislation model and the regulation of state-controlled shareholders.

1.1.1.2 Features of Corporate Governance

Although the TMSAFHC establishes some regulatory requirements for the corporate governance of Chinese FHCs, it is still at the stage of principle-based guidance, and

[23] State-owned FHCs can be divided into "state-owned companies by shares" and "wholly state-owned enterprises". In addition, "non-state-owned FHCs" is mainly discussed in one situation: "non-state-owned Mixed Ownership Companies"

[24] They are Beijing Financial Holding Group, CITIC Group, and China Merchants Group. However, it should be noted that another FHC, although originating from the CITIC Group, has a new name of China CITIC Financial Holding Company Limited (中国中信金融控股有限公司), which is still in the preparatory stage and has not been formally established. As a result, it does not currently have sufficient information for analysis.

[25] See Article 40–41, TMSAFHC. The PBOC reviews the major shareholders and controlling shareholders and their equity funds of FHCs and exercises penetrating supervision over their true shareholding structure, actual controllers, and the source, nature, and flow of equity funds.

it lacks a detailed programme. It is therefore more dependent on the exploration of internal governance mechanisms for FHCs. In this respect, research on corporate governance codes will fill gaps in regulation details.

In many jurisdictions around the world, corporate governance codes exist as a soft law regime following the "comply or explain" principle [28]. This means that companies have some freedom to comply with corporate governance codes, but they must give specific reasons for not doing so. However, Chinese corporate governance codes tend to be more of a hard law. There are currently no specific governance codes for FHCs in China. The current Chinese corporate governance codes include five main categories: listed companies, securities companies, securities investment fund management companies, small and medium-sized enterprises (SMEs), and bancassurance institutions.[26] Importantly, the last three types are only applicable to specific companies, which can be either listed or unlisted. However, if they are listed companies, they must also comply with the governance code for listed companies mentioned in the first one. The information published by the famous Chinese legal information platform PKULAW.com is classified as "Departmental Regulatory Documents[27]" (部门规范性文件) in Chinese law.[28] Under Chinese law, they are legally binding [37].

In current Chinese law, it should be noted that in documents from the Chinese government, the corporate governance of financial institutions needs to combine the modern enterprise system and the leadership of the Communist Party of China (CPC) to improve the imperfect corporate governance of Chinese enterprises.[29] It is an organisational governance system with Chinese characteristics and deserves in-depth research in the study of the protection of shareholder rights in FHCs [29]. The participation of the CPC in corporate governance has little relevant experience in other jurisdictions around the world. Therefore, it is a feature of current corporate governance in China.

[26] See Code of Corporate Governance of Listed Companies 2018 (上市公司治理准则 2018), Code of Corporate Governance of Securities Companies 2020 (证券公司治理准则2020修订), Code of Corporate Governance of Securities Investment Fund Management Companies (证券投资基金管理公司治理准则), Rules on Governance for Companies Listed on the National Small and Medium Enterprises Stock Transfer System (全国中小企业股份转让系统挂牌公司治理规则), Code of Corporate Governance for Bancassurance Institutions (银行保险机构公司治理准则 2021).

[27] For the translation in this Chinese term, see PKULAW.com. In Chinese law, it is a kind of regulatory instrument issued by a department with administrative powers.

[28] See Peking University Center for Legal Information.

[29] For example, according to Article 3 of "Regulations on the Basic Organisation Work of the State-owned Enterprises of the Communist Party of China (Trial)" (中国共产党国有企业基层组织工作条例(试行)), state-owned enterprises should insist on strengthening the leadership of the CPC and improving corporate governance, and integrate the leadership of the Party into all aspects of corporate governance. It has been implemented since December 31, 2019. At present, many FCHs in China are state-owned enterprises, so future governance should follow this principle.

1.1.2 *Financial Holding Companies Beyond China*

On the basis of the mechanisms for the protection of shareholders' rights, similar to the analysis of Chinese FHCs, the book focuses on the regulation and corporate governance of FHCs to explain their characteristics.

1.1.2.1 Financial Market Regulation

There are two key questions about the regulation of FHCs. First, does an FHC exist? Second, if so, how is it regulated? They will be explained next.

United Nations Member States with Financial Holding Companies

According to the United Nations (UN), there are currently 193 Member States[30] around the world in the UN, and they all have legal systems that are appropriate for their countries. Many of their legal texts can be searched through open channels. Although this book does not include the details of each country's situation with respect to FHCs, a general analysis and summary will enhance the understanding of the current development status of FHCs in the world from a macro-perspective.

FHCs involve different areas of the financial sector and their supervision. FHCs involve banking, insurance, and securities.[31] Even if there is no form of FHCs in some countries, if their country has banking, insurance, or securities business, it will necessarily involve the regulation model. The book can also predict that it involves the issue of shareholder rights protection. Therefore, the book summarises the banking, insurance, and securities regulatory agencies of 192 UN Member States except China. The specific content can be found in Appendix 1. Next, the book analyses the establishment of central banks and the presence of commercial banks, securities markets, and insurance companies in these countries.

According to data on Member States published by the UN, the legal systems of countries on the same continent are affected to varying degrees by each other due to their geographical proximity. Therefore, the book counts these countries according to different continents (see Table 1.1).

Through statistics, the book revealed that among the member states of the UN, in addition to China, a total of 117 countries have FHCs, accounting for approximately 60.94% of all countries. It is distributed on six continents worldwide. Among them, Europe has the highest proportion of countries with FHCs, accounting for approximately 86.36% of all European countries; in Oceania and African countries, the proportion of countries with FHCs is relatively low.

---

[30] For the information on UN Member States, see the UN website: https://www.un.org/en/member-states/. For information on FHC regulators in 192 Member States other than China.

[31] See Thomson Reuters Glossary: Financial Holding Company.

Table 1.1 FHC situation on different continents

Continent	Total number of countries with FHCs	Proportion of countries with FHCs to all countries on each continent
Africa	21	21/54 ≈ 38.89%
Asia	30	30/45 ≈ 66.67%
Europe	38	38/44 ≈ 86.36%
North America	15	15/23 ≈ 65.22%
Oceania	5	5/14 ≈ 35.71%
South America	8	8/12 = 66.67%
Total	117	117/192 ≈ 60.94%

According to data [20] published by the International Monetary Fund (IMF) in 2018, these countries with FHCs include both developed and developing countries. Thus, FHC is a very common form of firm in the world and has the value of being studied extensively.

Regulatory Modes of Financial Holding Companies

The regulation model has been of significant value. There are two kinds of regulation models: "regulation models based on different jurisdictions" and "Institution-based Regulation Models". These models can be built on them to identify the specific jurisdictions to analyse.

Regulation Models Based on Jurisdiction

Using statistics on the regulation of FHCs in the 192 UN Member States (excluding China) in Appendix 1, the book revealed that there are multiple types of regulation in different countries. It revolves around the regulators of banks, insurance companies, and securities markets as well as central banks in each country. Several studies provide support for this. For example, Thomson Reuters, a well-known legal database, categorises the operations of FHCs as banking, insurance, and securities. The categorisation falls within the context of defining an FHC as a bank holding company.[32] For the analysis of European FHCs, researchers have also focused on banks, insurance, securities, and regulators [17]. Therefore, both academics and practitioners tend to analyse the regulation of FHCs through the study of banking, insurance, and securities regulation. Prudently, it can be concluded that the analysis of the regulation of FHCs may also cover other services but should at least include banking, insurance, and securities market services [24]. The role of the central bank is necessarily one that cannot be ignored. For example, in the Organisation of Eastern Caribbean States (OECS), the main regulatory instruments for FHCs are developed

[32] See the explanation given in Westlaw.

by the Eastern Caribbean Central Bank.[33] According to regulations in different jurisdictions, the main models can be categorised as "unified regulation by the economic community", "national regulation", or both.

(1) Model of Unified Regulation by the Economic Community

The world's economic community model originated in the European Economic Community (EEC), where the main purpose was to increase regional competitiveness [15]. Today, the EEC has evolved into the European Union (EU).[34] However, in addition to the EU, there are other economic communities, including the West African Economic and Monetary Union (WAEMU) and the OECS, which are reflected in the regulation of FHCs. These economic communities have a common central bank and other financial regulators, but they do not have a separate central bank in Member States.

(2) Model of the Coexistence of the Economic Community and National Regulation

In terms of macro-regulation, there are both regional and national central bank supervisory models, and the world's leading economic community is currently the EU. The book will describe the regulators of the EU and its Member States with respect to FHCs. Among the 27 countries in the EU, their FHCs are not only subject to EU regulators but also have different regulators in their own countries to manage their FHCs. There are different types of regulation models in each country.

(3) Model of National Regulation

Apart from the two models, most of the remaining countries are essentially national regulatory models. However, due to the differences in their legal systems, different countries have different characteristics.

Institution-Based Regulation Models

With respect to the regulation of financial institutions, each country can conduct specific analyses from the perspectives of macro- and micro-level regulation. Macro-regulation focuses on national monetary policy and financial market stability. In general, the central bank undertakes national macro-financial regulation. Micro-regulation focuses on different financial sectors [11]. In terms of the statistical results of the regulation of FHCs, there are two main patterns: the "unified institutional model for macro- and micro-regulation" (1) and the "distinct institutional model for macro- and micro-regulation" (2).

(1) Unified Institutional Model for Macro- and Micro-regulation

Although macro-regulation and micro-regulation have different focuses in each country, according to the legal characteristics of different countries, there will be

---

[33] See Banking Act 2015.

[34] Ibid.

Table 1.2 Three models based on regulatory agencies

Models[36]	Number of countries
Single-regulatory-authority model	16
Two-regulatory-authorities model	37
Three or more-regulatory-authorities model	45

some differences in the specific responsible authorities. For example, in some countries, both macro-supervision and micro-supervision use the central bank to perform their functions in regulating FHCs. According to Appendix 1, seven such countries exist.[35]

(2) Distinct Institutional Model for Macro- and Micro-regulation

Notably, the book's classification on the basis of the statistical results in Appendix 1 is only for the supervision of FHCs, which may differ from the overall financial supervision model of various countries worldwide. For example, Thomson Reuters divided the regulation of U.S. FHCs into three areas: banking, insurance, and securities markets. However, the reality of U.S. financial markets encompasses more than just these three areas. Certainly, in each country, these three areas are the most critical for measuring FHCs and are among the greatest common factors in the regulation of FHCs in each country. In addition, according to some scholars, financial supervision models are divided into "single financial supervisor models", "two-peak supervision models", and "three pillar supervision models" [3]. However, it is aimed at the overall financial regulatory model of a country, not only related to banking, insurance, and securities business but also related to other types of financial services. What the book discusses here is only for FHCs. Specifically, the types of regulatory agencies that target the banking, insurance, and securities markets can be defined into three models (see Table 1.2).

1.1.2.2 Corporate Governance

Unlike the Chinese corporate governance codes, the governance codes of FHCs in other jurisdictions basically follow the soft law path and adhere to the principle of "comply or explain". However, there is some variation in different jurisdictions. For

[35] They are Liberia, Bahrain, Hungary, Ireland, Lithuania, Slovakia, Samoa.

[36] It is important to note that some scholars have proposed single-peak, twin-peak, and multiheaded regulatory models in their analysis of financial market regulation. The classification of models is mainly based on the classification of specific regulators for the banking, insurance, and securities markets, which is different from the models proposed by other scholars in their analysis of financial market regulation as a whole. For example, while the twin-peak model usually refers to the classification of prudential and operational regulation, the model of two regulators mentioned refers mainly to the fact that there are only two regulators for banking, securities and insurance. Thus, it echoes the model of regulation of FHCs being different from that of financial markets as a whole, but only one component of it.

example, the application of Singapore's corporate governance code is mandatory,[37] but the application of the Irish corporate governance code is voluntary.[38] The German corporate governance code adopts a two-tier structure, with a management board and supervisory board structure.[39] In contrast, in UK corporate governance, it has a one-tier structure, with a board of directors only.[40] Other countries, including France and Belgium, offer two options, which companies can choose at their own discretion.[41] However, these differences do not affect their nature as a soft law.

Sustainability, as represented by European corporate governance and corporate governance codes in many jurisdictions, has been incorporated into corporate governance codes and corporate practices. Although the relevant disclosure standards are still being studied,[42] they represent an increasing focus on long-term shareholder engagement.

In the digital age, new technologies such as blockchain and artificial intelligence are already gradually having an impact on corporate governance. For this reason, new technologies in corporate governance have been gradually incorporated into business practice and regulation.

1.2 Research Methodology

Legal methodology relates to how the research is argued. In the field of law, many research methods can be used, such as doctrinal analysis, comparative analysis, empirical analysis, and historical analysis [27]. However, it is understandable that the purpose of the research of legal methodology is to ensure the certainty of the law,[43] and the purpose is to make the research results more convincing. In many legal systems, different legal methods have different tendencies. For example, classic French legal methods are still doctrinal or "méthode de l'exégèse" [18]. In common law countries, in addition to traditional analytical methods, positivism is also developing rapidly, especially with respect to interdisciplinary research related to law [8]. However, regardless of the type of legal system, the legal methodology is used to study the scientificity of legal methods [1], or it can be called the identity of legal methods [8]. The book will utilise three main methodologies for analysis: doctrinal analysis, comparative analysis, and historical analysis.

---

[37] See the Code of Corporate Governance in Singapore, p. 3.

[38] See Corporate Governance Code for Fund Service Providers, p. 3.

[39] See German Corporate Governance Code.

[40] See UK Corporate Governance Code 2018.

[41] See the 2020 Belgian Code on Corporate Governance and Corporate governance code of listed corporations in France.

[42] It is a point made at the ECGI conference in May 2021 on Business Law and the Transition to a Net Zero Carbon Economy.

[43] Ibid.

1.2.1 Doctrinal Analysis

The doctrinal analysis method studies legal rules and principles. Specifically, it systematically analyses the specific legal provisions and the legal principles involved and logically explains the legal issues involved. The research objects are mainly legal provisions and case law and explore the consistency and certainty of the law to find the legislative purpose and possible effects [36].

1.2.1.1 Statutes and Regulations

From the perspective of common sense, for a legal issue, laws and regulations may involve not only existing laws and regulations but also those that have lapsed. Therefore, for researchers, do these all need to be studied? From the perspective of the application of law, it seems unnecessary to study invalidated laws and regulations because they are no longer binding on real life. However, from the perspective of legal research, ineffective laws and regulations reflect the legal characteristics of different historical periods. Therefore, it is of great reference significance for the systematic study of the development of a legal system.

1.2.1.2 Case Law

In both civil law countries and common law countries, case law plays a very important role in the legal system [13]. However, the judicial precedent represents the application of law in real life, which goes beyond the "law in books".[44] From the perspective of justice, the judge's judgement is based not only on formal laws and regulations but also on customary law, contracts, and so on.[45] In some countries, such as China, even though cases are not officially legal sources, judges still refer to them. Therefore, the study of case law is not only a study of the application of laws and regulations in the field of judicial practice but also a supplement to laws and regulations.

1.2.2 Comparative Analysis

This book looks to examine the mechanisms for the protection of shareholders' rights in Chinese FHCs in a global context. Two kinds of comparisons are needed:

[44] It is the concept proposed in an editorial of "Les Cahiers de la Justice" in the second issue of 2019. The title of the editorial is "Law in Books ou Law in Action?". Since there is no specific author, it is hereby explained.

[45] Ibid.

Table 1.3 Financial holding company regulation models

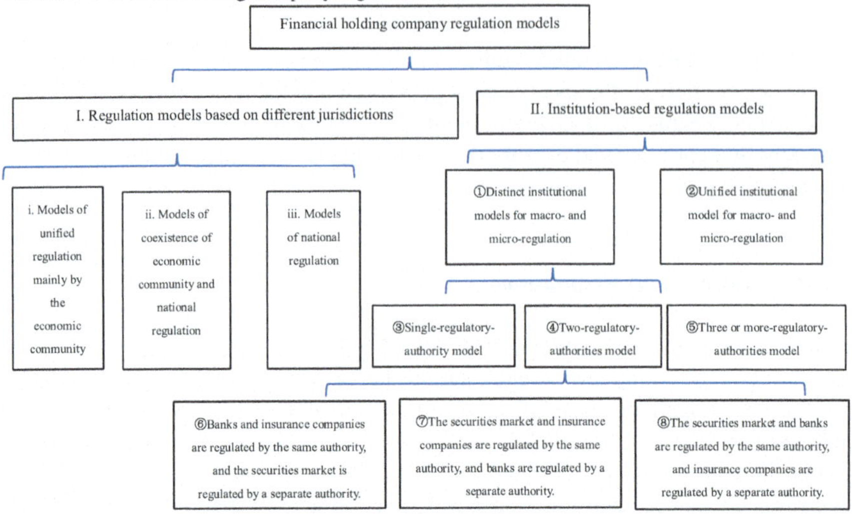

a comparison of the relevant regimes in different jurisdictions beyond China and a comparison between China and other jurisdictions.

1.2.2.1 The Choice of Jurisdictions

The book selects the subjects of the study on the basis of the jurisdictions to which these regulation models correspond according to three factors: continent distribution, gross domestic product (GDP) ranking,[46] and countries of special research value. The regulation modes are shown in Table 1.3.

From the "Models of Unified Regulation Mainly by the Economic Community", according to Appendix A, the book analyses the WAEMU and the OECS.

From the "Models of Coexistence of Economic Community and National Regulation", the book analyses the EU and its Member States as the main analysis objects. Among the Member States, combining their performance in "institution-based regulation models" and the GDP ranking in 2019, the book chooses Ireland, Germany, France, Belgium, and Italy as the research objects.[47]

---

[46] The reason for using GDP as an evaluation factor is that, through Appendix A, it has been found that countries where FHCs exist tend to be concentrated in countries that are in better economic shape across continents. Certainly, being in better economic shape does not necessarily mean that FHCs will emerge; but countries where FHCs exist must be better off economically. In addition, GDP is one of the most recognised international standards for measuring economic development.

[47] According to the 2019 GDP ranking, the five Member States of the EU are ranked in the order of Germany in 4th place, France in 7th place, Italy in 8th place, Belgium in 24th place, and Ireland in 32nd place. Furthermore, in terms of the regulatory model, Ireland is in ②; Germany is in ③, France is in ⑥, Belgium is in ⑦; and Italy is in ⑤.

From the perspective of "models of national regulation", combined with the performance of continent distribution, special research value, and "institution-based regulation models", the book chooses Uruguay, Australia, the UK, Singapore, Egypt, Mexico, and the U.S. as the analysis objects.[48]

The FHC regulation model filters out 12 countries and two economic communities from the 192 UN members, excluding China, which narrows the scope of the argument. However, it is still unrealistic to analyse all these regions in a single book. This conclusion is based on realistic needs. Thus, a reasonable narrowing of the scope must continue.

On the one hand, although it has been found through statistics that FHCs exist in approximately 60.94%[49] of countries, the legal concept of an FHC exists in two forms. First, in legal texts, FHCs are explicitly provided. Second, although there is no specific definition of an FHC in legal texts, some enterprises are named FHCs or are similar to them in real life. These are represented by Uruguay, Australia, Egypt, and Mexico.[50] As this book only examines the first form, these four countries will not be analysed.

On the other hand, although certain terms for FHCs can be found in the regulatory documents[51] of the WAEMU and the OECS, there is very limited information on these arguments from publicly available sources. Therefore, they will not be discussed in detail.

Finally, the eight remaining countries can be divided into two camps, namely the civil law system (France, Germany, Italy, and Belgium) and the common law system (U.S., UK, Singapore, and Ireland).[52] Given the requirements of the book, it is more appropriate to choose one representative country in each legal system. In combination with the "institutional-based regulation models" summarised above,

---

48 In terms of regulation models, Uruguay is in ②, located in South America; Australia and the UK are in ③, where Australia is in Oceania and the UK is in Europe, and the interaction of its FHC regulation with Europe is of interest due to the Brexit; Singapore is in ⑥, located in Asia; Egypt is in ⑦, located in Africa; Mexico is in ⑧, located in North America; and the U.S. is in ⑤, located in North America.

49 See the "United Nations Member States with Financial Holding Companies".

50 In the Australian and Mexican legal systems, they have some concepts that are similar to those of FHCs. For example, in Australia, there is the concept of a "financial sector company" (see Article 3, the Australian Financial Sector (Shareholdings) Act 1998); and in Mexico, there is a concept called "las sociedades controladoras de grupos financieros" (See Artículo 48, Ley para regular las agrupaciones financeiras in Mexico). In Uruguay and Egypt, they have companies that are named or treated as FHCs, such as Banco República in Uruguay and Cairo Financial Holding in Egypt. However, their laws do not contain the concept of an FHC.

51 See Article premiere, Deciston n° 014,124/06/2016/cmiumoa relatjve a la supervision sur base consolidee des etablissements de credit maisons-meres et oes compagnies financieres dans l'union monetaire ouest africaine (UMOA); Article 35, Banking Act 2015 in OECS. These articles are only intended to justify the existence of the FHCs in question, so a detailed discussion will not be analysed.

52 For information on the division between these two legal systems, see the information provided by the University of South Carolina Law Library: https://guides.law.sc.edu/c.php?g=315476&p=2108388 [accessed 1 February 2022].

France and the U.S. are more suitable for the main objects of analysis.[53] Considering that the UK's Brexit represents an alternative relationship between the EU Member States and the EU, which also concerns the future of the EU, the UK will also be the analysis subject, if necessary, which can be understood as special research value.

The choice of jurisdictions to analyse FHCs in a global context should provide a sound basis. This book takes a step-by-step approach to narrowing the scope of the study in terms of both the regulation model and the need for the book. It focuses on France, the U.S., and the UK as the subjects of analysis. On the basis of the analysis, this choice is not random and is representative. Certainly, EU law will be analysed where necessary, considering the relationship between the EU and the Member States.

1.2.2.2 Comparison Methods

With respect to methods of comparative research, from the perspective of basic logic, researchers should study the similarities and differences among research objects [10]. This means that researchers need to find connections between different systems, which arc valuable for comparative studies. For the specific theoretical aspects of comparative research methods, there are many theories. For example, Professor René David, a famous French comparative jurist, adopted the method of combining macro-comparison and micro-comparison in his research on comparative methods [26]. Macro-comparison focuses on comparisons between many different legal systems, whereas micro-comparison focuses on comparisons between different legal institutions under the same legal system.[54] This book also adopts this method. In particular, the book considers the systems of different countries in a balanced way when analysing regulatory modes on the basis of different geographical distributions and legal systems, which is an application of this method.

However, from a specific point of view, how should micro-comparisons be made? This is an issue that requires good design. German comparative law scholars Professor Konrad Zweigert and Professor Hein Kötz believe that the analysis of comparative law should focus on its function and analyse different systems by analysing the functions and effects of specific systems on society [38]. It can be assumed that analysing the legal systems of different countries from the perspective of institutional functions is

[53] The interpretation of this issue needs to be analysed in the context of the regulatory model for FHCs mentioned earlier, GDP and the value of special studies. In a common law country, the U.S. becomes the preferred option, considering the GDP. In the case of the civil law system countries, these four countries belong to the "single-regulatory-authority model", the "two-regulatory-authorities model", and the "three-or-more-regulatory-authorities model". Italy can be excluded because it is grouped into the same model as the U.S., and U.S. can already be used as a representative of "three-or-more-regulatory-authorities model". In the "two-regulatory-authorities model", the choice between France and Belgium should be made, as France has a higher GDP than Belgium, so France is the first choice. In the "single-regulatory-authority model", Germany and the UK can be chosen.

[54] Ibid.

conducive to fully understanding the role and effectiveness of the system in society. In addition, there is another kind of structuralism theory, which emphasises the comparative analysis of legal provisions, including the comparison of specific legal concepts, the analysis of the structure of the legal system, and the analysis of the elements of the law [32]. This approach is more nuanced.

Theories of comparative law are being updated over time [33], so there are more doctrines to look forward to being discovered in future. Cautiously, there are no absolute good or bad doctrines or theories alone, but when these are used to explain real-world problems, the researcher can make a choice. The research mainly adopts the analytical approach of the French jurist Professor René David. His theory looks at the global context, focusing both on the similarities and differences between different legal systems and on the relationships between specific systems within the same legal system [25]. Professor René David's theory is better suited to guide the analysis, as the book focuses on the protection of shareholders' rights in Chinese FHCs in a global context. It is a macro-comparison of the protection of shareholders' rights in different legal systems of FHCs in a global context. The development of FHCs in China currently has many different classifications. The studies of the shareholder rights protection mechanisms of these different categories of FHCs are micro-comparisons. In addition, as Professor René David argues that, logically, macro-comparisons precede micro-comparisons[55]; *thus*, the structure will also follow this line of thought. It will first analyse the shareholder rights protection mechanisms of FHCs in jurisdictions outside of China before focusing on Chinese FHCs.

More specifically, according to different FHCs regulation models, this dissertation has identified certain jurisdictions that need research. The book has introduced in detail the specific analysis parts of doctrinal analysis, including laws and regulations and judicial cases. It also compares specific regimes in these laws and regulations, and the book provides a comparative analysis in the context of real-life FHC cases.

1.2.3 Historical Analysis

Historical analysis of law is also a classical method of legal analysis. This emphasises the need to be critical in the analysis of the historical evolution of law, but it is not a criticism of history because history itself is objective and will not be changed by the analysis of historians or jurists. The historical analysis of law is an analysis of opinions, not an argument [9]. After the French sociologist Professor Pierre Bourdieu proposed the concept of "champ juridique" [19], there was a paradigm for the historical analysis of law. Through the sources of legal historical texts and the works of jurists, researchers can understand the role played by legal professionals in a specific historical background and the historical production process of laws and regulations. Therefore, what is the point of understanding throughout this history? The emergence and reform of a system always take place on the basis of history, and various

[55] Ibid.

factors influence the change in a system. Researchers can interpret them through various models, but this interpretation is ultimately very subjective. However, the development of history is objective, and researchers can find their desired answers from historical development, which is the enlightenment of history.

1.3 Innovation Points

From the perspective of the literature, current research on FHCs has focused mainly on financial regulation, whereas relatively few results have been produced from an integrated analysis of financial market regulation and corporate governance perspectives. Studies focusing on the protection of shareholders' rights are even rarer, and this book hopes to explore this topic from such a research perspective.

The research looks at the interaction between Chinese law and other jurisdictions in the regulation and governance of FHCs. It hopes to understand the lessons learned from Chinese and world experiences in the regulation and corporate governance of FHCs through doctrinal, historical, and comparative analysis. Particularly as China is currently at a transitional point in the financial market regulation of FHCs, such a study will allow us to understand the interplay between different legal systems and how they can come together to address future crises.

In addition to focusing on some basic issues of traditional corporate law and corporate governance regarding the protection of shareholders' rights, the book looks at new technologies, including blockchain and artificial intelligence, and their impact on the protection of shareholders' rights in FHCs. In addition, the book explores how FHCs should respond to the opportunities and challenges of sustainable development. These studies are expected to provide some reference for the future development of FHCs.

1.3.1 Why Study FHCs?

First, in all jurisdictions, FHCs have a strong influence on regional economies. Especially after the financial crisis of 2008, it has been recognised as a form of company that poses a threat to systemic crises; therefore, its study has research and practical value. Second, in the case of China, FHCs have moved from the exploratory stage to the legalisation stage, but the relevant research is still insufficient. This study is therefore expected to make some contributions to this end.

1.3.2 Why Focus on Shareholder Rights?

First, it is clear from the practice of FHCs that the protection of shareholders' rights remains a core concern for them. For listed companies, the focus of their disclosure is always how to ensure the realisation of shareholders' rights [23]. Second, despite criticism of shareholder primacy theory, stakeholder theory has received more attention in the context of sustainability, but this does not mean that shareholder rights protection is no longer important. In contrast, if stakeholder interests can be protected, shareholders need to be encouraged to participate in the long term, as has been demonstrated in several regulatory documents.[56] Finally, shareholder rights can be analysed as a whole or can be focused on specific types of shareholder rights, which can respond to two fundamental relationships in the protection of shareholder rights: the relationship between controlling shareholders and minority shareholders and the relationship between shareholders and management.

1.3.3 How Are the Mechanisms for the Protection of Shareholders' Rights Defined?

In an international context, financial market regulation is an external mechanism for the protection of shareholders' rights in FHCs, whereas corporate governance tends to be defined more as an internal mechanism [21]. The concept of corporate governance is considered by the World Bank as a process and structure concerning the control and management of a company.[57] Importantly, there are some regional differences in the concept of corporate governance. For example, as a concept originating from a common law system, the acceptance of the concept in French law has also gone through a long controversy. Currently, the concept exists only in listed companies, as management does not manage the common interests of shareholders well in the separation of "payeurs" and "décideurs" [31]. The interpretation of this concept in French law is not intended to emphasise the rights of shareholders but to restore their confidence in the market and thus achieve better corporate value.[58] However, on the whole, it is an internal mechanism that is recognisable. Financial market regulation, on the other hand, is a relationship in which the company interacts with its regulator and belongs to the external relationship management of a company. However, some scholars have also divided corporate governance into external and internal governance mechanisms [6]. In this model, the external governance mechanism is concerned with financial market regulation, whereas the internal governance

[56] For example, see Directive (EU) 2017/828 of the European Parliament and of the Council of 17 May 2017 amending Directive 2007/36/EC as regards the encouragement of long-term shareholder engagement.

[57] Ibid.

[58] Ibid.

mechanism is the disposition of the company's internal relationships.[59] For this book, there are limitations to this theory. Typically, the regulation of corporate governance can also be divided into two models: hard and soft regulation [30]. As a result, it has been argued that modern corporate governance has gradually moved towards an era of complexity and dynamic change [16]. Therefore, there is perhaps no consistent definition of what exactly corporate governance is, and it requires specific analysis in a specific context. To find common features in the different theories as well as in relation to the practical framework, this research explains the protection of shareholders' rights in terms of internal and external mechanisms, and corporate governance is used primarily to explain internal mechanisms.

1.3.4 How to Define "Global Context"?

This book examines the protection of shareholders' rights in Chinese FHCs in a global context. The "global context" is a very broad expression. Indeed, it would be impractical to analyse every jurisdiction in the world. The regulatory models of FHCs from the 192 UN Member States worldwide, excluding China, are considered; on this basis, 12 countries and 2 economic communities are filtered out. Considering the realistic requirements of the book, it has been narrowed down to France, the U.S., and the UK. Where necessary, EU law will also be analysed. Such a selection is not random; it has a sound basis, which is also in line with the principles of statistics. Hence, the analysis of the theories relating to these three countries can, to some extent, reflect the global context.

1.3.5 Why Beyond China and China?

On the one hand, the core of the research is to argue for a shareholder rights protection mechanism for FHCs in China, but it requires an understanding of the status of shareholder rights protection for FHCs in other jurisdictions. Therefore, it is necessary to address them separately. It is also in line with French comparative Professor Jenist René David's view that macro-comparisons precede micro-comparisons [25]. On the other hand, there are some peculiarities in the regulation and governance of Chinese FHCs, and these peculiarities make it difficult to correspond to the protection of shareholders' rights in FHCs in other jurisdictions. However, the peculiarities in the regulation and governance of Chinese FHCs also need to be argued. As such, it would be more appropriate that they be argued separately to provide a more comprehensive understanding of the commonalities and particularities in the regulation and governance of FHCs. It is also in line with the principles of universality and particularity in philosophy [2].

---

[59] Ibid.

References

1. Barraud B (2016) La méthodologie juridique, Aix-Marseille Université. https://hal-amu.archives-ouvertes.fr/hal-01367751/document#;~;text=Page%201-,Boris%20Barraud%2C%20%C2%AB%20La%20m%C3%A9thodologie%20juridique%20%C2%BB%2C%20in%20La%20recherche,167%20s.&text=Le%20droit%20est%20anim%C3%A9%20par,l'ensemble%20des%20activit%C3%A9s%20sociales. Accessed 19 Sept 2020
2. Bevir M (1999) Universality and particularity in the philosophy of history of E.B. Bax and R.C. Collingwood. Hist Hum Sci 1:3
3. Buttigieg CP (2013) The institutional models for financial supervision: an analysis. Accountant 13
4. Calabri MA (2009) Did deregulation cause the financial crisis? Cato Policy Report. https://www.cato.org/policy-report/julyaugust-2009/did-deregulation-cause-financial-crisis. Accessed 15 June 2020
5. Castres SF (1993) Les sociétés dites "holdings". Dissertation, Université Panthéon-Assas Paris II
6. Chen JJ (2010) A primer on corporate governance: China. Business Expert Press, New York
7. China Banking and Insurance News (中国银行保险报) (2022) Financial holding companies embrace a new phase of licenced operations (金控公司迎来持牌经营新阶段). China Banking and Insurance News. http://www.cbimc.cn/content/2022-03/21/content_458565.html. Accessed 25 Mar 2022
8. Cumyn M, Sqmson M (2013) La méthodologie juridique en quête d'identité (Legal methodology in search of an identity). Revue interdisciplinaire d'études juridiques (Interdiscip J Legal Stud) 71:1
9. Dubber MD (1998) Historical analysis of law. Law and History Review 16:159
10. Eberle EJ (2009) The method and role of comparative law. Washington University Global Studies Law Review 8:464
11. European Central Bank (2001) The role of central banks in prudential supervision, European Central Bank. https://www.ecb.europa.eu/pub/pdf/other/prudentialsupcbrole_en.pdf. Accessed 13 Aug 2020
12. Financial Services Agency (2017) Basic concepts concerning financial conglomerates supervision. Financial Services Agency. https://www.fsa.go.jp/en/refer/guide/conglomerate/01.html. Accessed 6 June 2019
13. Fon V, Parisi F (2004) Judicial precedents in civil law systems: a dynamic analysis. George Mason Law & Economics Research Paper. https://papers.ssrn.com/sol3/papers.cfm?abstract_id=534504. Accessed 22 Sept 2020
14. Francis JC, Ibbotson R (2005) Financial holding companies (FHCs). J Finan Liter 1:31
15. Gardiner B et al (2004) Competitiveness, productivity and economic growth across the European regions. Reg Stud J 38:1046
16. Gilson RJ (2018) From corporate law to corporate governance. In: Jeffrey NG, Wolf-Georg R (eds) The Oxford handbook of corporate law and governance, 1st edn. Oxford University Press, Oxford, p 19
17. Gruson M (2002) Supervision of financial holding companies in Europe: the EU directive on supplementary supervision of financial conglomerates. The International Lawyer 36:1230
18. Hakim N (2014) Méthodes du droit. In: Champeil-Desplats V(ed) Méthodologies du droit et des sciences du droit, 3rd edn. Dalloz, Paris, p 741
19. Halperin JL (2013) Droit et contexte du point de vue de l'histoire du droit. Revue interdisciplinaire d'études juridiques 70:119
20. IMF (2018). The world economic outlook database. IMF. https://www.imf.org/external/pubs/ft/weo/2018/02/weodata/groups.htm. Accessed 12 Aug 2020
21. International Finance Corporation (2010) Corporate governance manual. International Finance Corporation. https://www.ifc.org/wps/wcm/connect/topics_ext_content/ifc_external_corporate_site/ifc+cg/resources/toolkits+and+manuals/ifc+corporate+governance+manual. Accessed 20 Sept 2020

22. Jin S (2016) China's financial holding companies: mixed operation and separate supervision. Centre for Banking & Finance Law of National University of Singapore. https://law.nus.edu.sg/cbfl/publications/chinas-financial-holding-companies-mixed-operation-and-separate-supervision/. Accessed 12 Aug 2021
23. JPMorgan Chase & Co (2021) Annual report & proxy. JPMorgan Chase & Co. https://am.jpmorgan.com/blob-gim/1383229018341/83456/2020_Global%20Procedures%20and%20Guidelines_FINAL.PDF?segment=AMERICAS_US_ADV&locale=en_US. Accessed 25 July 2021
24. Lattre B (1975) Structure et pouvoir des groupes bancaires et financiers en France. Dissertation, Université Paris Dauphine
25. Legeais R (2005) Les grands systèmes de droit contemporains: une approche comparative (Major contemporary legal systems: a comparative approach). RTD Civ: 868
26. Liu Z (2020) Research method of comparative law, iolaw.org.cn. http://iolaw.cssn.cn/zxzp/200608/t20060831_4598664.shtml. Accessed 21 Sept 2020 (刘兆兴:《试论比较法的研究方法》, 载《中国法学网》)
27. Lqngbroek PM, Thomas MS (2017) Methodology of legal research: challenges and opportunities. Utrecht Law Review 13: 2–8
28. Magnier V (2017) Comparative corporate governance: legal perspectives. Edward Elgar Publishing, Cheltenham
29. Michael Bryane, GOO SH (2017) The case for the extraterritorial application of corporate governance standards in China, ResearchGate. https://www.researchgate.net/publication/322845205_The_Case_for_the_Extra-Territorial_Application_of_Corporate_Governance_Standards_in_China. Accessed 25 July 2021
30. Rapp MS, Schmid T, Wolff M (2016) Hard or soft regulation of corporate governance? SSRN. https://ssrn.com/abstract=1930847. Accessed 20 Sept 2020
31. Ripertg et al (2009) Traité de droit commercial. Tome 1 Volume 2. Les sociétés commerciales. LGDJ, Paris
32. Samuel G (2006) Droit comparé et théorie du droit (Comparative law and legal theory). Revue interdisciplinaire d'études juridiques (Interdiscip J Legal Stud) 57:23
33. Su J (2014) Crises and reform: a historical evolution of the UK banking regulatory system. J Gansu Administr Inst 1:120. (苏洁澈:《危机与变革:英国银行监管体系的历史变迁》,甘肃行政学院学报,2014年第1期,第120页)
34. Su J (2021) The constitutional review of government measures for financial crises--in case of failed bank resolution regime in the UK and US. Tribune Polit Sci Law 4:100. (苏洁澈:《金融危机干预措施的合宪性审查——英美处置破产银行及启示》, 政法论坛,2021年第4期,第100页)
35. Tombini A (2012) Universal banking: the view from Brazil. Quart Rev Econ Finan 1:154
36. Vibhute K (2009) Legal research methods: teaching material. Academia.edu. https://www.academia.edu/29384542/Legal_Research_Methods_Teaching_Material_Prepared_under_the_Sponsorship_of_the_Justice_and_Legal_System. Accessed 20 Sept 2020
37. Zhang Z (2017) Sectoral administrative law monographs. Law Press, Beijing. (章志远:《部门行政法专论》,北京:法律出版社,2017年,第25页。)
38. Zweigert K, KOTZ H (1998) An introduction to comparative law. Clarendon Press, Oxford

Chapter 2
Legal Analysis of the Concepts and Regulation Approaches of Financial Holding Companies Beyond China

Abstract To explore the external protection mechanisms of shareholders' rights in FHCs, the book has studied the development of FHCs in typical jurisdictions beyond China and has found that FHCs can be analysed from a legal textual perspective. The book has identified two different legal positions and two typical characteristics of FHCs, which provide an understanding of what an FHC is. In addition, the book has reflected on the summarised models for the regulation of FHCs. Through historical and comparative analysis, the book has identified the rationality of the models of FHC regulation. Finally, the book has identified two classic principles in the regulation of FHCs, namely, prudential regulation and consolidated regulation. These regulatory consensuses have gradually emerged in various jurisdictions since the financial crisis.

Keywords Consolidated regulation · Prudential regulation · Financial institutions · Bank holding company · Control relationships

To be able to make a full argument, the book presents three models for the regulation of FHCs, including "Models of Unified Regulation mainly by the Economic Community", "Models of Coexistence of Economic Community and National Regulation", and "Model of National Regulation". On this basis, thee U.S., the UK, and France have been chosen as the main subjects of analysis, with EU law and some relevant regional laws being covered where necessary, but they do not affect the main subject. Therefore, when the theoretical analysis is carried out, the book will also perform a comparative study of the relevant theories and legislation in these regions. On this basis, the book expects to discover the theoretical and legislative rules for the protection of shareholders' rights in these areas of FHCs.

Therefore, the regulation of FHCs in jurisdictions beyond China can be specifically analysed from the perspective of both legal concepts and financial market regulation approaches.

K. Ma, *Shareholder Rights Protection Mechanisms for Chinese Financial Holding Companies*, International and Comparative Law in the Asia Pacific,
https://doi.org/10.1007/978-981-97-9731-8_2

2.1 Two Aspects of the Legal Concepts

From the point of view of the literature, "legal concepts" can stand for some specific terms in legal provisions [18] but can also indicate the interpretation and analysis of certain terms [17]. In addition, in the book, it refers to the second one, which means that it will be useful for explaining and analysing FHCs. According to scholars, for the analysis of a concept, its definition, characteristics, and other useful aspects can be considered [17]. The research will use this approach to analyse legal texts to identify more specific ways of analysing the concept of FHCs. Such an analysis has several merits. As the French jurist Professor Drummond noted, as a product of a common law country, when the concept of a holding company enters the legal system of another country, it should first be accurately identifiable [8]. The same idea applies to FHCs.

The conceptual analysis of vocabulary can be carried out in terms of definitions, characteristics, and other aspects. Here, the book summarises the definitions and characteristics of FHCs from the legal text. From the point of view of legal doctrine, the study of law should be based on legal texts. The most direct relation should be legal documents such as the laws and regulations in force. On the basis of the main analytical jurisdictions, this research analyses the definitions of FHCs in the U.S., UK, and French legal systems. Considering the relationship between France and the EU, the content of EU law will also be analysed (see Table 2.1).

In summarising the conceptual features of each jurisdiction, there are two main purposes: first, to deconstruct the concepts in the legal text; second, to make a better comparison of the concepts. At this point, how can a comparative analysis be carried out? The analysis can be carried out specifically using the theory of structuralism advocated by French scholars. It is possible to analyse the constitutive elements of the concepts. Is there a uniform constituent element of legal concepts? Maybe not. For example, some EU law scholars have proposed five constituent elements of legal rules in EU law: access to justice and judicial review; legal certainty; proportionality; equality and nondiscrimination; and transparency [36]. Chinese scholars believe that legal concepts can be divided into three main elements, namely, assumptions, modes of conduct and legal consequences [41]. American scholars, on the other hand, argue that law may consist of rules, norms, and prescriptions [23]. In conjunction with the summary of legal texts, it appears that these theories do not allow for a uniform classification of the concepts in the legal texts of FHCs. Therefore, the point is to find some common features of the concepts of FHCs on the basis of the definitions in the legal texts. Specifically, it can be interpreted from both a macro perspective and a micro perspective. The macro perspective explains the nature of FHCs. It can be understood as the legal position. From the micro perspective, the specific features of the concepts of FHCs are analysed.

To provide a specific explanation of the FHC, as well as an accurate understanding of the concept, the legal positions from a macro perspective and specific characteristics from a micro perspective will be analysed.

Table 2.1 Definitions of FHCs in different jurisdictions

Jurisdictions	Definitions of FHCs
EU	According to regulatory requirements,[1] the defining FHC must meet simultaneously the following characteristics: • The FHC is a financial institution • Its subsidiaries are exclusively or mainly financial institutions or institutions • There is at least an institution for its subsidiaries • It is not a mixed FHC
France	According to regulatory requirements,[2] the defining FHCs must meet simultaneously the following characteristics: • The FHC is a financial institution • Its subsidiaries are exclusively or mainly financial institutions or institutions • There is at least an institution for its subsidiaries • It is not a mixed FHC
UK	According to regulatory requirements,[3] as for the definition of FHCs, it uses the EU regulations
U.S.	According to regulatory requirements,[4] the defining FHCs must meet simultaneously the following characteristics: • The FHC is a type of bank holding companies • The FHC can engage in a few extended financial activities • The FHC has sufficient capital and is well managed. All its depository subsidiaries have sufficient capital and are well managed. In addition, it has filed the certification documents with the board of directors

2.1.1 *Legal Positions*

"Legal positions" is not a specific legal term, but it is used in research. For example, a doctoral thesis in 2000 gives an example of "legal positions", where for a woman, in the family, the wife is a legal position for her [12]. However, in another study of war in international law, its interpretation of the legal position is linked to whether war is legally just or not [4]. Therefore, "legal positions" can be understood as the legal identity of a subject or the attitude of the law towards a phenomenon.

From the summaries, the book can initially determine that the legal positions of FHCs vary across jurisdictions. In general, the book can be classified into two categories: financial institution and bank holding company.

---

[1] See Article 4, Regulation (EU) No 575/2013 of the European Parliament and of the Council of 26 June 2013 on prudential requirements for credit institutions and investment firms and amending Regulation (EU) No 648/2012.

[2] See Article L517-1, Code monétaire et financier in France.

[3] The Financial Holding Companies (Approval, etc.) and Capital Requirements (Capital Buffers and Macroprudential Measures) (Amendment) (EU Exit) Regulations 2020. Under this regulatory requirement, the previous UK definition of an FHC followed the EU regulations.

[4] See Article (p), 12 U.S.C.A. § 1841 in U.S.

2.1.1.1 First Legal Position: Financial Institutions

An FHC is considered to be a financial institution[5] under the laws of both the EU and its Member States. Moreover, Member States' regulation of FHCs directly invokes EU law, as reflected in France and the UK. Importantly, the UK has left the EU, but according to the latest UK legislation on capital regulation of FHCs, which was completed in November 2020,[6] it still follows EU regulations. Therefore, the concept will remain the main regulatory basis for FHCs in the UK in the short term.

Notably, although the Member States have absorbed the EU regulations on FHCs, the EU definition of an FHC has been updated six times, which requires a historical analysis. The updates took place in 1978,[7] 1992,[8] 1993,[9] 2000,[10] 2002,[11] and 2013.[12] In terms of the legal position of FHCs, the EEC did not directly define FHCs in 1978.[13] However, from 1992 onwards, both the EEC and EU definitions of FHCs consider them to be a type of financial institution.[14]

---

[5] In EU law, financial institutions do not include credit institutions and investment firms, whose main activity is to engage in acquisition activities or certain authorised operations, and they include FHCs, mixed FHCs, a payment institution, and an asset management company, but excluding insurance holding companies and mixed-activity insurance holding companies (see Article 4, Regulation (EU) No 575/2013 of the European Parliament and of the Council of 26 June 2013 on prudential requirements for credit institutions and investment firms and amending Regulation (EU) No 648/2012).

[6] See Article 192O, the Financial Holding Companies (Approval etc.) and Capital Requirements (Capital Buffers and Macroprudential Measures) (Amendment) (EU Exit) Regulations 2020. Under this provision, matters such as the approval and regulation of relevant financial holding companies in the UK currently follow the provisions of previous EU law for the time being. Naturally, it is an option for the transitional phase. Once the UK has completed all Brexit procedures, it may change.

[7] See Fourth Council Directive 78/660/EEC of 25 July 1978 based on Article 54 (3) (g) of the Treaty on the annual accounts of certain types of companies.

[8] See Council Directive 92/30/EEC of 6 April 1992 on the supervision of credit institutions on a consolidated basis.

[9] See Council Directive 93/6/EEC of 15 March 1993 on the capital adequacy of investments firms and credit institutions Council Directive 2000/12/EC.

[10] See Directive 2000/12/EC of the European Parliament and of the Council of 20 March 2000 relating to the taking up and pursuit of the business of credit institutions.

[11] See Directive 2002/87/EC of the European Parliament and of the Council of 16 December 2002 on the supplementary supervision of credit institutions, insurance undertakings, and investment firms in a financial conglomerate and amending Council Directives 73/239/EEC, 79/267/EEC, 92/49/EEC, 92/96/EEC, 93/6/EEC, and 93/22/EEC and Directives 98/78/EC and 2000/12/EC of the European Parliament and of the Council.

[12] See Regulation (EU) No 575/2013 of the European Parliament and of the Council of 26 June 2013 on prudential requirements for credit institutions and investment firms and amending Regulation (EU) No 648/2012.

[13] See Article 5, Fourth Council Directive 78/660/EEC of 25 July 1978 based on Article 54 (3) (g) of the Treaty on the annual accounts of certain types of companies.

[14] See Article 1, Council Directive 92/30/EEC of 6 April 1992 on the supervision of credit institutions on a consolidated basis. The definition of an FHC in this clause clearly states that it is a financial institution.

Importantly, although EU legislation for FHCs dates back to 1978, the recognition or otherwise of this corporate form by Member States, at least in terms of name, reflects different time clues. In French law, for example, according to Professor Thierry BONNEAU's research, the name of the FHC emerged only in France in 2014 [7]. Prior to that, it would have been known as a financial company [7]. However, the two types of companies are clearly not the same. According to Professor Thierry Bonneau, the definition of an FHC in French law is an extension of the 2013 EU regulation [7]. Prior to this, French law on financial companies dates back to 1984,[15] when it was uncertain whether the legal position of a financial company was the same as that of a credit institution [7]. However, in 1993,[16] French law formally positioned financial companies as credit institutions [7]. In 1996, French law extended the legal positioning of financial companies, which is already very similar in substance to that of an FHC, but French law only called it an FHC in 2014.[17] Accordingly, Code monétaire et financier was updated in 2004,[18] 2007,[19] 2014,[20] and 2020[21] to accommodate the updating of financial companies or FHCs in legal regulation [7]. However, in general, the current definition and legal positioning of FHCs under French law follows the 2013 EU regulatory requirements. Parallels can be found in other Member States. It therefore also reflects the process of conflict and harmonisation of EU law with that of the Member States.

Therefore, the EU and its Member States consider an FHC to be a financial institution. It is a highly circumscribed concept in current EU law. It should not be overinterpreted. France and the UK have largely followed the rules of EU law. Importantly, some differences exist between the financial institutions referred to in the definition of an FHC under French law and those in the traditional French sense. With respect to the concept of an FHC, the concept of a financial institution strictly follows the definition of EU law and is highly restricted.[22] However, when talking about financial institutions in traditional French law, the concept is in fact very broad and includes mainly banks and financial companies [31].

---

[15] See Loi n° 84-46 du 24 janvier 1984 relative à l'activité et au contrôle des établissements de credit.

[16] See Loi n° 93-1444 du 31 décembre 1993 portant diverses dispositions relatives à la Banque de France, à l'assurance, au crédit et aux marchés financiers.

[17] Ibid.

[18] See Ordonnance n° 2004-1201 du 12 novembre 2004 relative à la surveillance complémentaire des établissements de crédit, des entreprises d'assurance et des entreprises d'investissement appartenant à un conglomérat financier.

[19] See Ordonnance n° 2007-571 du 19 avril 2007 relative aux établissements de crédit, aux entreprises d'investissement et aux sociétés de crédit foncier.

[20] See Ordonnance n° 2014-158 du 20 février 2014 portant diverses dispositions d'adaptation de la législation au droit de l'Union européenne en matière financière.

[21] See Ordonnance n° 2020-1635 du 21 décembre 2020 portant diverses dispositions d'adaptation de la législation au droit de l'Union européenne en matière financière.

[22] See Article L511-20, Code monétaire et financier.

2.1.1.2 Second Legal Position: Bank Holding Company

An FHC is defined as a type of BHC, which is clearly defined in U.S. law. Under the U.S. Bank Holding Company Act of 1956, a company that has control over two or more banks can be referred to as a BHC.[23] There are three types of control: control of more than 25% of the voting rights of a bank, control of the election of directors of a bank, and direct ownership of more than 25% or more of the voting rights of the bank.[24] Therefore, a BHC under this model is a type of holding company, and the only subsidiary of the BHC is the bank.

Importantly, in U.S. law, a BHC and a financial institution are two different concepts. For the purposes of the BHC Act, a financial institution is an institution whose business requires it to engage in financial activities [11]. The concept is different from that of European financial institutions. In addition, in the case of a BHC, its own operations do not require it to be physically involved in financial activities; it only needs to exercise control over those institutions that are involved in financial activities. Therefore, the concept of a BHC is broader than that of a financial institution. However, it is true that the concept of a BHC does not exist in Europe, and it is embodied mainly in U.S. law.

Thus, essentially, a BHC is itself a subconcept of a holding company. Since the creation of the holding company in 1824 [9], it has given rise to numerous updates. An FHC is a further innovation to the concept of a holding company within the concept of a BHC in U.S. law.

Therefore, the legal position of a BHC as an FHC is reflected mainly in U.S. law. Moreover, it is more inclined to be seen as a specific manifestation of a holding company, governed by relevant laws such as corporate law. Thus, the basic point about the identification of the legal position is that it must be analysed in the specific institutional context; it cannot be analysed through common sense judgements. There are two legal positions of financial institutions and BHCs as FHCs. On the one hand, it is based on the division of jurisdictions. As a general rule, the concept of a BHC does not exist in Europe, and even if the concept of a financial institution exists in the U.S., it is still distinct from that of a BHC. On the other hand, it is a division based on the particular legal connotations of specific terms. Although the concept of a financial institution exists in both the U.S. and Europe, the concept of a financial institution in EU law is highly restricted in regard to defining an FHC, whereas the concept of a financial institution in U.S. law is relatively more relaxed. Strictly speaking, they are not absolutely opposing concepts. However, in the study of comparative law, a division based on legal connotations and jurisdictions is necessary.

---

[23] See Section 2, U.S. Bank Holding Company Act of 1956.

[24] Ibid.

2.1.2 *The Two Common Characteristics*

The book has explained that a conceptual analysis of the term allows us to analyse its definition, characteristics, and other useful aspects, and here, it can look at the characteristics of an FHC to deepen the understanding.

By analysing the concept of FHCs in different jurisdictions, the book can identify two main common characteristics: emphasis on control relationships and special requirements for subsidiaries.

2.1.2.1 Emphasis on Control Relationships

All the FHCs in the jurisdictions studied emphasise that they have a controlling relationship over other companies or control over shares in other companies. This is one of the important purposes of FHCs. Importantly, this feature is shared with the general holding company mentioned by Professor Drummond [8]. In addition, it is particularly evident in European law. For example, in 1978, the sole purpose of an FHC was to make acquisitions of shares in other companies. The FHC does not participate in the actual operations of those businesses but rather helps the acquired companies make profits by managing those shares.[25] Although the EEC and the EU have made several adjustments to the concept of an FHC, they all continue to emphasise that the essential purpose of an FHC is the control of equity in other companies. The relationship is fully consistent with the relationship between parent and subsidiary companies in company law, where the subsidiary can operate and account for itself independently, without the parent company interfering too much with its actual operations.[26] Therefore, from this perspective, FHCs are often presented as parent companies.

Moreover, the means of control, whether direct or indirect, can achieve the purpose of control highlighted by FHCs. In terms of the legal definition of FHCs, some jurisdictions simply describe these forms of control, such as the UK, the EU, and France. If it is necessary to understand the detailed requirements of these forms of control, the book must adopt a systematic approach. In some jurisdictions, however, the control methods are described in detail directly in the definitions, as is the case in the U.S.[27] In French law, the Code de commerce divides the relationship of control

[25] See Article 5, Fourth Council Directive 78/660/EEC of 25 July 1978 based on Article 54 (3) (g) of the Treaty on the annual accounts of certain types of companies.

[26] It is also commonly understood in traditional company law.

[27] See 12 C.F.R. § 225.2. Under this provision, there are four main types of control over a company. First, a natural or legal person may own, or control, directly or indirectly or through others, 25% or more of the voting shares of a company. Second, a natural or legal person controls the election of a majority of the directors, trustees, or general partners of the company. Third, a natural or legal person has the right to exert a controlling influence, directly or indirectly, over the management or policies of the company. Fourth, where a person wishes to transfer 25% or more of the voting shares of another company, a natural or legal person may exercise significant influence over such transfer.

into three types.[28] On the other hand, Professor Oppetit considers the concept of control to be a question of fact, which will be decided specifically by the trial judge in each case [34]. The judges look at who actually has the power in the group in question [34]. In the internal governance of a company, this power may belong to the company's directors, as their personal role is too intrusive and tends to displace the role of the legal person, which can be understood as management control. In contrast, in relation to the control of a parent company over its subsidiaries, this relationship is often reflected as financial control. The corporate autonomy of the parent company is limited, as its dependence on the subsidiary increases. This argument is also used by Professor Drummond to explain holding companies [8]. Finally, in UK law, UK company law classifies control relationships into four types in terms of voting rights, the ability to appoint and remove the board, shareholder agreements, and substantial influence.[29]

Therefore, the control relationship is one important feature of the concept of an FHC,[30] and it reflects the fact that FHCs are a special manifestation of holding companies. However, the method of control is different in many jurisdictions. The main references in determining whether a control relationship exists are voting rights, the

[28] See article L233-3, Code de commerce. The interpretation of control in French law is divided into three cases. The first is determined by the share of voting rights. A natural or legal person is considered to have control when they hold, directly or indirectly, more than 40% of the voting rights and no other partner or shareholder holds, directly or indirectly, more than their share of the voting rights. Second, a natural or legal person may also be considered to have control when his share of the voting rights is less than 40%, if he can be granted a majority of the voting rights at a general meeting, obtain a majority of the voting rights by agreement, de facto decide on the decisions of the company's general meeting, or has the right to remove a majority of the members of the company's administrative, management, or supervisory bodies. Third, in addition to the above, two or more persons acting in concert are deemed to have control when they in fact determine the decisions taken by the general meeting of shareholders.

[29] See 89J (4), Companies Act 2006. For the purposes of those sections a person ("A") controls another person ("B") if (a) A holds a majority of the voting rights in B, (b) A is a member of B and has the right to appoint or remove a majority of the members of the board of directors (or, if there is no such board, the equivalent management body) of B, (c) A is a member of B and controls alone, pursuant to an agreement with other shareholders or members, a majority of the voting rights in B, or (d) A has the right to exercise, or actually exercises, dominant influence or control over B.

[30] It is important to note that in European legal texts, there are some other terms that are easily confused. For example, in a financial conglomerate, the control relationship is also an important feature. It is not clear and uniform in many EU legal texts. However, French law can provide some clues. For example, under Article L517-3, Code monétaire et financier, it is mentioned that a financial conglomerate can be formed when a group meets certain conditions. Therefore, a financial conglomerate is a special type of group. In addition, as far as the relationship between FHCs and financial conglomerates is concerned, essentially an FHC may be a special kind parent company in a financial conglomerate. According to the definition of a financial conglomerate, the combination of its subsidiaries is likely to be at least an insurance company and a credit institution or an insurance company and an investment company. In addition, while the subsidiaries of an FHC may contain at least credit institutions or investment companies, there is no mandatory requirement under EU law as to whether an insurance company needs to be its subsidiary, but there is no denial either. Therefore, it can be found that a financial conglomerate has higher requirements for its subsidiaries. Although the control relationship is not a unique feature of FHCs, it is essential for the interpretation of FHCs.

Table 2.2 Requirements for subsidiaries from 1978 to 2013

Year	Requirements for subsidiaries
1978	Not specified
1992	• They are either exclusively or mainly credit institutions or financial institutions • At least one subsidiary is a credit institution
1993	• They are either exclusively or mainly credit institutions, investment firms, or other financial institutions • At least one subsidiary is a credit institution or an investment firm
2000	• They are either exclusively or mainly credit institutions or financial institutions • At least one subsidiary is a credit institution
2002	• They are either exclusively or mainly investment firms or other financial institutions • At least one subsidiary is an investment firm • It is not a mixed FHC
2013	• They are either exclusively or mainly institutions or financial institutions • At least one subsidiary is an institution • It is not a mixed FHC

right to appoint and remove management, shareholder agreements, and influence over other shareholders, among others. These are features that are shared almost exclusively by French, UK, and U.S. law. Later, the description of the control relationship in Chinese law echoed these features.

2.1.2.2 Emphasis on Special Requirements for Subsidiaries

If an FHC merely exercises control over the shareholdings of other companies, then a holding company is sufficient for this purpose, so why would various jurisdictions need to create a further concept of a specific FHC? This leads to some of the special requirements of an FHC, specifically some specific restrictions on the subsidiary being controlled. However, the requirements for subsidiaries of an FHC vary from one jurisdiction to another at different points in history; at the same time, the provisions may also be different in many jurisdictions.

Special Requirements for Subsidiaries in Different Historical Stages

The differences between the different phases of the same jurisdiction are most evident in European law. As French and UK law follow these provisions of EU law, it also contributes to the understanding of the relevant national legal systems. The book can review the successive adaptations of the concept of FHCs in Europe. The EEC and EU have adapted the concept of FHCs six times: in 1978, 1992, 1993, 2000, 2002, and 2013 (see Table 2.2). The most significant difference between these adjustments is in the requirements for subsidiaries. The most obvious difference is in the presentation.

The generalisation and summary reveal several key terms, such as credit institutions, financial institutions, investment firms, mixed FHCs, and institutions.[31] If we wish to accurately understand the differences in the definitions of FHCs in the EU at different historical periods, the book must first focus on the differences in these different terms.

The definitions of some specific terms involved in analysing the concept of an FHC are explained in the previous paragraph.[32] Even though the legal term FHC was introduced in Europe as early as 1978, it was only in 1992 that its legal meaning became more enriched. In the five changes between 1992 and 2013, the legal meaning of the FHC was constantly adapted. The book can start by looking at the evolution of these legal terms over time.

Throughout the five changes, the basic meaning of "credit institutions" has not changed, mainly in terms of their basic functions. It comprises both the taking of public deposits and the granting of loans. In 1993, for example, the European definition of "credit institutions" was combined with the requirement for a solvency ratio.[33] In 2000, in addition to the definition in 1993, "credit institutions" included third country branches in Europe. However, in 2013, the legal definition of "credit institutions" reverted to the 1992 rules. Therefore, the book considers that the connotation of legal terms is historically recurrent.

This can be seen in two stages in the context of these five changes. The first was before 2013, when financial institutions were emphasised as not being credit institutions, and their main activity was the acquisition of shares in certain restricted activities. In 2013, however, the meaning of "financial institutions" was narrowed down, and they were defined as not being institutions, which in this case included both credit institutions and investment firms.

Among the five changes mentioned, the definition of investment firms first appeared in 1993 and was then defined in the 2000, 2002, and 2013 regulations. However, the year 2013 was still a turning point. There are three restrictions on investment firms: they are not credit institutions; they are not local firms[34]; and they exclude firms that only receive and transmit investor orders but do not hold client funds or securities. As to the three restrictions, in the regulation in 2013, the activities

[31] For the most recent definitions of these terms, see article 4, Regulation (EU) No 575/2013 of the European Parliament and of the Council of 26 June 2013 on prudential requirements for credit institutions and investment firms and amending Regulation (EU) No 648/2012. Credit institutions are mainly deposit-taking and loan-granting institutions. An investment company is any legal person whose regular business or professional manner provides investment services to third parties, but does not include credit institutions, local firms, and certain professional services which are not authorised. Institution only includes credit institution or an investment firm. A mixed FHC is a parent company which, together with its subsidiaries and several other entities, forms a financial conglomerate. It does not, however, include credit institutions, insurance companies, or investment firms.

[32] Ibid.

[33] See Council Directive 89/647/EEC of 18 December 1989 on a solvency ratio for credit institutions Council Directive 92/30/EEC.

[34] See Article 2-20, Council Directive 93/6/EEC of 15 March 1993 on the capital adequacy of investments firms and credit institutions Council Directive 2000/12/EC.

of the investment firms have been given more restrictions, which means more and more stringent regulation trends.[35] Therefore, from this perspective, the scope of companies restricted to the third category has narrowed, and the scope of companies that qualify as investment firms has expanded accordingly.

Among the changes examined, it was first introduced in 2002, and the concept of a mixed FHC has remained the same since the redefinition of FHCs in 2013. One of the most obvious qualities is that a mixed FHC is not one of the "regulated entities".[36] There are three types of regulated entities, namely, credit institutions, insurance undertakings, and investment firms.

In the five changes, the legal concept was defined in 1993, and in several subsequent legal changes, it involved credit institutions and investment firms. However, there is a difference in the logical relationship between the legal definitions, which began to change in 2000, and the definition has been used since then. Specifically, in 1993, institutions referred to credit institutions and investment firms.[37] From 2000 onwards, institutions refer to credit institutions or investment firms.[38] Therefore, the conditions for the application of institutions have been narrowed. Correspondingly, their scope of application has been expanded.

When analysing the successive changes in the definition of an FHC in Europe, several features can be identified. First, the conditions applicable to FHCs have become increasingly restrictive, but the minimum requirements for subsidiaries show a certain degree of historical repetition. For example, in 1992, at least one subsidiary was required to be a credit institution, and this requirement was followed in the regulation in 2000. However, the regulation in 1993 required at least one subsidiary to be a credit institution or an investment company, and the regulation in 2013 reverted to the regulation in 1993. Second, there is also a certain historical recurrence in the types of subsidiaries defined as FHCs, but there will be moments. For example, the definitions in 1992 and 2000 both required subsidiaries to be primarily or solely credit institutions or financial institutions; the definitions in 2013 and 1993 both required subsidiaries to be primarily or solely credit institutions, financial institutions, or

[35] See Article 4, Regulation (EU) No 575/2013 of the European Parliament and of the Council of 26 June 2013 on prudential requirements for credit institutions and investment firms and amending Regulation (EU) No 648/2012. In addition, it also need to refer to Directive 2004/39/EC of the European Parliament and of the Council of 21 April 2004 on markets in financial instruments amending Council Directives 85/611/EEC and 93/6/EEC and Directive 2000/12/EC of the European Parliament and of the Council and repealing Council Directive 93/22/EEC, it can be found Annex I of Section A, (1) Reception and transmission of orders in relation to one or more financial instruments; (2) Execution of orders on behalf of clients; (4) Portfolio management; (5) Investment advice.

[36] See Article 2-15, Directive 2002/87/EC of the European Parliament and of the Council of 16 December 2002 on the supplementary supervision of credit institutions, insurance undertakings, and investment firms in a financial conglomerate and amending Council Directives 73/239/EEC, 79/267/EEC, 92/49/EEC, 92/96/EEC, 93/6/EEC, and 93/22/EEC and Directives 98/78/EC and 2000/12/EC of the European Parliament and of the Council.

[37] See Article 2, Council Directive 93/6/EEC of 15 March 1993 on the capital adequacy of investments firms and credit institutions Council Directive 2000/12/EC.

[38] See Article 4, Directive 2000/12/EC of the European Parliament and of the Council of 20 March 2000 relating to the taking up and pursuit of the business of credit institutions.

investment companies. However, the year 2002 was a special moment because the subsidiaries of FHCs did not have to require the presence of credit institutions but rather, mainly, financial institutions or investment companies. Looking at the many historical changes, we can see that the regulation in 2002 is a very special case.

Therefore, there may be certain similarities in the definitions of FHCs at different stages of history, but the conditions for the regulation of FHCs have become increasingly varied, at the extreme of almost no special provisions in 1978, and increasingly rich in requirements later. Some lessons from history can be found.

Special Requirements for Subsidiaries in Different Jurisdictions

In terms of jurisdictions, the EU, France, and the UK maintain uniform definitions of an FHC, and those with significant differences are those in the U.S.

In the U.S., the definition of an FHC for subsidiaries requires an FHC to be the parent company of banks [25]. However, combining this with the EU's definition of an FHC in 2013, the requirements for the subsidiary of an FHC are also different. The legal terms that define an FHC under the EU legal framework, such as financial institutions and institutions, are also defined differently than those in other regions. This change is also reflected in French and English law. In addition, their national laws need to respond to these changes in EU law. The subsidiary requirements for European FHCs are more complex and stringent than those of U.S. law.

When reviewing the specific requirements for subsidiaries of FHCs in different legal systems, it is important to combine this analysis with other characteristics of FHCs. For example, the difference in the legal positioning of FHCs in Europe and the U.S. leads to differences in the specific requirements for their subsidiaries. Moreover, even within the same region, it is not invariable. For example, although the UK definition of an FHC still follows that of the EU, the requirements for FHC subsidiaries may also change in the future as the UK has left the EU.

Therefore, in jurisdictions outside of China, an FHC is a corporate form that exists as a parent company and whose subsidiaries are involved in financial activities, with a particular focus on control relationships. Specifically, it has the following main characteristics: (1) in the legal text of an FHC, it usually exists as a parent company. It may be legally positioned as a financial institution or as a bank holding company, which means that a nonfinancial company may equally well be the FHC. However, it is always a systemically important company; (2) it emphasises a controlling relationship over its subsidiaries, which means that it does not usually intervene directly in the management of its subsidiaries but helps them make a profit[39]; (3) it has some specific requirements for its subsidiaries. However, these requirements are updated

[39] Professor Drummond argues that holding companies do not have the means to carry out economic activities. In fact, this highlights the fact that it is not involved in the operations of its subsidiaries. It also echoes the important purpose of an FHC which is to gain control rather than to carry out operational activities.

continuously in different jurisdictions and at different points in the history of the same jurisdiction.

2.2 The Two Core Issues with Financial Market Regulation Approaches

The "regulation approach" provides a way of analysing the relationship between institutional forms and economic systems in response to changes in market dynamics, and it is designed to achieve stability and predictability in each economic context [21]. Specifically, some scholars have analysed this topic through regulatory strategies and regulatory principles [37]. Certainly, the interpretation of the regulation approach is not limited to this; it needs to be defined for specific needs.

On the basis of the meaning of the regulatory pathway, we explain it specifically from the perspective of both the regulation model and the regulation principles.

2.2.1 The First Core Issue: The Rationality of the Regulation Models

There are two different bases for the classification of regulatory models for FHCs, including "regulation models based on different jurisdictions" and "institution-based regulation models".[40] These two classifications each have a number of different submodels. These set the premise of the analysis.

The regulatory regimes of FHCs in different regions have different characteristics, particularly in terms of the role of the central bank and other different regulatory authorities in the regulation of FHCs. They are diverse in different jurisdictions. Therefore, why have so many models arisen? When choosing a specific model, how do regulators make such decisions? There must be some sound logic hidden behind this. The assumption of rationality is an important theory in the neoclassical model [13]. The book can explain these issues from a historical and comparative perspective.

2.2.1.1 Historical Legal Analysis of Rationality

The regulation of FHCs is part of the system of financial systems in a jurisdiction. The regulation of FHCs, then, must also evolve within the financial regulatory system of the region. This means that the regulation of FHCs cannot be independent of the financial regulatory system; rather, it is a specific manifestation of the financial regulatory system in a region. To answer the question of the rationality of the regulatory model of FHCs, it is necessary to review the main financial regulatory mechanisms

[40] See Chap. 1.

surrounding FHCs. It involves two main relationships: the relationship between the central bank and other regulators and the relationship between specific regulators of different businesses. A clear understanding of the history of financial regulation is needed.

Early financial regulation was mainly for banks. Its history has gone back a long way. When banks were first created, people were sensitive to their operations. In 1850, for example, the French Dictionnaire des idées reçues mentioned *Banquiers* [14]. However, in the Anglo–Saxon region, some scholars believe that the problems of financial regulation emerged mainly from the first banking crisis, such as the British Fringe bank crisis of 1973–1975, the Franklin Narional Failture of 1973, and the German Herstatt failure in 1974 [26]. During this phase, the central issue of contention lies in the role of central banks in regulation. In the 1980s, the debt crisis in Latin America dealt a fatal blow to the economies of poor countries, and it was accompanied by a reform of the international financial regulatory system [32]. By the mid-1990s, another major issue in the field of financial regulation emerged at this time: the regulation of different financial operations, such as banking, insurance, and securities. The concept of microprudential regulation was subsequently derived. The East Asian financial crisis of the same period triggered a renewed rethinking of regulatory governance [26]. In fact, this period was also an important historical period in which the U.S. FFC Act was enacted. By the stage of the global financial crisis in 2008, curiosity about macroprudential regulation was driven by this crisis. Therefore, building on this analysis, the period of focus on financial regulation is only approximately 40 years old.

This perspective is also partially confirmed in the eyes of European scholars. For example, historians Alexis Drach and Olivier Feiertag consider the period after 1970 to be an important turning point in financial regulation. However, when analysed from a historical perspective, the control and regulation of banks was born during the two world wars. In particular, the financial crisis of 1930 brought the issue of banking regulation to the fore [14]. Therefore, the financial crisis was a constant driver of regulatory reform. Every major financial reform has been the result of a reflection brought about by a crisis.

The regulation and governance of FHCs went beyond the control of banks to include other financial products, so the post-1970 period was a critical one in which FHCs began to be gradually taken seriously. It was also a period when global financial regulation entered an important turning point. At the same time, the initial reference to the earliest legal texts on the concept of FHCs dates back to 1978 in Europe, which also seems to confirm the observations of this period.[41] Thus, the historical analysis shows that the financial crisis led to a reform of the financial regulatory regime. The book can understand the regulatory regime for FHCs as a more specific strategy within a judicial regional financial system. Therefore, FHCs' regulations do not cover all aspects of the financial system.

[41] See Fourth Council Directive 78/660/EEC of 25 July 1978 based on Article 54 (3) (g) of the Treaty on the annual accounts of certain types of companies.

Table 2.3 Historical background of FHCs' legislation

Jurisdictions	Period of enactment	Brief historical background
EU or EEC	1978[42]	European banking crises have contributed to the development of prudential regulation. For example, the Fringe bank crisis in the UK in 1973–1975; the Herstatt failure in Germany in 1974 [14]
France	2004[43]	The EU Member States did not have some major financial crisis around the year 2000, and their legislation on FHCs was more in response to the embedding of EU law into national law. However, the timing of the legislation varies from country to country as Member States also have different circumstances
UK	2000[44]	In a historic change to increase the independence of the central bank, the UK pioneered the transfer of responsibility for banking supervision from the Bank of England to the Financial Conduct Authority in 1997 [14]
U.S.	1999[45]	The global impact of the 1997 Asian financial crisis had a knock-on effect on U.S. financial regulation. In addition, U.S. bankers saw increased competition and shortcomings between local banks and those in Europe and Japan. Reform was called for

To further substantiate this point, the following is an analysis of the first FHCs regulatory laws in some jurisdictions and their possible historical background. The specific analysis is found in Table 2.3.

From a historical perspective, the emergence of FHCs has been accompanied by financial crises and reforms. Overall trends are the result of economic globalisation and increased international competition in the financial sector [35]. The regulation of FHCs is necessary to improve the efficiency of overall financial regulation and to close systemic gaps and prevent systemic crises.

On this basis, different regulatory models have been presented, which are necessary and almost inevitable. The current regulatory mechanisms in various jurisdictions are the result of continuous reforms that were in place during the financial crisis during different periods of history before they were presented.

2.2.1.2 Comparative Legal Analysis of Rationality

In addition to historical experience, the book also reveals that many factors influence the regulatory culture of a region, such as the level of economic development and competition; globalisation; and geopolitics and economics. When these factors are analysed comparatively for different jurisdictions, the book will find that the current

[42] See Fourth Council Directive 78/660/EEC of 25 July 1978 based on Article 54 (3) (g) of the Treaty on the annual accounts of certain types of companies.

[43] See Code monétaire et financier 2004 in France.

[44] See Financial Services and Markets Act 2000 in the UK.

[45] See the Gramm-Leach-Bliley Act (GLBA) in the U.S.

regulatory regime on FHCs is regionally appropriate. When multiple models emerge, the book can also perform a deconstruction analysis.

First, the level of economic development and competition is fundamental to the choice of regulatory scheme. The development of FHCs is more dependent on the size of the local financial market. This is more profoundly demonstrated in the "Regulation Models Based on Different Jurisdictions".[46] Specifically, under this model criterion, there are three main classifications, namely, "Models of Unified Regulation Mainly by the Economic Community", "Models of Coexistence of Economic Community and National Regulation", and "Models of National Regulation".[47] The WAEMU in Africa and the OECS in the Caribbean rely more on regional central banks for their financial regulatory powers, and their Member States have few separate central banks, which means that monetary policy and financial stability within the Union are almost entirely dependent on the central banking institutions within the Union. However, the EU has a different character. The EU's central banking system is made up of the European Central Bank (ECB) and the central banks of the Member States. The ECB is primarily responsible for financial supervision, and the central banks of the Member States have a high degree of independence [16]. Why does such variability arise? It depends more on the regional level of economic development. European countries are traditionally rich countries, and their legal systems have all had a very important influence on the construction of the world's legal order, such as French law, German law, and Roman law. The EU and formerly the EEC, on the other hand, were designed to enhance Europe's international competitiveness to a greater extent [39]. The same applies to Africa and the Caribbean. However, unlike Europe, these regions have relatively low levels of economic development and small-scale financial markets. Therefore, the idea of a monetary union has become common to them to achieve economies of scale. In the case of WAEMU in Africa, all its member states are classified by the UN as "least developed countries", except for Côte d'Ivoire [20]. In addition, it seems that the idea of a central bank only began to be Africanized in 1973. Since small single countries seem incapable of creating an effective central banking mechanism, regional monetary unions as well as central banking mechanisms were created as a way of jointly regulating the financial operations of a region [20]. In contrast to European countries, in Europe, the world's first central bank was born, specifically Sweden's Riksbank, which opened doors in 1668 [10]. In other words, Europe has led the world trend in central bank regulation for more than 350 years. Therefore, the level of economic development and competition determines the relationship between the central banks of regional economic unions and the central banks of the member states. It also directly influences the regulatory model for FHCs.

---

[46] See Chap. 1.

[47] See Chap. 1.

Second, geopolitics and economics inevitably affect the regulation of FHCs in a region. For an explanation of this issue, the regulation of the EU and Member States, such as Ireland, is a good example. Ireland's financial market regulation is under the central bank's unified responsibility, including the banking, insurance, and securities businesses mentioned in understanding FHCs. Moreover, its central bank is also responsible for monetary policy and price stability in the market. Therefore, in this country, the central bank has absolute regulatory powers over financial markets. Why, then, has this led to this phenomenon? Irish academics argue that this function of the central bank is primarily in response to Ireland's status as a member of the Eurozone. Financial regulation is required to be more focused on the conduct of business. As a unified institution, the Central Bank of Ireland more easily communicates with other jurisdictions. Moreover, no institution was more reputable than the central bank was [38]. Therefore, in the view of Irish scholars, the reason why central banks regulate financial markets in a uniform way is that it is primarily to address the issue of coordination with the Eurosystem. From a macro perspective, it is exactly what geopolitics and economics bring to bear on financial regulation. The situation is similar in other European countries.

From a comparative perspective, several models of FHC regulation are recognised in each jurisdiction because of the size of the local financial market and different legal systems. At the same time, a decision is made by jurisdictions after geographical factors are considered and after relevant market variables are integrated. However, this section of the argument is not limited to the U.S., the UK, or France. However, to justify their models of FHC regulation, they need to be combined with different regulatory models. In Europe, the impact of EU law on France and the UK is long term, but the reforms brought about by other Member States to EU law will also affect France and the UK, which have left the EU.

2.2.2 The Second Core Issue: Financial Market Regulation Principles

Specifically, when browsing through the legal texts of the jurisdictions explored, the book reveals that the principles governing the regulation of FHCs are focused on two main areas, namely, consolidated regulation and prudential regulation.

2.2.2.1 Principle of Consolidated Regulation

According to the Association of Supervisors of Banks of the Americas (ASBA), consolidated regulation focuses on the overall assessment of a company's risk, which includes corporate entities as well as natural persons and is not limited to matters disclosed by the company [3]. In other words, if some matters pose a risk to the company's operations, these are the subject of the assessment. In the Chinese regulatory system, this type of supervision is also known as "the look-through supervision" [40]. It imposes higher regulatory requirements and standards on regulators, as it requires them to be able to identify not only existing risks but also potential risks. However, despite this, the principle has a long history. One of the more famous cases that established the principle dates back to the failure of Franklin National Bank in 1974 [27]. In this case, the central bank became concerned with the comprehensive supervision of commercial banks. It was followed by the Basel Committee on Banking Supervision (BCBS) in its 1979 report "Consolidated Supervision of Banks' International Activities" [5]. Since then, BCBS has refined the concept in four important documents[48] as time has changed. It has now become an internationally important principle for the supervision of financial conglomerates. Therefore, this principle applies not only to FHCs but also to other types of financial groups.

In addition, this concept of comprehensive analysis and regulation of corporate risk is necessary for FHCs. The important features of an FHC include an emphasis on control relationships, strict requirements for subsidiaries and special restrictions on operating activities. In view of this, it is conceivable that the control relationships of an FHC could be very complex and that any single problem could cause a chain reaction, which could easily lead to significant risks within thc FHC. As a pivotal presence in financial markets, the operational risks of an FHC could create a potential systemic crisis for the entire market, as has been demonstrated in the Lehman Brothers bankruptcy case in the U.S. For example, in the case of an FHC, regulation covers not only itself but also its subsidiaries, the financial groups they form together, and so on. It also covers not only the risks of its own operations but also those of its subsidiaries in other countries. The situation of each FHC may not be the same, relatively speaking, and therefore, the measures taken by the regulator may differ. The approach to regulation is therefore more targeted and focuses on the micro level of regulation.

Consolidated regulation was initially a regulatory scheme for banks, and following the emergence of FHCs, this approach was accordingly applied to FHCs. The reasons for this are understandable. On the one hand, some FHCs are themselves bank holding companies, such as those in the U.S. Therefore, it is natural that an FHC in this context can also implement the concept of consolidated regulation, as it is still essentially the regulation of banks. On the other hand, even in other jurisdictions, FHCs have broken away from banks and extended to other financial institutions.

[48] They are "1983 Principles for the supervision of banks' foreign establishments"; "1992 Minimum standards for the supervision of international banking groups and their cross-border establishments"; "1996 The supervision of cross-border banking"; "2006 Home-host information sharing for effective Basel II implementation".

However, the book still states in the legal texts that they follow the idea of consolidated regulation, as defined in the EU law in 2002, which emphasises the joint implementation of the consolidated regulation of FHCs by the EU regulators and the national regulators of the Member States. Notably, FHCs were required to be headquartered in the EU at this time.[49] This means that the FHCs must be a company incorporated in the EU and its Member States, which may ensure that the company is of European origin. Furthermore, it has also been argued that the consolidated supervision of companies is the responsibility of their home-country regulators [3]. If the theory is followed, then the requirement would almost certainly have to be met for the EU to be able to impose consolidated regulation on FHCs. In addition, the EU Member States have also implemented the concept of consolidated regulation into their national law.[50] The EU and the Member States have maintained uniformity in their regulatory principles. These situations also apply to France. Since 2010, French legislators have added antiabuse rules and imposed stricter regulations on transactions by groups of companies [24]. The UK has left the EU, but in the short term, this situation will not change significantly.

The U.S. consolidated regulation of FHCs also applies to other bank holding companies, pointing to controls on risk-based capital ratios.[51] From the analysis, the book finds that the interpretation of consolidated regulation in different jurisdictions has different emphases. However, all of them use the expression "consolidated regulation" at the same time. The book suggested that despite the differences in the expressions, the emphasis on the concept of regulation is similar and that it is necessary to understand the spirit inherent in consolidated regulation.

The principle of consolidated regulation of FHCs is therefore a response to the failure of banking supervision, an experimental reflection by regulators in the face of regulatory failures and the financial crisis. This principle has evolved so much that it is not only reflected in the legal texts of various jurisdictions but also implemented in some of the specific activities of FHCs.

---

[49] See Article 29, Directive 2002/87/EC of the European Parliament and of the Council of 16 December 2002 on the supplementary supervision of credit institutions, insurance undertakings, and investment firms in a financial conglomerate and amending Council Directives 73/239/EEC, 79/267/EEC, 92/49/EEC, 92/96/EEC, 93/6/EEC, and 93/22/EEC and Directives 98/78/EC and 2000/12/EC of the European Parliament and of the Council.

[50] In Belgium, see Art. 11, Titre 12 NOVEMBRE 2013. - Arrêté royal modifiant divers arrêtés royaux en vue de la transposition partielle de la Directive 2010/78/UE du 24 novembre 2010. In Italy, see Note all'art. 12, Decreto Legislativo 30 maggio 2005, n. 142. In Ireland, see Part 2, S.I. No. 475/2009—European Communities (Credit Institutions) (Consolidated Supervision) Regulations 2009. For the French ACPR regulations on the establishment of financial holding companies, see https://acpr.banque-france.fr/autoriser/procedures-secteur-banque/agrement-autorisation-ou-enregistrement/compagnie-financiere-holding-et-compagnies-financieres-holding-mixtes. In Germany, see (8a) BGBl. Nr. 532/1993 zuletzt geändert durch BGBl. I Nr. 20/2012. In these references to legal provisions, the term consolidated regulation is explicitly described.

[51] See 12 C.F.R. § 225.2 in U.S. Under this provision on a consolidated regulation basis, the total risk-based capital ratio of a BHC is maintained at or above 10.0%. It reflects the legal application of this principle.

2.2.2.2 Principle of Prudential Regulation

Prudential regulation is often a principle that goes hand in hand with consolidated regulation in the regulation of FHCs. For example, the BCBS, in its 2012 supervisory document, explains the use of prudential standards in the context of consolidated supervision [5]. It also sets out specific requirements for prudential regulation in 16 areas, including corporate governance; the risk management process; capital adequacy; credit risk; problem assets, provisions and reserves; concentration risk and large exposure limits; transactions with related parties; country and transfer risks; market risks; interest rate risk in the banking book; liquidity risk; operational risk; internal control and audit; financial reporting and external audit; disclosure and transparency; and abuse of financial services [5]. Therefore, prudential regulation already has a very detailed set of regulatory requirements at the international level. Thus, with respect to the concept of prudential standards, they must be analysed in the context of the specific legal framework. It is usually discussed in the context of the policy framework for financial market regulation, which is a set of standards with the primary objective of preventing risks in financial markets. It covers all aspects of the functioning of financial markets.

More specifically, prudential regulation is a risk-based approach and principle of macroregulation in financial markets [29], which has the primary objective of maintaining financial market stability. Guided by this fundamental principle, regulators set differentiated risk-based regulatory standards for different financial services and products, as they differ in market risk. Indeed, even for the same financial product or service, its impact on the stability of financial markets varies across different historical stages and market environments. However, the prudential principle is based on macro analysis, and the standards it sets are not specific to a particular market participant; rather, they are of concern whenever there is a risk of financial market instability. In current society, such market instability can manifest itself in various forms, such as violent fluctuations in the stock market, price inflation, and labour unemployment. These are all drawn from the various manifestations of financial crises throughout history. At the level of an FHC, the complexity of its shareholding structure and the richness of its financial products and services can make the instability it brings even more complex. Therefore, there is a strong need to design prudential standards for such companies to accurately identify risks.

Systemic risk is broadly defined as some form of system-wide financial distress or economic disruption that has a significant effect on the physical economy [2]. In the case of financial markets, this is often reflected in enormous fluctuations in the investment climate, which induce financial crises and generate a range of socioeconomic problems, such as inflation, corporate bankruptcies, and employee unemployment. The security of FHCs as a kind of behemoth in financial markets poses a systemic risk to the market.

Both consolidated regulation and prudential regulation are set up on the basis of risk. In other words, they are designed to prevent risks effectively and to respond quickly when they do occur, thereby minimising the damage caused by systemic risk. In terms of the regulation of FHCs, prudential regulation emphasises the need for regulators to manage the balance of interests between FHCs, financial consumers, and the government and is designed to protect different interests in the financial market, which can be interpreted as an "art of balancing". The consolidated regulation, on the other hand, places more emphasis on the market behaviour of FHCs, where the regulator must plan in a unified manner to discover the nature of the behaviour through market behaviour and thus gain a comprehensive understanding of the risks, which can be understood as an "art of discovery". Both regulatory principles need to be run consistently and in tandem with each other. Only in this way can the market risk of an FHC be reasonably controlled.

Therefore, prudential regulation and consolidated regulation together form regulatory principles for the protection of FHCs, which cut across specific regulatory actions in different jurisdictions and gradually reached regulatory consensus after the 2008 financial crisis.

References

1. AMF (2023) L'AMF est-elle compétente en matière d'assurance-vie (Does the AMF have jurisdiction over life insurance)? Paris. https://www.amf-france.org/fr/lamf-est-elle-competente-en-matiere-dassurance-vie-0. Accessed 29 July 2023.
2. Anand A (2016) Systemic risk, institutional design, and the regulation of financial markets. Oxford University Press, Oxford
3. Association of Supervisors of Banks of the Americas (2008) Consolidated supervision, Mexico. http://www.asbasupervision.com/en/todos/biblioteca-virtual-esp/i-publicaciones-asba/i-1-grupos-de-trabajo/757-gt04-2/file. Accessed 27 Jan 2021
4. Ballis W (1937) The legal position of war: changes in its practice and theory from platoin to vittel. Springer, Berlin
5. Basel Committee on Banking Supervision (2012) Core principles for effective banking supervision. Basel. https://www.bis.org/publ/bcbs230.pdf. Accessed 18 Jan 2021
6. Basurto X, Kingsley G (2010) A systematic approach to institutional analysis: applying crawford and ostrom's grammar. Polit Res Q 63:523
7. Bonneau T (2021) Droit bancaire. Dalloz, Paris
8. Castres SF (1993) Les sociétés dites "holdings" (So-called holding companies), Dissertation, Panthéon-Assas University Paris II
9. Couret A (1997) Les sociétés holdings (Holding companies). Presses universitaires de France (University press of France), Paris
10. Crowe C, Meade EE (2007) The evolution of central bank governance around the world. J Econ Perspect 21:69
11. Cuaresma JC (2002) The Gramm-Leach-Bliley Act. Berkeley Technol Law J 17:497
12. Cudjoe RV (2000) The social and legal position of widows and orphans in classical Athens. Thesis, University of Glasgow
13. Deakin S (2015) The evolution of theory and method in law and finance. In: Moloney N et al (eds) The Oxford handbook of financial regulation, 1st edn. Oxford University Press, Oxford, p 22
14. Drach A, Feiertag O (2018) Le sens de la mondialisation: surveillance bancaire et globalisation financière du xxe au xxie siècle (The meaning of globalization: banking supervision and financial globalization from the 20th to the 21st century). Monde(s) 13:133
15. Dulong D (eds) (2012) Sociologie des institutions politiques (Sociology of political institutions). La Découverte (The Discovery), Paris

16. European Parliament (2024) The European Central Bank (ECB), European Parliament. https://www.europarl.europa.eu/factsheets/en/sheet/13/the-european-central-bank-ecb. Accessed 27 Jan 2021
17. Gleeson S (2018) The legal concept of money. Oxford University Press, Oxford
18. Gubby H (2016) English legal terminology: legal concepts in language. Eleven International Publishing, Hague
19. Herrera PA, Huylenbroeck GV (2005) A generic four-step methodology for institutional analysis of governance structures, Researchgate. https://www.researchgate.net/publication/23509411_A_Generic_Four-step_Methodology_For_Institutional_Analysis. Accessed 20 Oct 2020
20. Jeanneney SG (2006) Independence of the central bank of west African states: an expected reform? Revue d'économie du développement 14:45
21. Jessop B (1997) Survey article: the regulation approach. J Polit Philos 3:288
22. Jia H (2016) The conventional practice of legal institutions- the analysis based on institutional theory of law. Xiamen University Law Review 1: 49. (贾焕银:《法律制度的惯例实践——基于制度法律理论的分析》,载《厦门大学法律评论》2016年第1期,第49页。)
23. Johnson AV (1977) A definition of the concept of law. Mid-Am Rev Sociol 2:49
24. Lo W (2020) La fiscalité des groupes de sociétés: entre incitation et restriction (Group taxation: between incentives and restrictions). Thesis, Toulouse 1 Capitole University
25. Ly KC (2017) Banking activities, insolvency risk, and mergers and acquisitions: the case of different bank structures in USA. University of Glasgow, Thesis
26. Masciandaro D, Quintyn M (2013) The evolution of financial supervision: the continuing search for the holy grail. In: Balling M, Gnan E (eds) 50 years of money and finance: Lessons and challenges, 1st edn. Larcier, Brussels, p 264
27. Mcclintock B (1996) International financial instability and the financial derivatives market. J Econ Issues XXX:28
28. Mishkin F (2013) Monnaie, banque et marchés financiers (Money, banking and financial markets). Pearson, Paris
29. Moloney N (2014) EU securities and financial markets regulation. Oxford University Press, Oxford
30. Murphy T (2006) Institutions of law: an essay in legal theory by Neil. Irish Jurist 41:140
31. Narassiguin P (2004) Monnaie : Banques et banques centrales dans la zone euro (Currency: Banks and central banks in the euro zone). De Boeck Supérieur, Paris
32. Ocampo JA (2014) The Latin American debt crisis in historical perspective. In: Stiglitz JE, Heymann D (eds) Life after debt: the origins and resolutions of debt crisis, 1st edn. Palgrave Macmillan, London, p 87
33. Ogus AI (2004) Regulation: legal form and economic theory. Hart Publishing, Oxford
34. Oppetit B (1963) Les rapports des personnes morales et de leurs membres (Relationships between legal entities and their members), Thesis, Ancienne université de Paris (Former University of Paris)
35. Perrut P (2012) La régulation financière après la crise des "subprimes" : quelles leçons et quelles réformes (Financial regulation after the subprime crisis: lessons and reforms)? Fondation Robert Schuman. https://www.robert-schuman.eu/fr/questions-d-europe/0246-la-regulation-financiere-apres-la-crise-des-subprimes-quelles-lecons-et-quelles-reformes. Accessed 23 Jan 2021
36. Rafael LA (2014) Essential elements of the rule of law concept in the EU. SSRN Electron J 1–2
37. Rahim MM (2013) Legal regulation of corporate social responsibility: a meta-regulation approach of law for raising CSR in a Weak economy. Springer, Heidelberg
38. Stewart J (2000) Financial regulation in ireland: should the regulator be the central bank? J Finan Regul Compliance 9:42
39. Vie-publique.fr (2021) Pourquoi une Europe unie? Vie-publique.fr. https://www.vie-publique.fr/fiches/20308-pourquoi-une-europe-unie. Accessed 27 Jan 2021

40. Ye L, WU Y (2017) An outline of look-through regulation of financial markets. Law Sci 12:12. (叶林和吴烨:《金融市场的"穿透式"监管论纲》,法学,2017年第12期,第12页)
41. Zhao S (2013) A query on the topic "legal rules" in Chinese jurisprudence. Legal Forum 5:123

Chapter 3
Financial Market Regulation of Shareholders' Rights in Financial Holding Companies Beyond China

Abstract There is a sound rationale for regulating the rights of shareholders in FHCs in jurisdictions beyond China. This approach addresses not only the challenges posed by controlling shareholders in relation to related party transactions and interference in business decisions but also the vulnerabilities in the protection of minority shareholders' rights and the multiple barriers to tort remedies. To achieve the regulation of shareholder rights in FHCs, appropriate measures should be adopted for controlling shareholders and minority shareholders. In terms of controlling shareholders, FHCs can limit the participation of controlling shareholders by limiting their control over the board of directors and by innovating voting systems. For minority shareholders, FHCs can use shareholder agreements and cross-border arbitration systems to achieve the goal of protecting minority shareholders' rights.

Keywords Related party transactions · Interference · Controlling shareholders · Voting systems · Cross-border arbitration

The protection of shareholders' rights is a frequently mentioned topic in commercial law, so what rights do shareholders have? First, shareholders' rights are statutory rights [3]. Second, the content of shareholders' rights and their enforcement need to be reflected by legal practice or case law [2]. However, although the rights of shareholders are described in legal texts, they lack generalizability. It seems to rely more on the findings and summaries of researchers. For example, in the works of French scholars, shareholder rights related to the right to vote, the right to dividends, and the right to information can be found [21]. Professor John Armour, a UK company law scholar, also specialises in summarising shareholder rights in common law countries and argues that shareholder rights can be analysed from different perspectives, including at the level of lawyers and at the level of institutions. In summary, he identifies seven areas of rights involving shareholders, including rights to pay cash flows, rights to control, rights to information, rights to have directors and officers comply with their fiduciary duties, enforcement by litigation, shareholder voting, and market pricing [3]. In addition, the rights of shareholders are defined in a study published by the European Parliament in 2012 [22]. In this report, shareholders are classified as

K. Ma, *Shareholder Rights Protection Mechanisms for Chinese Financial Holding Companies*, International and Comparative Law in the Asia Pacific,
https://doi.org/10.1007/978-981-97-9731-8_3

shareholders with voting rights, shareholders holding securities, shareholders acting in the interests of the company as a whole, and shareholders acting in concert. The content of shareholders' rights likewise varies between the different classifications. When shareholders have the right to vote, their specific rights include the right to be informed, the right to vote, and so on, whereas when shareholders hold securities, their rights include the right to dividends [22]. Therefore, although shareholders' rights are set out in legal texts, they need to be generalised by legal practitioners.

As statutory rights, shareholders' rights are established in legal texts and are therefore governed by hard law, including the enforcement of rights and the monitoring of rights. It can be found in several legal texts. In Europe, for example, its regulation of shareholder rights has undergone a long period of study. In 2007[1] and 2017,[2] the EU introduced specific acts on the regulation of shareholders' rights, which together form the European Shareholder Rights Directive.[3] Both Europe and the Member States have updated their shareholder rights regulations to emphasise the need for greater corporate transparency and to encourage long-term shareholder engagement [5]. For companies with offices in Member States, EU law requires that Member States ensure that companies have the right to identify their shareholders, but EU law sets a threshold of no more than 0.5%, which has been criticised by jurists because it creates disparities within the EU, and French law does not support this threshold provision [5]. With respect to the regulation of FHCs, the attitude of French law is positive. Given the complexity of control relationships in FHCs, accurate identification of shareholders is essential, guided by the principle of prudential regulation based on market risk prevention. Moreover, under the principle of consolidated regulation, the supervision of FHCs involves identifying not only the operational risks in the home country but also the risks faced by subsidiaries in other countries. Only when these shareholders are fully identified, including the controlling shareholder and the actual controller, can the objectives of prudential and consolidated regulation be achieved. The TMSAFHC in Chinese law also clearly indicates the need to strengthen the regulation of shareholders by comprehensively identifying the true identity of shareholders of FHCs. Therefore, there should be a consensus on shareholder governance.

In addition, in the case of FHCs, the law imposes greater requirements on the qualifications of their shareholders and strict regulations on the enforcement of shareholders' rights. This reflects the fact that shareholder rights can vary depending on the shareholders. In the U.S., UK, and France, the regulation of shareholders' rights can also be affirmed in company law and FHC regulatory legislation. Shareholder rights are regulated both to protect the statutory rights of shareholders and to prevent

---

[1] See Directive 2007/36/EC of the European Parliament and of the Council of 11 July 2007 on the exercise of certain rights of shareholders in listed companies.

[2] See Directive (EU) 2017/828 of the European Parliament and of the Council of 17 May 2017 amending Directive 2007/36/EC as regards the encouragement of long-term shareholder engagement.

[3] See Directive (EU) 2017/828 of the European Parliament and of the Council of 17 May 2017 amending Directive 2007/36/EC as regards the encouragement of long-term shareholder engagement.

abuse of those rights. To argue this point well, the following paragraphs answer the questions of why and how to regulate shareholder rights in FHCs.

3.1 Reasons for Regulating Shareholders' Rights

The regulation of shareholder rights in FHCs is an important proposition that seeks to mediate the conflicting interests of controlling and minority shareholders in FHCs.

3.1.1 Addressing the Challenges of Controlling Shareholders

In accordance with the principle of equal treatment of shareholders [34], the controlling shareholder has a greater voice in the FHCs.[4] This means that it can have a significant effect on the operations of the company and the interests of other shareholders. This approach is consistent with both the equality of the rights and obligations of shareholders as defined in the articles of association and the equal treatment of shareholders in relation to corporate decision-making [33]. For this reason, the legal systems in many jurisdictions impose strict restrictions on controlling shareholders. Their main purpose is to avoid the abuse of control by controlling shareholders [35].

In the case of FHCs, one of the things that distinguishes them from ordinary companies is the enormous impact they can have on the systemic risk of financial markets. This phenomenon has been demonstrated in several financial crises. Therefore, external regulation is needed. Two of the more prominent types of abuse of controlling shareholders' rights are related party transactions (RPTs) and interference in business decisions.

3.1.1.1 Challenges from Related Party Transactions of Controlling Shareholders

Compared with those of ordinary companies, the RPTs of controlling shareholders in FHCs require more regulation. It manifests itself in several ways. First, RPTs in FHCs are more complex and hidden, making them more difficult to detect. For the characteristics of FHCs, the book has identified that control relationships are central to this type of company and that there is a wide variety of subsidiaries, all of which are usually linked to credit institutions. If the definition of a related party of an FHC is followed, the FHC's related parties are often professionals in the field of financial services and have a wealth of financial fraud at their disposal when the controlling shareholder transacts with a subsidiary of the FHC. For nonprofessional shareholders,

---

[4] And the controlling shareholder has more shares than the minority shareholder, he or she has more influence on the company's decisions. This reflects the principle of equality of shareholdings.

it is difficult to detect fraud. Second, RPTs by the controlling shareholder of an FHC may expose the company to noncommercial risk. The controlling shareholder of an FHC can sometimes be the government [19]. In this context, the RPT practices of controlling shareholders can, in some cases, fall into political risk, which can be very reactive for commercial companies. It also explains the use of many provisions in the legislation on FHCs in many jurisdictions that specifically regulate the RPTs of FHCs.[5] This is one of the most frequent and important difficulties faced in the protection of the rights of shareholders in FHCs.

The case of *Acosta v. JPMorgan Chase & Co.*[6] in U.S. law provides a vivid explanation of the potential RPTs of a controlling shareholder of an FHC in cross-border business. The background to the case is set out in the United States District Court, where the plaintiffs were 339 individuals and corporate entities from Argentina, Uruguay, and Panama. In 1991, plaintiffs were persuaded by Compania General de Negocios (Uruguay) S.A.I.F.E. (CGN-SAIFE), General de Negocios S.A. (BGN), Banco Comercial Uruguay S.A. (Banco Comercial) to make investments in various financial investment vehicles. However, these three companies defrauded depositors, minority shareholders, and investors by setting up secret companies. These secret companies took the form of "twin" companies and Commercial Investment Holding Corp., which were very secretive. Fraudulent tactics included fraudulent purchases of U.S. Treasury bonds and potential undisclosed RPTs with JPMorgan Chase & Co in relation to the sale of Euronotes. These fraudulent practices ultimately led to one of the most famous bank failures in Uruguayan history. The plaintiff argued that JPMorgan Chase & Co, as the majority shareholder, should be jointly and severally liable to the plaintiff. However, the defendants refused this request. The judge finally dismissed the plaintiff's application. The judge gave the reason "forum noncon conveniens". The judge interpreted the case in three ways, namely, "degree of deference", "adequate alternative forum", and "balance of private and public interest factors". In addition, the case suffered from a few inconveniences, including the inconvenience of witnesses, the investigation of evidence, the Spanish language, court congestion, and the application of foreign law.

The case involves the FHC, JPMorgan Chase & Co [40], which is the controlling shareholder of Banco Comercial in Argentina and Uruguay and involves RPTs, making it an ideal subject for analysis. In the case of JPMorgan Chase & Co, the U.S. court did not investigate potential RPTs. However, through this decision, the

---

[5] For example, in EU law, see Article 170, 300, 303-306, Regulation (EU) No 575/2013 of the European Parliament and of the Council of 26 June 2013 on prudential requirements for credit institutions and investment firms and amending Regulation (EU) No 648/2012. Under this provision, if an institution acts as a member of a corporate clearing organisation and in this capacity acts as a financial intermediary between its clients and the central counterparty, its funds in respect of related transactions with the central counterparty will be strictly regulated. In U.S. law, see Subpart G of the BHC Act. Under this provision, for an FHC or a BHC, a range of assessment criteria is required for federally related transactions. These include cross-agency assessments, assessments regarding board guidance aspects, and so on.

[6] Acosta v. JPMorgan Chase & Co, 2006 WL 229196, 1-9 (United States District Court, S.D. New York, 2006).

book has identified many of the challenges faced by minority shareholders in FHCs in regard to monitoring the controlling shareholder's RPTs. The description of the facts of the case reveals that RPTs in FHCs can use a variety of hidden economic and legal measures that are too difficult for vulnerable stakeholders to detect. The consequences of these events were tragic, as best exemplified by the bankruptcy of Banco Comercial Uruguay.

In addition, with respect to RPTs between shareholders, the importance attached to this issue is repeatedly confirmed by EU law in its "Shareholder Rights Directive", which considers that RPTs by controlling shareholders can infringe on the interests belonging to the company and the rights of minority shareholders and therefore requires that significant RPTs within Member States must be submitted to the regulator or that the EU considers that RPTs by controlling shareholders can infringe on the interests of companies and the rights of minority shareholders.[7]

The regulation of controlling shareholders' RPTs in cross-border FHCs faces challenges from a few sources, especially when more complex situations such as cross-border litigation are involved. Case law has demonstrated the enormous difficulties faced in safeguarding the collective interests of FHCs in the absence of regulation.

3.1.1.2 Challenges from Interference in the Business Decisions of Controlling Shareholders

In fact, in case law, it is possible to find diverse types of shareholder rights disputes in FHCs. This echoes the importance of the research at the heart of the research. From a comparative law perspective, however, it is essential to select representative types of disputes, not only to balance the differences between different national legal systems but also, more importantly, to address disputes concerning the protection of shareholders' rights in Chinese FHCs, as discussed in a later section. It also responds to Professor René David's view that macro-comparisons precede micro-comparisons. The interference of controlling shareholders in business decisions is one such example. The importance of this issue is therefore not only that it is indeed controversial, as shown in the case law, but, more importantly, that it provides lessons for the analysis of shareholder rights disputes in Chinese FHCs.

In a profit-oriented company, the shareholders and directors of FHCs should make business decisions with the best interests of the company and all shareholders in mind

[7] See Article 42, Directive (EU) 2017/828 of the European Parliament and of the Council of 17 May 2017 amending Directive 2007/36/EC as regards the encouragement of long-term shareholder engagement. Under this provision, transactions with related parties may be detrimental to the company and its shareholders, as they may give the related party the opportunity to take possession of value belonging to the company. It is therefore important to provide adequate safeguards to protect the interests of companies and shareholders. To this end, Member States should ensure that significant related party transactions are submitted to shareholders or administrative or supervisory bodies for approval in accordance with procedures to prevent related parties from taking advantage of their position and to provide adequate protection for the interests of the company and shareholders who are not related parties, including minority shareholders.

[42]. On this basis, the business judgement rule was introduced in U.S. law [41]. Under this rule, directors are required to follow good faith, loyalty, or due care [19]. The court will not review a director's business decision to perform his duties in good faith. In civil law countries, such rules may differ. For example, in France, there is no business judgement rule. In France, public authorities can only intervene if there is a breach of law or noncompliance by a company. Otherwise, the government cannot substitute for the management of a company to judge whether a business decision is justified, and it can also be referred to as the "le principe de nonimmixtion" [36]. Furthermore, France has a civil liability regime for directors, and in the case of case law, France also recognises that directors should remain loyal to shareholders [30]. Nevertheless, regardless of how the system is designed, the core objective is that the company's business decisions should be made in the best interests of the company and all shareholders in FHCs.

Intervention by controlling shareholders in business decisions can be classified as either active or negative intervention in FHCs. This classification is derived from the doctrine of acts/omissions [18]. Active intervention in FHCs means that the controlling shareholder exceeds its authority under the law and takes active action to interfere with the decisions of the board of directors. This approach is illustrated in *Fairholme Funds, Inc. v. United States.*[8] Negative intervention in FHCs refers to a controlling shareholder's passive performance of its responsibilities in corporate governance, resulting in a breach of the rights of the company and minority shareholders. This was the French case in 2005.[9] Specifically, the regulation of the rights of controlling shareholders in FHCs can be divided into two categories: first, where the government acts as the controlling shareholder of an FHC, and second, where the controlling shareholder is an ordinary shareholder.

Challenges from Governments as Controlling Shareholders

There are several reasons why the government, as the controlling shareholder in an FHC, is prone to excessive interference in business decisions. On the one hand, it is due to political criteria and is not based on its management skills in corporate governance [26]. On the other hand, the current legal system does not provide sufficient regulatory strategies [19] when the government intervenes in business decisions as a controlling shareholder, which encourages government intervention.

It is not uncommon for the government to be the controlling shareholder in an FHC [19]. For example, in the aftermath of the 2008 financial crisis, the U.S. government became the controlling shareholder of Citigroup, which, according to the Sovereign

---

[8] Fairholme Funds, Inc. v. United States, 147 Fed.Cl. 1, 15-53 (United States Court of Federal Claims, 2019).

[9] The case comprised both a first trial and an appeal. See Tribunal de grande instance de Paris, 9e chambre 2e section, 12 janvier 2005, n° 04/06594; Cour d'appel de Paris, 24 mai 2007, n° 05/12291.

Wealth Fund Institute,[10] is a typical FHC. Moreover, this situation also exists in Europe, such as in France. Why do governments like to have shareholding in FHCs? FHCs can pose a potential systemic threat to local financial markets.[11] In the case of an FHC, one of the features is its control over the subsidiary, but it often cannot participate in the subsidiary's operations to avoid conflicts of interest; it only needs to assist the subsidiary in making a profit. There are some similarities between the functions of an FHC in this context and the objectives of the government, as the government itself is responsible for helping businesses grow and become profitable. The conflict-of-interest regulation of FHCs, in some cases, is similar to what is required by the government. The government's objective is to serve society and business but not to compete with business for profit. After considering the characteristics of the government and the FHCs, the government is indeed eligible to be a shareholder in an FHC. This not only provides adequate protection against a potential systemic crisis caused by the FHCs but also helps to realise the public interest of the business.

Internal governance can hardly be effective. One embarrassing aspect of corporate governance is that the government is both a participant in corporate governance and a rule maker at the same time. The government can influence other participants in corporate governance by changing regulatory laws, as illustrated in *Fairholme Funds, Inc. v. United States*.[12] At this point, the corporate governance strategy as an internal mechanism is weak. Other shareholders or management of an FHC may be able to rely on litigation to obtain redress. However, such cases often end up going beyond commercial litigation and into administrative litigation. It has not been easy to achieve success in many national legal systems. However, the French model of the Conseil d'État seems to offer a recommendable route for binding the government. However, the French model is rather unusual, as it is not common in other countries.

The U.S. law case *Fairholme Funds, Inc. v. United States*,[13] can be an example. In the midst of the 2008 financial crisis, the U.S. government enacted the Housing and Economic Recovery Act of 2008 (HERA), and the U.S. Congress established the Federal Housing Finance Agency (FHFA) to regulate businesses and undertake their restructuring and bankruptcy (FHFA-C). On 7 September 2008, the FHFA-C and the Treasury entered into a preferred stock purchase agreement (PSPA) with each enterprise. In return for the Treasury, the enterprises relinquished control, and the Treasury effectively became the controlling shareholder of the enterprises. In 2012, the Treasury pushed for an amendment to the PSPA, in which the enterprises pay quarterly dividends to the Treasury, but the dividends are 100% of the net profits of the enterprises. The U.S. Treasury was thus rewarded with U.S. $124 billion, but to

---

[10] The Sovereign Wealth Fund Institute is a leading research centre in the U.S. that analyses global companies.

[11] See Part 4, the Financial Holding Companies (Approval etc.) and Capital Requirements (Capital Buffers and Macroprudential Measures) (Amendment) (EU Exit) Regulations 2020. This part describes some of the measures in UK law for FHCs in terms of macroprudential regulation, including regulators, procedures for capital regulation and assessment.

[12] The trend is also present in France. Specifically, the law that came into force on 24 January 1984 (La loi du 24 janvier 1984) allows French banks to engage in noncredit operations.

[13] Ibid.

the detriment of the companies and other shareholders. All the profits of the business go to the Treasury, and no dividends are paid to other shareholders. It interfered with the business decisions of the company. As a result, Fairholme Funds, one of the shareholders sued the U.S. Government in the U.S. Court of Federal Claims to seek the return of money illegally collected. The judge upheld part of the plaintiff's claim, finding that the Treasury's unlawful disposition of the profits of the business exceeded its regulatory powers and failed to promote a valid business purpose by failing to exercise its judgement in good faith in relation to the business decisions of the business. The court, however, had no jurisdiction over the Treasury's fiduciary duties.

In this case, the Treasury was the controlling shareholder of Fairholme Funds. Its interference and dishonest representation of the company's business decisions violated the rights of many other shareholders, including the Bank of America and JPMorgan Chase & Co. Although the Treasury Department is acting as a commercial shareholder, it interferes with commercial decisions by administrative means. It creates a significant obstacle for other shareholders and companies to defend their rights. Similarly, government intervention in the commercial decisions of FHCs in the public interest is also present in EU law, as exemplified by the 2014 CJEU judgement in relation to the German FHC Portigon AG, which became the current German FHC following the restructuring of WestLB and in which the German government is the controlling shareholder. The crux of the EU case was whether the German government's state aid to WestLB was in line with the EU common market competition rules and whether the government had abused its administrative powers. The explanation given by the German government was that aid was based on a public interest need, and EU judges considered that the need for aid had to be fully justified, as the ownership structure and conflict of interest could lead to competition rules being impeded.[14] Thus, as FHCs are often closely linked to the occurrence of financial crises, government intervention in their business decisions as controlling shareholders is almost inevitable and will become more pronounced in the wake of the 2008 financial crisis guided by prudential regulation as the main regulatory principle. In the context of the common market, this case of EU law is equally exemplary for the protection of shareholders' rights in other Member States, such as French FHCs. Despite the UK leaving the EU, the impact of EU law will continue in the short term.

When the government is the controlling shareholder in an FHC, its active intervention in business decisions creates challenges for the protection of the rights of other shareholders and the exercise of management's power. These challenges are inescapable, and there are very limited measures that can be taken by other shareholders; hence, there is a need for the government to strengthen regulation through its own reforms.

---

[14] See case T-457/09 Westfälisch-Lippischer Sparkassen- und Giroverband v European Commission [2014] ECLI:EU:T:2014:683.

Challenges from Ordinary Controlling Shareholders

In FHCs, when the government is the controlling shareholder, some pressure is placed on the protection of the rights of the company's other shareholders beyond the commercial sphere, which is a special manifestation. On the other hand, ordinary controlling shareholders are widely present. The intervention of the ordinary controlling shareholder in commercial decisions differs somewhat from that of the government, as it lacks political influence, but it can intervene by controlling the board of directors in a commercial manner around capital influence.

The definition of a controlling shareholder is usually analysed by regulators in terms of voting rights and capital influence. The influence of the company, which is usually expressed in terms of the controlling shareholder having a significant influence on the election of the company's board of directors and management [6], is evident in almost all jurisdictions. However, from a purely voting point of view, the share of the controlling shareholder may be different; the situation in the US is based on 25% of the voting rights. In France, the French Commercial Code provides a 40% holding ratio of voting rights. In UK law, the situation is 30%.[15] Specifically, they have a pivotal vote on major corporate matters, and they can also have significant influence on a company's business decisions. However, the exercise of their rights is not well regulated. Therefore, it is not uncommon for voting rights to be abused. In UK law, for example, according to Westlaw's jurisprudence, there have been 126 cases of abuse of voting rights by controlling shareholders since 2000.[16] In these cases, interference in business decisions is a relatively frequent phenomenon. In theoretical terms, interference in commercial decisions takes several forms, such as delays in the payment of commercial dividends to the company and the use of the dominant position of control to induce irregularities in the company's guarantees [46].

[15] See Appendix 1, Listing Rules. The rules are not the same depending on whether the controlling shareholder is an individual or a company. When the controlling shareholder is an individual, it falls into four categories: (1) he or she is the individual's family; (2) he or she is the trustees of any trust of which the individual or any of the individual's family is a beneficiary or discretionary object; (3) in any company, the individual or any member of the individual's family which are directly or indirectly interested so that they are able to exercise or control the exercise of 30% or more of the votes at general meetings or to appoint or remove directors holding a majority of voting rights at board meetings; (4) he or she is any partnership in which the individual or any member of the individual's family are directly or indirectly interested so that they hold or control a voting interest greater than 30% in the partnership or at least 30% of the partnership. When the controlling shareholder is a company, it is divided into three cases: (1) it is any other company which is its subsidiary undertaking or parent undertaking or fellow subsidiary undertaking of the parent undertaking; (2) it is any company whose directors are accustomed to act in accordance with the controlling shareholder's directions or instructions; (3) it is any company in the capital of which the controlling shareholder and any other company and is able to exercise power of the type.

[16] Data from Westlaw UK. The statistic is not limited to FHCs.

Active intervention by controlling shareholders in business decisions is more common and represents an excessive exercise of their rights by controlling shareholders, whereas negative intervention by controlling shareholders in business decisions results from controlling shareholders not actively fulfilling their responsibilities. The requirement of legal regulation is that the controlling shareholder should exercise its rights reasonably and fulfil its obligations actively. Thus, these factors also become two aspects of the controlling shareholder's interference in business decisions. Specifically, a case on the French FHC Crédit Agricole S.A.[17] explains well the situation where the controlling shareholder interferes negatively with the business decisions of the company. In 1996, the French FHC Crédit Agricole acquired a 16% stake in the Argentine bank Banco Bisel, and in 1999, the share reached 70%, making Crédit Agricole the controlling shareholder of Banco Bisel. On 18 May 2002, Crédit Agricole sold Banco Bisel's assets to an entity controlled by la Banco de la Nation Argentina. This led to losses for a number of investors, minority shareholders and depositors, and 37 of these Argentines initiated proceedings against Crédit Agricole in Paris in 2003, seeking compensation from Crédit Agricole for their losses, including the amount of their original deposits in Banco Bisel, consequential material damage, and moral damage. The Tribunal de grande instance de Paris filed the case on 27 April 2004.

In that case, the plaintiff argued that all the promotional activities showed that Crédit Agricole had been interfering in the business decisions of Banco Bisel and that it claimed to be the first bank in France and the third bank in the world, among the most important banks in the world. It was on the basis of their trust in Crédit Agricole's reputation that these minority shareholders and investors had chosen Banco Bisel. Having become aware of Argentina's financial difficulties, Crédit Agricole could have continued to meet its financial obligations to these minority shareholders, investors, and depositors, but instead of actively meeting its responsibility to increase its financial support for Banco Bisel, it sold Banco Bisel's assets. The defendant Crédit Agricole, on the other hand, argued that there was no credit business in Argentina and that it had no subordinate relationship with Banco Bisel, which was merely its subsidiary and could exercise independent commercial judgement. Moreover, Argentine law did not require other shareholders, including the controlling shareholder, to increase their shareholding in such circumstances; therefore, Crédit Agricole did not breach its legal duties and obligations. The case was handed down on 12 January 2005. The judge did not uphold the plaintiff's claim for damage but found Crédit Agricole at fault. The plaintiff then appealed, and the Cour d'appel de Paris upheld the decision in 2007.

One of the issues in this case was whether the FHC Crédit Agricole had negatively interfered with the business decisions of its subsidiary Banco Bisel in Argentina. The French judge held, on the basis of Argentine and French law, that this negative interference did not exist because it did not violate its statutory financial obligations. On the one hand, it confirms that negative intervention is indeed a form of intervention in business decisions. On the other hand, it again highlights the relationship between

[17] According to the Sovereign Wealth Fund Institute, Crédit Agricole S.A. is a French FHC.

an FHC and its subsidiaries. As a kind of parent company, it is not directly involved in the subsidiary's business activities, but it is necessary to help it make a profit. Crédit Agricole's public campaign is designed to help Banco Bisel gain market acceptance and better profits. In that case, this promotional activity was the very reason why it was found to be at fault by the court. However, its legal liability was excluded on the basis of the relationship of control between the parent company and the subsidiary.

Therefore, in an FHC, negative interference by ordinary controlling shareholders is a reality in practice, but the process of proving it in specific commercial practices is very complex. For minority shareholders, the ability to obtain evidence is very limited. On the other hand, the internal institutional design of FHCs sometimes helps to insulate them from liability.

3.1.2 Providing Solutions to the Dilemmas of Realising the Rights of Minority Shareholders in Decentralised Shareholding Structures

In an FHC with a decentralised shareholding structure, the rights of minority shareholders also need to be regulated, as the rights of minority shareholders can also be abused. For example, in French law, the abuse of minority shareholders' rights more often manifests as negative abuse (l'abus négatif), which manifests as minority shareholders trying to prevent any modification of the social contract [28]. The case of l'arrêt Flandin also exemplifies this [4]. The analysis of this issue is approached from two main perspectives. First, the rights of minority shareholders are de facto vulnerable; second, dispute resolution for cross-border minority shareholders is under considerable pressure.

3.1.2.1 First Dilemma: Vulnerability to Minority Shareholders' Rights in Decentralised Shareholding Structures

The vulnerability of minority shareholders is a constant topic in the theory of corporate law. This problem is common to the theory of shareholder regulation of companies in almost all countries. Thus, the protection of the rights of shareholders in FHCs with decentralised shareholding structures cannot avoid this issue either. However, the more important reason is that it can provide a reference for the resolution of Chinese law. Indeed, in the case of an FHC with very concentrated shareholding, such as the German FHC Portigon, where there are only two shareholders and both are government shareholders [37], the protection of minority shareholders' rights is not a prominent issue. However, in the book, German law is not the focus of the analysis. In contrast, the shareholding structure of the U.S. and UK FHCs is very fragmented, while the shareholding structure of French FHCs is relatively concentrated but also has many minority shareholders when the protection of minority shareholders' rights becomes a focus of attention. In comparison, the shareholding structure of Chinese FHCs is quite concentrated, but Chinese law is currently undergoing mixed ownership reform, which means that the shareholding structure will become more diversified and that many minority shareholders will be created. However, as the Chinese FHC is currently in the early stages of the legalisation phase, it does not yet have sufficient experience to address all the problems associated with protecting the rights of minority shareholders in FHCs. Therefore, the protection of minority shareholders' rights in FHCs outside of China is analysed here. It also echoes the theories of Professor René David. In practice, these two rights require special attention from minority shareholders compared with controlling shareholders. They are analysed from the perspective of the right to vote and the right to information.

The right to vote is a fundamental right of shareholders in FHCs, which cannot be infringed upon or derogated from at will. All shareholders make decisions for the development of the company through the right to vote, which is a fundamental expression of shareholder democracy [39] in FHCs. However, under certain special arrangements, shareholders may choose to waive their voting rights in exchange for other benefits, such as preference shares. Such institutional arrangements are found in both civil law countries and common law countries.[18] In an FHC with a decentralised shareholding structure, there are various reasons why shareholder democracy is violated during the voting process. The vulnerability of minority shareholders' rights to vote can be demonstrated in case law, but such typical cases are not common from the perspective of FHC regulation. It will then be explained by comparing the relevant case law in France with that in the UK. The plaintiff in the case was a minority shareholder in Carlsbad National Bank (CNB), and the defendant was Carlsbad Bancorporation (Holding Company), who is an FHC. The case arose from the reverse triangular merger of CNB and New Carlsbad Bank on 21 April 1986, which resulted in Carlsbad Bancorporation. The merger was approved by the controlling shareholders and directors of CNB, with 82% of the voting shares. In return, CNB's controlling shareholders received cash equivalent to $48.05 per share and preferred shares in the Holding Company. The directors of the holding company will be elected by the controlling shareholders, and no rights will be granted to the minority shareholders. The dissenting minority shareholders were offered $35 per share by the Holding Company. The minority shareholders, including the plaintiff, believed that the merger was a securities violation and was sued for damage. Under Virginia law, mergers were not required to obtain the consent of minority shareholders. Moreover, during mergers, majority stockholders "froze out" minority

[18] For example, German law: § 139, AktG. Under this provision, shares with preferential rights in the distribution of profits (nonvoting preference shares) may exclude voting rights. Nonvoting preference shares may only be issued with a maximum of half of the share capital. French law: Article L228-11, Code de commerce. Under this provision, a company may create preference shares, either temporarily or permanently, during its incorporation or existence. Preference shareholders may or may not have voting rights and carry any type of specific rights. These rights are set out in the company's articles of association. UK Law: article 1241, Companies Act 2006. Under this provision, preference shareholders have no rights to vote.

stockholders. The minority stockholders argued that the merger did not comply with the principles of entire fairness in corporate law with respect to mergers. These factors created significant financial risks for CNB and minority shareholders. As a result, minority shareholders take action to prevent damage to defendants. Following the merger, the U.S. District Court for the District of New Mexico issued a conclusion judgement. The judge did not uphold the minority shareholder's request. The judge found that minority shareholders had not met the burden of proof to prove the causal link between the controlling shareholder and the directors in relation to the securities breach in the acquisition. Therefore, the judge did not uphold the minority shareholder's request for leave to appeal. In that jurisprudence, the voting rights of minority shareholders were virtually ignored, and their voting rights played little or no role in the FHC.

For shareholders' right to information, there may not be a uniform principle or definition in FHCs with decentralised shareholding structures, but some basis can be found in the lex specialis [28]. In this context, the book can return to the legal text. In general terms, shareholders have the right to participate in the basic decisions of an FHC and to be adequately informed. The information comes from the articles of association, the minutes of the general meeting of shareholders, or other documents concerning corporate governance. These findings have been confirmed by the legal documents of the various jurisdictions examined.[19] It is generally accepted that shareholders are entitled to inspect and obtain copies of these documents. Although the judges in *Cotten v. Weatherford Bancshares, Inc.*[20] differed in whether shareholders were entitled to copies, the Court of Appeals of Texas ultimately affirmed the right of shareholders of an FHC to obtain copies of corporate governance documents. The defendant in this case, Weatherford Bancshares, Inc. (WBI), was an FHC in which Cotton was a minority shareholder. In January 1996, Sharp and his daughter Statham became the controlling shareholders of WBI, reorganised the board of directors of WBI, and sent a letter to Cotton indicating that Cotton's shares had been redeemed. However, Cotton objected to the redemption, as he felt it was in breach of the Articles

---

[19] For EU, see Article 5, Directive 2007/36/EC of the European Parliament and of the Council of 11 July 2007 on the exercise of certain rights of shareholders in listed companies. In accordance with this provision, EU Member States shall ensure that for a continuous period commencing no later than 21 days prior to and including the date of the General Meeting, companies shall make information about the General Meeting available to shareholders on their internet websites.

For France, see Article L225-117, Code de commerce. Under this provision, any shareholder is entitled to have access at any time to the documents relating to the last three financial years of the company and to the minutes and attendance forms of the meetings held in the last three years.

For U.S., see "Delaware Court Clarifies Scope of Shareholders' Rights to Inspect Corporate Books and Records". In this document, the court has the power to determine the proper scope of books and records necessary for shareholders to supervise the operations of the company for legitimate purposes.

For UK, see s.116-358, Companies Act 2006. Under this provision, shareholders have the right to inspect and request copies and it is free of charge. For others, for a specific fee, they can obtain information such as the company's register of members.

[20] Cotten v. Weatherford Bancshares, Inc., 187 S.W.3d 687, 694–709 (Court of Appeals of Texas, Fort Worth, 2006).

of Association. Later, Cotton discovered inconsistencies in WBI's public records. In May 1997, Cotton continued to request access to corporate books and records, but Sharp and his daughter Statham supported Cotton's request at random. However, Sharp and his daughter Statham supported Cotton's request by means of random drawing. Thereafter, Sharp and his daughter Statham ceased to allow Cotton access to books and records. However, the trial court did not uphold Cotton's claim. Cotton then appealed to the Court of Appeals of Texas, where he raised key issues. Cotton argued that the trial court had erred on this issue because he was entitled to a copy of the corporation's books and records. However, WBI argued that Cotton was entitled only to extracts of the records, not copies, and that there was a lack of clarity in the definition of the term "extract". Ultimately, the Court of Appeal sided with Cotton. The Court of Appeal reversed part of the trial court's judgement, remanding the claims for trial on the issue of inspection claim and oppression. The Court of Appeal judge quoted the definitions of "extract" from Black's Law Dictionary and Webster's Dictionary to explain the dispute and held that the record was relevant to the accuracy of the facts provided to Cotton by the WBI, ultimately upholding Cotton's argument. The judge held that the record was relevant to the accuracy of the facts provided to Cotton by the WBI and ultimately upheld Cotton's view. The case exemplifies some of the controversies faced by minority shareholders in FHCs in regard to protecting the right to information. These controversies stem from the interpretation of the law. On the other hand, in this case, the controlling shareholder supported the minority shareholder's fulfilment of its right to information by means of a random drawing, which in effect did not provide complete disclosure to the minority shareholder. It was also an infringement of minority shareholders' right to information. In addition, the controlling shareholder's oppression of the minority shareholder in that case also created an obstacle to the minority shareholder's enforcement of its right to information.

3.1.2.2 The Second Dilemma: Barriers to Cross-Border Dispute Resolution for Minority Shareholders in Decentralised Shareholding Structures

When the rights of international minority shareholders in FHCs have been infringed upon, the laws of various jurisdictions recognise, to some extent, the availability of judicial remedies to shareholders. For example, in French law, it has been argued that the most frequently used way for minority shareholders to obtain systematic remedies is to use judicial proceedings [12]. U.S. law relies on the fiduciary duty doctrine for minority shareholder remedies. In UK law, directors' duties against unfair prejudices are a statutory remedy for minority shareholders, in addition to the "buy-out" of the petitioner's shares and shareholders' self-help [8]. However, the remedy of right is never easy. In particular, for cross-border dispute resolution, international minority shareholders face multiple obstacles, such as financial costs and differences in legal systems, which undermine their confidence. These obstacles cannot be effectively addressed from internal governance in FHCs, as they are beyond the scope of internal governance. Therefore, regulation is necessary. Specifically, the barriers to rights redress are mainly in the form of options for cross-border statutory remedies and the high cost of litigation.

Legal scholars distinguish between "disputes" and "conflicts". They argue that this is largely the result of disciplinary differences. Social scientists prefer to use "conflict", whereas legal scholars tend to use "dispute" [32]. Therefore, when considering minority shareholders facing disputes or having a conflict of interest, it is likely that the book is discussing the same issues. From the point of view of dispute resolution mechanisms, four methods are more common: litigation, mediation, arbitration, and negotiation [7]. However, negotiation is primarily a contractual mechanism, so from a regulatory perspective, the main mechanisms to discuss are litigation, mediation, and arbitration [38]. These systems are prevalent in jurisdictions and widely used in commercial activities.

There are limited options for international minority shareholders. Financial market regulation has provided three main methods of dispute resolution in legal practice. The practical value of mediation and arbitration for resolving shareholder disputes has been questioned [8], although scholars have argued that they are beneficial in terms of the cost to minority shareholders of resolving shareholder disputes [10]. However, in the context of minority shareholder rights disputes in international FHCs with a decentralised shareholding structure, it can be found through case law that they face various types of cost pressures in relation to litigation issues [12]. Certainly, they are more interested in being able to resolve disputes quickly than they are under these pressures. Do these alternative dispute resolutions (ADRs) be effective enough to resolve minority shareholders' dilemmas? This is something that needs to be supported by more evidence. Therefore, from a practical perspective, effective avenues of remedy applicable to minority shareholders' rights for cross-border business remain very limited.

As to the costly litigation for international minority shareholders, in numerous judicial practices, it is generally accepted that the obstacles for minority shareholders to assert their rights are limited by their costs [12]. However, where do these costs come from? Few studies have focused specifically on this topic. However, some researchers have identified four types of costs for consumers to defend their rights, including financial costs, time costs, human effort costs, and legal costs [15]. These four costs also apply to shareholder rights remedies. In *Acosta v. JPMorgan Chase & Co.*,[21] for example, minority shareholders were not U.S. citizens in a cross-border lawsuit. They came to the U.S. from Argentina, Uruguay, and Panama and hired lawyers. In 2006, they filed a lawsuit in the U.S. District Court, S.D. New York, and lost. They then appealed to the U.S. Court of Appeals, Second Circuit, in 2007 but still lost. All four of these costs were vividly illustrated throughout the litigation. In terms of theories of legal thought, the natural law school believes that good law should be associated with morality and should be consistent with the values of democracy, freedom, and equality. However, Hart, a representative of the modern analytical school of law, believes that law itself contains both good and bad laws and that one

[21] It refers to "the Banking Act of 1933", also known as "the Glass-Steagall Act".

can oppose it in the face of bad law [45]. In the history of Chinese legal thought, both ancient and modern Chinese jurists have argued that good law should conform to basic moral concepts [45]. Therefore, jurists believe that a good legal system should be in line with basic moral values, such as fairness. With respect to the effect of a good law on people, the French jurist Montesquieu has a description in De l'esprit des lois.

> Je ne regarde pas comme une bonne loi celle que fit Cyrus pour que les Lydiens ne pussent exercer que des professions viles, ou des professions infâmes. On va au plus pressé ; on songe aux révoltes, et non pas aux invasions. Mais les invasions viendront bientôt; les deux peuples s'unissent, ils se corrompent tous les deux. J'aimerais mieux maintenir par les lois la rudesse du peuple vainqueur qu'entretenir par elles la mollesse du peuple vaincu [43]

The statement by Montesquieu highlights the role of law: a good law should encourage people to assert their rights rather than choose to endure and be weak in the face of oppression. If international shareholders are unable to reduce the cost of defending their rights by means of an agreement, who should be more responsible for this? The regulator. In an FHC with highly dispersed shareholding, international minority shareholders must protect their violated rights at great cost, partly because of the design of the legal system and partly because of the suppression of the controlling shareholders. In addition, in the face of this, minority shareholders cannot be expected to protect their rights at any cost because it violates substantive justice in a good legal system. Only if the regulator reforms the rules of the game and imposes restrictions on the rights of controlling shareholders, can the cost of remedies for minority shareholders be reduced. In this context, it should be a part of the prudential regulation of FHCs.

3.2 Financial Market Regulation Strategies for Shareholders' Rights

Financial market regulation is a response to the regulatory rationale, which together explains the regulation of shareholder rights in FHCs. It has been argued that financial market regulation is necessary and urgent in response to the threat of controlling shareholders and the oppression of minority shareholders' rights [12]. It is also necessary to take separate measures for controlling shareholders and minority shareholders.

3.2.1 Regulation Strategies for Participating in Controlling Shareholders

Is "shareholder participation" a legal term? The French Reverso diction explains it as the ownership of shares in a company and a share of profits. French law also provides several explanations, including participation in the management of the company, sharing in profits, and being informed about the company's operations.[22] More specifically, one of the most important ways in which shareholders can participate in the management of a company is by attending the general meeting of shareholders [17]. In some cases, shareholder participation may involve more specific concerns, such as controlling shareholder activism and encouraging long-term shareholder engagement [27]. Therefore, shareholder participation is another interpretation of the protection of shareholders' rights in FHCs. It has been argued that controlling shareholders pose challenges to the rights protection of minority shareholders through RPTs and excessive interference in business decisions. Therefore, the book will also propose measures to limit the participation of controlling shareholders from the perspectives of limiting controlling shareholders' control of the board of directors and innovating the voting system for these two phenomena.

3.2.1.1 Restricting Controlling Shareholders' Control of the Board to Combat Related Party Transactions

Why can controlling shareholders' control of the board of directors be limited, which can effectively regulate illegal RPTs? On the one hand, the book explained the connotation of "related parties", which include the board of directors [33]. Therefore, by reducing the control of the board of directors by the controlling shareholder, the corresponding RPTs will be limited. On the other hand, in a principal-agent model, the board of directors is favoured to remain independent and responsible for monitoring shareholders and thus reducing the risk of RPTs. Therefore, in an FHC, it is important to avoid RPTs by limiting controlling the board of directors by controlling shareholders. From a shareholding perspective, the regulator's restrictions on controlling shareholders should be considered from two perspectives: the underlying requirements for control and the expansion of control. These two perspectives are concretely expressed in terms of the controlling shareholder's shareholding and the composition of the board of directors.

The restrictions on the controlling shareholder's shareholding vary across jurisdictions. For example, a controlling shareholder in a U.S. FHC is deemed to have more than 25% of the voting power in a company such as a bank, either directly or indirectly, and this does not distinguish between voting classes.[23] The French Commercial Code indicates three types of control of a company, including de jure control, joint control, and de facto control.[24] Therefore, the controlling shareholder's shareholding limit of an FHC will also be evaluated under prudential criteria. It is set

[22] See Article 1, Loi n° 94-640 du 25 juillet 1994 relative à l'amélioration de la participation des salariés dans l'entreprise. It demonstrates that employee shareholders can participate in the amendment of the articles of association through an extraordinary general meeting.

[23] See Article (n), 12 C.F.R. § 225.2.

[24] See Article L. 233–3, Code de commerce.

out in detail in the "Core Principles for Effective Banking Supervision" published by the Basel Committee on Banking Supervision.

For the composition of the board structure, in FHCs, the system of independent directors is an important step in limiting the control of controlling shareholders on the board. It is certainly not just a measure for regulators but also a central concern in the internal governance of companies. While the book will later explore the value of independent directorships in FHCs in terms of corporate governance code monitoring, the book will focus on the legal regulatory perspective. In some jurisdictions, one-tire is the dominant form of FHCs, although the two-tire structure is gradually becoming accepted. In this model, independent directors are required to form much of the board of directors. Examples include the U.S. and France.[25] France requires that independent directors be at least two-thirds of the board.[26] Moreover, it is an effective means of limiting controlling shareholder control of the board of directors by imposing higher requirements for independent directors on the board and thereby improving the structure of the board.

3.2.1.2 Innovating Voting Systems to Combat Excessive Interference in Business Decisions by Controlling Shareholders

The intervention of controlling shareholders in business decisions can manifest itself in many forms, such as the negative interventions mentioned in jurisprudence. However, in the case of active intervention by controlling shareholders, they are mainly through the exercise of voting rights. Therefore, to respond to the excessive interference of controlling shareholders in business decisions, the book can examine some of the current innovations introduced to the voting rights regime. The main innovations to voting rights are dual-class shares and the proxy solicitation system.

Preference shares and golden shares in a dual-class share structure are typically designed in response to excessive interference in business decisions by government controlling shareholders and ordinary controlling shareholders in FHCs. Among other things, preference shares refer to the giving up of voting rights in exchange for a greater financial return [32]. It can be used to address interference in business decisions by conventional controlling shareholders. The gold shares are also a special arrangement in a dual-class share structure, which is usually held by a government authority. This allows for the possibility that the government shares may still control

[25] For the U.S. section, see Code of Federal Regulations, § 229.407. Under this provision, its directors are all expected to maintain their independence.

For the France section, see Code de gouvernement d'entreprise des sociétés cotées. According to its provisions, in widely held companies without a controlling shareholder, independent directors should make up half of the board members. In controlled companies, independent directors should make up at least one-third of the board. Directors representing employee shareholders and directors representing employees are excluded from consideration in determining these percentages.

[26] See Article L225-22, Code de commerce. Under this clause, the number of directors of a company bound by a contract of employment may not exceed one third of the directors in office. In addition, also see the 2020 French Corporate Governance Code of Listed Corporations.

the voting rights of the company at a very low percentage, which is an operational method in the privatisation process [16]. It can be used to address interference in business decisions by controlling government shareholders.

In addition, why can the proxy solicitation regime form a constraint on controlling shareholders' interference in business decisions in FHCs? First, it is complementary to the dual-class share structure. For international minority shareholders, a dual-class share structure is a strategy that protects investment returns at the expense of voting rights, which has a positive effect on the long-term sustainability of FHCs. At the same time, however, this does not mean that international minority shareholders give up their participation in corporate governance, as they also need to express their views through the general meeting of shareholders. Given their low shareholding and the relatively expensive cost of voting in a decentralised FHC where minority shareholders are spread all over the world, proxy solicitation offers a new way of thinking for minority shareholders. Second, proxy solicitation is essentially a form of proxy voting, but it is also a further innovation to this system. In contrast to those of the controlling shareholder, the views of international minority shareholders collected through proxy solicitation are not necessarily fully counter to those of the controlling shareholder because of the greater share of voting power from the controlling shareholder. However, on the same matter, such as the appointment of directors and officers and dividend distribution, when the number of minority shareholder proposals is sufficient, it can also have a significant effect on important matters of corporate governance. For example, when proxy solicitation is combined with weighted voting rights, it ensures that the board of directors is not completely controlled by the controlling shareholder.

3.2.2 Regulation Strategies for the Realisation of Minority Shareholders' Rights

It has been argued that two difficulties are encountered in the protection of minority shareholders' rights: the vulnerability of minority shareholders' rights and the multiple obstacles to tort remedies [3]. To realise their rights for minority shareholders in FHCs, some measures should also be proposed to address these problems. Thus, the realisation of minority shareholders' rights protection is a continuation. In this context, shareholders' agreement and the cross-border arbitration system are two systems for achieving the protection of minority shareholders' rights.

3.2.2.1 First Strategy: Shareholders' Agreements in Decentralised Shareholding Structures

A shareholder's agreement is a way of organising the arrangement of rights and obligations between contracting shareholders, and key factors in its success include its confidentiality [29]. As such, it reflects the free will of shareholders and is an effective way for minority shareholders to protect their rights in the face of controlling shareholders. When the controlling shareholder breaches the shareholders' agreement, the minority shareholder can bring a lawsuit or take other compulsory measures to defend his or her rights. For example, in the U.S. law case of *McMinn v. MBF Operating Acquisition Corp*,[27] the minority shareholder brought an action against the controlling shareholder for breach of the shareholders' agreement by failing to pay dividends and granting excessive remuneration to the controlling shareholder. It has been demonstrated that shareholders' agreements can provide an effective legal tool in business practice to improve the vulnerability of minority shareholders' rights protection. A shareholder agreement is a very general description in which shareholders can agree on many matters of corporate governance. Given the vulnerability of minority shareholders in relation to the rights to vote and information, the book will also look specifically at both the voting agreement and the agreement on shareholders' right to information.

In an FHC with a decentralised shareholding structure, minority shareholders find it expensive to vote. Moreover, their shareholding is low, and their voting rights are more dispersed in regard to decisions on important matters, which does not create an effective binding force on the controlling shareholders. Therefore, voting agreements can help minority shareholders reduce the cost of voting and allow them to participate in corporate governance. These are indeed innovations in the protection of minority shareholders' rights. Currently, the proxy voting system is commonly used in FHCs, such as JPMorgan Chase & Co[28] and Crédit Agricole S.A. [11]. There are also other forms of voting agreements, such as the voting trust agreement, which is similar to proxy voting and was confirmed in U.S. jurisprudence in 1928. Judges have held that a voting trust agreement is valid and legally binding if it does not violate public policy or a positive prohibitory statute and does not constitute fraud to other shareholders.[29] It can therefore treat a voting agreement as a broad concept that can be continuously innovated if the law does not clearly define the content of this agreement if there is an agreement between the shareholders on voting matters and if it does not violate regulatory requirements. Voting agreements have been used in FHCs with decentralised shareholding structures to save the cost of voting for international minority shareholders and to achieve better participation when they can expand the voice of minority shareholders. Voting agreements also need to be regulated, especially in FHCs with decentralised shareholding structures. Faced with the innovation of voting agreements, regulators of FHCs should consider whether to recognise their effectiveness from a prudential and integrated regulatory perspective.

Unlike voting agreements, in business practice, it rarely seems to see an agreement specifically on the right to information. In theory, this is possible because it is consistent with the free will of shareholders. Rather, it is more common to see

---

[27] McMinn *v.* MBF Operating Acquisition Corp., 164 P.3d 41, 2-55 (Supreme Court of New Mexico, 2007).

[28] See JPMorgan Chase & Co: Annual Report & Proxy.

[29] Mackin *v.* Nicollet Hotel, 25 F.2d 783, 78-788 (Circuit Court of Appeals, Eighth Circuit, 1928).

a specific clause in a shareholders' agreement on matters relating to the right to information. For example, French lawyers have argued that enhanced information clauses can be provided in shareholders' agreements [13], and this approach has been recognised by researchers [25]. In addition, Anglo-Saxon scholars also support the view that the scope of information, the format, and the mechanism for providing information can be agreed upon in the shareholders' agreement [13]. It is therefore an enhancement of minority shareholders' right to be informed. The shareholders' right to information is agreed upon through a shareholder agreement, which helps to strengthen the protection of the international minority shareholders' right to information. Shareholder agreements complement laws and regulations in the protection of shareholders' rights to information. As shown in *Cotten v. Weatherford Bancshares, Inc.*,[30] although the law provides a legal basis for the protection of shareholders' rights to information, it does not provide detailed guidance, which provides a loophole for controlling shareholders to deprive minority shareholders of their rights to information. In addition, although jurisprudence provides detailed explanations of the protection of minority shareholders' right to information, it is always expensive for international minority shareholders to protect their rights through litigation. Provisions in shareholder agreements avoid the vague application of the law.

3.2.2.2 The Second Strategy: Cross-Border Arbitration in Decentralised Shareholding Structures

Cross-border arbitration is a typical alternative dispute resolution (ADR) mechanism [24]. Notably, the main obstacles to the protection of international minority shareholders' rights are the inadequacy and high cost of remedies [10]. ADR is a good option for addressing these problems in cross-border operations [24]. It is open-ended about some of the specific solutions it encompasses. For example, some scholars have grouped these mechanisms into three types: "traditional private alternatives", "court-annexed alternatives", and "administrative agency-annexed alternatives" [9]. However, owing to the differences between jurisdictions in their legal systems, arbitration and mediation are the two prevalent traditional ADR mechanisms. However, it is important to note that the current discussion of ADR in shareholder disputes is focused mainly on arbitration, which, on the one hand, is based on the exploration of the current judicial practice in some countries, such as the U.S. [10] and Singapore,[31] which is focused mainly on arbitration. On the other hand, this may be because mediation is less efficient than arbitration and is therefore not favoured by companies. The historical development of cross-border arbitration can currently be divided into two forms: traditional cross-border arbitration and online cross-border arbitration [24]. Two classifications of this system are then analysed: traditional cross-border arbitration and online cross-border arbitration.

[30] See Chapter VI, TMSAFHC.

[31] See the Singapore case law in 2016: Maniach Pte Ltd. v L Capital Jones Ltd. and another [2016] SGHC 6.

In terms of the jurisdictions researched, the jurisprudence of the U.S. confirms the role of the arbitration mechanism in the resolution of shareholder rights disputes. The Delaware courts are radical in this regard [10]. Furthermore, UK law is hesitant about this issue. In 2005, the Company Law Review Steering Group recommended that the arbitration regime can be incorporated into UK company law to increase the protection of minority shareholders' rights, but this was not accepted [20]. In contrast, the case law[32] in 2011 was widely debated from a public interest perspective, but ultimately, the courts did not uphold the applicability of arbitration in the context of shareholder rights disputes. Continental Europe, on the other hand, has been relatively conservative on this issue. EU law established a regulatory framework for ADR, including arbitration, in 2013,[33] but it was concerned primarily with disputes between consumers and companies. However, French law is exploratory in its approach to the arbitrability of shareholder disputes, although France relies on litigation for shareholder disputes [12]. Specifically, French case law recognises the possibility of litigated arbitration in matters related to the removal of a shareholder from a company but does not explicitly respond to the question of whether a shareholder's voting rights dispute is arbitrable [1]. Thus, French law is somewhere between U.S. law and UK law with respect to the arbitrability of shareholder disputes. U.S. law recognises this option; UK law does not support it, whereas French law offers the possibility for some issues. These developments can also be extended to cross-border arbitration of shareholder disputes in FHCs.

Compared with litigation, cross-border arbitration is often considered to reduce the cost to shareholders [24], which is particularly beneficial to international minority shareholders. The challenges facing the protection of international minority shareholders' rights are limited access to remedies and the cost of remedies. Cross-border arbitration not only provides minority shareholders with more options to defend their rights but also reduces the cost to shareholders in FHCs with decentralised shareholding structures. Therefore, why does it reduce costs? This is for the following reasons. First, it is a quicker and simpler process than litigation. Although domestic arbitration is not necessarily less costly than litigation in theory, it does provide a relatively economical option for minority shareholders in terms of cross-border disputes in FHCs with decentralised shareholding structures. Naturally, it depends on the specific type of case. However, more options will offer the possibility of lower costs. Second, from a practical perspective, although there is some dispute in different jurisdictions as to the arbitrability of shareholder disputes, it is a relatively mature system concerning cross-border arbitration itself. For example, the International Chamber of Commerce (ICC) can provide guidance in this area. If the future judicial system takes a more permissive approach to the arbitrability of international minority shareholder disputes, then international arbitration institutions can respond relatively quickly.

---

[32] Fulham Football Club (1987) Limited *v* Sir David Richards and Ors [2010] EWHC 3111 (Ch).

[33] See Directive 2013/11/EU of the European Parliament and of the Council of 21 May 2013 on Alternative Dispute Resolution for Consumer Disputes and Amending Regulation (EC) No 2006/2004 and Directive 2009/22/EC.

Online cross-border arbitration is a manifestation of online dispute resolution (ODR), which was developed in the 1990s as a new type of ADR in the context of the internet [44]. It differs from traditional cross-border arbitration in that it uses the internet to solve cross-border commercial disputes, which means that it no longer relies on offline meetings between disputants but is a form of electronic ADR [44]. For some specific procedures, an electronic file management system as well as a recognised online arbitration platform such as the NetCase platform offered by the ICC in Paris is needed [14].

Currently, there is no established case law on the use of cross-border arbitration for the resolution of shareholder rights disputes. In the jurisdictions mentioned, the use of traditional cross-border arbitration to resolve shareholder rights disputes is currently confirmed by jurisprudence in the U.S. and France. However, online cross-border arbitration is not currently being used to resolve shareholder rights disputes. In Europe, although the regulation of ODR was established in 2013,[34] such as the ADR regime, it is applicable only to the resolution of consumer-related disputes. However, since ODR can be used to resolve consumer disputes, it is equally possible to use online cross-border arbitration to resolve shareholder disputes.

In addition, in 2020, U.S. legal scholars focused on this area and devised a framework for online cross-border arbitration for resolving shareholder rights disputes, covering various areas such as procedures, resources, and evaluation [31]. Although online arbitration for shareholder disputes is still at a theoretical stage of exploration, its optimisation of costs has been sufficient to attract attention to the resolution of shareholder rights disputes in FHCs with decentralised shareholding structures. This approach can significantly reduce the costs for international minority shareholders in the cross-border shareholder rights dispute cases mentioned in the jurisprudence.

Finally, the current development of online arbitration is a reality. In 2019, a research report [23] provided by a group of French jurists for the ICC came to some basic conclusions about online arbitration: first, online arbitration as a commercial reality has existed for many years. The ICC and the World Intellectual Property Organisation have become the two leading online arbitration organisations. Second, there is currently a lack of adequate legal regulatory frameworks for online arbitration, whether in France, Europe, or other countries. Third, online arbitration has been gradually revolutionised by technologies such as blockchain and artificial intelligence, and regulators should design a sound regulatory framework for this. Fourth, while online arbitration has the advantage of resolving disputes, human judgement should always be ensured in the context of algorithmic justice.[35] These apply equally to shareholder dispute resolution in FHCs.

---

[34] See Regulation (EU) No 524/2013 of the European Parliament and of the Council of 21 May 2013 on online dispute resolution for consumer disputes and amending Regulation (EC) No 2006/2004 and Directive 2009/22/EC (Regulation on consumer ODR).

[35] Ibid.

References

1. ABI RN (2019) Les limites du droit français l'arbitrage international: Le rôle de la notion d'arbitrabilité dans l'évolution de la faveur à l'arbitrage international (The limits of French international arbitration law: The role of the notion of arbitrability in the evolution of international arbitration favors). Dissertation, Université Panthéon-Assas Paris II
2. Alcouffe A, Kalweit C (2003) Droits à l'information des actionnaires et actions sociales des associés en France et Allemagne (Shareholders' information rights and social actions by associates in France and Germany). Revue internationale de droit économique (International Review of Economic Law) 2:162
3. Armour J (2020) Shareholder Rights. Oxf Rev Econ Policy 36:314
4. Bamdé A (2018) L'abus de minorité ne peut jamais être sanctionné par la validation judiciaire de la résolution rejetée (Abuse of minority rights can never be sanctioned by judicial validation of the rejected resolution), Le Droit dans tous ses états (Law in all its forms). https://aurelienbamde.com/2018/01/04/labus-de-minorite-ne-peut-jamais-etre-sanctionne-par-la-validation-judiciaire-de-la-resolution-rejetee-cass-com-21-dec-2017/. Accessed 25 Aug 2020
5. Barban P (2020) Publication des seuils retenus en matière d'identification des actionnaires (Publication of shareholder identification thresholds). Banque & Droit (Banking & Law) 58
6. Bebchuk L (2017) Independent directors and controlling shareholders. Harvard University. https://corpgov.law.harvard.edu/2017/05/03/independent-directors-and-controlling-shareholders/. Accessed 21 Aug 2020
7. Been V et al (2012) Dispute resolution: negotiation, mediation, and other processes. Wolters Kluwer, New York
8. Boyle AJ (2002) Minority shareholders' remedies. Cambridge University Press, Cambridge, pp 100–102
9. Brunet EJ, Craver CB (2016) Alternative dispute resolution: the advocate's perspective. Carolina Academic Press, Durham
10. Cheung R (2008) ADR and shareholder disputes: the Anglo-American experience and Hong Kong chai lenges. Asian Dispute Rev 4:118
11. Crédit Agricole S.A. (2021) Crédit Agricole S.A. - Convocation en AG (Crédit Agricole S.A.—Notice of AGM), Crédit Agricole S.A. https://www.actu-juridique.fr/annonces-legales/credit-agricole-s-a-convocation-en-ag/. Accessed 25 July 2021
12. Girard C (2002) Les actionnaires minoritaires (Minority shareholders). Revue française de gestion (French Manage Rev) 141:202
13. Goluba JM (2019) Shareholder agreements: litigation perspectives. Corporate Counsel Rev 167
14. Hörnle J (2009) Cross-border internet dispute resolution. Cambridge University Press, Cambridge
15. Huo W (2019) Jurisprudential analysis of the cost of consumer rights protection. Dissertation, Shanghai Normal University. (霍未:《消费者维权成本问题的法理分析》,上海师范大学法学论文,2019年,第15–19页。)
16. International Finance Corporation (2015) A guide to corporate governance practices in the European Union, International Finance Corporation. https://www.ifc.org/content/dam/ifc/doc/mgrt/cg-practices-in-eu-guide.pdf. Accessed 15 July 2021
17. J. O. L (2010) Shareholders' participation in the affairs of public companies: an insight. Int J Advan Legal Stud Govern 1(1):4
18. Julien J (2020) Droit de la responsabilité et des contrats (Liability and contract law) 2021/22. Dalloz, Pairs
19. Kahan M, Rock EB (2011) When the government is the controlling shareholder. Texas Law Rev 89:1294
20. Kaya S (2019) Suitability of alternative dispute resolution for shareholders disputes. In: Corporate governance: search for the advanced practices, p 70

21. Kuyven F (2019) Droit des sociétés (Company law). In: Oertel RR et al (eds) Droit brésilien des affaires (Brazilian business law), 1st edn. Larcier, Bruxelles, pp 131–133.
22. Laprade FM (2012) Droits et obligations des actionnaires (Shareholders' rights and obligations), European Parliament. https://www.europarl.europa.eu/thinktank/fr/document/IPOL JURI_ET(2012)462463. Accessed 20 May 2020
23. Le Club des jurists (The Jurists' Club) (2019) L'arbitrage en ligne (Online arbitration), Le Club des jurists (The Jurists' Club). https://www.leclubdesjuristes.com/les-commissions/larbitrage-en-ligne/. Accessed 22 Mar 2022
24. Lekkas Z (2015) Disputes in the Digital era: the evolution of dispute resolution and the model ODR system. Dissertation, Université Toulouse 1 Capitole
25. Leroy C (2010) Le pacte d'actionnaires dans l'environnement sociétaire (Shareholders' agreements in the corporate environment), Dissertation, Université Paris-Est (Paris-Est University)
26. Loch M et al (2020) The government as shareholder and principal-principal conflicts in the Brazilian electric power industry. Braz Bus Rev 17:25
27. Magnier V (2017) Comparative corporate governance: legal perspectives. Edward Elgar Publishing Ltd., Cheltenham
28. Magnier V (2019) Droit des sociétés (Company law). Dalloz, Paris
29. Magnier V, Barban P (2019) Blockchain et droit des sociétés (Blockchain and corporate law). Dalloz, Paris
30. Mahieu F (2017) La business judgment rule aux Etats-Unis et son application en France (The business judgment rule in the United States and its application in France), MBDE. https://blogs.parisnanterre.fr/article/la-business-judgment-rule-aux-etats-unis-et-son-application-en-france. Accessed 20 Aug 2020
31. Martinez JK (2020) Designing online dispute resolution. J Disp Resol 1:11
32. Moffitt ML, Bordone RC (2005) The handbook of dispute resolution. Wiley, New Jersey
33. Mucciarelli FM (2010) Equal treatment of shareholders and EU law-case note on the Decision "Audiolux" of the European Court of Justice. Europ Company Finan Law Rev 1:162
34. OECD (2011) Corporate governance of listed companies in China: self-assessment by the China Securities Regulatory Commission. OECD Publishing, Paris
35. OECD (2012) Related party transactions and minority shareholder rights. OECD Publishing, Paris
36. Papantoni M (1995) L'immixtion dans le droit des sociétés (Interference in company law). Dissertation, Université Panthéon-Assas Paris II (Panthéon-Assas University Paris II)
37. Portigon (2021) Portigon single entity accounts 2020, Portigon. http://www.portigon-ag.de/acm/cm/content/portigon/i/de/portigon-ag/finanzinformationen/finanzberichte.html. Accessed 25 July 2021
38. Staff P (2020) What are the three basic types of dispute resolution? what to know about mediation, arbitration, and litigation. Harvard College. https://www.pon.harvard.edu/daily/dispute-resolution/what-are-the-three-basic-types-of-dispute-resolution-what-to-know-about-mediation-arbitration-and-litigation/. Accessed 15 July 2021
39. Storck M (2012) L'exercice du droit de vote dans les sociétés (Exercising voting rights in companies). In: Fromont M et al (ed) Droit français et droit brésilien (French and Brazilian law), 1st edn. Bruylant (Emile), Bruxelles, p 889.
40. SWFI (2021) List of 195 financial holding company profiles by region, SWFI. https://www.swfinstitute.org/profiles/financial-holding-company. Accessed 20 May 2020
41. Thomas RS, Thompson RB (2012) A theory of representative shareholder suits and its application to multijurisdictional litigation. Northwest Univ Law Rev 4:1786
42. Thompson RB (1993) The shareholder's cause of action for oppression. Bus Lawyer 2:701
43. Versini L (eds) (1995) De l'esprit des lois (On the spirit of the laws). Éditions Gallimard (Editions Gallimard), Paris
44. Wang FF (2009) Online dispute resolution: technology, management and legal practice from an international perspective. Chandos Publishing, Oxford
45. Xu A, Li G (2009) History of western legal thought (2nd Edition). Peking University Press, Beijing. (徐爱国,李桂林:《西方法律思想史(第2版)》,北京大学出版社2009年,第201页。)

46. Zhao X (2020) Controlling shareholders in corporate governance and their legal regulation. Chin J Law 4: 107. (赵旭东:《公司治理中的控股股东及其法律规制》,法学研究,2020年第4期,第107页。)

Chapter 4
Rethinking the Financial Market Regulation of Chinese Financial Holding Companies

Abstract China is in a transitional period in the financial market regulation of FHCs and is still in an era of pilot regulation. The book now reviews the regulation of FHCs in China, which is highly controversial in terms of the legislative model and the uniformity of regulation. Chinese legislation and regulation of FHCs are still in their early stages, and more reforms will emerge in the future. This is partly in response to the adjustments brought about by fintechs to the regulation of FHCs and partly to resolve the deep-seated conflicts in the regulation of FHCs in China with respect to central and local regulators. To address these potential conflicts of interest, Chinese regulators should integrate prudential regulation into the regulation of fintech, in addition to the imminent need for a coordination mechanism between regulators. The Financial Stability Board will play a better role in the future. It is also the experience of other jurisdictions with prudential regulation of FHCs after the financial crisis in 2008.

Keywords Legislative models · Regulation uniformity · Regulation models · Fintech · Prudential standards

The financial market regulation of FHCs in China is subject to rethinking because China is now in the transitional stage of legalising FHCs. Although China has now approved three FHCs,[1] this is not currently reflected in the fact that these are mainly exclusively state-owned companies, whereas the previously mentioned FHC pilot also includes nonstate-owned companies. As a result, the corresponding administrative procedures are not currently in place. Therefore, rethinking the overall regulatory regime is necessary. In addition, there are still some issues that need further clarification in terms of legislation and regulatory models for the current regulation of FHCs in China. Here, we introduce the reform of the legislation and regulation model of FHCs in China.

---

[1] See Chap. 1.

K. Ma, *Shareholder Rights Protection Mechanisms for Chinese Financial Holding Companies*, International and Comparative Law in the Asia Pacific,
https://doi.org/10.1007/978-981-97-9731-8_4

4.1 Controversies Over Chinese Financial Holding Companies Legislation

An FHC is a relatively special form of company, but it is still governed by company law and other commercial laws and regulations.[2] Therefore, is there a need for specific legislation for FHCs? Or is the existing Chinese legal system unable to meet the regulatory needs of FHCs? This was once a controversial topic in the context of the financial market regulation of FHCs in China [17]. However, the prevailing view is now in favour of specific legislation for FHCs [29]. The reason is that although existing laws and regulations are equally effective in binding FHCs, the original legal regime cannot achieve a targeted interpretation given the enormous influence of FHCs on systemic risk in financial markets and the complex control relationships of their subsidiaries [29]. In addition, overly broad legal interpretations and discretion have created loopholes in the regulation of FHCs. This approach is not in line with prudential standards for the regulation of international financial markets after the financial crisis in 2008 [28]. Therefore, introducing special legislation for FHCs has become an important consensus in Chinese judicial practice. The controversies can be divided into two areas: the controversy over the legislative model for FHCs in China and whether the legislation on FHCs in China should achieve uniform regulation.

4.1.1 Controversies Over Legislative Models

Although it is necessary to have specific legislation for FHCs, it must also be based on the existing legal system. It ensures uniformity and authority in the implementation of the law [18]. Therefore, Chinese regulators should analyse the legislation of FHCs in two dimensions. First, China should be aware of the forms of legislation on FHCs in other jurisdictions, which will provide some useful experience for Chinese legislation. At the same time, it will also provide a basis for transposition of the law. Second, Chinese legislators should conduct a macro analysis of the Chinese legal history and legal system, which will ensure that the legislation on FHCs is more in line with the actual situation in China.

4.1.1.1 Understanding Legislation in Jurisdictions Beyond China

When analysing FHCs on the basis of legal texts, there are two main legislative models: the first is the creation of a specific FHC Act voted by the highest legislative body, which is represented by the U.S. The second is the absence of a specific FHC Act but rather the addition of provisions for the regulation of FHCs to the pre-existing legal system. Jurisdictions that use this legislative model include the EU and

[2] It can be evidenced by the regulatory law for FHCs published by the French ACPR.

its Member States, such as France. In addition, the UK's exit from the EU has led to a shift between the two legislative models for FHCs in the UK, which should now fall within a transitional period.

The first model.—The model represented by the U.S. has created a specific regulatory act for FHCs. It is enacted by the highest legislative body. In the U.S., the GLBA was enacted in 1999 and was voted on by the Senate and House of Representatives in Congress. In addition, although the U.S. has enacted specific acts for FHCs, it has also adapted other laws on this basis. For example, in the U.S., the Code of Federal Regulations includes provisions on the regulation of FHCs.[3]

The second model.—In the case of the EU and Member State models, they do not have a specific act for FHCs but rather integrate them into other legal regimes. For example, EU law has specific provisions on the regulation of FHCs in the 2000,[4] 2002[5] and 2013[6] Directives. France has added provisions on FHCs to the original Code de commerce[7] and Code monétaire et financier.[8]

UK Brexit.—The UK's exit from the EU represents a paradigm shift in the UK's FHC legislation. Prior to Brexit, UK legislation on FHCs fell into the second category discussed, mainly in that its provisions on FHCs were set out in its Financial Services Bill[9] and banking law.[10] However, after the UK decided to leave the EU, its Parliament issued a "Regulation" for FHCs in 2020, which was an important shift. The reason is that it is a regulation specifically for FHCs and not a regulation to be integrated into other regulations. This model is somewhat similar to the first model, as it was also enacted by the highest legislative body in the UK. However, it is not a specific act.

---

[3] § 1841, 12 U.S.C.A. They are a series of regulatory articles. For example, it mentions that if a BHC wants to be an FHC, it and its subsidiaries should have a good record of capital position.

[4] Directive 2000/12/EC of the European Parliament and of the Council of 20 March 2000 relating to the taking up and pursuit of the business of credit institutions.

[5] Directive 2002/87/EC of the European Parliament and of the Council of 16 December 2002 on the supplementary supervision of credit institutions, insurance undertakings and investment firms in a financial conglomerate and amending Council Directives 73/239/EEC, 79/267/EEC, 92/49/EEC, 92/96/EEC, 93/6/EEC and 93/22/EEC, and Directives 98/78/EC and 2000/12/EC of the European Parliament and of the Council.

[6] Regulation (EU) No 575/2013 of the European Parliament and of the Council of 26 June 2013 on prudential requirements for credit institutions and investment firms and amending Regulation (EU) No 648/2012.

[7] Article L820-1, Code de commerce. This provision refers to FHCs, but it quotes the Code monétaire et financier, which requires one of its subsidiaries to be a credit institution.

[8] Article L517-1, Code monétaire et financier.

[9] Schedule 1, Financial Services Bill. These provisions, although they refer to FHCs, cover very little; it mentions prudential regulation and consolidated regulation, although no further description is given.

[10] Chapter 2, Banking Act 2009. These provisions establish that UK FHCs follow the definition of EU law.

The analysis of FHCs' legislation in jurisdictions can be somewhat representative of the main models of current legislation on FHCs in the world. The conclusion is also based on the approach to the selection of jurisdictions. The choice of jurisdiction is somewhat representative. Therefore, it is prudent to assume that both legislative models are equally representative. Therefore, why have these jurisdictions chosen such a legislative model? What are the advantages and disadvantages of each of these two legislative models? These are the legislative experiences to focus on.

Different jurisdictions should choose a reasonable model of FHC legislation. According to the book on legislation prepared jointly by European and American scholars, the rational logic of legislation is as follows [26].

> 'According to this ideal model of rationality, the rational subject takes optimal decisions in a context defined by the following characteristics (Simon 1958, p. 137 ff): she or he (a) is a human being, endowed with an intelligence that allows him or her to find the real solution to a given problem; (b) has clear and stable preferences; (c) knows all possible solutions; (d) can predict all the consequences of each option; and, finally, (e) has an objective criterion (utility, justice, security, etc.) according to which she or he is able to order all his preferences.'

When choosing between different legislative models, legislators can look to comparative law and legal history. When faced with multiple options, legislators can compare them by using different methods of analysis, such as cost–benefit analysis and risk analysis [28]. Specifically, the two legislative models of FHCs both aim to address the legal risks associated with the mixed operation of credit and investment businesses in international financial markets while providing legal protection to enhance financial competitiveness [28]. This is both the problem to be solved and the goal to be pursued by the legislation on FHCs. Therefore, how do these analytical approaches work in the assessment of legislation when faced with two legislative models? In the case of France, for example, according to the theory of cost–benefit analysis, efficiency is indeed an option to be considered in French legislation. As a codified country, the incorporation of the regulation of FHCs into the current code is clearly an efficient and effective way of doing so. This is in line with the French legislative tradition and the experience of civil law countries in comparative law studies. Therefore, in civil law countries, the second model has usually been chosen. Moreover, this model carries little risk for civil law countries, as it does not undermine their long-established legal traditions, which are more easily accepted by the population.

Similarly, from the legislative history of common law countries, many Acts have been created. For example, in the U.S., the Bank Holding Company Act was also enacted in 1956, prior to the enactment of the Financial Holding Company Act. Therefore, "Act" is a very common form of legislation in common law countries. This is consistent with their legislative history and with the comparative law experience of common law countries. This approach is more acceptable to the local population and less costly.

Specifically, the first legislative model has a good advantage in addressing the systemic risk analysis of FHCs. Moreover, it creates a very detailed act for FHCs, which is very specific and can be continuously amended afterwards. This makes the application of the law much easier. Its disadvantage, however, is that this legislative model has the potential to create conflicts in the application of different legal regimes, as it requires the revision and adaptation of all laws relating to it, which is an enormous undertaking. If such amendments are not completed in a timely manner, then conflicts in use between different acts may occur.

The second legislative model, on the other hand, involves less of a legislative burden. In addition, in codified countries, the adaptation of new concepts only needs to be performed in the code. Since this legislative model is already very familiar locally, it allows FHCs to respond well to the legal system. At the same time, however, it is inconvenient in that it may require more judicial and jurisprudential interpretations. Since not everyone can provide a systematic analysis and interpretation of the legal issues in the application of FHCs, this may cause some inconvenience to practitioners in the application of the law.

This process needs to be tested and explored to determine which model is more appropriate for the development of the region in terms of FHC legislation. However, before an attempt is made, the characteristics of the different models need to be understood. A jurisdiction may adapt between the two models, and the impact of Brexit on UK FHCs legislation is an example. The good and bad qualities of the two legislative models of regulation cannot be easily judged, but legislators can choose between them on the basis of their strengths and weaknesses, taking into account the national context. Here is just an indication.

4.1.1.2 Controversies Over the Legislative Models for Chinese Financial Holding Companies

The legislation on FHCs has been analysed by some scholars in the context of overall Chinese commercial and financial regulation [33], which involves the evolution of the overall Chinese financial regulatory legal system. It is a complex history. However, the book can return to the legislation on FHCs themselves. Overall, there are only seven instances in Chinese law that address FHCs. It dates back as far as 2006, when the Ningbo Central Branch of the PBOC issued a circular establishing a monitoring system for FHCs.[11] In Chinese law, its effect was limited only to the city of Ningbo. In 2008, the PBOC issued a circular to include deposits of FHCs in the reserve for deposits.[12] In 2009, the Chinese Ministry of Finance issued regulations on the financial management of FHCs.[13] In 2016, the Local Financial Supervision Authority

[11] Notice of the People's Bank of China Ningbo Central Sub-Branch on the Establishment of a Monitoring System for Financial Holding Companies (中国人民银行宁波市中心支行关于建立金融控股公司监测制度的通知).

[12] Notice of the People's Bank of China on the Inclusion of Deposits of Financial Holding Companies in the Scope of Deposit Reserve Deposit (中国人民银行关于将金融控股公司存款纳入存款准备金交存范围的通知).

[13] Certain Provisions on Financial Management of Financial Holding Companies (《金融控股公司财务管理若干规定》).

of Shandong Province, China, issued regulations on the development of FHCs,[14] but its effect was only valid in Shandong Province. In 2020, the PBOC issued the "TMSAFHC", which signalled an era of systematic and comprehensive regulation of FHCs in China. In 2021, the PBOC issued regulations on the governance of FHCs, which came into effect on 1 May 2021.[15] Among these seven regulatory documents, the earliest with national application was the 2008 PBOC regulation on deposit reserves. This may have been in part a response to the global financial crisis of 2008. However, the concept of an FHC was only established in 2020. Therefore, it represents a milestone in the regulation of FHCs in China.

Historically, the legislative controversy over FHCs in China has focussed on three legislative models [25]. The first model advocates the establishment of specific FHCs act by the Chinese People's Congress.[16] The second model aims to amend existing laws such as the Banking Law and the Company Law to include provisions on FHCs. The third model is for the Central Bank to enact specific regulations for FHCs.

From a comparative law perspective, the first model is that of common law countries, and the second model is that represented by the EU and its Member States. From the point of view of current Chinese judicial practice, at this stage, China opted for the third model. Therefore, how can the current choices made by Chinese legislators be viewed?

First, legislative choice is in line with the prudential requirements for the regulation of FHCs. The reason is that both the first and second models implemented in other jurisdictions have their own advantages and disadvantages. The first model implies the creation of a specific act by the highest legislative body of the country, which is the highest level of law in terms of legal hierarchy. The second model, on the other hand, represents a legislative orientation that does not treat the FHCs as very special. In contrast, the FHCs constitute only one component of the overall financial system; thus, an adaptation of the legal regime will suffice. In contrast, the third model falls somewhere in between these two models. This is a tentative regulatory solution. Under the third model, China has a specific regulatory law for the supervision of FHCs. However, in terms of the legislative level, it is not the highest level.[17] Therefore, it is a compromise solution, a prudent approach to legislation.

Second, this legislative model is more in line with the current basic national conditions in China. The analysis of this issue lies in the differences between China and other jurisdictions in terms of legal systems and levels of economic development. Specifically, the countries that insist on a specific FHC act, namely, the U.S., have a financial sector that occupies a very important place in the development of the entire

[14] Notice of the Shandong Local Financial Supervision Administration on the issuance of the Guidelines for the Regulation and Development of Local Financial Holding Companies in Shandong Province (Provisional) (《山东省地方金融控股公司规范发展指引 (暂行)》).

[15] Interim Regulations on the Administration of Filing of Appointment of Directors, Supervisors and Senior Management of Financial Holding Companies (金融控股公司董事、监事、高级管理人员任职备案管理暂行规定).

[16] The Chinese People's Congress is the highest legislative body in China.

[17] The highest legislative body in China is the National People's Congress. However, in 2020, the TMSAFHC were promulgated by the People's Bank of China (the Central Bank of China).

national economy.[18] A dedicated regulatory act also represents a high degree of local importance and reliance on financial markets. China's economic development has achieved good results, but the imbalance in its development is obvious. For example, the level of economic development in the eastern and south-eastern coastal regions of China far exceeds that in its western regions. The level of financial development of the country is still at the mid-range level [29]. This means that China is still a developing country. Therefore, at least at this stage, a specific FHC act seems to exceed the legal needs of China for FHCs at this stage.

For the jurisdictions of the second model, the stability that characterises the legal system of the EU and its Member States, for example, seems to determine the feasibility of this model. In the case of France, for example, the French regulation of FHCs can be traced to its commercial, monetary and financial codes. The codified character of the French legal system determines that it is a very stable legal system, which means that many new legal phenomena can be interpreted and regulated by means of amendments to the code. For the regulation of FHCs, very systemic regulation seems to be more conducive to their development. However, the Chinese legal system is different. However, the Chinese legal system has been profoundly influenced by the civil law state. However, its current legal system is still very loose and not very systematic.[19] Although the Chinese Civil Code, which had already entered into force in 2021, represents a trend in Chinese future legislation, at this stage, it still has a long way to go. Considering the development of the Chinese financial market and its current legal system, the choice of legislation is now more in line with current reality.

Finally, the choice of the current Chinese legislative model for FHCs is only beginning, not ending. The analysis reveals that current Chinese legislation on the regulation of FHCs is based on the extent of development of their financial markets and the characteristics of their legal system. Importantly, however, as a developing country, the Chinese economy and legal system are in a state of rapid flux. Therefore, when Chinese financial markets develop more expansively and the trend towards codification of the Chinese legal system represented by the Chinese Civil Code becomes more apparent, will the pattern of Chinese legislation on FHCs change? Some scholars believe that the current Chinese legislative model of FHCs is only at a preliminary stage and that in the future, China will still create a specific act on FHCs [18]. Indeed, the possibility also exists. In addition, Brexit has already led to signs of a shift in the UK's legislative model of FHCs. Therefore, the legislative model is not fixed. However, in any case, the current model of Chinese legislation on FHCs is only a start. Despite the controversy over three legislative models for FHCs in China

[18] The United States, as a highly developed capitalist country, is pivotal in the international financial markets.

[19] Some traces of this issue can be found in the legislative history of Chinese FHCs. For example, it was not until 2020 that the Central Bank of China specifically regulated the concept of an FHC. However, in 2006 the Ningbo branch of the People's Bank of China had already decided to establish a monitoring system for FHCs. Here an awkward phenomenon arises: what exactly is an FHC? Here there is a barrier to application.

and the fact that the Chinese legislation for 2020 already shows legislative bias, it is only the beginning.

4.1.2 *Controversies Over Regulation Uniformity*

Is regulatory uniformity an issue to be questioned in a sovereign state? Such a challenge exists in federal states, such as the U.S. [20]. In the context of Chinese law, it does not exist. However, the premise of this question is interpreted on the basis of sovereignty. However, regulatory uniformity does not refer to the issue of national sovereignty. The issue of uniformity in the regulation of uniformity in China is whether the performance of FHCs in different financial services is regulated uniformly or separately in a sovereign state. Furthermore, it also relates to the question of whether the authorities responsible for regulation are unified. The reason for this doubt is closely related to the regulatory regime of FHCs in China. The analysis of this issue also corresponds to models of FHC regulation in other jurisdictions [20]. The issue of regulatory harmonisation involves two main issues: harmonised regulation of different financial services (I) and a unified regulator (II). This will be analysed in more detail.

4.1.2.1 Controversies Over Regulation Uniformity for Different Financial Services

In the legislation governing FHCs in China, there is a great deal of controversy as to whether to adopt a unified approach to the regulation of different financial services and products. The reasons for this are largely determined by the current regulatory regime for FHCs in China. The Chinese FHCs regulation model has undergone a process of change [24]. The most important change occurred in 2018. Although, until 2020, Chinese FHCs lacked legal text for regulation, they were based on social reality. However, for FHCs that exist despite the lack of a legal definition, Chinese regulation before 2018 was regulated separately in relation to banking, securities, and insurance businesses. After 2018, Chinese insurance regulators and banking regulators merged to create the China Banking and Insurance Regulatory Commission (CBIRC). Thereafter, the insurance business and credit business were regulated by a unified authority, but the securities business was still regulated independently. Therefore, after 2018, the regulation of FHCs in China was carried out by two main authorities, the China Securities Regulatory Commission (CSRC) and the CBIRC. This regulatory model is similar to that of France.[20] However, in general, the regulation of FHCs in China is still in a sector regulation model.

[20] As shown in the Chap. 1, the French model of FHCs regulation is "two-regulatory-authorities-model".

With the legislation on FHCs in China in 2020, the regulation of FHCs entered a new phase at this time. One of the most important features of an FHC is the emphasis on control relationships and the special requirements for subsidiaries. In an FHC, it is entirely possible that the business carried out by the subsidiaries it controls may include securities, credit, and insurance operations. In this case, unified regulation seems to be more conducive to controlling systemic risk. Therefore, some academics and judicial practitioners believe that China is heading towards an era of mixed regulation in the future [33]. However, according to the documents recently published by the Chinese government, the idea of regulating FHCs within the model of sectoral regulation should be explored. Therefore, this controversy arises in relation to the legislation on FHCs: should a unified regulation be adopted for different financial services? The essence of this question is where the regulation regime for Chinese FHCs is heading in the future.

After analysing regulatory models from other jurisdictions, the book proposes two models based on institutions: "Distinct Institutional Models for Macro and Micro" and "Unified Institutional Model for Macro- and Micro-Regulations". In "Distinct Institutional Models for Macro and Micro", the book summarises three models based on other jurisdictions in the world: "single-regulatory-authority-model", "two-regulatory-authority-model", and "three or more-regulatory-authority-model".[21] On the basis of the history of the regulation of FHCs in China, before 2018, they belonged to the "three or more—regulatory-authority model". After 2018, it belonged to the "two-regulatory-authority-model". Therefore, is it possible that China will move towards the "single-regulatory-authority model" in the future after the implementation of the regulation of FHCs in China in 2020? The research argues that this is entirely possible. The Chinese government is inclined to innovate in the "two-regulatory-authority model".[22] However, either model is a variation of the "Distinct Institutional Models for Macro and Micro". Thus, is it possible for China to move towards a "Unified Institutional Model for Macro- and Micro-Regulation"? This depends on the development of FHC regulation.

The history of FHCs regulation was discussed earlier, but the history of financial regulation is not identical to the history of FHCs regulation. Since the founding of New China in 1949, the history of financial regulation in China has gone through five stages. These include the absence of financial regulation (1949–1978), the establishment of financial regulation (1979–1991), the establishment of sectoral regulation (1992–2003), the improvement of institutional regulation (2004–2017) and experimentation with functional regulation (2018–present) [31]. Importantly, the "Unified Institutional Model for Macro- and Micro-Regulations"[23] represented by Ireland and Uruguay represents the financial regulation of China from 1979 to 1991. The PBOC was subsequently responsible for all financial operations in China. This model is similar to the current model in Ireland and Uruguay. From 1992–2017, China had

[21] See Footnote 1.

[22] See Footnote 1.

[23] See Footnote 1.

three or more regulatory-authority models,[24] which were in place for 25 years in China. The year 2018 saw China move towards a "two-regulatory-authority model"; thus, financial regulation in China is constantly undergoing adjustments, but the ultimate trend should be in the "Distinct Institutional Models for Macro and Micro"[25] for flexible adjustment, which has been demonstrated in the two model changes approximately 2018. Therefore, it is unlikely that the Chinese financial regulatory regime will revert to the "Unified Institutional Model for Macro- and Microregulation".

The question of whether to move towards a "three or more—regulatory-authority model"[26] is possible in the long term. In the short term, however, the regulation of FHCs in China will be innovative within the "two-regulatory-authority-model", with functional regulation representing one such innovation [33]. The Chinese government's recent policy suggests that it will adhere to the model of sectoral regulation, which, in the current context, is reflected in the "two-regulatory-authority model".[27] It should still be limited by the short-term objectives of the government's work. After all, Chinese financial regulation has only started to change since 2018.[28] The former model has been in place for 25 years.[29] Therefore, the future legislation and regulation of FHCs in China will be innovative in the "distinct institutional models for macro and micro".[30]

4.1.2.2 Controversies Over Uniformity for Regulators

In the regulatory legislation for FHCs in China, apart from the legislative model, there is another controversy. This is what authority should regulate FHCs or what authority should be the primary regulator. This controversy arises mainly because there is some conflict of functions between the central bank and other regulatory bodies of the State Council in the Chinese model of FHCs regulation [21]. Coordinating in FHC legislation is one of the more difficult issues. The issue arises in relation to the regulatory model of FHCs in China. It is mainly in terms of whether the central bank should take the lead in promoting the legislation on FHCs or whether the central bank and other authorities should regulate and legislate at the same time. The Chinese FHCs regulatory model is based mainly on the "two-regulatory-authority-model". However, this model is premised on the central bank maintaining an independent regulatory status. In the context of Chinese law, the "two-regulatory-authority model" refers to the CBIRC and the CSRC.[31] It is a classification that arises for specific

[24] See Footnote 1.

[25] See Footnote 1.

[26] See Footnote 1.

[27] See Footnote 1.

[28] China has been experimenting with functional regulation since 2018.

[29] From 1992 to 2017, China has operated under a model of sectoral regulation.

[30] See Footnote 1.

[31] The CBIRC is China Banking and Insurance Regulatory Commission. In addition, the CSRC is China Securities Regulatory Commission.

financial operations. In addition, China created the Financial Stability Development Committee of the State Council in 2017, which is specifically responsible for the coordination of prudential regulation. In terms of the unity of the regulators of FHCs, the conflict centres on whether it is the central bank or another department of the State Council. Notably, in the Chinese legal regulatory system, the Central Bank is also part of the State Council. Therefore, in essence, the conflict over the uniformity of regulators is still centred on the internal agencies of the State Council in China.

Scholars who support having the central bank as the primary regulator of Chinese FHCs agree that the central bank is part of the State Council, along with the CBIRC and the CSRC[32] and the Financial Stability Development Commission of the State Council. However, they also argue that since 2003, the PBOC[33] has no longer been responsible for financial supervision, only for monetary policy, and that the independence of PBOC supervision has been mentioned in the wake of the financial crisis and the trend towards prudential regulation [19]. FHCs, then, as an integral part of the Chinese financial market, should also follow the current regulatory regime. Scholars who support separate regulations by different agencies argue that the current Chinese financial regulator is a situation where the central bank coexists with the CBIRC, the CSRC and the Financial Stability Development Commission of the State Council. However, they do not have a situation where one agency is dominant. Each of these proteins is responsible for different regulatory functions. Therefore, the regulation of FHCs can be independently passed between different agencies [32].

In the current legislation, Chinese legislators do not seem to support the idea of the uniformity of regulators, but there is some vagueness. The regulation for Chinese FHCs in 2020 does not include a unified regulator for FHCs, as the Central Bank, the financial administration of the State Council and the Ministry of Finance are each responsible for different aspects of the supervision of FHCs. Moreover, Chinese lawmakers advocate the establishment of an information sharing mechanism between different institutions.[34] This would seem to imply that the regulators of FHCs in China are not unified under the specific responsibility of one department but rather have a cooperative relationship. However, in terms of the actual legislative sequence, the PBOC issued the first regulation for FHCs in 2020. The other regulators have not issued specific regulations for FHCs. Therefore, this, in turn, creates a de facto situation where the central bank is leading the legislation and the other regulators are cooperating. However, Professor Jieche Su believes that giving the central bank too many functions affects the effectiveness and neutrality of its monetary policy [23]. This should be a cause for alarm for regulators. However, the future regulation of FHCs in China will not result in a situation where the central bank dominates the regulation, and a joint regulator seems to be the future trend.

---

[32] The CBIRC is China Banking and Insurance Regulatory Commission. In addition, the CSRC is China Securities Regulatory Commission.

[33] It is the People's Bank of China.

[34] See Article 4, TMSAFHC. Under this provision, the PBOC, together with the banking and insurance regulatory authorities, securities regulatory authorities and foreign exchange authorities will be responsible for supervisory cooperation and information sharing in respect of FHCs and the financial institutions they hold.

4.2 The Regulation Model Reform of Chinese Financial Holding Companies

Since the enactment of Chinese FHC regulatory legislation in 2020, the regulation of FHCs in China has entered a completely new phase, but its regulatory model is still in a constant state of flux. The future of FHCs regulation in China will be innovative in the "Distinct Institutional Models for Macro and Micro". However, in the short term, China will still explore the "two-regulatory-authority-model". The aim of this innovation will also be to make the model more relevant to the current development of Chinese society. Therefore, the reform here refers to the improvement of the "two-regulatory-authority-model".

4.2.1 The Reasons for Reforming the Regulation Models

Since China entered into reform and opening up in 1978, the reform of the Chinese legal system has been implemented mainly in response to the real needs of the economy and society, as well as to provide institutional safeguards for further economic development. This is evidenced by the successive processes of financial regulation in China [32]. In the specific case of the FHCs regulation model, the reform still follows this path. However, approximately 2020, the development of FHCs in China faced some new situations to which the reform needed to respond, as a reflection of Chinese reform and opening-up policies in this area. The current Chinese regulatory model for FHCs is still in a phase of continuous improvement following its reform in 2018. Short-term reforms will also focus on addressing some of the challenges encountered by Chinese FHCs during their development. This is done in two main areas: on the one hand, the challenges arising from fintech, and on the other hand, the focus on resolving the conflicts between central and local regulators faced in the regulation of FHCs in China.

4.2.1.1 Addressing the Challenges Posed by Fintech

Fintech has already had a significant effect on the development of FHCs in China. The development of fintech has made the systemic risk of FHCs more hidden and more difficult to identify. The development of fintech has led to the formation of a new type of market monopoly for FHCs. This is well demonstrated by the development and regulation of Ant Group, one of the eight FHC pilots announced in China.

Furthermore, this can also be evidenced by the series of measures taken by Chinese regulators. For example, the PBOC established a fintech Committee in 2017 to focus on the development and regulation of fintech. In the 2018 Financial Stability Report released by the PBOC, regulation and legislation on fintech became important parts of

Chinese future legislative planning.[35] The interaction between FHCs and fintech will also be key to improving legislation. In addition, the Chinese government released its 14th Five Year Plan in 2020, which states that from 2021 to 2035, China will focus on enhancing the development and regulation of fintech [5]. Therefore, fintech has far-reaching implications for the development of FHCs. The focus on fintech is a focus on the future regulation of FHCs.

However, there are some conflicts between innovation and regulation. On the one hand, the regulation of FHCs is based on the principles of prudential and consolidated regulation, but the development of fintech poses new challenges to the existing prudential standards. According to the World Bank report, this is the case mainly for financial products, payment instruments, transaction accounts, etc. [27]. For example, can bitcoin transactions be used in an FHC? How much leverage can be used for the financial products of FHC subsidiaries? How can the innovative payment instruments of FHCs be coordinated with the central bank's credit mechanism? These are all challenges to regulation in the current context. Many countries, such as France, which published a report on innovation from 2000 to 2015 in 2016, encourage financial innovation. The French government proposed that support for financial innovation can compensate for the impact of market failure and other public policy failure. To this end, France created la Commission nationale d'évaluation des politiques d'innovation (CNEPI) in 2014. However, how can the contradiction between innovation and regulation be captured in regulatory measures in the face of the development of fintech? It seems to depend more on the discretionary judgement of the regulator. However, French regulators and researchers are also paying close attention to the challenges that fintech poses to French law. For example, according to a research report in 2017, the Haut Comité Juridique de la Place Financière de Paris identified four areas of conflict that fintech poses to regulatory measures in French law, including confidentiality, security, standardisation and interoperability [14]. The situation is similar to that of Europe and France, where FHCs were first developed and where FHCs are themselves the financial innovation that will continue in the future [8]. The creation of the French CNEPI and the fintech Committee of the Chinese PBOC are perhaps responses to this question. However, the creation of a dedicated regulator is only the beginning. What criteria emerge for the future regulation and innovation of fintech? This approach is more dependent on future regulatory practices.

On the other hand, the exploration of fintech by FHCs is also facing anti-monopoly regulation. China introduced the Anti-Monopoly Guidelines on the Platform Economy Sector in 2021. It proposes regulations for fintech. For example, regulation focuses on ways to reach monopoly agreements through technological means, platform rules, data, and algorithms.[36] In fact, the antitrust issues arising

[35] See China Financial Stability Report 2018.

[36] See Article 7, Anti-monopoly Guidelines of the Anti-monopoly Commission of the State Council on Platform Economy (《关于平台经济领域的反垄断指南》第7条). Under this provision, operators in the platform economy and counterparties to transactions may enter into vertical monopoly agreements such as fixing resale prices and setting minimum resale prices through the following

from fintech products on internet platforms also have the same security, confidentiality, standardisation and interoperability issues as those referred to in French law. In this document, Chinese regulators argue that an important means of coordinating innovation and regulation is fair competition.[37] However, this still needs to be detailed in the future in relation to the four areas of conflict. It is not explicitly stated in the regulation of FHCs, but it is a challenge that must be faced for Chinese internet FHCs.

In addition to theoretical explanations, there is also some practical evidence of the conflict between regulation and innovation in current Chinese society, such as the Chinese FHC pilot: Ant Group, the most prominent internet FHC among the eight FHCs pilots announced by the Chinese government. Ant Group was originally listed on the Shanghai Stock Exchange in China on 5 November 2020. According to market projections, if Ant Group succeeds in listing, it will be the world's largest IPO [30]. However, on 2 November, the PBOC, the CBIRC, the CSRC and the SAFE[38] held a regulatory interview with Ant Group's substantive controllers [6]. On 3 November, its listing plan was announced to be suspended. According to an announcement issued by the Shanghai Stock Exchange, its listing plan was suspended because Ant Group's substantive controller, as well as its chairperson and general manager, was subject to a regulatory interview and because of changes in the fintech regulatory environment [22]. Subsequently, Ant Group issued a notice to investors and shareholders to clarify this matter. Thereafter, on 24 December 2020, Ant Group's parent company, Alibaba Group, was opened an antimonopoly investigation by the Chinese State Administration of Market Supervision and Administration and was fined RMB 18.228 billion on 10 April 2021. The case is an insightful exposure of the conflict between innovation and regulation in internet FHCs. The core lies in the challenges that fintech poses to the regulatory regime. It is a wake-up call for the reform of the Chinese FHCs regulation model, and it also signals a constant renewal of the Chinese future FHCs regulatory regime. In addition, there will be an increasing number of internet FHCs in China in the future; this case is a reminder of the development of internet FHCs. From a legal perspective, the conflict and balance between innovation and regulation will be an ongoing proposition.

---

ways: (i) Automatic setting of prices by technical means; (ii) Uniformity of prices by using platform rules; (iii) Direct or indirect price fixing by using data and algorithms; (iv) Limiting other trading conditions by using technical means, platform rules, data and algorithms to exclude or restrict market competition.

[37] See Article 1, Anti-monopoly Guidelines of the Anti-monopoly Commission of the State Council on Platform Economy. According to this article, this regulatory instrument is intended to prevent and stop monopolistic practices in the platform economy, protect fair competition in the market, promote the standardised and orderly innovation and healthy development of the platform economy, and safeguard the interests of consumers and the public interest.

[38] They refer, respectively to China Banking and Insurance Regulatory Commission (CBIRC), China Securities Regulatory Commission (CSRC), People's Bank of China (PBOC), and the State Administration of Foreign Exchange (SAFE).

4.2.1.2 Coordinating Central–Local Regulation Conflicts

The development of FHCs in China should not only remain at the policy level but also be implemented in the real environment. The complexity of the Chinese socioeconomic structure leads to differences in the understanding and implementation of the legal regime for FHCs at the central and local levels. This issue is key to the successful implementation of the regulatory regime for FHCs in China. Moreover, it is an issue that must be addressed in the current reform. The issue of central-local regulation of FHCs will be analysed here in terms of its blurred power boundaries and the problems of the system in terms of systemic risk regulation.

The future regulator of FHCs in China will be a joint regulator rather than a specific regulator. However, this regulatory regime in the current context remains at the central level, specifically at the level of the Chinese State Council.[39] Some blurred boundaries can be found between the regulatory powers of the central and local regulators. First, the financial regulatory authority in China has been concentrated mainly at the central level, and this trend has remained unchanged even since the merger of Chinese banking and insurance regulators that took place in 2018. However, different local FHCs tend to have different characteristics. For example, FHCs in Zhejiang Province are mainly internet FHCs, whereas those in Beijing and Shanghai are mainly state-owned exclusive FHCs. This then requires targeted regulation for local FHCs when financial risks arise. If regulatory authority is primarily centralised, how does one respond in a timely manner to the risk oversight of local FHCs? It appears to be subject to clarification. Second, the local FHCs regulators are not balanced. According to the TMSAFHC, the regulatory authorities include the PBOC, the CSRC, the CBIRC, the China Foreign Exchange Bureau and the Ministry of Finance of China. There are 34 provincial-level administrative regions in China, but in terms of the supervision of FHCs, there are three levels of financial supervision in China in terms of the establishment of local regulatory authorities. The People's Bank of China and the CBIRC are reasonably well placed at all three levels, but the Securities Regulatory Commission is only stuck at the first level in the arrangement for local provinces [6]. Therefore, when faced with the local regulation of FHCs, the Securities Regulatory Commission may not be able to achieve rapid coordination with other authorities in some cases. This problem may not be apparent in the current environment, but it will be a problem that will have to be faced in the future.

For the systemic risk in local FHCs, taking the regulatory law enacted by the Central Bank in 2020 as the boundary, the development of FHCs in China can be divided into two stages: before 2020, Chinese FHCs lacked clear financial market regulation and were based on social reality; after 2020, Chinese FHCs began to enter an era on the basis of legal texts. However, in the short term, the problems of those de facto FHCs will not be solved in the short term. On the one hand, Chinese FHCs legislation is still in its infancy, and regulation is not yet adequate; on the other

[39] According to the FHC supervisory authorities mentioned in the TMSAFHC, the PBOC, the CSRC, the CBIRC and the China Foreign Exchange Bureau and the Ministry of Finance of China are all departments of the State Council of China.

hand, the problems with Chinese FHCs are so deep-rooted that it will take time to adjust them. Systemic risk regulation is the most prominent issue. The problem of systemic risk in Chinese local FHCs is very prominent. This is due mainly to the very diverse types of local FHCs in China and the complexity of their affiliations. However, local regulators are still inadequate in their supervision of systemic risk. The reason is that although at the central level, China has established the Financial Stability and Development Commission of the State Council, this system has not yet been implemented in individual provinces and is still at an experimental stage.[40] Therefore, there is still a coordination problem between the central regulator and local regulators regarding the regulation of systemic risk in local FHCs.

4.2.2 The Proposals for Reforming the Regulation Models

The reform of the Chinese FHCs regulatory model should be based on the social reality of China and propose corresponding solutions to those reasons for reform, which is the right logic for constructing an external regulatory mechanism for Chinese FHCs. In response to the challenges encountered in the current Chinese FHCs regulatory model from fintech and the ambiguity between central and local regulatory powers, two reforms can accordingly be proposed: the introduction of prudential standards in fintech regulation and the construction of a central and local coordination mechanism under the leadership of the China Financial Stability Committee.

4.2.2.1 Incorporating Prudential Standards into Fintech Regulation

In line with the Basel requirements for prudential standards, Chinese regulators may consider including prudential standards for the use of fintech in FHCs.[41] There are a few arguments in favour of such a measure. First, fintech developments are always ahead of existing regulatory models,[42] which means that technological updates will always pose regulatory challenges. However, from a cost–benefit analysis, it is

---

[40] According to an announcement made by the PBOC on 14 January 2020, China will establish a local coordination mechanism for the Financial Stability Committee. Referring to the information disclosed by the State Council of China.

[41] Chapter 3, Notice of the People's Bank of China on Issuing the Financial Technology (fintech) Development Plan (2019–2021) (中国人民银行关于印发《金融科技 (fintech) 发展规划(2019-2021年)》的通知, 第三章). According to this chapter, in order to achieve the goal of prudential regulation of fintech, the Chinese government will work in four areas: first, establishing a legal framework for fintech regulation; second, enhancing regulatory coordination and combining fintech products with traditional financial products; third, improving penetrating regulation. For example, for financial holding companies, it should identify all shareholder relationships; fourth, improving the regulatory regime for financial innovation. It should clarify the bottom line of financial innovation, which is the minimum requirement for compliance.

[42] See Footnote 1.

unlikely that regulatory policy changes will be made quickly in the short term. Therefore, clear regulatory principles can be more responsive than specific regulations to issues arising from technological change. Second, prudential standards and evaluation are already well-established systems of assessment [4], and their integration into the regulation of fintech is realistically feasible.

With respect to the challenges that fintech poses to financial market regulation, which is a global proposition, the Basel Committee on Banking Supervision published a 2018 note on the impact of fintech on banks and banking supervisors. Among other things, it argues that the development of fintech can challenge existing prudential standards beyond the scope of current prudential standards. However, there is no description of the prudential standards for fintech, as this topic is still being studied. For example, in 2019 and 2020 [4], it sought views on prudential standards for bank crypto assets.[43]

In EU law, there are currently no regulations or prudential standards specific to fintech, but fintech companies need to be licenced if they perform services such as banking, payments, or financial markets [2]. In 2018, the EU adopted an action plan on fintech. This was followed by the adoption of the digital finance package on 24 September 2020. These are intended to enable regulators to better understand the relationship between fintech and prudential standards [11]. At present, the relationship between fintech and prudential standards is still an open question.

In terms of EU Member States, in France, for example, the Financial Markets Authority (AMF) and the Prudential Control and Resolution Authority (ACPR) are responsible for fintech regulation [22]. In July 2016, these two authorities jointly organised the fintech Forum to help regulators better identify the regulatory challenges posed by fintech and to strengthen the position of Paris as a financial centre after Brexit [1]. In terms of the relationship between fintech and prudential standards for FHCs, French jurists believe that future prudential standards cover the risks associated with the provision of financial services by platforms and technology companies, as well as by conglomerates and technology finance groups [9]. In addition, the ACPR published a paper for discussion in June 2020 on the issue of prudential standards for fintech,[44] which refers to the prudential regulation of algorithms, which are first validated within the banking group and need to be submitted to the ECB for prudential standard testing when the banking group deems it appropriate [10]. In addition, in terms of specific content, it presents the development and governance of artificial intelligence algorithms in the field of financial markets, including antimoney laundering and the fight against terrorism, credit evaluation and financial consumer protection. This study provides reference for the future development of French financial law, consumer protection law and corporate law. However, it is also important to note that it does not establish a complete prudential standard for fintech, as this standard is currently being studied and is not finished.

---

[43] It is a type of a fintech.

[44] For a description of prudential standards in prudential regulation, see Chap. 2. The prudential standards for fintech refer to a set of standards designed by regulators to prevent and manage the risks that fintech poses to financial markets, as part of prudential regulation of financial markets.

In U.S. law, U.S. regulators have adopted an ongoing approach to the regulation of FHCs by meeting with fintech companies to understand the risks of fintech to regulation, which is also known as "office hours" [27]. Therefore, the relationship between fintech and prudential standards is something that U.S. regulators are also looking at. However, it is worth noting that in 2018, the U.S. jurisprudence *Conference of State Bank Supervisors versus Office of Comptroller of Currency* on fintech companies referred to a constitutional principle in U.S. law, "prudential ripeness doctrine".[45] The judge held that under this principle, two issues must be clarified: first, whether the issues are fit for judicial decisions; second, whether withholding a decision will cause "hardship to the parties". It is a good reference for the prudential standard[46] for fintech. Financial regulation in the U.S. is shared between states and the nation. The Conference of State Bank Supervisors (CSBS) and the Office of the Comptroller of Currency (OCC), involved in the case, are the state and national regulatory authorities responsible for financial regulation in the U.S., respectively. Historically, the CSBS was responsible for granting charters to fintech companies, and later, the OCC wanted to grant national charters to fintech companies but did not take this forward. This resulted in fintech companies being unable to apply to the OCC. The judge ultimately held that the prudential ripeness doctrine counsels in favour of allowing time to sharpen this dispute before deciding it. This case is a good explanation of the conflict between financial innovation and regulation. If the regulator is to confer regulation, then it must be shown that the regulated is causing harm to the market. Otherwise, when the conflict is not inflamed, perhaps the regulator should encourage innovation.

In UK law, a public consultation was launched in February 2021 on the application of Basel standards to FHCs [3]. This is a further refinement of the prudential standards for FHCs, which will also be related to the regulation of fintech. In addition, the UK's best-known model for fintech regulation is Sandbox [12]. To date, the FCA has started a 6-cohort test, which covers payment services, blockchain applications and other fintech services, but prudential standards are still in progress, and there is no uniform statement now [13].

In China, regulators have adhered to the principle of inclusive and prudential regulation.[47] Chinese scholars have analysed this topic and believe that inclusive and prudential regulation should focus on preventing systemic financial crises, improving the market entry system for fintech companies, establishing an experimental regulatory system and improving the credit regulatory system [15]. Therefore, China currently does not have a detailed prudential standard for fintech regulation. However,

---

[45] According to the interpretation of this case, the "Ripeness doctrine" in U.S. law refers to the moment when a court can or should make a decision. Once the court has made its decision, the parties are left with ample scope to choose before they are bound by the administrative process to accept the court's decision, which avoids abstract disagreements between the courts about the administrative process and ensures that the corresponding administrative process is not interfered with by the courts. It is a restrained system of justice.

[46] See Chap. 2.

[47] Article 55, Regulation on the Optimisation of Business Environment (《优化营商环境条例》第55条).

in terms of future development, the prudential standards for fintech in Chinese FHCs adhere to the principles of prudential regulation and consolidated regulation. These two principles are fundamental to the regulation of FHCs. They also apply to the application of fintech in Chinese FHCs.

4.2.2.2 Improving the Coordination Mechanism Led by the Chinese Financial Stability and Development Committee

The coordination mechanism is necessary for the conflicting regulatory powers of the central and local authorities facing the regulation of FHCs. First, there is a practical need for the regulation of FHCs in China. Most FHCs in China are located in various local provinces. Among the eight pilot FHCs announced in China, only three are directly managed by the central government,[48] whereas the other five are all local FHCs. Thus, managing local FHCs is a very real issue. On the other hand, this is in line with the trend of the evolution of the Chinese financial regulatory legal system. The division between central and local financial regulatory authorities can be divided into four historical periods. First, before 2003, the financial regulatory authority was unified by the central government. Local governments had no financial regulatory authority; second, from 2003 to 2013, China began to explore joint regulation of the financial market by central and local governments; third, from 2013 to 2017, based on prudential regulation, the State Council established the Inter-Ministerial Joint Conference system for financial regulatory coordination, which was led by the People's Bank of China; fourth, after 2017, central and local governments' regulatory collaboration strengthened [7]. To demonstrate the coordination mechanism under the auspices of the Financial Stability Committee of China, the local coordinating authority and the systemic risk disposition cooperation of the local FHCs are presented here.

For the regulation of FHCs in China, the coordination of central and local regulators has gained the approval of current Chinese regulators. According to information disclosed by the Chinese government, the idea proposed by Chinese regulators is to set up a financial stability committee office in local governments to coordinate central and local financial regulatory powers, which would be led and supervised by the Financial Stability Development Commission of the State Council and not governed by local governments [5]. This plan was proposed in 2020, and it is still in the process of being studied on a pilot basis.

The division of powers between the central and local governments is not clear in regard to the regulation of FHCs. Despite attempts by Chinese regulators to harmonise the allocation of powers between the central and local levels in financial regulation, the Office of the Financial Stability Committee has been established in local governments, which is indeed a good example. However, legal obstacles remain. There are still serious doubts about the regulatory efficiency of the coordination mechanism.

---

[48] They are Everbright Group, CITIC Group and China Merchants Group, respectively.

The local coordination mechanism of the Chinese Financial Stability and Development Committee is still in the exploratory stage, and the EU's "act or explain" mechanism may serve as a reference.

There is considerable resistance to the regulation of systemic risk in local FHCs in China. It stems not only from the financial market but also from local governments. Many local FHCs have the government as a shareholder. For example, in eight Chinese pilot FHCs, there are four wholly state-owned enterprises in which the government is the only shareholder: the State-owned Assets Supervision Commission and the Administration Commission of the State Council (SASAC). However, there are many regulators involved in local financial regulation. From a central perspective, the SASAC and the Central Bank are parallel institutions, and it is difficult to determine who regulates whom. From a local perspective, the government regulators mentioned involve local financial supervisory authorities, the Banking and Insurance Regulatory Commission and the Security Regulatory Commission, as well as the local agencies of the central bank. However, in terms of power settings, the SASAC and SASAC are tiered agencies and have no subordination to each other. Even though the financial stability committee offices set up by local governments are directly responsible for the financial development and stability committees of the State Council, this still does not change the situation. In particular, the local branches of the central bank are also directly accountable to the central People's Bank. Therefore, how can the Financial Stability Commission Office, which has no independent supervisory powers, supervise the SASAC, the shareholder of an FHC? Perhaps Chinese regulators are aware of this, which is why they are emphasising coordination mechanisms. However, systemic risk regulation is concerned with timeliness in financial markets [16]. The efficiency of regulation under a coordination mechanism may face questions.

Under current Chinese regulation, the Chinese Financial Stability and Development Committee will set up offices in local governments to be responsible for specialised coordination. Therefore, there will be some clarity here. What is the status of this office? In fact, it will need to coordinate not only local financial regulators in China but also local governments. There are many FHCs whose shareholders are local governments. Therefore, cooperation on the systemic risk[49] disposal mechanism of local FHCs should address the following issues.

The first is to upgrade the status of the Financial Stability Board Office. There is no subordination between local financial regulators. However, based on the prudential supervision of systemic risk, the status of the Financial Stability Board Office can be appropriately increased. The Financial Stability Board Office is also required to issue recommendations in the case of disputes between different supervisory authorities on specific systemic risk supervision matters and that its opinion will be decisive.

The second is to construct a unified information sharing mechanism. In the "TMSAFHC",[50] the responsible authorities for the information sharing mechanism

---

[49] See Footnote 46.

[50] See Footnote 1.

are the People's Bank of China and the banking and insurance supervision and administration agency of the State Council, the securities supervision and administration agency of the State Council, and the SAFE. In terms of data sharing, in addition to the abovementioned departments, the finance department and the state-owned assets management department have also been added. However, this regulatory document does not explain how to establish such an information sharing mechanism, which is an important topic that needs to be addressed afterwards.

The risk disposal mechanism of local FHCs faces complex Chinese social realities, but it still offers a new way of thinking about the reform of the regulatory model of FHCs in China.

References

1. AMF (2016) The AMF, and ACPR launch the FinTech Forum, AMF. https://www.amf-france.org/en/news-publications/news-releases/amf-news-releases/amf-and-acpr-launch-fintech-forum. Accessed 21 Mar 2021
2. Baba C et al (2020) Fintech in Europe: promises and threats, IMF working paper WP/20/241. https://www.imf.org/-/media/Files/Publications/WP/2020/English/wpiea2020241-print-pdf.ashx. Accessed 21 Mar 2021
3. Bank of England (2021) PS17/21 | CP5/21—Implementation of Basel standards, Bank of England. https://www.bankofengland.co.uk/prudential-regulation/publication/2021/february/implementation-of-basel-standards. Accessed 21 Aug 2020
4. Basel Committee on Banking Supervision (2019) Designing a prudential treatment for crypto-assets, Basel Committee on Banking Supervision. https://www.bis.org/bcbs/publ/d490.htm. Accessed 21 Mar 2021
5. The Central People's Government of the People's Republic of China (2020) Will establish a local coordination mechanism for the financial stability development committee office of the state council (我国将建立金融委办公室地方协调机制), Central People's Government of the People's Republic of China. http://www.gov.cn/xinwen/2020-01/14/content_5469125.htm. Accessed 21 Sept 2020
6. Chen B (2020) Optimisation of the allocation of central and local financial supervisory powers: a perspective on the supervision of local shadow banks. Mod Law Sci 1:104–105. (陈斌彬:《论中央与地方金融监管权配置之优化—以地方性影子银行的监管为视角》,现代法学,2020年第1期,第104–105页。)
7. Chen P (2020) Central-regional financial regulatory collaboration: experience, review and prospect. Southwest Financ 4:26. (陈盼:《央地金融监管协作:经验、回顾与展望》,西南金融2020年第4期,第26页。)
8. Dargacha-sablé S (1992) Et si on créait une société holding?: réalités juridiques et fiscales (Why not set up a holding company? Legal and tax realities). Dissertation, University of Bordeaux
9. D'esclapon T (2020) Pour une stratégie en matière de finance numérique pour l'UE—Thibault de Ravel d'Esclapon (A digital finance strategy for the EU—Thibault de Ravel d'Esclapon), RTD Com: 894
10. DuPont L, Fliche O, Yang S (2020) Gouvernance des algorithmes d'intelligence artificielle dans le secteur financier (Governance of artificial intelligence algorithms in the financial sector), ACPR. https://acpr.banque-france.fr/gouvernance-des-algorithmes-dintelligence-artificielle-dans-le-secteur-financier. Accessed 21 Mar 2021
11. European Commission (2021) Digital finance, European Commission. https://ec.europa.eu/info/business-economy-euro/banking-and-finance/digital-finance_en. Accessed 21 Mar 2021

12. FCA (2021) FCA innovation-fintech, regtech and innovative businesses, FCA. https://www.fca.org.uk/firms/innovation. Accessed 21 Aug 2020
13. FCA (2021) Regulatory sandbox—cohort 6, FCA. https://www.fca.org.uk/firms/regulatory-sandbox/regulatory-sandbox-cohort-6. Accessed 21 Sep 2020
14. Haut Comité Juridique de la Place Financière de Paris (High Legal Committee of the Paris Financial Center) (2017) Réponse à la consultation publique de la Direction Générale du Trésor sur le projet de réformes législative et réglementaire relatif à la Blockchain (Response to the Treasury Department's public consultation on the draft legislative and regulatory reforms relating to Blockchain.), Haut Comité Juridique de la Place Financière de Paris (High Legal Committee of the Paris Financial Center). https://www.hcjp.fr/marches-financiers. Accessed le 18 Mar 2022
15. Hou D, Tian S (2020) Research on financial technology inclusive prudential supervision system. Nanjing J Soc Sci 10:91–93. (侯东德,田少帅:《金融科技包容审慎监管制度研究》,南京社会科学,2020年第10期,第91–93页。)
16. Lecourt B (2014) Le gouvernement d'entreprise dans les banques: lorsque le droit des sociétés doit s'adapter au droit bancaire (Corporate governance in banks: when company law must adapt to banking law). Revue des sociétés (Company Review): 335
17. Li H (2007) Legal study on the risk prevention system in Chinese financial holding company. Dissertation, Hunan University. (李晗:《论我国金融控股公司风险防范法律制度》,湖南大学法学博士论文,2007年,第5页。)
18. Li M (2017) Research on legal issues of financial holding company supervision system in China. Dissertation, Zhejiang University. (李敏:《我国金融控股公司监管制度法律问题研究》,浙江大学法学论文,2017年,第23页。)
19. Liu Y (2014) On the legalisation of the financial supervisory function of the central bank in China—a perspective on macroprudential supervision. Contemp Law Rev 3:120. (刘迎霜:《论我国中央银行金融监管职能的法制化——以宏观审慎监管为视角》,当代法学,2014年第3期,第120页。)
20. Metzger GE (2015) Through the looking glass to a shared reflection: the evolving relationship between administrative law and financial regulation. Law Contemp Probl 78:138
21. Qing T (2016) Study on the coordination mechanism of macroprudential supervision function of central bank. Dissertation, Southwest University of Political Science & Law. (青彤:《中央银行宏观审慎监管职能协调机制研究》,西南政法大学法学论文,2016,第34页。)
22. Stucki D (2021) FinTech in France: overview, Thomson Reuters. https://uk-practicallaw-thomsonreuters-com.proxy.scd.u-psud.fr/w-016-8308?transitionType=Default&contextData=(sc.Default)&firstPage=true. Accessed 21 Mar 2021
23. Su J (2021) The constitutional review of government measures for financial crises: in case of failed bank resolution regime in the UK and US. Tribune Polit Sci Law 4:113. (苏洁澈:《金融危机干预措施的合宪性审查——英美处置破产银行及启示》,政法论坛,2021年第4期,第113页)
24. Wan W (2018) Study on the development and regulation of Chinese financial holding companies. Southwest Fin 6:14. (万魏:《我国金融控股公司发展及监管问题研究》,西南金融2018年第6期,第14页。)
25. Wang X (2011) Research on the legislative issues of Chinese financial holding companies. Dissertation, Party School of the Central Committee of the CPC. (王熙麟:《我国金融控股公司的立法问题研究》,中共中央党校法学论文,2011年,第32页。)
26. Wintgens LJ, Oliver-lalana AD (2009) The art of legislating. Springer, Cham
27. World Bank Group (2019) Prudential regulatory and supervisory practices for fintech: payments, credit and deposits, World Bank Group. https://openknowledge.worldbank.org/handle/10986/33221. Accessed 21 Mar 2020
28. Wymeersch E (2012) Financial regulation and supervision: a postcrisis analysis. OUP Oxford, Oxford
29. Yan W (2011) Analysis of the differences in the level of regional financial development in China. J Yunnan Fin Econ Univ 4:69. (严武军:《中国区域金融发展水平差异分析》,云南财经大学学报(社会科学版) ,2011年第4期,第69页。)

30. Yang J, Gao J (2020) Ant Group raises about US$34.4 billion, making it the world's largest IPO. China Securities Journal. (杨洁,高佳晨:《募资约344亿美元 "蚂蚁"擎起全球最大IPO》,中国证券报,2020) http://www.cs.com.cn/xwzx/hg/202010/t20201027_6105312.html. Accessed 21 Mar 2020
31. Yin Z (2020) A review of Chinese financial regulatory reform and future prospects. Financial Times. (尹振涛:《中国金融监管改革的历程回顾与未来展望》,金融时报,2020.) https://www.financialnews.com.cn/ll/xs/202003/t20200309_183647.html. Accessed 21 Mar 2020
32. Zhang D (2018) On the theory and practice of Chinese construction of the modern financial system since the 18th party congress of the Communist Party of China. Dissertation, Hebei Normal University. (张岱:《党的十八大以来中国健全现代金融体系的理论与实践探索》,河北师范大学法学博士论文,2018,第146页。)
33. Zheng Y (2020) On the separate basis of functional regulation under financial law. Tsinghua University Law Journal 2:113. (郑彧:《论金融法下功能监管的分业基础》,清华法学2020年第2期,第113页。)

Chapter 5
Rethinking the Financial Market Regulation of Shareholders' Rights in Chinese Financial Holding Companies

Abstract This chapter analyses the mechanisms for protecting the two core rights of shareholders of FHCs in China, namely, the right to vote and the right to information. With respect to the right to vote, logically, the protection of voting rights for shareholders of FHCs is concerned with two important issues: who votes and how they vote. With respect to the former, the voter is identified as the shareholder, and the share of the shareholder is closely related to the right to vote, so the focus on shares is a fundamental issue in realising shareholders' voting rights. In terms of how to vote, the current cumulative voting system in the Chinese legal system can be examined, and adherence to mandatory cumulative voting under prudential standards can be argued. In relation to the right to information, there is an urgent need to improve the regulation of disclosure regarding shareholder information in China. It is based partly on the shortcomings of the current Chinese disclosure regime and aims to achieve Chinese financial regulatory objectives in the future.

Keywords State shares · Cumulative voting system · Rights to information · Disclosure standards · Liability regime

It is a very important step in the construction of an external mechanism for the protection of shareholders' rights in FHCs in China to reflect the regulation of shareholders' rights in FHCs. The reform of FHCs is closely related to the regulation of shareholder rights in FHCs. The current Chinese law on the regulation of FHCs already explains the regulation of shareholder rights in terms of both day-to-day operations and shareholder qualifications.[1] However, it does not explain these areas specifically; therefore, it will need to be detailed in the future. Current reflections are necessary.

Given that the regulation of FHCs needs to be rethought, it is necessary to rethink the protection of shareholders' rights in Chinese FHCs in the light of the regulation of shareholder rights protection in other jurisdictions. It is based on the pressure that international financial competition is putting on the reform of Chinese FHCs [14].

---

[1] See Article 6, TMSAFHC.

K. Ma, *Shareholder Rights Protection Mechanisms for Chinese Financial Holding Companies*, International and Comparative Law in the Asia Pacific,
https://doi.org/10.1007/978-981-97-9731-8_5

On the other hand, China is accelerating the regulation and legislation of FHCs, one of the most important parts of which is the regulation of shareholders' rights.[2] From a legal perspective, shareholder rights remain a very important aspect of shareholder regulation. This chapter focuses on two fundamental rights of shareholders in FHCs: the right to vote and the right to information.

5.1 The Two Priorities for the Regulation of Shareholders' Rights to Vote: Reforms of the State Shares and the Cumulative Voting System

The importance of shareholders' voting rights to the overall interests of shareholders has been demonstrated in legislation and legal practice in other jurisdictions [3]. It applies equally to the protection of shareholders' rights in Chinese FHCs. However, how to choose key issues when voting rights can be interpreted from many perspectives may be questioned.In this context, the research incorporates the key issue in the current corporate governance reform in China, namely, the reform of the state shares in the context of mixed ownership reform [25]. Indeed, the study of the reform of state-owned shares is not only in line with the basic idea of the current social reform in China but also in line with some of the characteristics of shareholders in FHCs. This book also focuses on a fundamental issue of shareholder voting rights, namely, the shareholder voting system [17]. However, having a good voting system in FHCs does not necessarily mean that shareholder rights are adequately protected. If the voting system in FHCs is inherently flawed, then the risk of shareholder voting rights being infringed upon is greatly increased. This book discusses the state-owned shares of Chinese FHCs and the cumulative voting system from a reform perspective.

5.1.1 Reform of the State Shares

The reform of state shares is a topic of interest in regard to the regulation of shareholder rights. However, why should state shares be reformed? It is true that in other jurisdictions, there are abuses of control by the state as a controlling shareholder and that corporate governance has only a limited role to play when the state as a shareholder abuses its control. The greatest problem with the corporate governance of Chinese SOEs is that the dominance of one share of state-owned shares is very serious, which has given rise to many drawbacks [29]. As a result, China has started to implement mixed ownership reforms in recent years, in which it is important

[2] For example, in 2020 China enacted "TMSAFHC" "Decision of the State Council on Implementation of Administration of Admission of Financial Holding Companies (国务院关于实施金融控股公司准入管理的决定)". In 2021, the People's Bank of China issued a regulation governing the filing of director and supervisor positions in FHCs.

to limit the control of state-owned shares and the exit and transfer of state-owned shares.[3] This is very evident in FHCs. Chinese FHCs fall into several categories: state-owned exclusive enterprises, mixed-ownership enterprises, and private enterprises [20]. These three types of enterprises are regulated differently. For example, in a state-owned exclusive enterprise, the government is the sole shareholder, who goes beyond the protection of shareholders' rights, and there is no difference between controlling and minority shareholders. In contrast, there are no state-owned shares in private enterprises, so the book here focuses only on mixed-ownership FHCs.[4] FHCs under a mixed ownership model, in relation to the reform of state shares, focus on control and the exit of state shares.

5.1.1.1 Reform on the Relationship Between State Shares and "Control"

For the study of the control of Chinese owned shares in FHCs, several aspects need to be considered. First, how is control in FHCs achieved? Second, why is it important for government shares to maintain control in FHCs? Third, what is the purpose of the reform of the control of government shares in FHCs? Fourth, how should the reform of state share control of FHCs be carried out? Responses to these questions can help to better understand the relationship between state shares and control. To provide a comprehensive analysis of the reform of state-owned shares in FHCs in China, two perspectives are considered: the experience of other jurisdictions and reform in China.

It is not uncommon in other jurisdictions for the government to take a stake in an FHC and even become the controlling shareholder. From a case law perspective, there have been instances where the government has abused its control as a controlling shareholder, as do other jurisdictions considering reforming state ownership. The answer is yes. The legal basis for this can be found in jurisdictions such as Europe. For example, the report on SOE reform in the EU in 2016 noted that the scope of public ownership in SOE reform is decreasing, as it is in France [9]. Each of the four issues raised at the beginning can then be explained.

Control in an FHC is not limited to government shareholders. It is manifested in multiple ways, and it can be found the basis for this in the legal texts of various jurisdictions. In general, there are two methods of control: direct control and indirect control.

This can be evidenced by the legal systems of the EU and its Member States, such as France, the U.S., and the UK.[5] In the case of direct control, there is often direct

---

[3] See Opinions on Several Policies Concerning the Pilot Program of Deepening the Mixed-Ownership Reform (关于深化混合所有制改革试点若干政策的意见). All the elements of this legal regulatory measure explain this.

[4] Among the pilot FHCs in China, the representative of a mixed-ownership FHC is Ping An Insurance.

[5] For descriptions of the control relationships in these three national legal systems, see previous Chapters.

regulation of the proportion of voting rights. For example, in U.S. law, it is required to be 25%. On the other hand, indirect control means that although the proportion of voting rights does not meet the requirements for direct control, it can control the appointment and removal of officers such as directors of the FHCs.

In an FHC, does the government share have to be controlling? This may not be the case. The simple proof is that among the FHCs, there are also private FHCs in which the government is not involved. However, why does the government need to gain control in an FHC where the government is involved? It is often needed under specific conditions. For example, in U.S. law, the government began to take an equity stake or a controlling interest in U.S. FHCs, mainly from the summer of 2008, which was during the financial crisis [15]. In the EU case law,[6] the German FHC Portigon AG is currently controlled by the German government Land NRW,[7] formerly WestLB AG, which fell on hard times during the 2008 financial crisis and was eventually created in 2011 with the consent of the EU. This EU law jurisprudence is equally instructive for French law. Therefore, the government's shareholding or ownership of the FHCs was, to a large extent, influenced by the 2008 financial crisis.

According to the "TMSAFHC" promulgated in 2020 in China, the regulators of FHCs in China are concerned with the substantial control of shareholders, which includes both holding and substantive control.[8] In turn, shareholders can obtain 50% of the voting rights of an FHC either directly or indirectly when they obtain substantial control. In the case of effective control, there are at least three scenarios, namely, control by agreement,[9] the right to appoint or remove most of the members of the board of directors, and most of the voting rights on the board of directors. Thus, the form of control in the current regulation enacted for FHCs in China is similar to the situation in other jurisdictions.

It is a historical fact that China has shares in Chinese FHCs as controlling shareholders. From the three pilot FHCs announced by the Chinese government in 2002, CITIC Group is a state-owned exclusive enterprise where the government is the sole shareholder; Everbright Group is a state-controlled enterprise where the government is the controlling shareholder; and Ping An Insurance is a state-participating enterprise where the government shares only a certain percentage but is not a controlling shareholder.[10] Therefore, the control of state-owned shares discussed here mainly refers to state-owned exclusive enterprises and state-controlled enterprises. However, in regard to the protection of shareholders' rights, the main concern is state-controlled enterprises, as there is no difference between controlling and minority shareholders in state-owned exclusive enterprises.

---

[6] Case T-457/09 Westfälisch-Lippischer Sparkassen- und Giroverband v European Commission [2014] ECLI:EU:T:2014:683.

[7] See Portigon AG 2020Annual Report.

[8] According to Article 3 of the TMSAFHC, control by agreement can be divided into two forms: obtaining a majority of the voting rights of an FHC through an agreement and actually dominating the company's actions through an agreement.

[9] Ibid.

[10] Information from China National Enterprise Credit Information Public Notice System (中国国家企业信用信息公示系统).

Where should the reform of state-owned shares in Chinese FHCs occur? This introduces the way in which the state-owned shares of Chinese FHCs have been reformed. In other jurisdictions, privatisation and shareholding reform are the two main approaches. However, in the current Chinese context, shareholding reform is perhaps the only viable way, and it is the main way in which mixed ownership reform is currently taking place in China. In the context of Chinese FHCs pilots, SOEs are unlikely to hand over full ownership to the private sector, mainly because FHCs are a type of systemically important company.[11] Under Chinese regulatory policy, privatisation of SOEs is unlikely to occur. For example, in Beijing's 2014 SOE reform programme, Beijing SOEs increased the concentration of state capital, with public service SOEs reaching over 80% and special function SOEs increasing their state capital to over 60% [27]. Therefore, for FHCs, if they are originally SOEs, it is unlikely that state-owned capital will be privatised. For private FHCs, on the other hand, state capital may instead try to participate. Therefore, the central issue is the question of how much of the state share is to be in the FHCs. This is the key to mixed ownership reform.

5.1.1.2 Reform on the Exit of State Shares

There is no specific definition of the "exit of state shares". Like this concept, it is found that there is also "the termination of state ownership" and "divestment". However, according to the OECD, "the termination of state ownership" includes both the bankruptcy of state enterprises and the privatisation of state enterprises [22]. In contrast, according to the OECD, "divestment" focuses on the privatisation of SOEs.[12] However, the shareholding reform of Chinese FHCs is not a privatisation process but is more likely a shareholding reform. Chinese scholars argue that the reform of SOEs in China cannot be defined in general terms as public or private but rather as whether the controlling interest belongs to the state or to a private party [28]. Therefore, in the context of Chinese law, privatisation of a state-owned FHC may refer to a situation in which the government shares are not controlling or shareholding in the FHC. However, Chinese mixed ownership reform emphasises the need for the government to hold a controlling stake in key areas. This is evidenced by the mixed ownership reform proposal put forward by the Beijing government. Therefore, this expression can also lead to some ambiguity. With respect to the concept of the "exit of state shares", scholars have argued that "exit" refers to the planned withdrawal of an investor or shareholder from an investment, which is equivalent to the sale of

---

[11] Article 1, the Guidance on Improving the Supervision of Systemically Important Financial Institutions (关于完善系统重要性金融机构监管的指导意见). Under this provision, systemically important financial institutions are those that are large, structurally and operationally complex, highly interconnected with other financial institutions and provide irreplaceable key services in the financial system. If they were to experience a significant risk event and become unsustainable, it would have a significant adverse impact on the financial system and the real economy and could lead to systemic risk. FHCs may also be considered to be systemically important.

[12] Ibid.

shares in the company [7]. Therefore, according to this concept, the "exit of state shares" emphasises the planned withdrawal of state shares from an FHC. The state shares may still be the controlling shareholder, or they may simply participate in or exit the FHC altogether. Therefore, this formulation is more in line with the Chinese mixed ownership reform programme and is also evidenced in the laws and regulations promulgated by the Chinese government.[13] For the exit of state shares in a mixed-ownership FHC, two issues are of concern: the role of the state and the manner of exit.

Among the eight FHC pilots announced in China, the Chinese government's representation in FHCs is mainly divided into the Chinese SASAC, the Ministry of Finance, and state-owned exclusive enterprises. The Ministry of Finance is a shareholder of the Everbright Group but not a controlling shareholder; Ping An Insurance's state-owned shares are in a state-owned exclusive enterprise, but its only shareholder is SASAC; CITIC Group, Beijing Financial Holding Group, Shanghai International Group and China Merchants Group all have only SASAC as a shareholder. Withdrawal of state-owned shares in an FHC requires compliance with certain procedures, and the direct identity of the state-owned shares in China when acting as the controlling shareholder of an FHC is the SASAC. However, the exit of state-owned shares also requires approval, one of which is to obtain the approval and consent of the SASAC. A very awkward phenomenon arises at this point. The SASAC is both the controlling shareholder of the state-owned FHC and the regulator of shareholder exit applications. Therefore, only when the real role of the government is clarified can the supervisory authority be rationalised in the process of the exit of state-owned shares. With respect to the regulation of state-owned FHCs, the role of the government is important. However, regulatory reform of Chinese state-owned FHCs is being called for in the face of the dual role of regulators and controlling shareholders.

In the context of mixed ownership reform, the exit of state-owned shares in Chinese FHCs requires several basic principles. First, the laws of the market should be respected, and the government should reduce unnecessary intervention. Chinese regulators also recognise this, as evidenced by the report of the SASAC.[14] Second, regulators should respect the business decisions of FHCs. The FHCs have different characteristics, so it is unlikely that there will be a uniform standard for them in the context of mixed ownership reform. Third, information disclosure and disclosure regulations should be strengthened in the context of mixed ownership reform. Since most current Chinese FHCs pilots are not listed and do not have good disclosure systems in place for key issues in mixed ownership reform, regulators should strengthen their transparency regulation to prevent the transfer of benefits and loss of state assets.

---

[13] Guidelines on Market-Oriented Banks' Debt-for-Equity Swaps (关于市场化银行债权转股权的指导意见). This legal document as a whole provides the corresponding legal basis.

[14] Special Report of the State Council on the Management of State-owned Assets of Enterprises under the Supervision of the State-owned Assets System for the Year 2019 (国务院关于2019年度国资系统监管企业国有资产管理情况的专项报告). This report refers to the importance of reducing unnecessary government intervention.

The essence of the issue of the entry and exit of state shares in Chinese FHCs is all about the adjustment of control. The reason is that it comes back to the control of state shares itself. In Chinese FHCs, the participation of state shares has historical and practical significance. However, the disadvantage of state share participation is that the company has limited means of preventing the abuse of control. It is a rational choice to keep state shareholding within a reasonable range for more regulated corporate governance.

5.1.2 Reform of the Cumulative Voting System

The voting system is the basis and prerequisite for the realisation of shareholders' voting rights. In addition, according to Chinese Company Law, the voting system practiced by Chinese companies is the "Cumulative Voting System" [27]. This system was confirmed in the Chinese Company Law reform in 2005. Moreover, regardless of the form of company, the voting system for shareholders of Chinese companies has remained uniform.[15] It is conceivable, then, that the reform of the voting system for shareholders of FHCs does not concern only the FHCs themselves. This is, in fact, about the basic design of Chinese company law for the shareholder voting system. As Chinese company law was confirmed to be amended in 2018, formal legislation on the regulation of FHCs will be a matter for consideration in the revision of Chinese company law. Moreover, company law is a very important legal basis for the regulation of FHCs, as seen in the regulation of FHCs in other jurisdictions. This can be confirmed by the legal systems of many countries, such as the UK and France.[16] From a comparative legislative perspective, then, it is necessary for the reform of Chinese Company Law to draw on the regulatory experience of these jurisdictions. In addition, it helps maintain the uniformity and authority of the effectiveness of Chinese Company Law. In the context of the reform of shareholder voting rights in Chinese FHCs, why and how to reform the voting system will be analysed here.

5.1.2.1 Reasons for Reforming the Cumulative Voting System

The "Cumulative Voting System" was confirmed in the 2005 reform of Chinese Company Law and has been used since then.[17] The basic idea is to leave the choice of such a voting system to shareholders. In other words, the significance of the Chinese Company Law for this system is that it confirms the legitimacy of this system.

[15] Article 105, Chinese Company Law (revised 2018) (中国公司法2018). This article explains what is meant by cumulative voting. It means that in the election of directors or supervisors at a general meeting, each share has the same number of votes as the number of directors or supervisors to be elected, and the voting rights owned by shareholders can be used centrally.

[16] Ibid.

[17] Chinese company law arose in 1993 and five amendments have occurred since then. They occurred in 1999, 2004, 2005, 2013 and 2018, respectively.

However, it does not interfere much with the use of this system, which is reflected in "permissive cumulative voting".[18] On 24 December 2021, draft amendments to the Chinese Company Law were published for public consultation. It was also reconfirmed, but no changes were proposed. There is some justification for this legislative model. Moreover, minority shareholders can exercise their voting rights centrally and thus elect directors and supervisors to represent their interests, thus avoiding oppression by controlling shareholders [11]. However, when discussing the application of this voting system to FHCs, this permissionist model has several shortcomings. The reason why the book proposes a reform of the shareholder voting system in FHCs is that, on the one hand, the current "cumulative voting system" is inadequate. On the other hand, it also considers the special characteristics of FHCs. The argument here will analyse the shortcomings of "permissive cumulative voting" and a review of the Chinese shareholder voting system from the perspective of prudential standards.

"Permissive cumulative voting", as currently practiced in Chinese Company Law, is designed for all types of companies.[19] Therefore, the design of this system can be understood as a choice that balances the values of freedom and order. However, in the case of FHCs, this system has several shortcomings. These are mainly in the following areas. First, such a system may not protect the rights of nonstate shareholders in a mixed ownership reform. It has already been mentioned that state-owned companies and state-owned holding companies make up most current Chinese FHC pilots. When nonstate capital is introduced, according to the current Chinese mixed ownership reform strategy, the reform of SOEs involves following a shareholding system, but government shares still hold a controlling position.[20] Therefore, the current situation is that the government will still be the controlling shareholder in a state-owned FHC. Although "permissive cumulative voting" offers opportunities for nonstate shareholders, the articles of association may not always be able to protect minority shareholders. Second, the differences between the provisions of the company law and the code of governance for listed companies pose several challenges for the current regulation of FHCs in China. The Chinese Company Law uses "Permissive Cumulative Voting", but the Chinese Code of Governance for Listed Companies uses Mandatory Cumulative Voting. Therefore, "Permissive cumulative voting" has its justification in company law, but it has certain disadvantages in the case of FHCs. The regulatory regime for FHCs is in the process of being improved. It is therefore timely to examine it currently.

In addition to the shortcomings of "permissive cumulative voting", the importance of the FHC voting regime is that the protection of shareholders' rights should itself be a factor of systemic risk and should have been included in the prudential evaluation

---

[18] Article 105, Chinese Company Law (revised 2018) (中国公司法2018).

[19] See Footnote 18.

[20] Circular of the General Office of the State Council on the Guidance of the State-owned Assets Supervision and Administration Commission on Promoting the Restructuring of State-owned Capital and State-owned Enterprises (国务院办公厅转发《国资委关于推进国有资本调整和国有企业重组指导意见》的通知). It proves the point as a whole, and it covers all the articles.

criteria.[21] However, the current regulatory regime for FHCs in China does not respond to this. Therefore, the "cumulative voting system" should be reformed from the perspective of protecting the rights of shareholders of FHCs. It is also crucial in building a good system for the protection of shareholders' rights in Chinese FHCs.

5.1.2.2 The Proposals for Reforming the Cumulative Voting System in Chinese Financial Holding Companies

The implementation of the regulation of FHCs in China is a challenge to the Chinese Company Law regime, but it also provides some opportunities for the reform of Chinese Company Law. In response to the voting system in the reform of state-owned shares in FHCs, the book argues for two reasons for reform. On this basis, the research also proposes two reform initiatives accordingly. These include changing the current "cumulative voting system" regime from a permissive model to a compulsory model and introducing prudential criteria into the assessment of the voting system.

"Permissive cumulative voting" has shown some shortcomings in the shareholder voting system of FHCs. On this basis, our idea of reform is to still follow the "cumulative voting system" in company law, a voting system whose advantages have moved from theory to practice since its introduction by the Chinese legislature in 2005, which has been somewhat proven. However, the advantages of this system are better at the theoretical level than at the practical level. In addition, "Permissive Cumulative Voting" has made the system misleading in its practical use. Therefore, the reform proposed is a reform for the way used in practice, and "Mandatory Cumulative Voting" should be used in FHCs. The "Mandatory Cumulative Voting" applied to the regulation of FHCs does not undermine the structure and legislative spirit of Chinese Company Law. It is a stricter voting regime based on prudential standards proposed to protect the entry of nonstate capital into FHCs. This eliminates the opportunity for controlling shareholders to oppress minority shareholders from the constitution.

It has been argued that "Permissive cumulative voting" does not meet the prudential regulatory requirements for FHCs and that "Mandatory cumulative voting" also complies with prudential regulatory standards. The book also supports the introduction of prudential standards into the voting regime for FHCs in China. However, it is also important to note that the prudential standard is manifested not only in the use of "Mandatory Cumulative Voting". A more nuanced set of arrangements should exist. Specifically, it should contain the following main aspects. First, the scope of use of "Mandatory Cumulative Voting" should be clarified. According to the Chinese Company Law and the Code of Governance of Listed Companies, the "Cumulative Voting System" will only be used for the election of directors and supervisors at a

[21] With regard to the evaluation of prudential standards, Chinese law does not provide a nuanced explanation. For regulators, it leaves a lot of room for interpretation. However, overall, it remains risk and macro based. It is consistent with the analysis of prudential regulation and prudential standards mentioned in the previous paragraphs.

general meeting of shareholders.[22] However, matters to be voted on at general meetings may also include amendments to the articles of association, capital increases or reductions by shareholders.[23] It can be found that shareholders are left to determine whether the "cumulative voting system" can be applied to other major voting matters other than the election of directors and supervisors by agreement through the articles of association. Second, "Mandatory Cumulative Voting" should follow prudential standards in the annual general meeting (AGM) process. It includes the manner of voting, the manner of counting votes, and so on. In Chinese FHCs, there are fewer shareholders in either state-owned exclusive FHCs or mixed-ownership FHCs. The shareholding structure is therefore highly concentrated. However, in either type of FHCs, when they attract investors or shareholders to the FHCs through the public listing channel, the number of shareholders currently increases, although minority shareholders do not hold a high percentage of shares.

In response to this situation and to reduce the cost of voting for minority shareholders, both China and other jurisdictions are now focussing on protecting the rights of shareholders to vote electronically. For example, in 2005, the CSRC's proposal to improve the online voting system for shareholders' meetings was approved by the Chinese State Council.[24] In 2014, the SASAC of Henan Province in China issued guidelines for state-controlled listed companies, which require that state-owned listed companies should include an online voting system in their articles of association.[25] The EU confirmed the right of shareholders to e-vote in its 2017 revised Directive on the protection of shareholders' rights.[26] In terms of Member States, the French Code de commerce, for example, confirms this right for shareholders.[27] This right

[22] Article 105, the Chinese Company Law (中国公司法). With regard to its contents, see *supra*, n° 338. Also see Article 17, the Code of Governance for Listed Companies (中国上市公司治理准则). According to this provision, the election of directors and supervisors shall fully reflect the views of small and medium-sized shareholders. The cumulative voting system shall be actively implemented in the election of directors and supervisors at general meetings. Listed companies in which a single shareholder and persons acting in concert with him own 30% or more of the shares shall adopt the cumulative voting system. Listed companies that adopt the cumulative voting system shall stipulate the implementation rules in their articles of association.

[23] Article 103, the Chinese Company Law. This paragraph explains its content.

[24] Notice of the State Council on Approving and Forwarding CSRC's Opinions on Improving the Quality of Listed Companies (国务院批转证监会关于提高上市公司质量意见的通知). It proves the point as a whole, and it covers all the articles.

[25] Notice of Henan Securities Regulatory Bureau and Henan Provincial State-owned Assets Supervision and Administration Commission on the Issuance of the Guidance on Improving the Governance of State-controlled Listed Companies in Henan (河南证监局、河南省国资委关于印发《关于完善河南国有控股上市公司治理的指导意见》的通知). It proves the point as a whole, and it covers all the articles.

[26] Article 3c, Directive (EU) 2017/828 of the European Parliament and of the Council of 17 May 2017 amending Directive 2007/36/EC as regards the encouragement of long-term shareholder engagement. Under this provision, Member States shall ensure that electronic confirmation of receipt of a ballot paper is sent to the voter when voting by electronic means.

[27] Article R225-61, Code de commerce. According to this provision, if the articles of association allow shareholders to vote at meetings by electronic means, then the company should establish a website dedicated to this purpose.

of shareholders has been confirmed on several occasions in U.S. jurisprudence, such as *Broadridge Financial Solutions, Inc. v. Inveshare, Inc.*[28] These practices are also found in other jurisdictions.

However, in practice, there have been some controversies regarding e-voting, for example, in the Chinese judicial case *Dandong Port Group Company Limited v Wanlian Securities Company Limited*,[29] which was a result of inconsistencies between the agreement on the articles of association and the actual implementation of e-voting. Therefore, prudential standards should also be introduced in the implementation process of the future voting system of FHCs.

5.2 The Key for the Regulation of Shareholders' Rights to Information: Reform of the Disclosure Regulation

Traditional theory considers information asymmetry among shareholders to be a key factor in the violation of shareholders' right to information, and it is particularly true for the protection of minority shareholders' rights [17]. The development of internet technology has increased the transparency of information. However, in the case of FHCs, the problems with shareholders' right to information could include both insufficient and excessive information perspectives. Therefore, shareholders want to provide correct and critically important information. The reform of information regulation for FHCs should ensure that this aim prevails. This section analyses why Chinese FHCs urgently need to reform their disclosure regulatory regime and how this can be improved.

5.2.1 Reasons for Reforming the Disclosure Regulation

There seems to be no precise definition of "Disclosure Regulation". In addition, traces can be found in many legal documents. For example, the European disclosure regulation on environmental, social, and governance (ESG) [8] and the corporate disclosure on climate issues [10]. China has also introduced a series of disclosure requirements for mixed ownership reforms, such as the disclosure of corporate capital increase projects [10]. Therefore, disclosure regulations are aimed at information that should be disclosed. The purpose of the French AMF is to improve transparency [2].

Therefore, why is it important to improve transparency? In the governance of FHCs, information asymmetry under the principal–agent model may lead to the

---

[28] Broadridge Financial Solutions, Inc. v. Inveshare, Inc., 2012 WL 1,245,723, 1–16 (United States District Court, D. Delaware, 2012).

[29] Dandong Port Group Ltd. versus Wanlian Securities Co. (丹东港集团有限公司诉万联证券股份有限公司, 最高人民法院 (2018) 最高法民辖终336号民事裁定书).

infringement of minority shareholders' rights by the board of directors and controlling shareholders.[30] From the perspective of protecting minority shareholders' rights, disclosure regulation is a necessary measure. In Chinese law jurisprudence, *Shenzhen Qianhai Huineng Financial Holding Group Co., Ltd., and the Defendants Tianma Bearing Group Co., Ltd., Xu Maodong and Fu Miao*[31] demonstrate the importance of disclosure regulations for the protection of minority shareholders' rights in an FHC.

There are two reasons for reforming the information regulation of Chinese FHCs. On the one hand, from the perspective of the protection of shareholders' rights in Chinese FHCs, the current information disclosure regime has several deficiencies, which make it difficult to meet the needs of shareholders' rights protection. On the other hand, it is also judged from the objective of overall economic development in China.

5.2.1.1 The Shortcomings of the Legislation on Disclosure in Chinese Financial Holding Companies

The shortcomings of the disclosure regime in the Chinese corporate legal system have been revealed [3]. The regulator has also recognised the shortcomings of the original system, such as the lack of specific guidance for FHCs in the current regime and insufficient sanctions for breaches of disclosure regulation.

In the Chinese FHC regulation enacted in 2020, the standards for disclosure are truthfulness, accuracy, and completeness.[32] However, it lacks detailed guidance on the specific application, which is a challenge for the regulation of disclosure in Chinese FHCs. It is located mainly in the following areas. First, with respect to the disclosure standards for FHCs, which refer to truthfulness, accuracy, and completeness, are they consistent with the regulations of other companies? It is not explained in detail, and the three standards are not fleshed out. It is too principled for practitioners. In addition, four of the eight current Chinese pilot FHCs are wholly state-owned enterprises. Although there is no legislation in Chinese law that specifically addresses disclosure standards for state-owned exclusive enterprises, some local governments have issued guidance on the status of wholly state-owned enterprises.

---

[30] Ibid.

[31] Shenzhen Qianhai Huineng Financial Holding Group Co Ltd. v Tianma Bearing Group Co Ltd, Xu Maodong, Fu Miao and others (深圳前海汇能金融控股集团有限公司诉天马轴承集团股份有限公司、徐茂栋、傅淼，深圳前海合作区人民法院(2019)粤0391民初3161号民事判决书).

[32] Article 37, TMSAFHC. According to this provision, FHCs shall follow the principles of truthfulness, accuracy and completeness in disclosing information in a timely manner in compliance with laws, administrative regulations and the requirements of the PBOC. They shall be liable for false records, misleading statements and material omissions in information disclosure in accordance with the law.

In Shanghai[33] and Guangxi,[34] for example, the disclosure standards for wholly state-owned enterprises are required to be in line with those criteria, including "truthful, accurate, complete, timely and fair". However, it conflicts with the disclosure standards of FHCs. Therefore, how will this apply in the future? This ambiguity may make disclosure regulation a mere formality. Second, from a practical point of view, of the current eight pilot FHCs in China, only Ping An Insurance is a listed company, and Everbright Group is an unlisted public company, whereas the other six companies are limited liability companies. Past Chinese legislation indicates that the regulation for disclosure is mainly for public companies. In the context of Chinese law, it is expressed as a joint stock company. However, for closed companies, such as limited liability companies, is it subject to explicit disclosure regulation? This is not reflected in Chinese law.

With respect to the regulation of disclosure, in addition to the overly principled nature of disclosure regulation, another notable problem is that the penalty mechanisms for breaches of the disclosure regime are inadequate or too superficial to have a substantial effect. Some examples of this can be found in the judicial data. Since 2007, there have been a total of 36,090 cases[35] in which Chinese companies have been settled in litigation concerning information disclosure issues. Of these, only 2 cases related to FHCs occurred in 2015 and 2019.

From a regulatory perspective, the current information disclosure penalties for FHCs are inadequate in two main areas: first, incomplete information disclosure liability. According to the "TMSAFHC", there are three types of information disclosure acts for which an FHC is liable: false statements, misleading statements, and material omissions.[36] However, in the section on legal liability, it only provides for liability for false statements.[37] Therefore, how should one be liable for the other two types of conduct? The regulation gives no explanation. Second, the regulation

---

[33] Guidelines on the Articles of Association of Shanghai Wholly state-owned enterprises 2020 (上海市国有独资公司章程指引 (2020版)). It proves the point as a whole, and it covers all the articles.

[34] Guidelines on the Articles of Association of Wholly state-owned enterprises in the Guangxi Autonomous Region 2015 (广西自治区国有独资公司章程指引2015版). It proves the point as a whole, and it covers all the articles.

[35] Information from the China Judgement Online (中国裁判文书网).

[36] Article 37, TMSAFHC.

[37] Ibid., Article 51. According to this provision, if the promoter, controlling shareholder or de facto controller of an FHC violates the provisions of these regulations and commits any of the following acts, the PBOC shall order rectification within a certain period of time, confiscate the illegal proceeds and impose a fine of not less than one and not more than five times the illegal proceeds. If there is no illegal income or the illegal income is less than RMB 500,000, a fine of not less than RMB 500,000 and not more than RMB 5 million shall be imposed. Where the circumstances are serious, the administrative permit shall be revoked in accordance with the provisions of the Administrative Licensing Law of the People's Republic of China; and where it is suspected of constituting a crime, it shall be transferred to the relevant authorities for investigation of criminal liability in accordance with law: (a) Providing a false letter of undertaking. (b) False capital contribution, circular capital injection, using entrusted funds, debt funds and other nonowned funds to fund. (c) Illegal holding of equity interests in FHCs through entrusting others or accepting entrustments from others, and so on. (d) Providing false information or concealing material facts.

does not address the issue of CSR disclosure. Second, the liability for penalties is low. As an institution of systemic importance to the financial market, an FHC, from a risk prevention perspective, should have a heightened duty to disclose information. However, from the perspective of Chinese law, the disclosure liability of FHCs has not increased. This is mainly in comparison with securities law and the duty to disclose information for listed companies. For example, the disclosure liability of FHCs is based mainly on fines. In the absence of illegal income, fines against controlling shareholders and beneficial owners will not exceed a maximum of RMB 5 million; fines against directors and management will not exceed a maximum of 1 million.[38] In contrast, the disclosure liability regime in Chinese listed companies is based on the provisions of the Chinese Securities Law,[39] where the maximum fine for the controlling shareholders and the beneficial owner will not exceed RMB20 million, and the maximum penalty for the directors and management will not exceed RMB10 million, in the absence of illegal income.[40]

The disclosure regulation of FHCs in China is still in its early stages, both in terms of the content of disclosure and the duty to disclose, and it is subject to continuous improvement in the future. However, given that China has already started to improve the regulatory regime for FHCs, it is very urgent in the current legislative context.

5.2.1.2 The Achievement of Regulation Objectives for Chinese Financial Holding Companies (2021–2035)

One of the reasons why the disclosure reform of FHCs needs to be researched, in addition to the current problems of the disclosure system, is also based on Chinese regulatory objectives. In 2020, China published its economic plan for the period from 2021–2035, in which it mentioned the need to achieve transparency reforms in the financial and economic sector.[41] In other words, this is another proof that Chinese lawmakers are aware of these issues. Therefore, it is important to address

---

[38] Ibid.

[39] Article 54, Measures for the Administration of Information Disclosure by Listed Companies (2021) (上市公司信息披露管理办法 (2021)). According to this provision, listed companies that evade their disclosure and reporting obligations by concealing their affiliation or by other means are punished by the CSRC in accordance with the Securities Law.

[40] Article 181, Securities Law of the People's Republic of China (Revised 2019) (中华人民共和国证券法 (2019修订)). Under this provision, the controlling shareholder and the person in effective control of the issuer who conceals material facts or fabricates materially false information shall forfeit the proceeds of the offence and be liable to a fine of not less than 10% of the proceeds of the offence and not more than double the proceeds of the offence; if there are no proceeds of the offence or the proceeds of the offence are less than RMB 20 million, a fine of not less than RMB 2 million and not more than RMB 20 million shall be imposed. The person in charge and other persons directly responsible shall be liable to a fine of not less than one million RMB and not more than ten million RMB.

[41] Outline of the Fourteenth Five-Year Plan for National Economic and Social Development of the People's Republic of China and Vision 2035 (中华人民共和国国民经济和社会发展第十四个五年规划和2035年远景目标纲要). It proves the point as a whole, and it covers all the articles.

these issues in the future economic planning. In the future reform of FHCs in China, in the context of Chinese policy, two main objectives of disclosure regulation are considered here: meeting the transparency standards of modern financial regulation and the requirements of sustainability.

The transparency standard for modern financial regulation is not a specialist legal term. Therefore, it needs to be explained here exactly what this standard is. In the Chinese context, it appears in Chinese government documents and is one of the Chinese goals for the years 2021–2035.[42] It is therefore a political term at this point. According to the explanation of Guo Shuqing, Chairperson of the CBIRC, the modern standard on transparency in financial regulation in a political context refers to the international disclosure standard represented by the Basel framework [13].

Why does this standard apply to Chinese FHCs? On the one hand, after Chinese FHCs start to have a clear legal status in 2020, their future development will inevitably have to be adapted to international competition. Therefore, the so-called standards of modern financial regulation are essentially designed to attract international investors.[43] In other words, standards that are agreeable to different shareholders and investors should be the direction of regulatory reform for Chinese FHCs. In this context, a moderate balance between the Chinese legal system and the international financial regulatory framework is needed. Specifically, improved standards should be developed on the basis of the Basel framework, considering the actual situation of Chinese FHCs, such as supervisory transparency and accountability. In response to the "essential criteria"[44] proposed for disclosure and transparency, Chinese FHC regulation should examine how to embed them in the Chinese legal system in the future.

Sustainability disclosure has become an international trend in the field of financial market regulation. From a regulatory perspective, in 2014, the EU identified the need for public interest entities to publish corporate sustainability reporting on an integrated regulatory basis, which includes environmental matters, social matters and treatment of employees, respect for human rights, anticorruption and bribery, and diversity on company boards.[45] In 2019, the EU included sustainability risk in transparency criteria.[46] France has introduced EU regulation into its national law

---

[42] Ibid.

[43] Outline of the Fourteenth Five-Year Plan for National Economic and Social Development of the People's Republic of China and Vision 2035, *supra*, p. 207.

[44] See "Disclosure requirements" in the Basel Framework. In addition, the standard was updated on 22 January 2021.

[45] Directive 2014/95/EU of the European Parliament and of the Council of 22 October 2014 amending Directive 2013/34/EU as regards disclosure of nonfinancial and diversity information by certain large undertakings and groups. It proves the point as a whole, and it covers all the articles.

[46] Article 3, Regulation (EU) 2019/2088 of the European Parliament and of the Council of 27 November 2019 on sustainability-related disclosures in the financial services sector. According to this provision, financial market participants should publish on their websites information about their policies for incorporating sustainability risks into their investment decision-making process.

and requires companies to state their reasons for not disclosing sustainability risks.[47] Moreover, France is a pioneer in the treatment of environmental issues and corporate governance [19]. In fact, France has been concerned with the social and environmental performance of listed companies in their reports by law on *les Nouvelle Régulations Économiques* since 2001 [1].

Sustainability disclosure in Chinese law can be traced back to the 2008 Guidelines on Environmental Information Disclosure for Listed Companies on the Shanghai Stock Exchange, issued by the Shanghai Stock Exchange. It encourages listed companies to publish CSR reports in accordance with the disclosure rules of the securities law, mentioning that CSR is closely related to the protection of shareholders' rights and that listed companies should pay attention to the rights of their stakeholders.[48] Moreover, if companies fail to disclose timely, accurate and complete information on environmental protection, then disciplinary measures will be taken depending on the severity of the circumstances. However, it does not specify the specifics of the liability regime for breaches of environmental information disclosure.

The Guidelines on Corporate Social Responsibility for Financial Institutions in the Banking Sector in China mention that CSR disclosure needs to include information on economic, social and environmental aspects[49] and encourage enterprises to establish a CSR disclosure system and submit annual reports to the China Banking Association, with third-party independent institutions being encouraged to be responsible for authentication and to make them public.[50] Thereafter, in 2010, the Guidelines on the Disclosure of Environmental Information by Listed Companies (Draft for Public Comments) were issued by the former Chinese Ministry of Environmental Protection (now known as the Ministry of Ecology and Environment), which provides detailed instructions on disclosure reports. However, unfortunately, thus far, it is still in draft form. These are not legally binding.

Returning to the sustainability disclosure of FHCs, Chinese law does not currently provide for the sustainability disclosure of FHCs. However, according to the policy

---

[47] Article L533-22-1, Code monétaire et financier. According to this provision, portfolio management companies shall make available to their subscribers and to the public a document setting out their policy on the inclusion in their investment strategy of environmental, social and governance quality criteria and the means used to contribute to the energy and ecological transition, as well as a strategy for implementing this policy. They shall indicate how the voting rights attached to the financial instruments resulting from these choices are exercised.

[48] Notice of the Shanghai Stock Exchange on Strengthening the Social Responsibility of Listed Companies and Issuing the Guidelines on Environmental Information Disclosure for Listed Companies on the Shanghai Stock Exchange (上海证券交易所关于加强上市公司社会责任承担工作暨发布《上海证券交易所上市公司环境信息披露指引》的通知). It proves the point as a whole, and it covers all the articles.

[49] Article 1, Guidelines on Corporate Social Responsibility for Banking Financial Institutions in China (中国银行业金融机构企业社会责任指引). According to this regulation, it is formulated to urge banking and financial institutions to assume CSR and promote harmonious and sustainable development of the economy, society and the environment.

[50] Ibid., Article 25.

objectives issued by the Chinese government (2021–2035),[51] sustainability disclosure will be a legislative priority in the future. Furthermore, according to Le Monde, the Chinese government wanted to achieve carbon neutrality by 2060 and contribute to global environmental protection, although it has been questioned whether this goal will be achieved [12]. However, this also means that the Chinese government's statements are subject to international scrutiny. In this context, sustainability disclosure will be an important tool for the Chinese government to achieve this ambitious goal. It extends to the sustainability disclosure of FHCs as well.

5.2.2 *The Proposals to Reform the Disclosure Regulation*

In response to some of the problems with the disclosure regulation of Chinese FHCs and Chinese economic development goals, Chinese regulators should act on these issues in the future. It is very important. This is an inevitable issue in terms of the development of Chinese FHCs, and early measures can only be taken to effectively address the challenges ahead. In addition, from the perspective of legislation, China has already started to legislate on FHCs. According to the theory of cost–benefit analysis of legislation, it is important to respond and design well to these issues in the legislative process. It will reduce legal barriers to future economic development while also reducing the cost of legislation while ensuring benefits.

In response to the urgent need for disclosure regulation of FHCs in China, two targeted recommendations are made here: the promulgation of specific standards for FHCs disclosures and the reform of the disclosure liability regime.

5.2.2.1 Establishing Dedicated Disclosure Standards for Chinese Financial Holding Companies

In terms of the specific content of disclosure, Chinese legislators can draw on some of the basic ideas of traditional disclosure regulation, including the discloser, the form of disclosure, and the liability regime for disclosure.[52] However, legislators should pay attention to some of the special features of disclosure regulation for FHCs. Its specificity is reflected mainly in the implementation of two regulatory principles.[53] More specifically, attention is given here to some salient issues in the protection of minority shareholders' right to information, namely, the concealment and fraud of minority shareholders by controlling shareholders in RPTs and accounting disclosure.

---

[51] Outline of the Fourteenth Five-Year Plan for National Economic and Social Development of the People's Republic of China and Vision 2035.

[52] For example, the Administrative Measures for Disclosure of Information by Listed Companies (上市公司信息披露管理办法). It proves the point as a whole, and it covers all the articles.

[53] They are prudential regulation and consolidated regulation.

The RPTs of controlling shareholders in FHCs connect transactions between management, which results in the infringement of minority shareholders' rights. Moreover, it is a very regular and frequent form of infringement of minority shareholders' interests by major shareholders.[54] Therefore, the issue needs to be taken seriously in the reform of the disclosure regulatory regime. Prudential standards should be adhered to in future reviews of the disclosure regulation of RPTs. There are several specific reasons for this. First, it is in line with international disclosure standards. According to the principles set out in the Basel framework for effective regulation, the disclosure of RPTs should be subject to prudential standards. Second, it is in line with the regulatory requirements for FHCs in China and the legislative experience of Chinese commercial law. The TMSAFHC currently issued in China proposes that the establishment and operation of FHCs should adhere to prudential requirements.[55] The prohibition on RPTs is also clearly stated.[56] However, how RPTs are to be disclosed in accordance with prudential standards is not explained. A comprehensive analysis of the Chinese legal system revealed that prudential regulation of RPT disclosure was only specifically provided for commercial banks in China in 2004.[57] It contains detailed provisions on related parties, the types and management of RPTs, and the liability regime.

Given that prudential regulation can be applied to the disclosure of RPTs, how does it work? It can be broken down into several areas. First, the prudential standard for the disclosure of RPTs should be categorised and prescribed according to the different types of FHCs. From the perspective of current Chinese FHC pilots, Chinese FHCs fall into three main categories: state-owned exclusive FHCs, mixed-ownership FHCs, and private FHCs. Among private FHCs, internet FHCs are very new. The prudential standard for the disclosure of RPTs then needs to focus not only on the differences in the disclosure of government and nongovernment shares but also on traditional RPTs and RPTs in internet technology. Clearly, how should the use of internet technology in RPTs, such as those completed using virtual currencies, be regulated? These factors

[54] Ibid.

[55] Article 6, TMSAFHC. According to this article, where nonfinancial enterprises, natural persons and approved legal persons substantially control two or more financial institutions of different types, and the total asset size of the financial institutions substantially controlled or the total size of the assets entrusted to them for management does not meet the standard, but the PBOC deems it necessary to establish an FHC in accordance with macroprudential supervision requirements, they must establish an FHC.

[56] Ibid., Article 11. According to this article, the controlling shareholder or beneficial owner of an FHC shall not have the following circumstances: (a) Evading the regulation of the FHC by means of a specific purpose vehicle or entrusting others to hold shares. (b) Numerous related parties, complex and nontransparent shareholding relationships, or disputes over ownership, carrying out connected transactions in bad faith and using connected relationships in bad faith. (c) Abuse of monopoly position in the market or technical superiority to carry out unfair competition. (d) Manipulating the market and disturbing the financial order. (e) Transferring the shares held in the financial holding company within five years.

[57] Administrative Measures on Affiliated Transactions between Commercial Banks and their Insiders or Shareholders (商业银行与内部人和股东关联方交易管理办法). It proves the point as a whole, and it covers all the articles.

present a greater challenge to prudential regulation. Second, RPT disclosure should focus not only on the protection of shareholders' rights but also on sustainability disclosure. Sustainability disclosure is an inescapable aspect of future disclosure regulation for FHCs. It should then be responded to in the context of RPT disclosure regulations. Third, the list of responsibilities in the disclosure of RPTs is based on prudential standards. RPTs significantly harm the interests of shareholders, and they need to be regulated in a focussed manner. Throughout the regulatory provisions, the shortcoming of the disclosure regulation was that the liability regime was not comprehensive or standardised, which led to the binding effect of the disclosure regulation being reduced. In the context of systemic crisis prevention, the disclosure regulation of FHCs in China should receive sufficient attention.

Consolidated regulation is an important regime for accounting disclosures and is widely used in the regulation of financial conglomerates and multinational enterprises. The book explains the legal basis for the principle of consolidated regulation.[58] Putting this into practice, then, in relation to accounting disclosure, it can adhere to the following ideas. First, there is the penetrating regulation of the shareholding structure.[59] The shareholding structure of an FHC is very complex. Therefore, in the context of disclosure regulation, comprehensive regulation of the shareholding relationship is needed. This can also be referred to as penetrating regulation in the formulation of Chinese law. This is reflected in the accounting information as changes in shares. This includes the number of changes, the percentage of changes and the reasons for the changes. Typically, it is disclosed in the annual reports of the FHCs. However, the disclosure in the annual report often varies according to the accounting year. In practice, some cases are divided into a half-yearly report and an annual report.[60] In some cases, only the annual report is disclosed [4]. Therefore, this type of disclosure is slow. Penetration regulation at this point should adhere to an ongoing basis.

Second, the consolidated statements of FHCs should be improved. Consolidated statements are an expression of consolidated supervision. As a kind of parent company, the financial statements of an FHC should adequately reflect its financial relationship with its subsidiaries. The regulation of FHCs in China has been of particular concern in the context of the current mixed ownership reform. One of the ways in which mixed ownership reforms can be carried out through acquisitions has already been discussed.[61] In 2014, the Chinese Supreme People's Court issued regulations suggesting that companies should avoid using consolidated statements

---

58 Ibid.

59 Article 5, TMSAFHC. According to this article, the PBOC, in conjunction with the relevant authorities, conducts comprehensive, continuous and penetrating regulation on the capital, conduct and risks of financial holding groups in accordance with the principle of substance over form, to prevent the transmission of financial risks across industries and markets.

60 See JPMorgan Chase & Co 2020 Annual Report.

61 Ibid.

and managerial acquisitions to appropriate state assets.[62] It is also something that should be considered in the future regulation of accounting disclosure in FHCs.

5.2.2.2 Reform of the Liability Regime on Disclosure

In response to the inadequacy of current FHCs' disclosure regulation legislation, dedicated FHC disclosure regulation can help provide detailed guidance on FHCs' disclosure. In addition, in response to the lack of sanctions, the liability regime for disclosure needs to be taken seriously. To clarify the liability regime of an FHC disclosure regime, it is necessary to reflect on foreign models to consider what impact they may have on the liability regime of an FHC disclosure regime in China. Two models are more typical: the controlling shareholder fiduciary duty model in common law countries and the French civil liability model for directors.

The common law model of fiduciary duty arose in the UK.[63] This model has since been widely accepted in common law countries.[64] With respect to the definition of fiduciary duties, some scholars have found it difficult to provide a clear definition, but the courts have held that the relationship is based on trust and confidence. In the jurisdictions explored in the book, it is found in UK law and U.S. law. However, the duty of confidence in English law has common law and equitable differences. In common law, it is embodied as a duty of care; in equity, it is embodied as a duty of loyalty. In U.S. law, it is divided directly into a duty of loyalty and a duty of care, with no distinction between common law and equity [11]. Therefore, as a rule, fiduciary duties are expressed in two main manifestations: the duty of loyalty and the duty of care. When directors breach these duties, they may be liable to shareholders; in exceptional circumstances, they may also be criminally liable [16].

The duty of fiduciary duties is not enshrined in the regulatory act for FHCs in China. However, in Chinese Company Law, directors owe a duty of fidelity and a duty of diligence to the company.[65] Some scholars believe that Chinese law has adopted the common law duty of the fiduciary duty regime. Although there are differences in the specific formulation, the duty of fidelity in Chinese law corresponds to the duty of loyalty in common law, whereas the duty of diligence in Chinese law corresponds to the duty of care [11]. According to Chinese Company Law, if a director breaches the relevant provisions and thus causes the company to suffer losses, the director should

---

[62] Guiding Opinions on Judicial Protection by the People's Courts for Mergers and Acquisitions of Enterprises (关于人民法院为企业兼并重组提供司法保障的指导意见). It proves the point as a whole, and it covers all the articles.

[63] Ibid.

[64] Such as the U.S. and Singapore.

[65] Article 147, Chinese Company Law. According to this article, directors, supervisors, and senior management shall comply with the laws, administrative regulations and the articles of association of the company and have a duty of loyalty and diligence to the company. They shall not use their authority to accept bribes or other illegal income and shall not misappropriate the property of the company.

be liable to the company for compensation.[66] However, according to Chinese jugements online, there are only 16 cases related to this duty of directors, of which only 6 have been successful.[67] These cases did not involve FHCs or subsidiaries. Chinese scholars have called for the reform of corporate governance in China in recent years, and one of these calls has been the abuse of power by directors and other managers [30]. By analysing these unsuccessful cases, one of the common reasons given was that it was impossible to find sufficient evidence that the directors had breached their duty of loyalty and diligence. In addition, shareholders want to obtain sufficient evidence, which requires adequate disclosure by directors in corporate governance. Therefore, the key issue emerges. How can directors determine whether they have adequately discharged their duties of loyalty and diligence in relation to the disclosure of information by shareholders? This is not a question that has found a suitable answer in current Chinese law [23]. There is currently no provision for fiduciary duties in FHCs, either for directors or controlling shareholders. Although Chinese Company Law provides for directors' fiduciary duties, this regime does not work as well as it should in judicial practice, and it does not adequately protect shareholders' right to information for disclosure. Therefore, in the face of prudential regulation of FHCs, the regulator may choose to set strict rules of evidence and evaluation criteria for the duty of fidelity and diligence of directors on disclosure in the company law or may choose to introduce other liability regimes to regulate the behaviour of directors. With respect to the liability of controlling shareholders, prominent Chinese company law scholars are also calling for a stronger design of liability for controlling shareholders [30]. Therefore, is fiduciary duty a recommended model? This may still be questionable at the level of FHC regulation.

The model adopted in French law for dealing with agency conflicts between shareholders and management is to impose additional restrictions on the liability of directors. Under this model, management has a significant responsibility for the disclosure of information about the company. In French law, management is the agent of shareholders [18]. At this point, the directors are part of the management. Therefore, this liability regime also applies to directors [20]. The liability of directors under French law dates to la loi de 1925 (pour les SARL) [18], which provides for exceptions to the criminal liability of directors. As French business practices developed, jurisprudence confirmed the duty of the loyalty of directors. In addition, French scholars consider that directors have a duty of care and a duty of information [6]. When directors fail to comply with these duties, they may face civil liability, criminal liability, and responsabilité scales. French law has developed a relatively rigorous system of arguments for these duties of directors. The civil liability of directors is most notable, for example, in the case of director liability, which is premised on fault, which in addition requires actual damage to the company and a causal link between the fault and the actual damage [21]. It is characteristic of French

[66] Article 149, Chinese Company Law. According to this article, directors, supervisors and senior management shall be liable for any damage caused to the company in the performance of their duties in violation of the laws, administrative regulations or the articles of association of the company.

[67] See China Judgments Online (中国裁判文书网).

law that such a regime may rely not on a fiduciary relationship between shareholders and directors but only on a contractual relationship. The common law model of fiduciary duties is based on a relationship of trust, but French law has structured a regime for directors around a contractual relationship in a principal agency. Since the interests of shareholders are in many cases aligned with those of the company, the directors' duties to the company can also be indirectly expressed in terms of their duties to the shareholders. First and foremost, civil liability arises from the civil law system. It is only in exceptional cases that criminal liability, or "responsabilité fiscal", arises. Moreover, in the European context, although there has long been some controversy over the doctrine of group companies in France, since the 1960s, Germany has been a relatively early adopter of legislation on group companies [24]. However, as an FHC is a form of parent company, the liability regime in this context is in German law converging on French law [5]. The treatment of French law is therefore representative of the European context.

Given that French law defines the liability of directors on disclosure on the basis of the civil law system, it is necessary to reflect on the provisions of Chinese Company Law. Chinese scholars argue that Chinese Company Law has adopted a fiduciary duty system to bind directors, supervisors, and senior management. However, judicial practice has not established a complete set of liability standards for determining the duty of fidelity and diligence. Perhaps the French law model of director liability could be used as a model. The reason is that the Chinese Civil Code was implemented in 2021, and Chinese commercial law scholars are considering the future direction of Chinese commercial law. For example, some scholars believe that China does not currently have plans to develop a commercial code, probably because the long-standing controversy over the relationship between civil law and commercial law has not been resolved [25]. From a practical point of view, then, the application of civil law theory to directors' liability has become the recommended approach. Moreover, company law and jurisprudence have not brought into play a complete doctrine that strictly defines the liability arising from a director's duty of loyalty and diligence. The French law model serves as a model.

Furthermore, it is feasible in the context of Chinese law. The regulation of FHCs does not currently specifically set out the obligations of their directors, although it does not prevent company law from binding them. However, the provisions of company law do not fully comply with the requirements of the prudential regulation of FHCs. It can be argued that the fiduciary duty regime in common law provides a foundation regime for Chinese Company Law. The French law model, however, allows this regime to become more detailed and systematic in the context of Chinese law. This is in line with the long-term trend in Chinese legislation. Chinese law does not tend to directly copy a particular system from another country but tends to synthesise comparative analysis and borrowing. The development of the supervisory board system in China has demonstrated this. The directors' liability regime on disclosure could then also go further in this legislative history.

Following the advent of the Chinese Civil Code era, from a practical perspective, the French law model provides an institutional reference for clarifying the liability of directors for disclosure arising from their duty of loyalty and diligence. It not only is in line with the long-established legislative experience of Chinese law but is also consistent with the requirements of prudential regulation of FHCs. This approach can provide a more complete design of liability for the protection of shareholders' right to information.

References

1. Abadie P (2013) Entreprise responsable et environnement: recherche d'une systématisation en droits français et américain (Corporate responsibility and the environment: the search for a systematization in French and American law). Dissertation. Université Paris 1 Panthéon-Sorbonne (University of Paris 1 Panthéon-Sorbonne)
2. AMF (2021) Règlement disclosure: l'AMF donne des clés de lecture sur la consultation en cours des autorités européennes de surveillance (Disclosure regulation: the AMF provides an overview of the current consultation with the European supervisory authorities), AMF. https://www.amf-france.org/fr/actualites-publications/actualites/consultation-des-autorites-europeennes-de-surveillance-sur-le-reglement-disclosure-lamf-donne-des. Accessed 21 Sept 2021
3. Ba S, Shen C (2013) Trends in international financial regulatory reform and policy options for financial regulatory reform in China. Southwest Financ 8:10. (巴曙松和沈长征:《国际金融监管改革趋势与中国金融监管改革的政策选择》,西南金融,2013年第8期,第10页)
4. Crédit Agricole SA (2021) Rapport financier annuel document d'enregistrement universel 2020 (Annual financial report universal registration document 2020), Crédit Agricole S. A. https://www.credit-agricole.com/finance/finance/communiques-de-presse-financiers/mise-a-disposition-du-document-d-enregistrement-universel-et-rapport-financier-annuel-2020-de-credit-agricole-s.a. Accessed 25 July 2021
5. Desoutter V (2012) La responsabilité civile de la société mère vis-à-vis de sa filiale: comparaison entre l'Aktiengesetz allemande et le droit français des groupes (Civil liability of the parent company vis-à-vis its subsidiary: a comparison of German Aktiengesetz and French group law). Dissertation, Jean Moulin Lyon 3 University.
6. Dondero B (2017) Droit des sociétés (Company law). Dalloz, Paris
7. Draxler J (2009) Private equity exit: strategie und vertragsgestaltung (Private equity exit: strategy and contract design). Springer, New York
8. European Banking Authority (2021) Joint regulatory technical standards on ESG disclosure standards for financial market participants, European Banking Authority. https://www.eba.europa.eu/regulation-and-policy/transparency-and-pillar-3/joint-rts-esg-disclosure-standards-financial-market-participants. Accessed 21 Sept 2021
9. European Commission (2016) State-owned enterprises in the EU: lessons learnt and ways forward in a postcrisis context, European Commission. https://ec.europa.eu/info/publications/economy-finance/state-owned-enterprises-eu-lessons-learnt-and-ways-forward-post-crisis-context_en. Accessed 21 Sept 2020
10. European Commission (2019) Corporate disclosure of climate-related information, European Commission. https://ec.europa.eu/info/business-economy-euro/banking-and-finance/sustainable-finance/corporate-disclosure-climate-related-information_fr. Accessed 21 Sept 2021
11. Fan J (2018) Company law. Law Press, Beijing. (范健:《公司法》第五版,法律出版社,2018年)
12. Garric A, Lemaître F (2020) La Chine surprend en s'engageant à atteindre la neutralité carbone d'ici à 2060 (China surprises by committing to carbon neutrality by 2060), Le Monde. https://www.lemonde.fr/climat/article/2020/09/24/la-chine-surprend-en-s-engageant-a-atteindre-la-neutralite-carbone-d-ici-a-2060_6053402_1652612.html. Accessed 21 Sept 2021

13. Guo S (2020) Improving the modern financial regulatory system (完善现代金融监管体系), The People's Bank of China. http://www.pbc.gov.cn/redianzhuanti/118742/4142474/4143008/4137411/index.html. Accessed 21 Sept 2021
14. Jiang L (2005) On the legal issues of financial holding companies. Dissertation, East China University of Political Science and Law. (姜立文,《金融控股公司法律问题研究:国际比较与中国对策》,华东政法大学博士论文,2005年,第1页)
15. Kahan M, Rock EB (2011) When the government is the controlling shareholder. Tex Law Rev 89:1299
16. Lee R (2018) The fiduciary duties of directors, LexisNexis. https://advance.lexis.com/api/document?collection=news&id=urn:contentItem:5TBV-F7W1-JCF2-82HY-00000-00&context=1516831. Accessed 21 Sept 2020
17. Li J (2012) The hierarchy of shareholders' right to information and its development - a comparative study of legislation in eight countries and regions as a background. Jinan J (Philos Soc Sci) 8:42. (李建伟:《股东知情权的层级结构及其展开—以八个国家、地区的立法比较研究为背景》,暨南学报(哲学社会科学版),2012年第8期,第42页。)
18. Magnier V (2019) Droit des sociétés. Dalloz, Paris
19. Magnier V (2019) Old-fashioned yet innovative: corporate law, corporate governance and sustainability in France. In: Beate S, Christopher MB (eds) The cambridge handbook of corporate law, corporate governance and sustainability. Cambridge University Press, Cambridge, p 278
20. Maria CRA (2011) Les fondements de la responsabilité civile des dirigeants des sociétés: étude franco-colombienne (The foundations of corporate officers' civil liability: a Franco-Colombian study). Dissertation, Pantheon-Assas University
21. Mestre J, Velardocchio D (2021) Le Lamy sociétés commerciales (The Lamy commercial companies). Wolters Kluwer France, Paris
22. OECD (2015) State-owned enterprise governance: a stocktaking of government rationales for enterprise ownership, OECD. https://www.oecd-ilibrary.org/governance/state-owned-enterprise-governance_9789264239944-en. Accessed 21 Sept 2020
23. Ren Z (2017) Research on the standard of diligence duty of company directors. In: Long W, Wang Q (eds) Beihang faxue 20 zhounian jinian wenji. China Legal Publishing House, Beijing, p 112. (任自力:《公司董事的勤勉义务标准研究》,载龙卫球和王琪全主编:《北航法学20周年纪念文集》,北京:中国法制出版社,2017年,第112页)
24. Saïd I (2015) Les groupes de sociétés: étude de droit tunisien à la lueur du droit français (Company groups: a study of Tunisian law in the light of French law). Dissertation, University of Paris 1 Panthéon-Sorbonne
25. Wang J (2021) Where does Chinese commercial law go in the era of codification? (法典化时代,中国商法何去何从?), the Chinese Civil and Commercial Law Net. https://www.civillaw.com.cn/t/?id=37733&security_verify_data=3830302c363030. Accessed 21 Sept 2021
26. Wang X (2015) Study on the legal system of state-owned enterprises. Central Compilation and Publishing House, Beijing. (王新红:《国有企业法律制度研究》,北京:中央编译出版社,2015年第20页。).
27. Wang Y et al (2018) The next step in mixed reform: new ideas for mixed ownership reform in the new era. Tsinghua University Press, Beijing. (王勇(等):《混改下一步:新时代混合所有制改革的新思路》,北京:清华大学出版社,2018年)
28. Zhang Y (2016) Modernising the governance of state-owned enterprises. National Academy of Administration Press, Beijing. (张银平:《国有企业治理现代化》,国家行政学院出版社,2016年,第60页)
29. Zhao X (2020) Controlling shareholders in corporate governance and their legal regulation. Chin J Law 4:93
30. Zhao X (2021) Dilemmas and pathways of Chinese corporate governance system. Mod Law Sci 2:89. (赵旭东:《中国公司治理制度的困境与出路》,现代法学,2021年第2期,第89页。)

Chapter 6
Legal Analysis of Shareholders' Rights Protection in the Corporate Governance Codes for Financial Holding Companies Beyond China

Abstract This chapter examines mechanisms for the internal protection of shareholder rights in FHCs in jurisdictions beyond China, with a specific focus on corporate governance codes and annual reports. The book analyses two objectives of shareholder rights protection in FHCs at both the theoretical and practical levels: effective governance and sustainable success. These two objectives are reflected in the corporate governance codes of other jurisdictions. Specifically, one of the most typical institutional designs of corporate governance for achieving the goal of effective governance is the "Independent Board Member". Furthermore, the book also reflects on the true binding nature of corporate governance codes, which are still subject to other commercial practices despite their lack of mandatory legal binding force. However, monitoring the implementation of corporate governance codes should be strengthened, which is a weak point in the current corporate governance codes. Sustainability success is not only based on systemic risk considerations but also on realising the right to a long-term return on shareholders' dividends. Therefore, FHCs need to focus not only on the protection of shareholders' rights but also on the balance of interests between shareholders and other stakeholders.

Keywords Corporate governance codes · Effective governance · Sustainable success · Independent board member · Sustainability

Why study corporate governance codes? First, it responds to the internal mechanisms for the protection of shareholders' rights in FHCs. The Corporate Governance Code, in turn, proposes a range of institutional arrangements for the internal governance mechanisms of companies. It has been widely accepted from the jurisdictions studied. In the case of European countries, for example, the French regulator AMF conducted a summary and analysis in 2016 of the corporate governance codes of the EU Member States [3]. According to this study, despite the EU's commitment to a harmonised corporate governance framework within a single market, there are some differences in the design of specific systems in each member state due to the specificities of their legal systems. Second, it is consistent with the practical application of FHCs. From the disclosures of FHCs in many jurisdictions, FHCs analyse

K. Ma, *Shareholder Rights Protection Mechanisms for Chinese Financial Holding Companies*, International and Comparative Law in the Asia Pacific,
https://doi.org/10.1007/978-981-97-9731-8_6

compliance with local corporate governance codes and provide explanations. In a 2014 survey, 89% of directors of European listed companies considered corporate governance code compliance to be important [20]. Finally, there is considerable debate as to whether the corporate governance codes have a regulatory effect. The more common perception is that it is soft law and lacks legal binding force. This means that its implementation is more dependent on the internal decisions of the company. Therefore, analysing corporate governance codes from the perspective of internal mechanisms may be more appropriate.

Can corporate governance codes be applied to FHCs? This is an issue that needs to be clarified in advance. The analysis of the issue must be performed in the context of the specific jurisdiction. For example, France updated its code of governance for listed companies in 2020. Although there is no direct statement in French law that the code is applicable to FHCs, it is clearly applicable to listed FHCs, such as Crédit Agricole. France has issued a code of governance for listed companies, which applies primarily to listed companies.[1] However, not all FHCs have chosen to be listed. Therefore, how should corporate governance codes be applied to unlisted FHCs? This is a difficult issue for corporate governance in China. When analysing corporate governance codes in other jurisdictions, the meaning of the "code" should first be understood in this context. Most jurisdictions that have developed codes are in the form of a "code". Among the jurisdictions defined in the book, those represented in this way include France and the UK. In addition to the "code" form, another form is the "principle", such as in the U.S. As such, an FHC does not depart from the type of company as defined by traditional company law and is still subject to corporate governance codes.

From a more specific perspective, this chapter analyses the objectives of shareholder rights protection from the perspective of corporate governance codes and FHCs.

6.1 The Theoretical Objectives of Shareholders' Rights Protection in Corporate Governance Codes

There are multiple models for the legal analysis of corporate governance, but the protection of shareholders' rights is indispensable. Given the international community's focus on sustainability, the balance between shareholders and other stakeholders is a key concern in corporate governance. This concern is also reflected in the case of FHCs, and only by re-examining the objectives of shareholder rights protection can the right measures be taken in corporate governance to adapt to the trends in the governance of FHCs. The corporate governance code contains two objectives for the protection of shareholder rights in FHCs. The first is the effective governance of the FHCs, and the second is sustainable success.

---

[1] See Corporate governance code of listed corporations 2020.

6.1.1 First Objective: Effective Governance

"Governance" usually refers to the board and leadership of a company [24]. "Effective governance" is intended primarily to address agency conflicts in corporate governance [7]. This view is recognised because it finds its basis not only in the research literature but also at the practical level. For example, some company operators have specifically studied the relationship between effective governance and the company board [30], and the book also adopts this view.

The relationship between the protection of shareholders' rights and effective governance appears to be one of mutual achievement. If the protection of shareholders' rights is the goal, then effective governance is the means to achieve that goal. However, if effective governance is the goal, shareholder rights protection is equally the means to that end. Therefore, which approach should be chosen? Perhaps it would be more appropriate to aim for effective governance. The doctrine of shareholder primacy has been challenged, and shareholder rights protection can be found with the very aim of achieving better development for FHCs. Therefore, the protection of shareholders' rights should serve the interests of the company. From this perspective, shareholder rights protection can be understood as a way of achieving effective governance. Some scholars may have different views of what effective governance means. However, the understanding of effective governance here will take a restricted interpretation, which refers to the relationship between shareholders and management. Conflicts in agency relationships in the governance of FHCs are precisely the issues that corporate governance codes focus on.

Some of the conflicts between shareholders and management are discussed in Part I. This research focuses on some of the key designs for resolving these conflicts, including the "Independent Board Member" and the implementation of corporate governance codes.

6.1.1.1 The "Independent Board Member" Under the Prudential Standard in the Corporate Governance Codes

An independent board member is a neutral expression and has two meanings: an independent director and an independent member of the supervisory board [20]. The reason for this divergence is mainly based on the corporate governance structures in different jurisdictions. In terms of global corporate governance practices, there are two main types of corporate governance structures: the one-tier structure and the two-tier structure [29]. In the one-tier structure, independent directors are designed to play a supervisory role on the board of directors, and there is no supervisory board in this model. Typical jurisdictions are represented by common law countries such as the U.S. and the UK. In contrast, there are no independent directors in a two-tier structure, and the supervisory board is the organisation in the company that oversees the board of directors, which also has independent members. It is represented by Germany. In addition, there are countries with corporate governance codes that take a neutral approach to the choice of these two corporate governance structures, leaving the choice to the company. It is represented by France.[2]

Why is it necessary to evaluate independent board members through prudential criteria? On the one hand, it is dictated by the special nature of FHCs. As a type of company with systemic risk to financial markets, all aspects should be included in a prudential evaluation system, which is in line with the trend in corporate governance in various jurisdictions after the crisis in 2008. For example, the OECS was issued in 2011 for banks the "Corporate Governance Principles for the OECS".[3] This standard applies to the board of directors of banks, including independent directors. On the other hand, from the perspective of the prudential standard itself, the Basel framework's corporate governance principles for banks require directors to perform their duties of care in a "prudent person" manner [4]. The independent board member is then naturally evaluated through the prudential standard. The member is also evaluated through the prudential standard.

Under prudential standards, how should independent board members be specifically designed in corporate governance? This requires addressing two core issues. The first is how to ensure the independence of independent directors, and the second is the understanding and practice of the relationship between the independent board system and the protection of shareholders' rights.

A very important reason why independent board members are recognised is their independence. It is a very important design in FHCs. The controlling shareholders of an FHC can be divided into the government and ordinary controlling shareholders with great capital power. In the presence of these two highly influential giants, the protection of minority shareholders' interests relies heavily on the role of independent directors. Moreover, in the case of agency conflicts, the independent board member is an important tool for easing the relationship between shareholders and management, but the achievement of this purpose is dependent on its independence. In addition, case law provides some explanations for these issues. For example, the French Code of Corporate Governance refers to the assessment of the independence of the director as an employee corporate officer within the past 5 years, and from the point of view of the Code of Governance, it can be found that to ensure the independence of the director, he or she must not have an "employee corporate officer" relationship with the company. What proportion of the board of directors should such a director represent? The corporate governance code indicates that the proportion of independent directors should be two thirds.[4] In the case law, the judge cited the law and explained that no more than one-third of the board of directors can have an "employee corporate officer" relationship.[5] It is in line with the requirements of the Corporate Governance Code. At this point, although this provision of the Code is soft law and not enforceable,

---

[2] See the 2020 French Corporate Governance Code of Listed Corporations.

[3] See the Corporate Governance Principles for the OECS.

[4] See Article 5.3, 2020 French Corporate Governance Code of Listed Corporations. According to its description, the Board was advised to establish an ad hoc committee with at least two-thirds of its members made up of independent directors, with the executive officers not included.

[5] Cour de cassation, civile, Chambre sociale, 29 juin 2017, n° 16–15.814.

if it conflicts with existing regulations, the law prevails. These authors also find a similar basis in the case law of other jurisdictions, which will not be explained in detail here. The effect of soft law is therefore freedom since it does not contradict existing financial market regulation.

Why do independent board members protect shareholders' rights? The independent board member was created to resolve the agency conflict between shareholders and management. The reason for this judgement requires a review of the reasons why agency conflicts between shareholders and management arise, which encompass the following aspects. First, in corporate governance, the separation of ownership and management has resulted in shareholders being removed from the running of the company, which has led to increased demands on management. However, as the objectives of shareholders and management are not fully aligned, this leads to conflicts between the two [14]. Second, in an FHC, the controlling shareholder, whether it is the government or another entity, may also be a member of the board of directors.[6] In this case, the oppression of minority shareholders comes not only from the controlling shareholder but also from the board of directors. The cost for minority shareholders to monitor the controlling shareholder and the board of directors is expensive [17]. The agency conflict between minority shareholders and the board of directors is therefore magnified.

Theoretically, the value of the independent board member system lies in the avoidance of these causes of conflict and thus the effective protection of minority shareholders' rights. First, it is closely related to the function of the independent director. The function of the independent director is related to the ownership structure of the company. Whether it is a one-tire or two-tire structure, they maintain convergence in the design of independent directors [16]. Specifically, in an FHC with dispersed shareholding, independent directors are required to protect the interests of shareholders against management abuses.[7] In contrast, in an FHC with concentrated shareholding, independent directors are required to protect the interests of minority shareholders. Second, it is related to the reputation of independent directors, and the value of their human capital depends on their expertise in this area [2]. The corporate governance codes of various jurisdictions set several criteria for the independence of independent directors. If independent directors meet these criteria, then the book may consider them to be independent. In this case, independent directors tend to have a social reputation and expertise that can help reduce agency costs and thus help minority shareholders realise their right to information, vote and other important rights in the company.

Whether it is a one-tire or two-tire structure, an independent board member has a positive effect on the protection of shareholders' rights in FHCs. However, given the limitations of the system, it needs to be improved.

---

[6] It is evident in the case of Chinese FHCs. In other jurisdictions, reference can be made to Portigon AG.

[7] Ibid.

6.1.1.2 Implementation of the Corporate Governance Codes

A good system design does not necessarily lead to good results; the key also lies in the implementation of the system. The independent board member system represents an institutional arrangement at the theoretical level of corporate governance and is a tool for the alignment of interests between shareholders and management. Therefore, how effective is this system? This depends on feedback in the governance practices of FHCs. To argue for the governance of FHCs in concrete implementation, the book explains in this section the binding effect of corporate governance codes on FHCs and the monitoring of implementation.

A corporate governance code is widely recognised as a soft law tool [22]. Therefore, how effective is it in protecting the rights of shareholders in an FHC? The book hopes to explore the following questions. First, how can corporate governance codes have a binding effect on the protection of shareholder rights in FHCs? Soft law tools are not usually considered to have the enforcement power of law. It is common to use the term soft law to characterise the environment in which cooperation institutions operate and, in particular, to refer to the nature of the rules they adopt [5]. However, an important reason why this tool is revered in corporate governance practice in many jurisdictions is that it does have some binding effect on corporate governance. Second, corporate governance codes are binding through the principle of complying with or explaining. It is the principle followed by almost all corporate governance codes. In this model, the binding effect of a code of corporate governance is left to the market. Researchers believe that companies follow corporate governance codes because they are in the interest of the company and create confidence in the market. When they provide untrue or misleading information to the market, the market imposes penalties, which include share price volatility and investor withdrawal [38].

How can the binding nature of corporate governance codes in the protection of shareholder rights in FHCs be evaluated? First, the limited binding effect has several advantages for corporate governance practices. Since FHCs are not of the same type and the actual operation of each company varies, the soft law route offers a great deal of flexibility. While soft law is not legally enforceable, it does not prevent binding forces from being created by other means. From a business perspective, noncompliance with corporate governance codes may not break hard law, but it can lead to lower business performance or even bankruptcy. It is unacceptable to shareholders and management alike. Therefore, this binding force is perhaps more effective. The legal requirements are fixed, but market pressures are omnipresent. Second, there are some limitations to this binding effect. While the book recognises that FHCs follow corporate governance codes, it can be monitored by the market. However, in cases where the comply or explain model is followed, the market may not be able to respond in a timely manner. This relies on truth in disclosure and oversight, and such cases are not uncommon, as the book can find evidence of various corporate scandals, such as the famous Madoff investment scandal in the U.S., in which unethical behaviour, from publicly available sources, continued for at least 16 years until the financial crisis in 2008, when it was discovered by the market. In this case, it was particularly detrimental to minority shareholders. Moreover, minority shareholders are not nearly as resilient to risk as large shareholders are. In a situation where the market is unable to react in a timely manner to the unethical behaviour of an FHC, this sends the wrong signal to minority shareholders, and the blowback can be devastating. Ultimately, rules exist to resolve conflicts. If the rule is designed by good legislators but is only at the theoretical level and does not achieve a fair and reasonable disposition of the conflict, then it will ultimately be useless. It is more like a poseur. Therefore, soft law is sometimes more effective than hard law in terms of flexibility in resolving disputes. When the remedy of hard law is sought, it is often expensive. However, the pressure in the soft law model tends to stem less from those rules that are visible and more from those that are invisible because they cannot be precisely controlled.

Although a code of corporate governance is not legally enforceable, it is also expected to be well enforced. To achieve this goal, monitoring implementation is necessary. From the corporate governance codes of the jurisdictions studied, the content of supervision of the governance codes of FHCs can be divided into two main categories. The first category is functional oversight in corporate governance, which manifests itself primarily as internal oversight. This is reflected in the internal arrangements within the corporate governance structure and manifests itself in the monitoring of management, the monitoring of financial reporting, and the monitoring of the company's operations. The second category is the supervision of the overall implementation of corporate governance standards. It manifests itself primarily as external oversight. It refers to the monitoring and evaluation of the overall governance of the FHCs.

Different jurisdictions each have different approaches to internal and external oversight of corporate governance. First, there are also some differences in the one-tire model. In France and the UK, the board of directors and the audit committee perform internal oversight. In the U.S., it is mainly the board of directors.[8] Second, there are some differences in the external supervision of FHCs. For external oversight. In France, a high committee is responsible for the annual disclosure of corporate governance reports. However, external oversight is not described in the corporate governance codes in the U.S. and the UK.[9]

Therefore, monitoring the implementation of the corporate governance code for FHCs has led to a renewed understanding of the effectiveness of the corporate governance code and its relationship with hard law. It is characterised differently in different jurisdictions. The soft law effectiveness of corporate governance codes is more limited to internal monitoring. In terms of external monitoring, soft law and hard law work together.

---

[8] The sections of the presentation can all be found explained in the corporate governance codes of the respective jurisdictions.

[9] Ibid.

6.1.2 Second Objective: Sustainable Success

What is "sustainable success"? In the governance of FHCs, the protection of shareholders' rights requires not only dealing with the agency relationship of the company but also with the conflicts between shareholders and other stakeholders. It is referred to as "sustainable success" in the UK Corporate Governance Code.[10] Its focus is on promoting the contribution of shareholders to the development of society as a whole rather than being limited to shareholder interests. This is the second objective of shareholder rights protection in FHCs. To fully argue this point, the importance of "sustainable success" for FHCs and how this can be achieved will be explained here.

6.1.2.1 Importance of Sustainable Success in Corporate Governance Codes

In the context of FHCs, "sustainable success" has gradually gained acceptance by regulators in many jurisdictions, as evidenced by a few regulatory initiatives in recent years. For example, in 2018, the EU published the "Action Plan on Sustainable Finance", in which corporate sustainability disclosures have been incorporated into the legislative framework, which also promotes green investment in sustainability [11]. The Paris Agreement has become more deeply entrenched as one of the regulatory standards for corporate governance in Europe. In addition, in 2020, the EU launched an initiative on sustainable corporate governance to encourage long-termism in corporate governance [12]. This initiative has received support from member states, such as the Mouvement des Entreprises de France (MEDEF), which has expressed its support for the EU initiative but also its desire to place more emphasis on the development of SMEs [13]. The UK government called for corporate governance reform in 2017 and invited the Financial Reporting Council to improve the long-termist governance model in its corporate governance code to create sustainable business [37]. Therefore, sustainability is also recognised in the future governance reform of FHCs, although research and regulation in this area is still in progress. For both financial market regulation and corporate governance, sustainability has gained widespread acceptance [33]. There are many broad perspectives from which the book can explain this phenomenon. However, on the basis of the protection of shareholder rights in FHCs, two perspectives can be analysed on the basis of a systemic risk analysis and a shareholder's right to dividends perspective.

Why does the "sustainable success" of FHCs in terms of shareholder rights protection have a relationship with systemic risk? This is the first question to be answered. This can be explained from three perspectives. First, according to principal–agent

[10] See Article 18, 2018 UK Corporate Governance Code. According to its description, all directors should be subject to annual re-election. The Board should set out in the document accompanying the resolution to elect each director the specific reasons why their contribution is important to the long-term sustainable success of the company.

theory, the directors and shareholders of an FHC and its subsidiaries are responsible for the sound operation of the FHC [25]. Whether based on fiduciary duties in common law countries or the directors' duties in French law, the effect of directors and shareholders on the governance of an FHC, as a systemically important institution, extends beyond the FHCs to the financial markets. In other words, the failure of governance in one FHC may cause a chain reaction that could lead to a financial crisis, as illustrated by the bankruptcy of Lehman Brothers. Second, environmental and social issues, as represented by the climate crisis, have formed an important variable in the systemic risk of financial markets. The book has analysed, from a historical perspective, that part of the economic crisis in the OECS region was caused by the climate crisis.[11] The reflection on environmental and social issues triggered by the spread of COVID-19 has forced us to confront the fact that sustainable success is the right path to prevent systemic crises [34]. Thus, "sustainable success" in shareholder rights protection for FHCs is a tool to avoid systemic risk and, to some extent, market turbulence, but it does not have a decisive impact.

Why does "sustainable success" in FHCs correlate with shareholders' rights to dividends? Realistically, "sustainable success" has a direct effect on shareholders' earnings. This can also be justified by legal theory because shareholders' rights to dividends are influenced by several factors. "Sustainable success" is one of the most important aspects of corporate governance. With respect to the dividend policy of shareholders, the right to dividends is guaranteed in the laws of every jurisdiction.[12] In principle, shareholders' rights to dividends are limited by the proportion of their capital contribution or the amount of their investment [27], but shareholders may also agree otherwise in the company's articles of association. In addition to legal protection and the agreement in the articles of association, shareholders' access to dividends also depends on the performance of the FHC [36]. When an FHC is difficult, the shareholder's right to dividends may be interfered with by the regulator. Therefore, if an FHC is in a systemic crisis due to a crisis such as climate change, the shareholders' right to dividends will be restricted [10]. This means that if the FHC can achieve sustainable success, the shareholders' right to dividends will be greatly protected. However, if there are problems with this aspect of sustainability,

---

[11] Ibid.

[12] For EU law: Article (7), Directive (EU) 2017/828 of the European Parliament and of the Council of 17 May 2017 amending Directive 2007/36/EC as regards the encouragement of long-term shareholder engagement. According to its description, the company is required to keep the necessary records relating to the general meeting of shareholders, including information on the validity of its resolutions, the company's fulfilment of its obligations in respect of the manner in which dividends are paid. It proves the shareholders' right to dividends.

For French law: Article L232-12, Code de commerce. According to its description, after approval of the annual accounts and confirmation of the existence of distributable amounts, the General Meeting determines the shares to be distributed to the partners in the form of dividends.

For U.S. law: § 316, 26 USCS. According to its description, the term "dividend" refers to any distribution of property by a company to its shareholders.

For UK law: Section 830, Companies Act 2006. The clause confirms that the company can distribute its profits to its shareholders and that the profits available for distribution by the company are its accumulated, realised profits. It is in fact the shareholders' right to dividends.

then shareholders' rights to dividends will also be negatively affected. Thus, "sustainable success" in FHCs contributes to the realisation of shareholders' rights, particularly in relation to dividend rights. However, excessive interference from shareholder activism should also be avoided in the sustainable strategy of FHCs. To this end, the corporate governance of FHCs could encourage more innovative measures.

6.1.2.2 Realisation of Sustainable Success in Corporate Governance Codes

In terms of regulation and corporate governance practices, sustainability has moved from theory to reality. In this context, Europe became the first jurisdiction in the world to design a sustainability disclosure system that can support sustainable corporate governance [32]. According to the EU disclosure, the EU Public consultation on sustainable corporate governance has been concluded, and the relevant regulation will be published shortly [12]. It is foreseen that the corporate governance guidelines of the EU Member States will also be updated. Other jurisdictions will also follow suit. In addition, in terms of FHC practices, the book examines different FHC disclosures. All of them disclose environmental, social and governance (ESG) issues in their annual reports,[13] which are analysed in detail and are not presented in detail here. However, it has been noted that the sustainability of FHCs is already in practice and will be more regulated in the future. Here, the book discusses the shareholders' right to vote and the shareholders' right to information.

From the perspective of shareholders' rights to vote, the achievement of sustainability in FHCs requires the engagement of shareholders, while the realisation of shareholder rights protection is one of the component evaluation criteria of "sustainable success". Therefore, to facilitate the achievement of sustainable development in FHCs, it is important that this strategy is reflected in the protection of shareholder rights. However, the discussion of the realisation of voting rights in the context of corporate governance is more often considered to be specific to FHCs with decentralised shareholdings. The issue of voting rights does not seem to be an issue of concern in FHCs with highly concentrated shareholdings. When the book discusses shareholder voting rights, the main conflict is the conflict between the controlling shareholder and the minority shareholder. However, in the case of decentralised FHCs, there is a very close relationship between the realisation of shareholders' voting rights and the company's "sustainable success", which is more evident in Anglo-Saxon countries. This can be explained in two ways. First, minority shareholder activism can impede a company's "sustainable success" through voting rights. Shareholder activism tends to be more focussed on short-term interests, which is more evident among minority shareholders, and voting rights become a tool for them to impede this process. In FHCs, the controlling shareholder is often a government or other wealthy consortium,[14] which may be more patient about long-term returns than

[13] Ibid.

[14] It has already been dealt with in Part I.

minority shareholders are. Second, controlling shareholders may abuse their voting rights to interfere excessively with the "sustainable success" of an FHC. When the government is the controlling shareholder, the sustainability initiative is not just a corporate decision; it can also be a political mandate. Therefore, when the government is the controlling shareholder of an FHC, activism for sustainability may overlook minority shareholder participation and transparency. Therefore, in the governance of an FHC, the design of shareholders' voting rights can have a significant and sometimes decisive effect on a company's sustainable success. Both controlling and minority shareholders have a certain legitimacy in the attitude they adopt in the face of a sustainability strategy.

From the perspective of shareholders' right to information, the realisation of "sustainable success" can be analysed from two relevant aspects of the argument. First, how should corporate governance respond in the absence of clear regulatory standards in the face of the disclosure challenges posed by sustainability? Setting standards may not be easy. However, within the existing corporate governance model, the development and improvement of the "Code of Ethics" and "Code of Conduct" for FHCs should be considered. Second, more professional staff should be added to independent board members. Whether it is a one-tire or two-tire governance structure, they have oversight responsibilities over the directors and management of the company. In the face of sustainability issues such as climate change, independent board members could consider bringing in experts with different knowledge structures so that relatively effective oversight can be achieved. Therefore, the protection of shareholders' rights to information in FHCs can have a positive effect on the achievement of sustainable corporate success. In the face of unknown or unclear sustainable corporate governance issues, FHCs can improve the "Code of Ethics" and "Code of Conduct" and monitoring systems on existing corporate governance models.

6.2 Business Practices of Shareholders' Rights Protection in the Three Financial Holding Companies

To better understand the role of corporate governance codes in the protection of shareholders' rights in FHCs, this chapter presents the protection of shareholders' rights disclosed by three FHCs in their annual reports.[15] These three FHCs are Crédit Agricole S.A. in France, HSBC in the UK, and JPMorgan Chase & Co. in the U.S.[16] These three companies were chosen to provide a basis for subsequent analysis of Chinese FHCs. To gain a full understanding of the role of corporate governance codes in the protection of FHCs, two aspects are analysed here. First, this research analyses the internal measures taken by FHCs for the protection of shareholders'

[15] Due to differences in the timing of disclosure of annual reports of FHCs in different jurisdictions, only their latest published annual reports will be selected.

[16] Information sourced from the Sovereign Wealth Fund Institute (SWFI).

rights from a practical perspective. Second, on the basis of the case study of FHCs, the book reflects on the theoretical analysis from a jurisprudential perspective to better validate the role of corporate governance codes in the protection of shareholders' rights in FHCs.

6.2.1 *Measures for Shareholders' Rights Protection in the Three Annual Reports*

The information contained in a company's annual report is voluminous. Here, the book reflects on whether the theory has gained practical acceptance through a comparative case perspective. In a specific analysis, the independent board member regime and sustainability disclosure in these FHCs will be analysed here.

6.2.1.1 The Design of an "Independent Board Member" to Protect Shareholders' Rights

The three FHCs have a one-tier structure, with only a board of directors in their corporate governance and independent directors as supervisors. However, the French Code of Corporate Governance is neutral in the choice of corporate governance structure, but studies show that most listed companies still favour the one-tier structure and do not have a supervisory board [23], so that independent directors are an essential option, as is Crédit Agricole S.A. Therefore, the term "Independent Board Member" is used here to refer to the system of independent directors. In terms of internal protection mechanisms, the book has chosen to analyse the internal design of the company from the perspective of the shareholders or management of the FHC. From a legal perspective, the designs of the three FHCs for independent board members and their compliance with the recommendations of local corporate governance codes will be analysed here.

The independence of the independent board member in the governance of an FHC is crucial to the effective governance of an FHC. Therefore, how does this system manifest itself in corporate governance at a practical level? Considering the information disclosed in the annual reports of the three companies, it is believed that a comparative analysis can be made from two perspectives: the composition of the independent board member and the performance of their duties. The independent directors of the three companies all focus on balancing the diversity of independent directors from different criteria.[17] For example, in the cases of Crédit Agricole S.A. in France, the HSBC in the UK and JPMorgan Chase & Co. in the U.S., the disclosure of the background of independent directors is more abbreviated. Only the "senior independent director" is disclosed by the HSBC, and only the "lead independent

[17] These analyses are based on the 2020 annual reports of these three companies.

director" is disclosed by JPMorgan Chase & Co. The functions of the "senior independent director" and the "lead independent director" are similar; for example, they are both responsible for calling other independent directors.

With respect to the performance of independent board members, in JPMorgan Chase & Co.'s annual report, the independent directors meet regularly to discuss topics they see fit, with the lead independent director being responsible for convening them. The HSBC specifically addresses the role of the senior independent director through a report that sets out a total of 10 tasks, which are subsidiary to the annual report. It is stated that the Senior Independent Director's primary role is to support the Chairperson and to oversee the Chairperson with the other Nonexecutive Directors as and when required [18]. Crédit Agricole S.A.'s annual report identifies four committees on which the independent directors maintain oversight: le Comité des risques, le Comité d'audit, le Comité des rémunérations, le Comité des nominations et du gouvernement. In each of these four committees, the independent directors constitute a majority.

With respect to compliance with the disclosure of independent board members, compliance analysis refers not only to corporate governance codes but also to regulatory laws [31], as explained in the three FHCs. However, at this point, the book has chosen to focus on compliance analysis of corporate governance codes only. For corporate governance codes, owing to their soft law effect, in much of the literature and research, companies use the "comply or explain" approach. However, through the analysis of the three FHCs, it can be found that this was not the case. Specifically, the only companies that use the "comply or explain" approach in their annual reports are Crédit Agricole in France and the HSBC in the UK. JPMorgan Chase & Co. in the U.S. does not have compliance statements or analysis.

The number of independent directors is explained in Crédit Agricole S.A.'s annual report in a specific statement entitled "Points de nonconformité au Code Afep/Medef". The proportion of independent directors at Crédit Agricole S.A. is only one-third, which is a reasonable measure given the shareholding structure of Crédit Agricole S.A., although it does not comply with the French corporate governance code, which expects most independent directors. The HSBC follows the UK Corporate Governance Code, and in relation to independent directors, an independent director will not be reelected because he has worked for more than nine years, which may affect his independence. It is in accordance with the UK Corporate Governance Code.

Thus, the Corporate Governance Code is primarily for listed companies. With respect to the "comply or explain" principle of corporate governance, companies in France and the UK perform well. Compared with the U.S., it is also a European model.

6.2.1.2 Disclosure on Sustainability to Protect Shareholders' Rights

"Sustainable success" is an important objective in the governance of FHCs. The three FHCs all disclose the actions they take. However, it is also noted that their disclosure of this component differs. The main difference is in the form of disclosure, which is divided into two main types: disclosure in the company's annual report and the publication of a separate report to supplement the annual report. Specifically, JPMorgan Chase & Co. in the U.S. reported on sustainability initiatives. The HSBC in the UK and Crédit Agricole S.A. in France all chose to detail the measures they have taken in relation to sustainability disclosure in their annual reports. Furthermore, in terms of the form of disclosure, all three companies have taken to publish ESG reports or sustainability reports to disclose their actions. In addition, Crédit Agricole S.A. in France adopted an innovative disclosure measure in addition to issuing a report. In 2020, an ESG performance management system was implemented to improve transparency. This is a step forward in sustainability disclosure. The relationship between sustainability disclosure and shareholder rights protection for the three FHCs will be analysed, along with a compliance analysis of their disclosures.

"Sustainability disclosure" is an expression of shareholder engagement and a way for boards to ensure that shareholders' right to information is realised. Scholars believe that companies should establish effective dialogue mechanisms and engagement processes with shareholders to coordinate the relationships among the board, management, and investors [8]. Sustainability disclosure is one of these communication mechanisms. This is evidenced by the explanations in the annual reports and ESG reports of the three FHCs. JPMorgan Chase & Co, for example, consider that the purpose of an ESG report is to establish a voluntary and consistent way of disclosing relevant financial risk, which is one of the main ways in which FHCs discuss ESG disclosure issues with their stakeholders, including shareholders.[18] The HSBC in the UK sees sustainability disclosure as a statement of intent that expresses the long-term opportunities that the company offers to other stakeholders, including shareholders [19]. Crédit Agricole S.A. in France sees sustainability disclosure to ensure that a sustainable and equitable development model for the company is achieved, which benefits all stakeholders, including shareholders.[19] Judges in French law have already rejected automatic liability as to whether an FHC is liable for environmental damage to its subsidiaries [1]. Such an attitude could be applied equally to disclosure reports. That is, in the annual report of an FHC, the FHC, as the parent company, may not necessarily be liable if there is an error in the subsidiary's statement on sustainability disclosure. Therefore, all three FHCs have taken steps towards sustainability disclosure, which is a necessary action taken by the board of directors to fulfil their agency responsibilities and is a step towards the realisation of shareholders' rights and participation.

With respect to sustainable disclosure compliance, corporate governance codes provide recommendations on sustainability disclosures. The book uses the corporate governance codes of these three jurisdictions as examples, which can be divided into two types. First, sustainability disclosures are required to be reflected in annual

[18] JPMorgan Chase & Co does not make specific disclosures about ESG in its annual report, but instead publishes a specific report: "Environmental Social &Governance Report".

[19] See Crédit Agricole S. A. Annual Report 2020.

reports. It is represented by the UK Corporate Governance Code.[20] Second, corporate governance codes require companies to safeguard shareholders' access to the necessary information on sustainability through greater transparency. It is represented by France and the U.S.[21] Specifically, with respect to the compliance analysis of sustainability disclosures, the book has demonstrated the representativeness of European countries, so how do Crédit Agricole S. A. and HSBC respond in their annual reports? All companies have analysed and explained their compliance with the Codes of Corporate Governance in relation to their employees and shareholders.[22] However, there is no analysis of environmental and community responsibilities. Therefore, if sustainability disclosures are linked to ESG issues, the current compliance analysis of sustainability disclosures is focussed mainly on governance. The environmental and social aspects of governance compliance are not disclosed. Therefore, from the analysis of the annual reports of FHCs, compliance analysis of corporate governance codes can be applied to corporate sustainability disclosures, but as such, sustainability disclosures still lack clear corporate governance standards. This finding is also in line with what was shown in a study published by the French AMF in 2016 for corporate governance codes [3]. Therefore, this topic should be improved in the future.

6.2.2 Reflections on Shareholders' Rights Protection in the Three Annual Reports

The explanation of the relationship between the protection of shareholders' rights in the annual reports of FHCs in different jurisdictions is based on a practical perspective. It does provide additional reference. It can help regulators, corporate governance standard setters and researchers understand how rules are applied in practice. The book can use this to reflect on the differences between the theory and practice of governance codes for FHCs and the direction of future efforts. Here, two objectives

[20] See Part 1, UK Corporate Governance Code 2018. According to it, the annual report should describe how the company considers and addresses the opportunities and risks to the future success of the business, the sustainable nature of the company's business model, and how the company's governance contributes to the implementation of its strategy.

[21] See Part I, 2016 U.S. Principles of Corporate Governance". According to its description, shareholders may seek a say in the strategic direction and decision-making of the company—areas that have traditionally fallen squarely within the domain of the board and management. Shareholders seeking this influence should recognise that this type of empowerment necessarily involves a certain level of responsibility for the goal of creating long-term value for the company and all shareholders. Better transparency is therefore necessary.

Also see Article 4.3, French Corporate governance code of listed corporations. According to its description, the Board should ensure that shareholders and investors receive balanced and relevant information and that they are fully aware of the strategy, the development model, the nonfinancial considerations that are important to the company and its long-term sustainable prospects.

[22] See "Points de nonconformité au Code Afep/Medef" in "Crédit Agricole S. A. Annual Report 2020" and "Statement of compliance" in "HSBC Holdings plc's Annual Report 2020".

in the governance of FHCs are reflected upon in the light of feedback from the practice area. On the one hand, the book will assess the achievement of the objective of shareholder rights protection in these three companies, and on the other hand, the book will analyse future trends on this basis.

6.2.2.1 Realisation of the Objectives of Shareholders' Rights Protection in the Corporate Governance Codes

The corporate governance code explains the objectives of shareholder rights protection in FHCs and sets out several criteria. Therefore, have the FHCs achieved these objectives in their operations? There are a few questions before the book looks at the criteria for the realisation of shareholders' rights. How can the objective of shareholder rights protection be assessed? In fact, it is a vague criterion. However, from the perspective of the evaluation mechanism, the corporate governance code already represents a nonbinding best practice of corporate governance [22]. Therefore, from the perspective of the corporate governance code, the question of whether the objective of shareholder rights protection has been achieved translates into two aspects: first, whether the FHC has complied with the requirements of the corporate governance code; second, in the case of noncompliance with the requirements of the corporate governance code, whether the FHC has complied with the requirements of the corporate governance code. The second is whether the explanations given by the FHC for noncompliance with the requirements of the code are reasonable. On the basis of the analysis of the criteria for achieving shareholder rights protection, the book assesses the "effective governance" objective and the "sustainable success" objective for the protection of shareholder rights in FHCs.

"Effective governance" is designed primarily to resolve conflicts in agency relationships, which is the path to protect the rights of shareholders. To this end, the book examined the design of three FHCs for independent board members. The book then analysed their compliance with the corporate governance code. Some explanations are given for noncompliance with the corporate governance code, but are their explanations for noncompliance sufficient? Similar questions have been raised by company law scholars. In 2014, for example, UK company law scholars argued that the provisions of the UK and European corporate governance codes for "comply or explain" were problematic in business practice in two ways: the lack of shareholder engagement and the fact that the company's explanations were too abbreviated [22]. The same problem persists in the annual reports of the FHCs. However, the corporate governance code adopts a self-regulation approach to the strategy, which means that it is up to stakeholders to make a judgement on explanations that do not comply with the corporate governance code. If they accept the company's explanation, then what does it matter if the company's explanation is vague? Therefore, as required by the corporate governance code, these companies follow the "comply or explain" rule, and if shareholders do not question it, then the book considers this governance to be effective. Therefore, the evaluation of disclosure in a company's annual report by shareholders and other stakeholders is key to whether "effective governance" is achieved.

For the three FHCs in terms of sustainability disclosure, only the European companies have conducted a compliance analysis. Therefore, for FHCs in France and the UK, in terms of sustainability disclosure, why is there no compliance analysis for issues such as environmental and social issues? Sustainability disclosure is an issue that has been studied in a very broad sense. The disclosure of shareholder- and employee-related issues certainly does respond to sustainability disclosure. However, these do not seem to be sufficient compared with the current encouragement of long-term shareholder engagement and the repeated emphasis on ESG issues. The reality, however, is that corporate governance codes still lack standards for environmentally and socially relevant sustainability disclosures. This means that, thus far, FHCs still lack a credible commitment to the sustainability of corporate governance. In the absence of a system of verification for sustainability objectives, researchers believe that the current actions of companies tend to be more of a public relations exercise and lack practicality [15]. Although the book has promoted initiatives and research in these areas, it must be admitted that it is still in its infancy. In the absence of corporate governance standards, these companies simply disclose their efforts to this end without conducting a compliance analysis. It is in line with the reality of the situation and the legal requirements.

In response to the assessment of the sustainability success of FHCs, future sustainability disclosure standards should be developed in corporate governance codes and guided by a soft law path. It applies not only to future European companies but also to the sustainability of FHCs in other jurisdictions around the world, including U.S. companies. Moreover, more professionals should be included on boards of directors in corporate governance mechanisms, thus highlighting the value of science in sustainable development decisions [1].

6.2.2.2 Trends in Shareholders' Rights Protection

By analysing the status of the protection of shareholders' rights in the corporate governance of three global FHCs, the book has identified the implementation of their corporate governance codes. Moreover, further improvements are needed to achieve the two objectives of shareholder rights protection. This leads us to reflect on future trends in the governance of FHCs. From the analysis and assessment of the annual reports of the three FHCs, the book highlights two main trends in the future protection of shareholder rights in FHCs: risk-based corporate governance and the ongoing redefinition of shareholder rights.

Risk-based corporate governance can be analysed from a shareholder engagement perspective. In the assessment of the objective of effective governance, it has been argued that, in response to the interpretation given in the corporate governance codes, FHCs should take steps to encourage shareholder participation and oversight. It is indeed where the FHC currently falls short in relation to this objective. Therefore, why is shareholder engagement needed? Researchers have argued that if a company is at risk of legal sanctions, the quality of its explanations will be compromised when they are given in response to matters that do not comply with corporate governance codes. However, corporate governance codes are based on voluntarism, which is a form of self-regulation. Whether an FHC will be sanctioned for the explanations it gives depends entirely on whether the shareholders are satisfied. Therefore, shareholder engagement is precisely about reducing potential risks and creating oversight in FHCs' governance. In addition, it echoes the principle of risk-based prudential regulation of FHCs.

In addition, in the analysis of sustainability disclosure compliance, it has been argued that a sustainability disclosure standard under the soft law model should be developed. FHCs respond to risks in ESG governance. French researchers have reported that since 2016, the financial sector has started to report climate-related risks and that capital may be reallocated [28]. Moreover, it has been confirmed by the disclosures in the annual reports of the FHCs. JPMorgan Chase & Co, for example, believe that they will manage climate-related risks in reference to credit risk criteria in their future corporate governance [21]. The HSBC has disclosed its sustainability risk policies. They expect their financial services to not pose unacceptable risks to people or the environment and are working to find better practices [19]. Risk-based corporate governance has thus become a consistent approach to achieving both shareholder rights, and this needs to be explored further, both in practice and in theory.

With respect to the redefined shareholders' rights, from protecting the shareholders' rights, the relationship between shareholders' rights and the company is the theoretical basis for the construction of a mechanism for the protection of shareholders' rights in FHCs. Although an FHC has several important features that distinguish it from other types of companies, it is still bound by the theory underlying company law. In 2020, by tracking the historical evolution of corporate governance in 21 developing countries around the world from 1995–2014, researchers found that shareholder primacy had become a consistent trend. This trend slowed after the financial crisis in 2008, but it has not completely changed [35]. Therefore, while shareholder primacy has been widely criticised, it still enjoys support in developing countries. Under this theory, shareholder rights are based on the identity of shareholders as owners of the company.

In response to criticisms of shareholder primacy theory, scholars have rethought the identity of shareholders. For example, shareholders are regarded as ordinary unsecured creditors [26]. Under this theory, then, shareholder rights essentially become the rights of creditors. It would also be subject to the rights of other creditors. Indeed, this could indeed break the foundation of shareholder priority theory. Some explanations for this can be given by civil law theory. The interpretation adopted by the French Civil Code is representative. Instead, the French Civil Code has devised a series of droit de préférence regimes, and the rights of ordinary unsecured creditors are subject to the rights of other creditors who hold priority [9].

Although new theories on the redefinition of shareholder rights have emerged, they are perhaps still in the early stages of theoretical research. If shareholder rights are limited by other stakeholders, then it implies that other stakeholders are involved in the governance of the company. However, from the three FHCs, it was common practice to disclose their efforts towards employees, the community, and the environment but not how these stakeholders were involved in the governance of the FHC. For example, JPMorgan Chase & Co discloses the extensive training they do for their employees and the benefits they provide to them in the ESG report, but it is still essentially the operation and management of the company and does not change in terms of governance structure. In other words, shareholder rights have not been diminished as a result. Therefore, in essence, perhaps the redefined theory of shareholder rights is still at the stage of theoretical exploration and needs more time to be tested before it can be applied commercially. However, the business community still lacks more models for reference. The PACTE Act, introduced by French society in 2019, already reflects a rethinking of the nature of business by both the government and society.[23] Although it is still not perfect, both the government and business have made attempts to rethink shareholder rights, and it can be believed that more practices in the future will drive the reform of corporate law theory.

An analysis of the disclosures of FHCs reveals that despite the critique of shareholder primacy theory, it remains an inescapable reality of the business world. Both FHCs and governments have made attempts to explore the sources of shareholder rights and the involvement of other stakeholders, but further studies are needed. The trend should be fast-tracked in the context of encouraging long-term shareholder engagement.

References

1. Abadie P (2013) Entreprise responsable et environnement: recherche d'une systématisation en droits français et américain (Corporate responsibility and the environment: the search for a systematization in French and American law). Dissertation, University of Paris 1 Panthéon-Sorbonne
2. Anand A, Milne F, Purda L (2010) Monitoring to reduce agency costs: examining the behavior of independent and nonindependent boards. Seattle University Law Review 4:813
3. Autorité des marchés financiers (2016) Étude comparée: les codes de gouvernement d'entreprise dans 10 pays européens (Comparative study: corporate governance codes in 10 European countries), Autorité des marchés financiers (French Financial Markets Authority). https://www.diva-portal.org/smash/record.jsf?pid=diva2:1327377. Accessed 2 Sept 2021
4. BIS (2015) Corporate governance principles for banks. BIS. https://www.bis.org/BCBS/publ/d328.htm. Accessed 21 Sept 2020
5. Bonneau T (2018) Régulation bancaire et financière européenne et internationale (European and international banking and financial regulation). Bruylant, Bruxelles
6. Chen JJ (2010) A primer on corporate governance: China, New York. Business Expert Press, New York; Schiller S (1999) Les limites de la liberté contractuelle en droit des sociétés: les connexions radicales (The limits of contractual freedom in corporate law: radical connections). Dissertation, Université Panthéon-Assas Paris II (Panthéon-Assas University Paris II)
7. Clarke T, Branson D (2012) The SAGE handbook of corporate governance. SAGE Publications, London

[23] Ibid., p. 287.

8. Dallas G, Pitt-watson D (2016) Corporate governance policy in the European Union through an investor's lens. CFA Institute. https://www.cfainstitute.org/en/advocacy/policy-positions/corporate-governance-and-ESG-disclosure-EU. Accessed 21 Sept 2020
9. Delebecque P, Mauriès V (2019) Le lamy droit des sûretés. Wolters Kluwer France, Paris
10. European Commission (2018) Climate change. European Commission. https://commission.europa.eu/energy-climate-change-environment/topics/climate-change_en. Accessed 21 Sept 2020
11. European Commission (2018) Sustainable finance: making the financial sector a powerful actor in fighting climate change. European Commission. https://ec.europa.eu/commission/presscorner/api/files/document/print/en/ip_18_3729/IP_18_3729_EN.pdf. Accessed 21 Sept 2021
12. European Commission (2020) Sustainable corporate governance. European Commission. https://ec.europa.eu/info/law/better-regulation/have-your-say/initiatives/12548-Sustainable-corporate-governance. Accessed 21 Sept 2021
13. European Commission (2020) Feedback form: Mouvement des Entreprises de France (MEDEF), 2020. https://ec.europa.eu/info/law/better-regulation/have-your-say/initiatives/12548-Sustainable-corporate-governance/F583963. Accessed 21 Sept 2021
14. Gao N (2014) Research on the effectiveness of independent directors with offshore background. Posts & Telecom Press, Beijing. (高楠:《境外背景独立董事的有效性研究》,北京,人民邮电出版社,2014年,第20页。)
15. Goffaux CG, Biron J (2016) La juridicité des engagements socialement responsables des sociétés: regards croisés Québec-France (The legality of corporate social responsibility commitments: a Quebec-France perspective). Les Cahiers de droit (The Cahiers of law) 57:489
16. Gordon JN (2015) Convergence and persistence in corporate law and governance. In: Jeffrey NG, Wolf-Georg R (eds) The oxford handbook of corporate law and governance. Oxford University Press, Oxford
17. Hansmann H, Squire R (2015) External and internal asset partitioning: corporations and their subsidiaries. In Jeffrey NG, Wolf-Georg R (eds) The oxford handbook of corporate law and governance. Oxford University Press, Oxford
18. HSBC (2020) HSBC senior independent nonexecutive director, HSBC. https://www.hsbc.com/-/files/hsbc/our-approach/corporate-governance/pdfs/200218-senior-independent-non-executive-director.pdf?download=1. Accessed 25 July 2021
19. HSBC (2021) Annual report and accounts 2020, HSBC. https://www.hsbc.com/-/files/hsbc/investors/hsbc-results/2020/annual/pdfs/hsbc-holdings-plc/210223-annual-report-and-accounts-2020.pdf. Accessed 25 July 2021
20. International Finance Corporation (2010) Corporate governance manual. International Finance Corporation. https://www.ifc.org/wps/wcm/connect/topics_ext_content/ifc_external_corporate_site/ifc+cg/resources/toolkits+and+manuals/ifc+corporate+governance+manual. Accessed 20 Sept 2020
21. JPMorgan Chase & Co (2019) Understanding our climate-related risks and opportunities. JPMorgan Chase & Co. https://www.jpmorganchase.com/content/dam/jpmc/jpmorgan-chase-and-co/documents/jpmc-cr-climate-report-2019.pdf. Accessed 21 Sept 2020
22. Keay A (2014) Comply or explain in corporate governance codes: in need of greater regulatory oversight. Leg Stud 2:279
23. Levin K (2021) France: corporate governance. Kramer Levin. https://www.kramerlevin.com/images/content/4/8/v2/48943/190222-The-Legal-500-Reid-Feldman-France-Corporate-Governance.pdf. Accessed 21 Sept 2021
24. Lipson B (2012) Effective governance: a guide for small and diaspora NGOs, INTRAC. https://www.intrac.org/resources/effective-governance-guide-small-diaspora-ngos/. Accessed 21 Sept 2021
25. Macey JR, O'Hara M (2015) Vertical and horizontal problems in financial regulation and corporate governance. In: Jeffrey NG, Wolf-Georg R (eds) The oxford handbook of corporate law and governance. Oxford University Press, Oxford
26. Magnier V (2017) Comparative corporate governance: legal perspectives. Edward Elgar Publishing Ltd., Cheltenham
27. Magnier V (2019) Droit des sociétés. Dalloz, Paris

28. Magnier V (2019) Old-fashioned yet innovative: corporate law, corporate governance and sustainability in France. In: Beate S, Christopher MB (eds) The Cambridge handbook of corporate law, corporate governance and sustainability. Cambridge University Press, Cambridge
29. Mallin CA (2013) Corporate governance, 4th edn. Oxford University Press, Oxford
30. Nadler DA et al (2005) Building better boards: a blueprint for effective governance. Jossey-Bass, San Francisco
31. Ouassini SM (2014) La responsabilité de la société mère du fait de ses filiales (Liability of the parent company for its subsidiaries). Dissertation, Paris Dauphine University
32. Pacces AM (2021) Sustainable corporate governance: the role of the law. University of Oxford. https://www.law.ox.ac.uk/business-law-blog/blog/2021/02/sustainable-corporate-governance-role-law. Accessed 21 Sept 2021
33. Rahim MM (2013) Legal regulation of corporate social responsibility: a meta-regulation approach to raising CSR in a weak economy. Springer, Heidelberg
34. Ramani V (2020) Addressing climate as a systemic risk: a call to action for financial regulators. Harvard Law School Forum on Corporate Governance. https://corpgov.law.harvard.edu/2020/06/28/addressing-climate-as-a-systemic-risk-a-call-to-action-for-financial-regulators/. Accessed 21 Sept 2020
35. Samanta N (2019) Convergence to shareholder primacy corporate governance: evidence from a leximetric analysis of the evolution of corporate governance regulations in 21 countries. Corp Gov 5:849
36. Schiller S (1999) Les limites de la liberté contractuelle en droit des sociétés: les connexions radicales (The limits of contractual freedom in corporate law: radical connections). Dissertation, Panthéon-Assas University Paris II
37. UK Government (2017) Corporate governance reform: the government response to the green paper consultation, UK Government. https://assets.publishing.service.gov.uk/government/uploads/system/uploads/attachment_data/file/640631/corporate-governance-reform-government-response.pdf. Accessed 21 Sept 2021
38. Wymeersch E (2005) Enforcement of corporate governance codes, SSRN. https://ssrn.com/abstract=759364. Accessed 21 Sept 2020

Chapter 7
Legal Analysis of Shareholders' Rights Protection in Financial Holding Companies Governance Beyond China in the Context of New Technologies

Abstract This chapter examines the internal mechanisms surrounding the protection of shareholder rights in FHCs, focusing on how they deal with the protection of shareholder rights in the face of the opportunities and challenges presented by new technologies in jurisdictions beyond China. In this chapter, two technologies, blockchain and AI, have gained widespread attention in corporate law. Specifically, blockchain and AI provide new solutions for the protection of shareholder rights in FHCs. Primarily, blockchain technology improves the rights to vote and information for shareholders, increases the transparency and security of shareholder engagement, optimises agency costs, and reduces the threat posed by insider control. In addition, AI technology can provide data standards for ongoing board evaluation and enhance the effectiveness of board evaluation by improving transparency standards. However, new technologies also pose some challenges to the internal governance of shareholder rights protection in FHCs. The challenges arise both from within the company and from the limitations of the technology itself.

Keywords Blockchain · Principal-agent relationships · Artificial intelligence · Shareholder activism · Disputes

In an era of technological change, new technologies have brought about a number of changes to corporate governance, which at the same time have implications for the protection of shareholder rights in FHCs. In the current environment, it is important to study new technologies and the protection of shareholder rights in FHCs. For example, in 2018, the relationship between corporate governance and new technologies was explored in the Roundtable organised by the European Corporate Governance Institute. In this conference, participants from academia and business discussed the impact of technologies such as blockchain and artificial intelligence (AI) on shareholder engagement and argued that a change in technology in corporate governance is inevitable [21].

In addition, regulators are already working on legislation for new technologies. For example, in April 2021, the EU published a proposal for the regulation of AI [23],

K. Ma, *Shareholder Rights Protection Mechanisms for Chinese Financial Holding Companies*, International and Comparative Law in the Asia Pacific,
https://doi.org/10.1007/978-981-97-9731-8_7

in which Member States are encouraged to establish a framework for governance,[1] supervision, and liability through regulatory sandboxes. There is also a penalty clause for corporate governance.[2] Therefore, how should corporate governance respond to this? Although the relevant legislation has not yet been formally enacted, there is no doubt that the regulation of new technologies is still in a transitional period in various jurisdictions. Real regulation will come soon.

From the perspective of shareholder rights protection, FHCs should actively make corresponding explorations to improve their compliance systems. Indeed, FHCs are already taking action. For example, Crédit Agricole S.A. in France disclosed in its annual report that they are actively using new technologies to improve ESG transparency in an effort to contribute to European standards.[3] As a result, there is a consensus between regulators and FHCs that new technologies will bring profound changes to the protection of shareholders' rights in FHCs. In terms of building internal mechanisms for the protection of shareholders' rights in FHCs, FHCs should strengthen their research in this regard. This chapter analyses the impact of new technologies on the protection of shareholders' rights in FHCs in terms of both opportunities and challenges.

7.1 Opportunities for Shareholders' Rights Protection

Currently, there are a wide variety of new technologies, including blockchain, cloud computing, big data, AI, and the Internet of Things.[4] All these technologies may, to varying degrees, have unexpected impacts on areas such as corporate law, corporate governance, and financial regulation. Blockchain technology and AI may play a greater role in addressing the problems faced in protecting the rights of shareholders in FHCs, including RPTs and interference in business decisions by controlling shareholders, as well as the protection of minority shareholders' rights to vote and information. From a corporate governance perspective, the book should also analyse the impact of these new technologies. The opportunities offered by blockchain and AI for the protection of shareholders' rights in FHCs will be analysed here.

---

[1] See Article 5.2.6, EU Artificial Intelligence Act. According to its description, at EU level, the proposal establishes a European Committee on Artificial Intelligence (the "Committee"), composed of representatives of Member States and the commission. The committee will facilitate the smooth, effective and coordinated implementation of the regulation by promoting effective cooperation between national regulators and the commission, and by providing advice and expertise to the commission. It will also collect and share best practices among Member States.

[2] See Article 71, EU Artificial Intelligence Act. Under this provision, the penalties are mainly administrative regulation. Member States shall establish rules on penalties, including administrative fines, applicable to infringements of this regulation and shall take all necessary measures to ensure that these rules are properly and effectively enforced. The penalties provided for shall be effective, proportionate, and dissuasive.

[3] See Crédit Agricole S.A. Annual Report 2020.

[4] See the new technologies listed in Chapter 13 of the Outline of the 14th Five-Year Plan and Vision 2035 of the National Economic and Social Development of the People's Republic of China.

7.1.1 Opportunities Offered by Blockchain Technology for Shareholders' Rights Protection

The protection of shareholders' rights in FHCs requires the resolution of two main conflicts, namely, the conflict between controlling and minority shareholders and the potential conflict between shareholders and management. The book has already analysed the issue from a legal and regulatory perspective. Here, the book focuses on the corporate governance perspective. It can be believed that blockchain technology has the potential to play an important role in resolving these two conflicts in the future. Specifically, the positive impact of blockchain on improving shareholder rights disputes and principal–agent relationships will be analysed here.

7.1.1.1 Opportunities in Improving Shareholders' Rights Disputes

One of the conflicts in the protection of shareholders' rights in an FHC manifests itself in the controlling shareholder and minority shareholder. The controlling shareholder's RPTs and interference in business decisions have infringed on the interests of minority shareholders [5]. Blockchain technology, on the other hand, can help improve the vulnerability of minority shareholders in terms of the rights to vote and information. The role of blockchain technology in improving rights to vote and the right to information will be analysed to explain the positive impact of blockchain technology on improving shareholder rights disputes.

There are different interpretations of the concept of blockchain technology. For example, technologists consider blockchain to be a distributed ledger of transactions, which is implemented in the form of data batched into blocks, using cryptographic verification to link the blocks together 4]. This book does not explore the principles of this technology from a technical point of view. However, from a legal point of view, blockchain is an information technology processing method that is characterised primarily by decentralisation, openness, and anonymity, which increases the transparency of the participants and reshapes their legal rights and obligations.

Blockchain technology helps provide a new way of operating the voting system in FHCs, which is an institutional innovation for the protection of minority shareholders' rights. This is for the following reasons. First, blockchain technology is already being used for shareholder voting. In 2019, for example, the Society for Worldwide Interbank Financial Telecommunication (SWIFT) announced a proof-of-concept (PoC) on e-Voting in the Asia Pacific region to implement a blockchain-based shareholder voting method, which was supported by Singapore's FHC DBS [46]. It is not uncommon in the U.S., France, or the UK. Second, there are some new features of voting with blockchain technology compared with the traditional shareholder voting system. Some academics argue that these features are in four main areas: blockchain voting is more secure, more transparent, and more streamlined, while also encouraging shareholder democracy [30]. The explanation for this observation is that smart contract code is executed redundantly by the underlying blockchain-based network, which cannot be manipulated unilaterally by any party; therefore, translating legal rules into smart contract code means that no centralised operator can modify these rules or prevent their execution [17]. These arguments can be supported. Although the legal systems of various jurisdictions stipulate that companies should guarantee the right of shareholders to vote electronically,[5] some researchers have questioned the validity of internet voting. For example, in 2009, French engineers questioned this method of voting, mainly from a technical and legal point of view, arguing that there are technical and democratic flaws in internet voting. In terms of democracy, the secrecy and transparency of voting on the internet cannot be fully guaranteed [22]. Therefore, the application of blockchain technology to shareholder voting in FHCs is already a reality; it is helping to improve shareholder relations and will play a greater role in the future.

In addition, the use of blockchain technology in FHCs can effectively change the information asymmetry between shareholders of FHCs, which can better protect the interests of minority shareholders. This functionality is mainly found in FHCs with decentralised shareholdings, such as JPMorgan Chase & Co and HSBC, which the book has analysed. This is due to the following reasons. First, blockchain technology makes shareholder information and company information more transparent. In FHCs, shareholders' right to information is reflected not only in the voting system. Although some scholars have analysed this aspect, blockchain-based voting systems can improve the quality of voting by enhancing shareholders' right to information [26]. Moreover, it helps to better identify shareholders [6]. For the governance of FHCs, the accurate identification of their controlling shareholders and beneficial owners is an important tool in achieving the objectives of prudential regulation and consolidated regulation. Second, blockchain technology offers a new solution for remedying shareholders' rights to information. Remedies are obtained through litigation, which is often expensive.[6] In contrast, remedies from within the company can be obtained relatively quickly and inexpensively. Blockchain enables the supervisor of an FHC to have an identical copy of the public ledger and no special user rights through a smart contract, which allows the supervisor of the company, including independent directors, the supervisory board, and the audit committee, to intervene, thus enabling minority shareholders to obtain redress.

Blockchain technology provides a new technical solution for the protection of minority shareholders' rights in FHCs. It protects shareholders' right to information in that it can effectively reduce disputes over shareholders' rights, thus avoiding the cost of defending rights. In addition, internal governance can reduce the cost of supervision for supervisors to obtain evidence and monitor, thus enhancing the efficiency of corporate governance.

---

[5] *Ibid.*

[6] *Ibid.*

7.1.1.2 Opportunities in Improving Principal–Agent Relationships

In addition to resolving conflicts of interest between shareholders, the protection of shareholders' rights also requires good relations between shareholders and agents. The major conflicts faced between management and shareholders are agency costs and insider control issues [5]. Blockchain technology offers a new way to solve this problem. Blockchain's improvements to agency relationships are mainly in the form of reduced agency costs and a new solution to the problem of insider control.

The application of blockchain technology in FHCs can help optimise agency costs between shareholders and management. The theory of agency costs is not a legal concept; however, scholars of corporate law and corporate governance have focused on this issue. In 1976, scholars Michael C. Jensen and William H. Meckling defined agency costs in their paper as three types of costs: monitoring expenditures by the principal, bonding expenditures by the agent, and residual loss [31]. This theory seems to be widely accepted; for example, in 2019, scholars similarly adopted this view when studying the relationship between blockchain and corporate governance [32]. This theory can also be used to explain agency costs in FHCs. From a practical explanation, the book is already seeing such attempts by start-ups, represented by the UK start-up Colony [12], whose idea is to remove agents from corporate governance through blockchain technology and achieve autonomy among shareholders. This firm believes that most companies define corporate rules in documents and legal contracts. The boundaries and hierarchies of shareholders, executives, and employees are no longer so strict. This firm wants to implement simple rules between people and help them organise themselves by aligning incentives around common goals. They believe that blockchain can help them achieve this goal [13]. Although it is a start-up company and much of the business model still needs time to be proven, it is a worthy experiment. However, even if this model is possible in some companies, it still faces many tests in the case of FHCs. FHCs have maintained prudent standards in their use of technology. Therefore, it may take time to verify that blockchain technology increases agency costs for FHCs.

In corporate governance, internal control and insider control are two different concepts. Insider control is a concept introduced by Japanese economist Mahahiko Aoki in 1994 [14]. It refers to the phenomenon where management conspires with employees to gain de facto control of a company, resulting in a loss of control by shareholders [2]. In 2015, Capitol City Bank & Trust Company was taken over by the Federal Deposit Insurance Corporation in the U.S. [24], making it a classic example of a bank failure where insider control led to a failure of corporate governance oversight [45]. Moreover, the phenomenon is more evident in economies in transition, as evidenced by the transition period of privatisation of state-owned enterprises in Russia [25]. Chinese state-owned FHCs are also facing mixed-ownership reforms at a time when they should also be highly alert to the phenomenon of insider control. When insiders conspire with employees to create a situation of insider control that jeopardises the rights of shareholders, the challenge for shareholders is to detect such conspiracies effectively and develop effective oversight, as it is often relatively hidden. The monitoring of insider control may rely on a system of internal control that emphasises the enforcement and efficiency of the corporate governance system, not only for management but also for all employees [5]. Therefore, this system is an important form of corporate governance. The role of blockchain lies in the new solutions offered to the internal control system of FHCs.

Internal controls in an FHC need to identify, analyse, and respond to risks and then minimise the risks faced by the company by means of manual, automated, preventive, and discovery controls. The application of blockchain in this context is mainly in the form of smart contracts to improve the risk identification and analysis capabilities of insider controls. In addition, the risk response prevents the risk of insider control due to increased transparency. Overall, it has improved the efficiency of the response to insider control.

7.1.2 Opportunities Offered by Artificial Intelligence Technology for Shareholders' Rights Protection

With respect to the definition of AI, some researchers have summarised eight definitions that focus on two levels: thought processes and reasoning and behaviour. It can be analysed from four perspectives: thinking humanly, thinking rationally, acting humanly, and acting rationally [42]. Therefore, this study focuses on the relationship between machines and humans from the perspective of thinking and behaviour. In terms of shareholder rights protection, the book has shown that FHCs take action using AI. For example, HSBC in the UK is fighting corruption within businesses as well as financial crime, including among directors and other employees, through the use of AI technology. In addition, in its corporate governance, it has introduced independent directors with an AI background. JPMorgan Chase & Co. in the U.S. has used AI to increase investor experience and improve its technological infrastructure. Crédit Agricole S.A. in France uses AI to increase the efficiency and transparency of corporate governance.[7] As a result, this technology is working in practice.

AI technology is already at work in the governance of FHCs, and its potential will be better demonstrated in the future. Here, the book analyses the role of AI in the internal mechanisms of shareholder rights protection in FHCs from a corporate governance perspective. Specifically, the book analyses the value of AI in board evaluation and in encouraging shareholder engagement in the governance of FHCs.

7.1.2.1 Opportunities for the Evaluation of the Board of Directors

There is a general consensus on the assessment of the board of directors in corporate governance codes. Both the one-tyre model and the two-tyre model can be found for the corresponding basis in the corporate governance codes. In terms of corporate governance, provisions corresponding to the corporate governance codes

[7] See their annual reports in 2020.

in all the jurisdictions studied can be found.[8] The French code of corporate governance is the most straightforward in terms of the relationship between the evaluation of the board of directors and the protection of shareholders' rights: "the Board of Directors should evaluate its ability to meet the expectations of the shareholders".[9] The corporate governance codes of other jurisdictions do not directly state the relationship between the evaluation of the board of directors and the protection of shareholders' rights, but they all follow principal-agent theory. In the agency model, the principal and the trustee are in a contractual relationship, so does the trustee follow the wishes of the principal? The day-to-day running of a company needs to be assessed. Therefore, board evaluation is a way to ensure that management protects the rights of shareholders as they should. The application of AI technology in FHCs has helped improve board evaluation in corporate governance, mainly through reforming evaluation criteria and enhancing the effectiveness of soft law in board evaluation.

For the corporate governance codes, there is no uniformity in the criteria used to assess the board of directors. These can be reflected in the following areas. First, how often are evaluations conducted? The one-tier model can be divided into two categories: the European model and the other models. In European countries, their corporate governance codes stipulate a minimum of every three years,[10] as seen in France and the UK. In the U.S., it does not specify the timing of the assessment. Second, what is assessed? It can also be divided into two models: enumeration and general description. Under the general description model, the U.S. considers that the overall performance of the board of directors should be assessed,[11] but this is not explained in detail in the corporate governance principle. Under the enumeration model, the assessment of the composition, diversity, size, and effectiveness of the board is more consistent, as is evident in the corporate governance codes of France and the UK.[12] Third, who is responsible for the assessment? It can be divided

---

[8] They are France, the UK, and the U.S.

[9] See Article 10.1, 2020 French Corporate Governance Code of Listed Corporations.

[10] France: see Article 10.3, 2020 French Corporate Governance Code of Listed Corporations. According to its interpretation, there should be a formal evaluation at least once every three years. It could be done under the leadership of an appointment or nomination committee or an independent director, with the assistance of external advisors.

UK: see Article 21, 2018 UK Corporate Governance Code. According to its description, there should be a formal and rigorous annual evaluation of the performance of the board, its committees, the chairperson, and individual directors. The chairperson should consider having external assistance in conducting regular board evaluations. In FTSE 350 companies, it should be done at least once every three years.

[11] U.S.: see Article V, 2016 U.S. Principles of Corporate Governance. According to its recommendations, the board should have an effective mechanism to assess its performance on a continuous basis. Meaningful board evaluation requires an annual assessment of the effectiveness of the full board, the functioning of board committees and the contributions of individual directors. The results of these evaluations should be reported to the full board and any issues and concerns arising from the evaluation should be followed up.

[12] France: see Article 10.1, 2020 French Corporate Governance Code of Listed Corporations.

into external and internal assessments. In the U.S., the Nominating/Corporate Governance Committee is jointly responsible,[13] which is an internal assessment. In France, three approaches are proposed: the leadership of the appointments or nominations committee or of an independent director assisted by an external consultant.[14] In the UK, the nominations committee and the external assessor are jointly responsible.[15] Thus, European countries tend to favour a combination of internal and external assessments. In contrast, U.S. tends to favour internal assessment.

How will AI technology structure the evaluation criteria for the board of directors of an FHC? The main areas of performance are as follows. First, AI will provide the data standard for ongoing board evaluation. While corporate governance codes in many jurisdictions require an assessment of the board at least every three years, more important is the day-to-day monitoring of the board. It cannot be effectively achieved through humans, but machines can do it. Therefore, machine learning can be used to establish big data standards for the day-to-day evaluation of boards. Second, AI can improve the effectiveness of boards of directors by increasing transparency standards. The book explained that Crédit Agricole S.A. has begun to explore the use of AI technology to improve the transparency and efficiency of its services to investors and shareholders. Although it is still in the exploratory phase, it is a good start. In the governance of FHCs, insider control occurs mainly because of the covert nature of this form, which can manifest itself in the finances as well as in the day-to-day operations of the company. If shareholders want to access this information, it relies on the information disclosed. However, in a manual model, how can you ensure that the information available to shareholders is valid? In business, this can be difficult. However, machine intervention seems to provide shareholders with a faithful tool. It can be imagined that if the role of a robot is added to the operation of the board and the way in which the robot is controlled is known only to the shareholders, then this seems to put a loyal pair of eyes on the board for the shareholders. If there is a problem with the robot, then the shareholders will be alerted. This would lead to a reform in the criteria for board evaluation. In practice, it also involves many issues of privacy as well as business ethics, but AI does offer a new possibility.

The soft law effect of corporate governance codes has been widely recognised in academic circles, and it can be found on some basis in the analysis of the annual reports of three FHCs. The book has also shed new light on the binding nature of corporate governance codes. It is true that a code of corporate governance is not legally enforceable, but it may be binding in other ways.[16] For example, if an

---

UK: see Article 16, 2018 UK Corporate Governance Code. According to this description, all directors should have access to the advice of the company secretary, who is responsible for advising the board on all governance issues.

[13] U.S.: see Article IV, 2016 U.S. Principles of Corporate Governance. Under this provision, the board, under the leadership of the Nominating/Corporate Governance Committee, shall periodically consider the method or combination of methods by which the Board and its committees can be meaningfully evaluated.

[14] France: see Article 10.3, 2020 French Corporate Governance Code of Listed Corporations.

[15] UK: see Articles 21, 2018 UK Corporate Governance Code.

[16] *Ibid.*

assessment shows that the board of directors has not acted in the best interests of the corporation.[17], thereby infringing on the interests of the shareholders, what is the responsibility of the board of directors in this case? The book has identified many jurisdictions where the board is evaluated by a nominating committee. The job of the nominating committee is to appoint and remove directors. It certainly involves taking action on this. In addition, the U.S. Principles of Corporate Governance suggest that the results of the evaluation may also affect the CEO's compensation.[18] Therefore, the results of the evaluation of the board of directors mainly affect the qualifications of the directors. However, it may not be sufficient. In common law countries, directors have a fiduciary duty. Under the French model, directors are also subject to civil liability. However, this arises only if the conditions for legal remedies are met. Suppose that a director fails to actively discharge his duties, resulting in a loss to the shareholder, but the criteria for legal remedy are not met; how should the shareholder's loss be made good at that point? The use of the soft law route may be controversial. However, in real life, such examples may not be uncommon. With respect to independent directors in particular, although independent directors have a supervisory role, it is questionable whether they actually play that role. Especially in FHCs where there is a controlling shareholder, the role of the independent director may be suppressed by the controlling shareholder, and the interests of minority shareholders may be compromised as a result [5]. Perhaps it should not be too critical of the independent directors at this point, as it is a result of the shareholding structure of the company. However, owing to the passive nature of independent directors, the role of the system is not reflected, and ultimately, the system is ineffective. This is an embarrassing situation.

The use of AI technology in FHCs may lead to new interpretations of the soft law effect of corporate governance codes. It is mainly based on the theory of "code is law" [35]. The theory suggests that each historical period has had different regulators. In nineteenth-century England, social norms were considered to constitute a form of regulation; in the twentieth century, there was concern about injustices of the market; and in the network society, code became the alternative regulator of the age [34]. It can be considered a regulatory lever and thus has an impact on many areas beyond the law [17]. Therefore, AI is not the latest proposition for the interpretation of soft law. The subject was discussed when the internet was created. In the two decades of the twenty-first century, the development of AI has gradually moved from ideas to commercial practice. The role of AI as a binding force in a networked society may be better demonstrated in corporate governance.

---

[17] France: see Article 20, 2020 French Corporate Governance Code of Listed Corporations. According to its description, the directors are authorised by all shareholders and should act in the best interests of the company in all circumstances.

[18] U.S.: see Article VI, 2016 U.S. Principles of Corporate Governance. According to its recommendation, the results of the CEO's evaluation should be communicated to the CEO by a representative of the independent directors in an executive session in a timely manner and used to determine the CEO's remuneration.

7.1.2.2 Opportunities Offered by Artificial Intelligence Technology for Shareholder Engagement

"Shareholder engagement" is a legal term that is described in research works and policy documents. For example, in 2017, the UK Department for Business, Energy & Industrial Strategy proposed incentivising companies to obtain remuneration reports by enhancing shareholder engagement rights [49]. With respect to the concept of shareholder engagement, it seems difficult to define it from a policy perspective. However, researchers have explained that shareholder engagement refers to the right way for shareholders to engage with decision-makers, other investors, and other constituencies to make their voices heard [29]. The concept is recognisable. In civil law countries, such a concept is explained by case law. French case law, for example, explains whether shareholders need to be heard in a merger, such as *les engagements des actionnaires*.[19] AI technology has a role in encouraging shareholder participation in the governance of FHCs. This is demonstrated mainly by the fact that it provides a simulation tool to encourage long-term shareholder engagement and by the fact that it offers a new option for protecting shareholder rights in complex business decisions.

The long-term engagement of shareholders is important for FHCs. In an FHC with fragmented shareholding, minority shareholder activism manifests itself in a focus on short-term interests rather than ensuring sustainability [11]. When faced with voting problems, abuses by minority shareholders also take the form of the passive exercise of voting rights.[20] The realisation of shareholders' rights is often closely linked to general meetings, and voting is an important means of realising shareholders' rights, such as the right to information and the right to dividends [8]. Therefore, long-term shareholder involvement is not only directed at controlling shareholders but also includes minority shareholders. In the case of sustainability issues, shareholder participation is encouraged to be able to obtain the support of shareholders on major issues of the company.

In corporate governance, AI can be used as a simulation tool.[21] The book can also provide an in-depth analysis of its value for long-term shareholder engagement. Therefore, how does AI technology encourage long-term shareholder engagement? It is akin to a sandbox exercise. The book identified the short-sighted behaviour of shareholders in the previous analysis.[22] However, ultimately, shareholders invest in companies in pursuit of returns, such as financial returns [7]. Moreover, what is called short-sighted behaviour is truly a case in which shareholders are unsure of the opportunities and risks that this investment presents for them. Institutional investors may have professional tools and techniques to obtain sufficient information. However, for minority shareholders, it is difficult for them, so they take a conservative approach to investing. Thus, the short-sightedness of minority shareholders is criticised in both

[19] Cour d'appel de de Versailles, 12ème chambre sect. 2.7.24 février 2005, n° 03/07294.

[20] *Ibid.*

[21] It was a point made by the European Corporate Governance Institute at its 2018 conference on "Technology and Corporate Governance".

[22] *Ibid.*

corporate law and the theory of corporate governance. However, from a realistic point of view, they are justified. Can the book expect a company to invest in areas of unknown risk in the operation of the company? This does not seem to be in line with the principle of cost effectiveness. Central to this question is not a focus on long-term or short-term investments but rather that shareholders should be given a clear understanding of the risks and opportunities facing the company in terms of sustainability. In the case of long-term investments by shareholders, AI has been created to address this issue. For example, on the basis of big data analysis, AI can help shareholders of FHCs predict the risks and opportunities of ESG investments over the next ten years. When shareholders are aware of investment opportunities in this area, they will naturally want to participate.

In addition, many FHCs are multinational corporations, which means that their investors and shareholders may come from different jurisdictions around the world. This then makes it difficult for shareholders from different jurisdictions to participate in the governance of an FHC because of multiple factors, such as language, costs, and time zones. For example, the EU regulation published in 2017 encouraged long-term shareholder participation. However, the identification of shareholders indicates that for cross-border shareholders, there can be some barriers to shareholder identification due to the presence of multiple intermediaries.[23] In addition, researchers have identified the costs of cross-border voting as an issue that cannot be ignored, which may include information, organisation, and communication costs, among others. However, these factors cannot be avoided when encouraging long-term shareholder engagement [36].

AI technology helps resolve these conflicts to some extent. Robotics, a real-life application of AI, is already at work in several business sectors. Faced with cost issues and other potential difficulties for shareholders in terms of cross-border engagement, robots seem to offer a convenient way to do so. For example, in cross-border engagement, there are situations where shareholders do not understand English or French because they may come from all parts of the globe. However, some commercial applications for translation bots exist. While there is enormous scope for all of these in the future development of AI, these offer a wealth of possibilities for cross-border shareholder engagement.

---

[23] See Article 3a, Directive (EU) 2017/828 of the European Parliament and of the Council of 17 May 2017 amending Directive 2007/36/EC as regards the encouragement of long-term shareholder engagement. According to this provision, a Member States may require that a company with its registered office in its territory may only require the identification of shareholders holding more than a certain percentage of shares or voting rights. Such a percentage may not exceed 0.5%. This provision was criticised by jurists because it would have created enormous differences within the EU.

7.2 Challenges for Shareholders' Rights Protection

New technologies offer many advantages for the protection of shareholder rights in FHCs, and these advantages are being realised in concrete applications in several companies. Therefore, the book proposes the following hypothesis: can technology replace humans in the future of FHC governance? In modern companies, some of the company's jobs are already being replaced by machines; for example, the well-known finance company Deloitte has developed Robotic Process Automation [18], which is a financial robot. Shareholders are not going to be replaced because if shareholders are machines, then it seems to evolve into a robot crisis. However, can the management of a company be replaced? This suspicion has already been raised by corporate law scholars [3]. Indeed, new technologies pose challenges for improving the governance of FHCs. It stems not only from the company but also from the technology.

7.2.1 Challenges from the Company

In theory, new technologies can have a positive effect on the protection of the rights of shareholders in FHCs. However, when analysed from a practical point of view, is good technology always applied in practice? Not truly. It has been demonstrated throughout the history of human technology, for example, by scientists who have argued that cloning can help solve many problems but that genetically modified food can have safety problems and have a negative impact on the environment. In addition, a number of ethical issues associated with cloning have prevented many technologies from being applied [9]. Therefore, advanced technology may not be used commercially; rather, it relies more on nontechnical factors. This logic also applies to addressing the relationship between new technologies and the governance of FHCs. Returning to the protection of shareholder rights in FHCs by new technologies, it is subject to several questions and challenges from both the theoretical and practical spheres. These challenges arise from the actions of shareholder activism on the one hand and from the questioning of traditional principal-agent theory on the other hand.

7.2.1.1 Conflicts Between Shareholder Activism and New Technologies

Some conflicts may arise between shareholder activism and new technologies. For example, in the 2019 case of the French merger between Altran and Capgemini, Capgemini argued that the merger facilitated the development of new technologies, including cloud computing, AI and 5G, but les associations de défense des actionnaires, representing Altran's minority shareholders, argued that the merger was detrimental to the participation of minority shareholders. In this case, the judge interpreted the "conséquences manifestement excessives" under French law, which can only be applied if the consequences are irreversible and clearly excessive.[24] This jurisprudence highlights some of the conflicts between shareholder activism and the development of new technologies, although it focuses on minority shareholders' right to participate. However, controlling shareholders can also act in the face of new technologies. Although this jurisprudence did not occur in an FHC, it has demonstrated the judicial remedy for this real conflict. Conflict can manifest itself in terms of shareholders interfering with the use of new technologies on the basis of their own interests and concerns about privacy issues.

Blockchain and AI can have positive effects on the rights of minority shareholders. In other words, technologies that benefit minority shareholders may have a limiting effect on the interests of controlling shareholders. The book has analysed through case law that controlling shareholders in FHCs can interfere excessively or negatively with corporate decision-making [5]. Logically, then, the question arises as to whether a controlling shareholder would allow a technology to be applied to the company that could be detrimental to the interests of the controlling shareholder. It does not seem logical to do so.

How do shareholders intervene? On the one hand, they can exert pressure on management. The book has already demonstrated the importance of board evaluations. According to the French code of governance for listed companies, board evaluation is designed to meet the expectations of shareholders [7]. When a director's agency effectiveness is called into question, it may be replaced by a new director. Therefore, shareholders can use board evaluation to put pressure on management. On the other hand, they can intervene through voting rights at shareholder meetings. In the case of the takeover of Gree Electric in China, shareholders made use of this approach.

While new technology has facilitated the protection of shareholder rights in FHCs, it has also raised concerns about privacy protection for shareholders. This phenomenon is even more evident in FHCs with highly dispersed shareholdings. It is also based on the principle of the application of blockchain and AI technologies. For both blockchain and AI, their use in FHCs is data-based in their application. For both board evaluation and shareholder engagement, the construction of databases is key if effective governance is expected to be achieved through new technologies. The construction of databases, in turn, is linked to privacy issues. In the context of human–machine interaction, researchers cite the "reasonable expectation of privacy" [39] to explain the issue of privacy protection in the development of AI. Confidentiality should not be used as a precondition for privacy protection [9]. Moreover, as French jurists have noted, with respect to the protection of information in financial markets, we cannot expect the legislator to be able to intervene at every time, as it could pose a threat to potential freedoms [10]. Therefore, what are the reasonable expectations of shareholder protection when new technologies are used in corporate governance? It seems to be something that should be set out in the code of conduct.

In the context of FHCs, the conflict between shareholder privacy protection and shareholding transparency in the context of new technologies manifests itself in

[24] Cour d'appel de Paris, Pôle 5–Chambre 15, 18 décembre 2019, n° 19/18938.

two main ways. The first is the disclosure of minority shareholdings in FHCs with dispersed shareholdings. In companies such as JPMorgan Chase & Co and HSBC, which have highly dispersed shareholdings and tens of thousands of investors, it is difficult to find information on all shareholders when looking at their shareholding structure, which is often the case for the top 10 shareholders.[25] However, the use of new technologies, including blockchain and AI, can make it possible to disclose information to all shareholders, including cross-border investors. The second is the scope of shareholding disclosure. In 2017, the Thai Ministry of Commerce requested companies in the country to provide a list of shareholders, information on shareholdings and audited accounts, which included the shareholders' ID numbers and passport numbers, which led to the risk of disclosure of shareholders' personal privacy. Moreover, under Thai law, shareholders are not obliged to provide personal information to the Ministry of Commerce, which presents some awkward situations at this point [48]. For FHCs, owing to the complexity of the shareholding structure and the intricate control relationships, equity disclosure should be thorough under the principles of prudential and comprehensive supervision. However, if new technologies are used to disclose shareholding structures, how does that come to protect shareholder privacy? The immediate conflict here lies between the prudential nature of FHC disclosure and shareholder privacy, and for a solution to this problem, perhaps new technology can provide a solution. The same story that happened in Asian countries could also happen in the future in France, the UK, and the U.S.

7.2.1.2 Pressures on Traditional Agency Theory

Agency theory is not a jurisprudential concept, but it is often used to analyse certain phenomena in corporate law and corporate governance. The purpose of the history of this theory here is to show that each of its developments has been accompanied by certain changes in the social context, a situation that also applies to the era of technological change. While the use of new technologies in corporate governance is a trend, there are also many challenges to overcome. On the one hand, one may wonder whether AI will change the existing agency relationship between shareholders and management. On the other hand, the full application of AI, as well as blockchain, to the governance of FHCs currently lacks a business environment.

The use of AI technology in company operations is not new. The book has also identified the measures taken by three FHCs with respect to new technologies from their annual reports. However, the governance of FHCs is based on prudential standards, so its practical application in the protection of shareholders' rights in FHCs may have to wait until the technology matures. At present, these technologies are still in their early stages.[26] Returning to the goal of shareholder rights protection in FHCs, how can the use of robots in management be viewed? For a long time, it has been an innovation that is unlikely to end the original principal–agent relationship.

[25] See the annual reports of JPMorgan Chase & Co and HSBC in 2020.

[26] Evidence of this can be found in the annual report disclosures of the three FHCs.

There are several reasons to explain this view. First, the selection of management in FHCs adheres to prudential standards, and FHCs have greater requirements than ordinary companies do. It is set out in current laws and regulations and in corporate governance codes. For example, in France, according to the French prudential regulator ACPR, the appointment and removal of the management of an FHC is subject to a declaration to the ACPR, which may object if it considers that the management does not meet the requirements, in which case the FHC is required to re-elect the management. The company will then need to choose a new management approach [1]. Therefore, if a robot acts as a manager, it also needs to be approved before it can do so. Second, from a systemic risk prevention perspective, the direct replacement of humans as management by such technology is also difficult to achieve in the short term. In a hypothetical scenario, replacing humans with robots for management could reduce some of the drawbacks of the traditional principal-agent model, particularly agency costs. However, a study in 2021 showed that robots based on big data may not perform better than humans do, especially in regard to environmental, social, and other sustainability issues, which require good interaction between participants. However, robots do not feel that way, as confirmed by experiments with teaching robots, and future research should make robots better at assisting humans in more complex environments [37].

In addition, the positive role that new technology can play in the governance of FHCs and the challenges it poses have been understood. However, its challenges stem not only from the impact on traditional principal-agent theory but also from the challenges it faces in achieving commercial application in the future. A very important reason is the lack of business custom. Although corporate governance codes are based on the soft law approach, their implementation needs to consider the current market and legal environment. In the absence of business practices, although the soft law path allows for compliance or explanation, does it make sense for this model to be embedded in a corporate governance code if none of the companies in the market have adopted it? Not sure. A good corporate governance code should consider not only future trends but also practical applications.

In this context, how can the new technology be applied in the context of the FHC's objective of protecting the rights of shareholders? First, it could take precedence over its application within the company, which is an internal innovation. It can be used as a sandbox model for corporate governance [4]. As the internal application matures, the technology can then be used to address external relationships. Second, in cases where the FHC endorses the model but other companies do not yet recognise it, it could present a dilemma for commercial application. However, it could also be a new opportunity. At this point, the FHC should focus on building a commercial ecosystem, but this will require the long-term engagement of shareholders. This is something that is promoted in Europe and in many jurisdictions in corporate governance[27] because these visions can be realised only if shareholders are engaged in the long term.

[27] See Directive (EU) 2017/828 of the European Parliament and of the Council of 17 May 2017 Amending Directive 2007/36/EC As Regards the Encouragement of Long-term Shareholder Engagement.

7.2.2 *Challenges from the New Technology*

The challenge of applying new technologies to the protection of shareholder rights in FHCs stems not only from concerns within the company about the future of the technology but also from the limitations of the technology itself. Corporate governance needs to be flexible in dealing with complex environments [6], which places greater demands on technology. The exploration of this question perhaps goes beyond FHCs, which remains a response to the following question: can machines replace management in corporate governance? The interpretation of this question was analysed from the perspective of the company's shareholders; here, it is a different perspective, namely, the shortcomings of technology in corporate governance. The flaws in the application of blockchain and AI in FHCs are analysed separately here.

7.2.2.1 Challenges from Blockchain Technology

In the history of blockchain development, several failures have occurred. A typical example is the hacking of the DAO in 2016, a very well-known application[28] in the history of blockchain development. However, in the 2016 incident, $60 million in U.S. dollars was stolen by hackers. Researchers believe that this is due mainly to the vulnerability of its complex code and decentralised decision-making framework [38]. Moreover, the use of blockchain in corporate governance poses a challenge. French researchers have reported that it is difficult to reassess the effectiveness of technology when these unknown failures occur [27]. These challenges are also present in the governance of FHCs. Blockchain can improve conflicts between shareholders and between shareholders and management in FHCs. However, the application of this technology in corporate governance also raises some concerns, which mainly stem from the governance efficiency and moral hazard of blockchain technology in corporate governance.

The concept of efficiency, which derives from welfare economics, can provide the basic methodology for assessing legal rules [16]. To this end, scholars have developed two concepts: "external legitimacy" and "internal efficiency" [40]. According to the distinction between these two concepts, the internal governance of a company is about efficiency, which is the focus of corporate governance. Therefore, how is efficiency understood in the context of corporate governance specifically? The view of corporate law scholars is that shareholders should drive companies to respond quickly to a changed competitive environment [28]. Therefore, perhaps the efficiency of corporate governance can be used as a test of a company's ability to adapt and the cost of adaptation.

On the basis of the analysis of efficiency in corporate governance, the book can analyse the efficiency of blockchain technology in governance. First, can blockchain

[28] It is important to note that "The DAO" here is a company or product application. It should be distinguished from the DAO (Decentralised Autonomous Organisation) as it is commonly understood. In the context of blockchain technology, the latter is often considered an infrastructure.

truly improve the monitoring efficiency of FHCs? The application of blockchain technology to the governance of FHCs is based primarily on its improvement in transparency. However, effective oversight of governance through improved transparency is predicated on the accuracy and security of data. However, the view of scientists is that business judgements based on the analysis of data are not necessarily better than human analysis [37]. This means that by improving transparency through blockchain technology, the actual results it brings to corporate governance are not necessarily better than what is currently the case. Furthermore, in terms of security, an attack on the DAO occurred in 2016. Second, can it help shareholders and boards of directors of FHCs respond quickly to a changing business environment? Blockchain offers a new way of thinking to address agency costs in corporate governance. However, it depends on whether it can solve the problems encountered in the reality of corporate governance. The main feature of blockchain technology is that it offers a decentralised mindset, with improvements in transparency and security. However, there seems to be a lack of sufficient evidence of its application to scenarios involving complex business environments. If it is to be commercialised at this time, it would also not meet the prudential standards of an FHC.

In the application of blockchain to the governance of FHCs, there are some concerns about it; in addition to the efficiency of governance, there is also the issue of moral hazard. The moral hazard of blockchain technology in commercial transactions has been demonstrated in the case of the DAO [50], the world's largest crowdfunding project, in 2016. Although this incident did not occur in an FHC, it has raised concerns about the technology. Therefore, when FHCs are returned, why may moral hazard pose to the protection of shareholder rights in FHCs? First, the concept of moral hazard can be analysed. Moral hazard is not part of a legal vocabulary, but it is often used for analysis of the economics of law. For example, a document compiled by the legal expert Stéphane Rousseau on the basis of a conference organised by Faculté Jean Monnet de l'Université Paris XI in 2008 demonstrated the application of moral hazard in the economics of law and noted that moral hazard was developed by the field of insurance and that it corresponds to opportunism [41]. Second, moral hazard arises from blockchain in the governance of FHCs. In an FHC, its subsidiaries may be banks, insurance companies, or securities companies, to name a few [5]. Therefore, the concept of moral hazard, which originated in insurance contracts, is likely to occur in FHCs. The application of blockchain in the contractual space is mainly in the form of smart contracts, which are in fact already being used in some insurance products. However, according to a study by computer scientists in 2020, the code of smart contracts is vulnerable, and many instances of smart contracts, including the Parity Wallet hack [43] in 2017 in addition to the DAO incident, have been attacked. For this reason, the French jurist believes that regulation is necessary and that the Central Bank of France, the Autorité des marchés financiers (AMF), and the Autorité de contrôle prudentiel et de résolution (ACPR) are responsible for jointly studying and balancing the innovation of blockchain technology with potential risks [33].

7.2.2.2 Challenges from Artificial Intelligence Technology

At this stage of AI commercialisation, several failures demonstrate the inadequacy of AI in current society. One of the better knowns is the 2017 case concerning voice recognition at the HSBC. The HSBC developed a voice recognition tool in 2016 through AI technology that allowed consumers to log into their accounts by voice, which the bank considered to be a secure tool. However, a pair of twin brothers actually managed to log into each other's bank accounts repeatedly in 2017 after imitating each other's voices, a case that has prompted thoughts about AI security [44]. Clearly, the case of HSBC illustrates that even under current standards of prudence, issues of technological security are still inevitable. The application of AI technology in FHCs holds great promise, and it can offer unique technological advantages for both board evaluation and encouraging long-term shareholder engagement. However, its application in the field of corporate governance is still in the exploratory stage. Some thought has been given to its drawbacks. This approach mainly considers both data justice and systemic risk perspectives.

Researchers have explained the concept of data justice as a rational state of informational fairness, where factual evidence and knowledge are taken into account in decision-making [20]. In addition, some legal scholars have suggested three elements of data justice: visibility, engagement with technology, and anti-discrimination [47]. Therefore, data justice in this context refers to people being treated fairly in the presence of data. In the context of FHCs, is it truly in the interest of shareholders' rights that the underlying data based on AI technology are useful for the board's evaluation or for the company's business decisions? With respect to the discussion of justice, there has always been a distinction between formal and substantive justice in legal theory. Therefore, is the use of AI technology in corporate governance a formal or substantive protection of shareholders' rights? The concepts of data justice and net neutrality both require the nondiscriminatory treatment and equal treatment of users.

In addition, the use of AI technology in FHCs may pose a threat to systemic risk, largely on the basis of prudential standards. Systemic risk arises from "malicious actors". According to scholars, "malicious actors" refer to those who profit from creating instability with the aim of destabilising the financial system [15]. The twins' testing of the HSBC's AI application in the HSBC voice recognition case may not fall into this category. However, if the other party deliberately mimics the other party's voice to gain access to the other party's bank account without the knowledge of the other party, such behaviour is already a situation that endangers financial stability.

Why might the use of AI in FHCs threaten systemic risk? On the one hand, this is due to the existence of "black boxes" in algorithms. The complexity and technical opacity of AI algorithms obscure the inner workings of the technology [19]. The "black boxes" provide the interface for the existence of risks. Here, the EU's GDPR establishes a right to explain algorithms, and they need to be explained in regard to important issues.[29] The potential conflict in corporate governance is how to reconcile

[29] See Article (71), General Data Protection Regulation (GDPR). According to this provision, in order to ensure fair and transparent processing of data subjects, taking into account the specific

these conflicts when shareholders demand an explanation if the algorithm is a trade secret. On the other hand, it is also an analysis based on cost–benefit theory. Scholars argue that the regulation of AI is expensive and that the more regulation there is, the greater the cost is for stakeholders such as investors and consumers of financial services. This reduces the growth of the economy, and in an innovative environment, it may be subject to many challenges [15]. Corporate governance, then, has a limited role in the face of systemic risks that may arise from "unknown-unknowns" in an underregulated environment [35]. This explains why many AI applications are now basic and rudimentary.

The new technologies represented by AI are subject to legal, cultural, and other restrictions in their current development. If it is used brutally when humans are not ready to govern it, it can significantly harm the interests of the shareholders of an FHC, which can manifest itself as an affront to the rights of the whole. In addition, it can confuse the governance of the FHC and prevent it from achieving its sustainability goals. In the worst-case scenario, it could induce a financial crisis. Therefore, it needs to be regulated in due course with respect to the use of AI in FHCs. In addition, corporate governance codes should respond to the corporate governance issues raised by technology.

References

1. ACPR (2021) Compagnie financière holding et Compagnies financières holding mixtes, ACPR. https://acpr.banque-france.fr/autoriser/procedures-secteur-banque/agrement-autorisation-ou-enregistrement/compagnie-financiere-holding-et-compagnies-financieres-holding-mixtes. Accessed 28 Sept 2021
2. Aoki M, Kim HK (1995) Corporate governance in transitional economies: insider control and the role of banks, The World Bank. https://documents.worldbank.org/curated/en/912861468324888594/pdf/multi-page.pdf. Accessed 21 Sept 2021
3. Armour J, Eidenmueller H (2019) Self-driving corporations? SSRN. https://ssrn.com/abstract=3442447. Accessed 10 Sept 2021
4. Bambara JJ et al (2016) Blockchain: a practical guide to developing business, law, and technology solutions. McGraw-Hill Education, New York
5. Banks E (2004) Corporate governance: financial responsibility, controls and ethics. Palgrave Macmillan, Hampshire
6. Barban P (2019) Les marchés financiers et la blockchain: esquisse d'une infrastructure blockchain (Financial markets and blockchain: sketching out a blockchain infrastructure). In Magnier V, Barban P (ed) Blockchain et droit des sociétés (Blockchain and corporate law), Dalloz, Paris

circumstances and context in which personal data are processed, the controller shall carry out analyses using appropriate mathematical or statistical procedures and apply appropriate technical and organisational measures to ensure that, in particular, factors leading to errors in personal data are corrected and that the risk of error is minimised. To prevent discriminatory effects of racial or ethnic origin, political opinions, religion or beliefs, trade union membership, genetic or health conditions or sexual orientation on natural persons, data analysis is only permitted under certain conditions.

7. Boffo R, Patalano R (2020) ESG investing: practices, progress and challenges, OECD. www.oecd.org/finance/ESG-Investing-Practices-Progress-and-Challenges.pdf. Accessed 10 Sept 2020
8. Bonneau T (2018) Régulation bancaire et financière européenne et internationale (European and international banking and financial regulation). Bruylant, Bruxelles
9. Brown TA (2016) Gene cloning and DNA analysis: an introduction, 7th edn. John Wiley & Sons, West Sussex
10. Chacornac J (2014) Essai sur les fonctions de l'information en droit des instruments financiers (Essay on the functions of information in financial instruments law). Dalloz, Paris
11. Chiu I (2008) The meaning of share ownership and the governance role of shareholder activism in the United Kingdom. Richmond J Glob Law Bus 8:144
12. Colony (2021) About the Vision, Colony. https://colony.io/about. Accessed 21 Sept 2020
13. Colony (2022) Whitepaper, Colony. https://colony.io/whitepaper.pdf. Accessed 10 April 2022
14. CSRC (2009) Study on insider control of listed companies (上市公司"内部人控制"问题研究), CSRC. http://www.csrc.gov.cn/shandong/xxfw/sszypy/200911/t20091113_168065.htm. Accessed 21 Sept 2020
15. Danielsson J et al (2020) Artificial intelligence and systemic risk, SSRN. https://ssrn.com/abstract=3410948. Accessed 10 Sept 2020
16. Deakin S (2012) The juridical nature of the firm. In: Thomas C, Branson D (ed) The SAGE handbook of corporate governance, SAGE Publications Ltd, London
17. Defilippi P, Wright A (2018) Blockchain and the law: the rule of code. Harvard University Press, Cambridge
18. Deloitte (2021) Leviers technologiques et solutions d'automatisation (Technological levers and automation solutions), Deloitte. https://www2.deloitte.com/fr/fr/pages/strategie-et-innovation/solutions/leviers-technologiques-solutions-automatisation.html. Accessed 10 sept 2021
19. Diakopoulos N (2017) Algorithmic accountability reporting: on the investigation of black boxes, Columbia Academic Commons. https://academiccommons.columbia.edu/doi/https://doi.org/10.7916/D8ZK5TW2. Accessed 10 Sept 2020
20. Duarte ME (2020) Ruptured knowledge ecologies in indian country. In: Taylor L et al (ed) Data justice and covid-19: global perspectives, Meatspace Press, London
21. ECGI (2018) Technology and corporate governance, ECGI. https://ecgi.global/content/technology-and-corporate-governance. Accessed 21 Sept 2020
22. Enguehard C (2009) Vote par internet: failles techniques et recul démocratique (Internet voting: technical flaws and democratic backsliding). Revue internationale de droit politique (International Journal of Political Law) 2:4–17
23. European Commission (2021) Proposal for a regulation laying down harmonised rules on artificial intelligence (Artificial Intelligence Act), European Commission. https://digital-strategy.ec.europa.eu/en/library/proposal-regulation-laying-down-harmonised-rules-artificial-intelligence-artificial-intelligence. Accessed 27 July 2021
24. FDIC (2020) Failed bank information for capitol city bank & trust company, Atlanta, GA , FDIC. https://www.fdic.gov/resources/resolutions/bank-failures/failed-bank-list/capitolcity.html. Accessed 21 Sept 2020
25. Filatotchev I et al (1999) Privatisation, insider control and managerial entrenchment in Russia. Econ Transit 7:481
26. Goffaux CG (2019) Blockchain et droits des actionnaires (Blockchain and shareholder rights). In: Magnier V, Barban P (ed) Blockchain et droit des sociétés (Blockchain and corporate law), Dalloz, Paris
27. González M et al (2017) Challenging anti-fragile blockchain applications, HAL. https://hal.inria.fr/hal-01653986. Accessed 10 Sept 2020
28. Gordon JN (2015) Convergence and persistence in corporate law and governance. In: Gordon JN, Ringe W (ed) The oxford handbook of corporate law and governance, Oxford University Press, Oxford
29. Gorman A (2017) Exit vs. Voice: a comparison of divestment and shareholder engagement. New York University Annual Survey of American Law 72: 125

30. Guégan E (2019) Blockchain and shareholders' meetings. In: Magnier V, Barban P (ed) Blockchain et droit des sociétés, Dalloz, Paris
31. Jensen MC, Meckling WH (1976) Theory of the firm: managerial behavior, agency costs and ownership structure. J Financ Econ 4:310
32. Kaal WA (2019) Blockchain solutions for agency problems in corporate governance, SSRN. https://ssrn.com/abstract=3373393. Accessed 21 Sept 2020
33. Legeais D (2019) Blockchain et actifs numériques (Blockchain and digital assets). LexisNexis, Paris
34. Lessig L (2000) Code is law: on liberty in cyberspace. Harvard Magazine 1
35. Lessig L (2006) Code: and other laws of cyberspace (code version 2.0). Basic Books, New York
36. Magnier V (2017) Comparative corporate governance: legal perspectives. Edward Elgar Publishing Ltd., Cheltenham
37. Mahdi QS et al (2021) Evaluation of robot professor technology in teaching and business. IT Industry 1:1192
38. Morrison R et al (2020) The DAO controversy: the case for a new species of corporate governance? Policy Pract Rev 3:6
39. Pagallo U (2013) Robots in the cloud with privacy: a new threat to data protection? Comput Law Secur Rev 5:501
40. Roberts J (2012) Between the letter and the spirit: defensive and extensive modes of compliance with the UK code of corporate governance. In: Thomas C, Branson D (ed) The SAGE handbook of corporate governance, SAGE Publications Ltd, London
41. Rousseau S (2009) L'analyse économique du droit (Economic analysis of law). In: Lienhard A (ed) Recueil dalloz. Dalloz, Paris
42. Russell S, Norvig P (2016) Artificial intelligence: a modern approach (third edition). Pearson Education Limited, Essex
43. Sarwar S et al (2020) Smart contract: attacks and protections. IEEE Access 8:24419
44. Simmons D (2017) BBC fools HSBC voice recognition security system, BBC. https://www.bbc.com/news/technology-39965545. Accessed 10 Sept 2020
45. Sun T et al. (2020) Lessons from the collapse of overseas financial institutions by bad shareholders ("坏股东"拖垮海外金融机构的教训及启示), FinancialNews. https://www.financialnews.com.cn/ll/gdsj/202008/t20200810_197830.html. Accessed 21 Sept 2020
46. SWIFT (2019) SWIFT launches DLT e-Voting PoC, SWIFT. https://www.swift.com/swift-resource/203826/download?language=en. Accessed 21 Sept 2020
47. Taylor L (2017) What is data justice? The case for connecting digital rights and freedoms globally. Big Data Society 1
48. The Bangkok Post (2017) 2017 poses new risks to shareholders' privacy. https://www.bangkokpost.com/business/1262679/2017-poses-new-risks-to-shareholders-privacy. Accessed 10 Sept 2020
49. UK Government (2017) Corporate governance reform: government response, UK Government. https://assets.publishing.service.gov.uk/government/uploads/system/uploads/attachment_data/file/640470/corporate-governance-reform-government-response.pdf. Accessed 10 Sept 2020
50. Wu X (2016) The DAO robbery highlights blockchain technology and ethical risks (The DAO 被劫，凸显区块链技术及道德风险), China Times. https://www.chinatimes.net.cn//article/59751.html. Accessed 10 Sept 2020

Chapter 8
Rethinking the Shareholder Governance of Chinese Financial Holding Companies from the Perspective of Shareholders' Rights Protection

Abstract This chapter examines the internal mechanisms for the protection of shareholders' rights in Chinese FHCs, focusing specifically on shareholder governance, including both controlling shareholder engagement and minority shareholder rights protection. In terms of controlling shareholder engagement, the main problem of Chinese FHCs is the excessive engagement of controlling shareholders, which has been demonstrated in both listed and unlisted companies. On this basis, future Chinese FHCs should limit the engagement of controlling shareholders, which incorporates Chinese mixed-ownership reform. With respect to the protection of minority shareholders' rights, the governance of FHCs in China needs to focus on both the role of the CPC and the governance structure. First, the participation of the CPC in corporate governance is an issue that cannot be avoided in the current governance of FHCs in China and that urgently needs to be addressed. In addition, the governance structure of Chinese FHCs breaks away from the traditional "one tyre" and "two tyres" structure, where the supervisory board and independent directors can coexist. Therefore, Chinese FHCs should actively address the governance gaps in the current governance structure.

Keywords Shareholder engagement · Shareholder equality · Control · Communist party of China · Governance structures

Shareholder governance is a technical term that belongs to one of the aspects of corporate governance. It can be found in the academic literature. For example, scholars in common law countries consider the existence and use of statutory freedoms to be central to shareholder governance [14]. This view is shared by other scholars and suggests that shareholders can obtain governance rights through contracts, such as voting agreements [4]. In addition, scholars in civil law countries have endorsed this concept. For example, French scholars argue that the purpose of shareholder governance is to ensure efficient management of corporate ownership by dispersed shareholders, despite differences in the interests and risks of shareholders and management [16]. In Chinese law, the concept of shareholder governance also seems to follow this concept. For example, researchers have divided the problems of corporate governance

K. Ma, *Shareholder Rights Protection Mechanisms for Chinese Financial Holding Companies*, International and Comparative Law in the Asia Pacific,
https://doi.org/10.1007/978-981-97-9731-8_8

in China into two categories: the dominance of one share by the controlling shareholder, which falls under the category of shareholder governance, and insider control [19]. The TMSAFHC imposes a number of specific requirements on the controlling shareholders of Chinese FHCs, including restrictions in areas such as shareholding substitution, antimonopoly, and share transfer. It is also an expression of the response to shareholder governance.[1] Thus, shareholder governance is a concept in corporate governance that is an aspect of the internal protection mechanism of shareholders' rights and focuses on achieving a balance of rights between different shareholders through contractual means.

In other words, shareholder governance is concerned with the relationship between controlling and minority shareholders and between shareholders and management, and these relationships need to be addressed for the protection of shareholders' rights. Given that the main conflict in corporate governance in China is focused on the relationship between controlling and minority shareholders, this Chapter analyses shareholder governance and shareholder rights protection in FHCs in terms of controlling shareholder participation and minority shareholder rights protection.

8.1 Rethinking the Engagement of Controlling Shareholders

Shareholder engagement refers to the need for shareholders to communicate with other stakeholders, express their views and make their voices heard in corporate governance. Controlling shareholder engagement, then, refers to corporate governance in which controlling shareholders express their views and balance their relationships with other stakeholders in major decisions of the company. In Chinese corporate governance, the involvement of controlling shareholders is manifested in the dominance of one share and excessive engagement. This is the reflection of Chinese scholars on corporate governance in China [21]. This is likewise reflected in the governance of Chinese FHCs. However, it cannot be ignored in the light of the future development trends of Chinese FHCs. To fully explain the significance of this phenomenon for the development of FHCs, this section explains the development of controlling shareholder engagement in Chinese FHCs and, on this basis, reflects the theory of corporate governance in China.

[1] See Article 11, TMSAFHC. A controlling shareholder of an FHC shall not have the following circumstances: (1) He evades the regulation of the FHC by means of a specific purpose vehicle or by delegating shareholding to others; (2) he has numerous related parties, complex and opaque shareholding relationships or disputes over ownership, carries out related transactions in bad faith and uses related relationships in bad faith; (3) he abuses his monopoly position in the market or technical superiority to engage in unfair competition; (4) he manipulates the market and disrupts the financial order; (5) he transfers his shares in the FHC within five years.

8.1.1 The Reality of Engagement in Controlling Shareholders

An analysis of the development of the involvement of controlling shareholders in Chinese FHCs is useful for understanding the particularities of the governance of Chinese FHCs. The study revealed that the equity bodies in FHCs in the U.S. and the UK are highly dispersed. In contrast, the FHCs in France have relatively concentrated shareholdings. However, the currently announced pilot FHCs in China include both private companies with dispersed equity and state-owned enterprises with concentrated equity. Therefore, by examining the current development of these companies in China, the differences between Chinese FHCs and those in other jurisdictions can be identified, and an appropriate corporate governance path for the protection of shareholders' rights in Chinese FHCs can be found. To fully justify the implications, the book analyses the main issues of the governance of FHCs in China and the future direction of reform.

8.1.1.1 Excessive Engagement of Controlling Shareholders

The protection of shareholder rights in Chinese FHCs relies on internal mechanisms of corporate governance. In the current pilot development of FHCs in China, the most obvious governance issue is the excessive engagement of controlling shareholders. The reasons for the excessive engagement of controlling shareholders are, on the one hand, the lack of effective financial market regulation of controlling shareholders in the current Chinese commercial legal system [20]. On the other hand, it is also strongly linked to the shareholding structure of Chinese FHCs. The pilot FHCs in China all have government shareholdings, and four are wholly state-owned companies. In the context of Chinese law, there is still a lack of effective internal governance mechanisms for government shareholders. In addition, the governance of a listed FHC is very different from that of an unlisted FHC. Therefore, separate explanations are provided here for listed FHCs and unlisted FHCs.

According to the financial stability report published by the PBOC in 2018, there are two patterns of FHCs in China, one dominated by financial institutions and the other dominated by nonfinancial institutions.[2] However, the Chinese government has announced only eight pilot FHCs thus far. Therefore, at least for now, there is not enough analysis of this pattern. Among these, Ping An Insurance, Suning.com, and CITIC Group are listed companies. Therefore, the governance model of these three companies will become very important representatives of the governance of listed FHCs in China in future. However, it is also important to note that FHCs, including the Everbright Group and China Merchants Group, hold many listed companies in the form of parent companies, although they are not listed.[3] At present, no typical

[2] See China Financial Stability Report 2018(中国金融稳定报告2018).

[3] See Chap. 1.

cases against the excessive engagement of controlling shareholders in listed FHCs in China have emerged. However, considering the historical development of listed companies in China, the following areas should be guarded against in the future development of listed FHCs. First, irregular guarantees by controlling shareholders are needed. A listed company's external guarantee should respect its articles of association, and as a rule, it should be voted on at the AGM of shareholders. It is also a requirement of the Chinese Company Law[4] and the Stock Exchange.[5] Second, controlling shareholders conspire to manipulate share prices. The act of controlling shareholders of a listed company conspiring to manipulate share prices and the act of listed companies manipulating share prices are in fact different. However, the behaviour of controlling shareholders can easily be transformed into the behaviour of a listed company. This was demonstrated in case law in 2019.[6] The judge found that the controlling shareholder manipulated the content and timing of the disclosure by failing to disclose timely, truthful, accurate, and complete information about the listed company, which led to misjudgement by investors and SMEs.

In terms of the current shareholding structure of the pilot FHCs, nonlisted FHCs can be divided into three types, namely wholly state-owned enterprises, nonstate-owned mixed-ownership companies, and state-owned companies by shares. Among the current nonlisted FHC pilots, wholly state-owned enterprises include China Merchants Group, Shanghai International Group, and Beijing Financial Holdings Group. The nonstate-owned mixed-ownership companies [20] are Ant Group and Ping An Insurance,[7] and the state-owned company by shares is the Everbright Group.[8] However, in terms of the governance engagement of controlling shareholders, the main reference is to nonstate mixed-ownership companies and state-owned companies by shares. The excessive engagement of controlling shareholders in governance has increased because the conflict between controlling and minority shareholders is the main conflict in Chinese corporate governance [21]. In addition, encouraging the engagement of controlling shareholders in governance essentially aims to better balance the conflicting interests of controlling and minority shareholders. However, in a wholly state-owned company, the government is the only shareholder, and there is no conflict between controlling and minority shareholders.

---

[4] See Article 16(2) of the Chinese Company Law provides that where a company provides a guarantee for a shareholder or person in substantive control of the company, it must be resolved by a shareholders' meeting or general meeting.

[5] According to Rule 9.11 of the Rules Governing the Listing of Stocks on the Shanghai Stock Exchange, matters relating to the "provision of guarantees" by a listed company shall be submitted to the board of directors or the general meeting for consideration and timely disclosure.

[6] Die-Color Asset Management (Shanghai) Co. v. China Securities Regulatory Commission (蝶彩资产管理(上海)股份有限公司诉中国证券监督管理委员会,北京市高级人民法院(2019)京行终2328号行政判决书).

[7] According to the disclosed information, among the shareholders of Ant Group, the National Council of Social Security Fund is the state-owned capital, and the other shareholders are nonpublic capital.

[8] Everbright's shareholders include Central Huijin (61.16% of shares) and the Ministry of Finance (38.84% of shares).

In nonstate-owned mixed-ownership companies and state-owned companies by shares, there are no particularly classic examples of excessive engagement by controlling shareholders. This is also because FHCs in China are still in the pilot stage. However, the book has also identified negative effects of the engagement of control ling shareholders and the actual controller of the company on the company as a whole and on minority shareholders. The ant group is an example. According to its 2020 prospectus, its controlling shareholders are the Hangzhou Junhan Equity Investment Partnership and Hangzhou Jun'ao Equity Investment Partnership, with Mr. Jack Ma as the de facto controller. Ant Group was originally scheduled to be listed on the Shanghai Stock Exchange in November 2020, but according to the disclosure, Ant Group's listing was suspended in November 2020 after Mr. Jack Ma criticised the traditional Chinese banking system at the Shanghai Financial Forum in October 2020. According to the regulator's disclosure, the suspension of Ant Group's listing plan was due to compliance issues. The controlling shareholder and the beneficial owner of an FHC should take this seriously in future.

In addition, similar to the analysis of listed FHCs, the book can also invoke the excessive engagement of controlling shareholders in mixed-ownership companies in Chinese history as a warning for the future development of FHCs in China. Through case law, in mixed-ownership companies, the excessive engagement of controlling shareholders manifests itself in two ways. First, the choices to withdraw capital and RPTs are more frequent when faced with major corporate decisions, which do not involve normal procedures in corporate governance and undermine the rights of minority shareholders.[9] Second, the controlling shareholder interferes with the normal decisions of the company in terms of environmental protection and fair competition without listening to the advice of other shareholders, thus exposing the company to litigation disputes.[10]

8.1.1.2 Governance Reform: Limiting the Excessive Engagement of Controlling Shareholders

Controlling shareholder engagement in Chinese FHCs is mainly for nonstate-owned mixed-ownership companies and state-owned companies by shares. The excessive engagement of controlling shareholders is a key concern for the governance of Chinese FHCs in future. This is not only true for FHCs but also for future corporate governance reform in China. In terms of the internal mechanisms for the protection of shareholders' rights, this reform trend manifests itself differently in these two types of FHCs. The reform of Chinese state-owned FHCs by shares and nonstate-owned FHCs by mixed ownership will be analysed separately.

---

[9] Xian Jinxian v. Zhengzhou Songlou Coal Mine Coal Industry Co. (鲜金贤诉郑州市宋楼煤矿煤业有限责任公司,河南省郑州市中级人民法院(2018)豫01民终3731号民事判决书).

[10] Fangda Carbon New Material Technology Co. v. Agricultural Bank of China Limited Shaanxi County Subbranch (方大炭素新材料科技股份有限公司诉中国农业银行股份有限公司陕县支行,最高人民法院(2012)民二终字第35号民事判决书).

"State-owned FHCs by shares" refers to an FHC in which the government has a controlling stake but whose shareholding structure is not limited to the government. In Chinese law, such companies are presented as limited companies by shares rather than as limited liability companies. The governance reform of Chinese state-owned enterprises (SOEs) lies mainly in adjusting the shareholding ratio of state capital by introducing various types of investors. The government promotes this by means of overall listing, mergers, and acquisitions, restructuring, and issuing convertible bonds.[11] Therefore, SOEs will gradually shift to a mixed-ownership model. In the case of state-owned FHCs by shares, the thinking on controlling shareholder participation is aimed mainly at preparing for future reforms, as they are now in a transitional phase. Given the special characteristics of SOEs, they should pay attention to the design of controlling shareholder engagement at the early stage of their future move towards a mixed-ownership model to avoid the excessive interference that exists in the areas of RPTs, environmental protection, and fair competition. In this regard, the following questions will be discussed. First, is the choice between listing in China or overseas? An overall listing of an FHC is an effective way to limit the excessive involvement of state capital in corporate governance as a controlling shareholder, and CITIC Group has already practised this approach. The choice of where to list, however, is complex. The book analyses it here only from the perspective of effectively limiting the participation of controlling shareholders and regulating corporate governance. There is a lack of complete statistics on the global listing destinations of Chinese companies. However, apart from mainland China, the main destinations for Chinese companies are the U.S.,[12] Europe [18], Singapore,[13] and Hong Kong.[14] In the case of FHCs, there are two main methods of listing: one in Hong Kong[15] and one in both Hong Kong and mainland China.[16] Second, China should develop a governance code for unlisted FHCs. The listing of a state-owned FHC by shares is a complex and long-term planning matter. In the short term, China should consider developing a choice of models for corporate governance codes for unlisted FHCs and proceed with implementation. Specifically, there are two possible models: developing a governance code specifically for unlisted FHCs and applying an effective corporate governance code by reference.

The reform of nonstate mixed-ownership FHCs in China encompasses not only listed companies but also unlisted companies. In the context of corporate governance, restrictions on the participation of controlling shareholders have the following main implications. First, it helps improve the internal governance mechanism of

[11] See Opinions of the State Council on the Development of Mixed Ownership Economy by State-owned Enterprises (国务院关于国有企业发展混合所有制经济的意见). It proves the point as a whole, and it covers all the articles.

[12] Such as Alibaba.

[13] China Everbright Water Limited.

[14] Examples include CITIC Group and the Industrial and Commercial Bank of China.

[15] Take the CITIC Group as an example.

[16] In the case of Ant Group, for example, the option at the time was to list on both the Shanghai Stock Exchange and the Hong Kong Stock Exchange, despite the current suspension of the listing plan.

shareholders of FHCs. Among the current FHC pilots in China, four companies,[17] both listed and unlisted, qualify as mixed-ownership FHCs, three of which are nonstate mixed-ownership enterprises, whereas CITIC Group[18] is a state-owned limited company by shares. In the corporate governance of some companies, there is not a complete separation of ownership and operations between management and controlling shareholders. The position of management should then be given more importance in future developments, which will help improve the internal governance mechanism. Second, the reform measures adopted in these FHC pilots provide experience for the future development of governance codes for FHCs in China. One of the important reasons for the criticism of the governance of listed companies in China is the ineffectiveness of corporate governance. Reform is difficult. However, corporate governance guidelines for Chinese FHCs have not yet been established. Therefore, a study of these pilot companies at this time will provide a valuable reference for the future, which will lead to the establishment of an effective governance code for FHCs in China. Thus, for nonstate-owned mixed-ownership FHCs, restrictions on the engagement of controlling shareholders should be aimed at providing valuable lessons for future FHC governance codes, specifically in the areas of shareholder agreements and management incentives.

8.1.2 Reflections on the Engagement of Controlling Shareholders

With respect to the participation of controlling shareholders in Chinese FHCs, the book has analysed its main problems and the future direction of reform. The analysis here is an extension of the analysis. Through the analysis here, the book seeks to answer a fundamental question: why does excessive engagement of controlling shareholders necessarily need to be reformed? The book has identified excessive engagement of controlling shareholders in Chinese FHCs; therefore, it is expected to change. It is logical. However, it could also go on to be asked: is it a must to make changes? Can it maintain the status quo? In fact, many issues are left on the back burner, even though it may be wrong. For example, environmental pollution needs to be addressed, but it always exists. As a result, some of the theories underlying corporate governance need to be rethought. These include the principle of shareholder equality and the understanding of control.

---

[17] These are CITIC Group, Ping An Insurance, Ant Group and Suning.com. It should be noted that CITIC Group is still registered as a wholly state-owned company in mainland China, but it is listed in Hong Kong.

[18] Although the Chinese government approved China CITIC Financial Holdings Limited which is a subsidiary of CITIC Group to become an FHC in 2022, this subsidiary is still in the preparatory stage and has not actually been established. Therefore, the analysis in the book will still be conducted with CITIC Group as the main entity.

8.1.2.1 Revisiting the Principle of Shareholder Equality

To provide a comprehensive analysis of the principle of shareholder equality in Chinese FHCs, a comparative approach is taken here to present an interpretation of the principle of shareholder equality in jurisdictions other than China to reflect the relationship between the equality of shareholders and majority rule in the reform of Chinese FHCs. Importantly, this principle has not been specifically addressed, despite the specific analysis of the governance and regulation of FHCs in other jurisdictions. Instead, the analysis here is valuable for the Chinese issue. Therefore, the book has devoted the analysis to the principle of shareholders' equality in other jurisdictions.

In jurisdictions outside China, the principle of equality for shareholders can be found in their legal systems.[19] In general, the principle of equality of shareholders is one of the fundamental principles of the corporate system, which not only means that different shareholders should be treated equally but also that the same information should be provided to different shareholders [2]. However, the law is relatively concise in its formulation of the principle of equity of shareholders. In general, it consists of two aspects: being treated equally in terms of shareholder status and being treated equally in terms of the information provided. To recapitulate, it should be equally treated in terms of shareholder engagement.

In this context, it is useful to look at jurisprudence for a better understanding of this principle. In a U.S. case from 1995,[20] the judges held that shareholders have the same rights to remedies against infringements of their rights by the company and should be treated equally. It is a confirmation of the principle of the equality of shareholders in relation to the equality of remedies. The principle of equity of shareholders was confirmed by a French case in 2002,[21] where the judge held that the decision of the majority shareholder on the basis of a majority vote was also an expression of the principle of shareholders' equality, which did not violate the principles of shareholders' equality and transparency under French law. It can also be understood as the principle of proportionality or geometric equality to which Professor Drummond refers [3]. This case in French law is an important reference for the governance of controlling shareholders in Chinese FHCs. On the basis of this principle, many jurisdictions have introduced innovations in corporate governance, such as dual-class shares and preference shares. Among the more controversial of these are dual-class shares. One of the more controversial of these is dual-class shares,

---

[19] France: see Article L433-1, Code monétaire et financier. Under this article, financial instruments issued by the AMF for companies domiciled in France are allowed to be traded on the French market, in order to ensure shareholder equality and market transparency.

UK: see Rule 11. Nature of consideration to be offered, The Takeover Code. Under this provision, the panel may offer securities against all other holders of shares of the class on an equal basis. It is a confirmation of the principle of equality for shareholders in the UK commercial legal system.

U.S.: see the principle of equality of shareholders in U.S. law is demonstrated by the U.S. case of Epstein v. MCA, Inc. The adherence to the principle of equality of shareholders in U.S. law is evidenced by the case of Epstein v. MCA, Inc.

[20] Epstein v. MCA, Inc., 50 F.3d 644, 649–668 (U.S. Court of Appeals, Ninth Circuit, 1995).

[21] Cour d'appel de Paris, 1ère chambre, 19 mars 2002, n° 2001/17786.

and the book therefore analyses this innovative mechanism here to better understand the principle of shareholder equality. The book has analysed the development of this system in different jurisdictions, and the controversy has not ceased.[22] Proponents of this theory generally argue that dual-class shares can attract international investment and improve local financial competitiveness through their flexible design of the voting rights system [8]. Opponents, on the other hand, argue that such a system violates the right to shareholder equality. Therefore, the question that arises at this point is why many jurisdictions still choose to have dual-class shares if it infringes on the right to equal shareholders. Is this an innovation or a step backwards?

It can be concluded that the interpretation of shareholder equality in laws, regulations, and corporate governance codes includes equal treatment of shareholders and equal provision of information to shareholders.[23] However, this may not have been interpreted in the same way before. For example, in 2002, French scholars interpreted the equality of shareholders as equal treatment in equal circumstances and as not constituting discrimination under criminal law (gender discrimination, religious discrimination, racial discrimination, and so on) [7]. The interpretation of discriminatory treatment may not be explained by modern concepts. However, it can be believed that this should be a fundamental human right. Therefore, in the case of a two-tier shareholding structure, is there equal treatment in equal circumstances? If it is necessary to look at it from the point of view of shares, a two-tier shareholding structure is a breakthrough in this matter. However, the idea of "equal treatment" implied by a dual-class shareholding structure may not be limited to the number of shares but also considers the situation of the shareholders themselves.

Thus, can democracy be an erosion of equality? Despite these doubts, it seems to be recognised by company law, for example, in the case of preference shares. The preference share regime itself can also be seen as a different interpretation of the principle of shareholder equality, but the law and corporate governance respect the views of shareholders when they redefine it through shareholder agreements. Why? It can be assumed that shareholder equality is a right of shareholders but that shareholders are free to dispose of this right to equal. When shareholders agree to adjust their equality rights, it is important to respect the shareholders' free choice.

The relationship between the principle of shareholders' equality and the majority rule of capital is an important theory for the proper treatment of the reasonable engagement of controlling shareholders in Chinese FHCs. The Chinese Code of Governance for Listed Companies does not specifically provide for a shareholder voting system, which means that it follows the setting of the Chinese Company Law. Under Chinese Company Law, shareholders exercise their voting rights on the basis of the proportion of capital contribution, but exceptions can be made to the company's articles of association.[24] A 2019 case law confirmed the application of this article in

[22] *Ibid.*

[23] *Ibid.*

[24] See Article 42, Chinese Company Law. According to this provision, the right to vote at meetings of the shareholders' meeting is exercised by the shareholders in proportion to their capital contribution, unless otherwise provided for in the articles of association.

judicial practice, where the judge held that the prerequisite for shareholders to follow majority rule should be the genuine intention of the shareholders.[25] Thus, under the "one share one vote" system in Chinese law, majority rule is itself an expression of the principle of shareholders' equality. It is also affirmed in French case law.[26] This finding is reasonable when considering the overall perspective of corporate governance in China. FHCs in China, however, have been echoed in the "TMSAFHC". However, under Company Law, exceptions to majority rule can be agreed upon in shareholders' articles of association. This essentially grants shareholders the freedom to adjust through the internal mechanisms of corporate governance. However, in the case of FHCs, shareholders' articles of association are subject to review and approval by the People's Bank of China.[27] Therefore, the internal mechanisms for the protection of shareholders' rights are also subject to regulation.

8.1.2.2 The Boundaries of "Control" Over Controlling Shareholders

In the context of the reform of Chinese law and to understand more specifically the control relationship in FHCs, the book will explain two aspects here. First, the book analyses the control and abuse of rights in Chinese FHCs. Second, the book analyses the relationship between the control relationship and the fiduciary duties of the controlling shareholder.

The book revealed that the main problem in the governance of Chinese FHCs is the excessive engagement of controlling shareholders and explained some specific directions for future reform. In addition, the book argued that the rationality of controlling shareholder control is based precisely on the principle of shareholder equality. At this point, the book reflects on a foundational issue, which concerns the relationship between control and abuse of rights in Chinese FHCs. Chinese scholars advocate the affirmation of controlling shareholders' control position in corporate governance, along with their strict monitoring [21]. The reasons for this are considered by most of the literature to be the abuse of rights by controlling shareholders and the protection of minority shareholders' rights. This is certainly in line with the trend in corporate governance in China and other jurisdictions. However, there is perhaps a logical gap here as to why controlling shareholders' control must lead to abuse of rights. The book does find some evidence of this through case law,[28] but this does not seem to prove a necessary relationship, which would seem to require statistical evidence. A large amount of data analysis would require disclosure by the regulator to be available, but the book has found no such statistics at present. Therefore, it can be proven only by logical deduction.

[25] Xu Peng v Jinan Baker & Hambone Food Technology Co. (许鹏诉济南贝克汉邦食品科技有限公司,山东省济南市中级人民法院(2019)鲁01民终7995号民事裁定书).

[26] Cour d'appel de Paris, 1ère chambre, 19 mars 2002, n° 2001/17786.

[27] See Article 15, TMSAFHC. Under this clause, if the company amends its articles of association, this requires the approval of the PBOC, which indicates that the will of the shareholders is restricted.

[28] *Ibid.*

It cannot be assumed that control rights necessarily lead to an abuse of rights. The book has shown that it is reasonable for controlling shareholders to gain control, on the basis of the principle of shareholders' equality. Logically, good corporate governance is indeed effective in avoiding abuse of rights [15]. However, good governance is achievable. Or is it just our ideal? If this is not achievable, then how can abuse of rights be avoided? Therefore, the fundamental question of what the criteria for good corporate governance truly are remains. Reflecting on the corporate governance codes of the other jurisdictions studied, such as France. The French Code of Corporate Governance states that what is set out in the code is the standard of good corporate governance.[29] In addition, the Chinese Code of Corporate Governance for listed companies sets out five criteria: sound, effective, and transparent; balanced internal and external oversight; protection of shareholders' legal rights; and ensuring that they are protected. In addition, the Chinese Code of Governance for listed companies sets out five standards: sound, effective, and transparent; balanced internal and external oversight; protection of shareholders' legal rights and ensuring that they are treated fairly; respect for the fundamental rights of stakeholders; and enhancement of the overall value of the enterprise.[30] Therefore, the Code of Corporate Governance in fact explains what good corporate governance is. In addition, is this good practice? A philosophical analysis of truthfulness and objectivity seems to be involved here [5].

> 'Hart's conception of social rules implicitly invokes the concept of minimal objectivity. What rules require is minimally objective, not fixed by the beliefs of particular agents, but by the convergent behavior and shared understandings of the majority of the population.'

According to this theory, the book can assume that an FHC achieves good governance when its governance meets the requirements of the corporate governance code. Even if it does have abuses of rights, it is difficult to detect. This interpretation seems to be recommended. It provides a truly definitive standard for social practice. In addition, there is no such thing as the best governance, only better governance.

In terms of corporate governance codes in other jurisdictions, corporate governance codes are soft laws that follow the "comply or explain" principle.[31] However, as explained earlier, in terms of legal effects, the Code of Corporate Governance of Chinese listed companies is a "departmental regulatory document (部门规范性文件)" in the context of Chinese law, which is in fact a form of hard law [17]. However, in terms of the content of the code, it does not provide for a liability regime. In addition, in pilot FHCs, there are nonlisted companies in addition to listed companies, and there is currently no legal documentation to clarify whether the controlling

---

[29] See Preamble, 2020 French Corporate Governance Code of Listed Corporations. It demonstrates that the purpose of a governance code is to provide a standard of good governance.

[30] See Article 3, Code of Governance for Listed Companies in China. According to this article, the governance of listed companies should be sound, effective, and transparent, with enhanced internal and external checks and balances. It should safeguard the legitimate rights of shareholders and ensure that they are treated fairly, respect the fundamental rights of stakeholders and effectively enhance the overall value of the enterprise.

[31] *Ibid.*

shareholders of nonlisted companies have fiduciary duties. In addition, it should be improved in future.

8.2 Rethinking the Engagement of Minority Shareholders

With respect to the protection of shareholders' rights in Chinese FHCs, the participation of controlling shareholders is one of the important aspects, whereas the protection of minority shareholders' rights is another angle of analysis. In fact, as a relatively weak party in corporate governance, the protection of minority shareholders' rights has always been a core concern. This is also reflected in the case of FHCs. However, it is important to note that among Chinese FHCs, the mixed-ownership model and state-owned shareholding FHCs are at the centre of attention. The pilot FHCs studied do not include wholly state-owned companies, where the state is the sole shareholder and the issue of minority shareholder rights protection does not naturally arise. There are two perspectives that are of great interest in the governance of FHCs in China. On the one hand, the Communist Party of China plays a role in the governance of FHCs with respect to the protection of minority shareholders' rights. On the other hand, there is a focus on the shareholding structure.

8.2.1 Relationships Between the Communist Party of China and the Engagement of Minority Shareholders

The Communist Party of China (CPC) is a very special phenomenon in Chinese corporate governance. It is a manifestation of the involvement of a country's ruling party in corporate governance. In accordance with Chinese company law, the establishment of a party organisation in a company is achieved in accordance with the constitution of the CPC.[32] In addition, in the constitution of the CPC, the party organisation in an enterprise is a grassroots party organisation.[33] If there are three or more members of the CPC in the enterprise, then the enterprise should establish a party organisation.[34] In addition, according to the provisions of the company law, the company should provide the necessary conditions for the activities of the party organisation.[35]

---

[32] See Article 19, Chinese Company Law.

[33] See Article 30, Constitution of the Communist Party of China (amended in 2017) (中国共产党章程(2017修改)). According to its interpretation, in enterprises, rural areas, organs, schools, scientific research institutes, street communities, social organisations, People's Liberation Army units and other basic units, where there are three or more official party members, all should set up a basic-level party organisation. In addition, companies are a type of social organisation.

[34] *Ibid.*

[35] See Article 19, Chinese Company Law.

In the jurisdictions studied, it is difficult to find a similar situation. The relationship between political parties and corporate governance is indeed not a new topic. Under Chinese law, the CPC is encouraged to participate in corporate governance, particularly in state-owned enterprises (SOEs). In 2017, the Chinese government issued regulations to clarify the legal status of the CPC in the corporate governance structure of state-owned enterprises. The rights, responsibilities, and working modalities of the CPC in all aspects of decision-making, implementation, and supervision of state-owned enterprises should be clarified.[36] However, the relationship between political parties and "good governance" is controversial [9]. Political parties can win elections by making policy rather than making policy through elections [1]. In the field of corporate governance, the policy preferences of the left and the right are different; for example, leftist governments encourage patient or dedicated owners of capital [9]. Nevertheless, the governance of Chinese FHCs should respect the Chinese context; otherwise, it will only worsen because it extends beyond corporate governance to a wider range of political, economic, and cultural factors.

On the basis of the Chinese corporate governance codes and the documents issued in relation to the governance of FHCs, the engagement of the CPC in the governance of FHCs is an issue that cannot be avoided in China, and this trend will continue in future. Given the history of corporate governance in China, this pattern has been in place since China began to focus on corporate governance. Therefore, it is necessary to examine the characteristics of the CPC in the governance of FHCs in China. To fully argue this point, this section analyses it from two perspectives. First, the role of the CPC in the governance of FHCs is important. Second, there is a relationship between the CPC and the protection of minority shareholders' rights.

8.2.1.1 Rethinking the Role of the Communist Party of China

The role of the CPC is crucial in the construction of a mechanism for the protection of shareholders' rights in Chinese FHCs and is therefore specifically discussed here. Regarding the governance of FHCs, China does not currently issue a specific governance code or similar document. However, it can be analysed in terms of the types of FHCs. From the perspective of a listed FHC, current Chinese corporate governance codes can be applied therein. From the perspective of an unlisted FHC, Chinese governance documents for unlisted companies can also provide a reference, such as the Code of Corporate Governance for Banking and Insurance Institutions, which is still in draft form. In addition, the Chinese FHC regulation released in 2020 provides a specific explanation of the governance of FHCs.

---

[36] See Article 5, General Office of the State Council on Further Improving the Corporate Governance Structure of State-owned Enterprises (国务院办公厅关于进一步完善国有企业法人治理结构的指导意见). It is mentioned here that the legal status of party organisations in the corporate governance structure of state-owned enterprises should be clarified, and the work of party organisations should be incorporated into the statutes of state-owned enterprises, so that party organisations become an organic part of the corporate governance structure of enterprises.

In Chinese law, there is a rich legal basis for the engagement of the Communist Party of China (CPC) in corporate governance, including company law and corporate governance codes.[37] Therefore, what role does the CPC play in corporate governance in China? One view sees it as a leader; for example, some scholars argue for supporting the leadership of the party committee in the corporate governance structure of state-controlled enterprises [10]. Another view sees it as a participant; for example, some scholars have analysed the ways in which the CPC is involved in Chinese enterprises in terms of political and economic participation [11]. Both perspectives explore the governance of Chinese enterprises in general terms rather than just for FHCs. How, then, is the role of the CPC positioned in FHCs? It should be treated differently for SOEs and nonSOEs. First, in terms of current Chinese legislation, the regulation of FHCs, which came into force in 2020, does not specify this. Chinese company law only indicates that companies should provide conditions for the activities of the CPC but does not further explain the position of the CPC in corporate governance. Second, from the perspective of corporate governance codes, there are five main specific documents in current Chinese corporate governance codes [20]. Among them, the code of governance for banking and insurance institutions is still in the draft stage. Moreover, in the other four corporate governance code documents, the role of the CPC in corporate governance is not clearly explained. However, in the governance code for bancassurance structures, which is currently being developed, a distinction is made between state-owned bancassurance structures and nonstate-owned bancassurance institutions. In state-owned bancassurance structures, the CPC is expected to play a leading role in corporate governance.[38] In the case of nonstate-owned bancassurance institutions, the CPC plays a role in safeguarding the interests of employees, building corporate culture, and promoting state and party policies.[39] This reflects the fact that Chinese legislators will continue to strengthen their political intervention in the governance of state-owned enterprises in future.

Currently, for the governance of FHCs, there are no specific corporate governance codes to explain the role of the CPC. According to the concept of an FHC, an FHC usually exists in the form of a parent company whose subsidiaries may be banking and insurance institutions. However, the governance model for the subsidiary may not be suitable for the governance of the parent company, which is not in line with the governance principles of consolidated regulation. Moreover, judging from current Chinese legislation on governance codes for bancassurance institutions, the future governance of Chinese FHCs may also be interpreted in accordance with the

[37] See Article 19, the Chinese Company Law.

[38] See Article 9, Code of Corporate Governance for Bancassurance Institutions. According to this provision, state-owned bancassurance institutions should integrate the leadership of the CPC into all aspects of corporate governance and continue to explore and improve the modern financial enterprise system with Chinese characteristics.

[39] See Article 14, Code of Corporate Governance for Bancassurance Institutions. According to this provision, private bancassurance institutions are required to establish party organisational structures and strengthen political leadership in accordance with the relevant provisions on the establishment of party organisations.

distinction between state-owned enterprises and nonstate-owned enterprises with respect to the role of the CPC. In addition, it is important to clarify that state-owned enterprises in Chinese law currently refer mainly to wholly state-owned companies and enterprises in which state-owned capital is in a controlling position [17]. In the FHCs, those in which state-owned capital is in a controlling position are represented mainly by state-owned companies by shares[40] and mixed-ownership FHCs in which state-owned capital is in a controlling position. Among the eight pilot FHCs currently regulated in China, five companies belong to the SOEs here.[41]

Among the eight pilot FHCs in China, four are wholly state-owned companies,[42] which are not the subject of the analysis. The book analyses the remaining four groups, including Ping An Insurance, Ant Group, Suning.com, and Everbright Group. The book can analyse them according to state-owned FHCs and nonstate-owned FHCs.

The analysis revealed that the role of the CPC in the current Chinese FHC pilots is largely in line with the trend reflected in the current Chinese regulatory documents. However, it is necessary to reflect on the future positioning of the CPC in Chinese FHCs from the macro-perspective of Chinese corporate law and corporate governance. First, should the Chinese Company Law be amended? The provisions of Article 19 of the Chinese Company Law do not distinguish between specific companies but rather require companies to facilitate the activities of the CPC uniformly. In practical terms, however, nonstate and foreign-invested enterprises are not active in the establishment of the CPC in corporate governance [6]. Moreover, Chinese regulators have distinguished between state-owned and nonstate-owned enterprises in terms of the role of the CPC. Thus, the provisions of Article 19 of the Company Law may also need to be amended and adjusted. Otherwise, this would undermine the authority of Chinese company law as a basic Chinese commercial legal system. Second, is there a need for a governance code for FHCs? Currently, there is no governance code for FHCs in China, but given the status of Chinese FHC pilots, it has broken out of the scope of listed companies, securities companies and banking and insurance institutions, as it usually exists as a parent company.[43] Therefore, current Chinese corporate governance codes are unable to meet the needs of FHCs. Moreover, in facing the difficult issue of the positioning of the CPC in corporate governance, it also needs to be clarified in the future code of governance for FHCs. As China is still in the early stages of research on the governance of FHCs, it is important to clarify

[40] According to the Chinese Company Law, there are two types of companies: limited companies by shares, and limited liability companies. The "state-owned companies by shares" are one of these companies. In addition, Chinese FHCs are primarily a type of company. Therefore, the analysis of FHCs also needs to be done in the context of company law.

[41] They are China Merchants Group, Shanghai International Group, Beijing Financial Holdings Group, Everbright Group and CITIC Group. The remaining three companies, including Ping An Insurance, Ant Group and Suning.com, are not state-owned enterprises.

[42] These are China Merchants Group, Shanghai International Group, Beijing Financial Holdings Group, and CITIC Group. It should be noted that although CITIC Group is listed in Hong Kong, it is still a wholly state-owned company in its registration documents on the mainland.

[43] See Chap. 1.

the current position of the CPC, as this will reduce the influence of historical factors on Chinese past economic development and provide a good governance framework for the future governance of FHCs.

8.2.1.2 Rethinking the Role of the Communist Party of China in the Engagement of Minority Shareholders

In the internal governance mechanism of Chinese FHCs, the relationships between the protection of minority shareholders' rights and the CPC are closely linked. Therefore, what role does the CPC play in the protection of minority shareholders' rights? It should be explained separately according to state-owned FHCs and nonstate-owned FHCs.

State-owned FHCs refer mainly to FHCs in mixed-ownership FHCs where state-owned capital occupies a controlling position. The reason is that in a wholly state-owned company, the issue of protection of minority shareholders' rights does not exist. Moreover, in a state-owned FHC by shares, the issue of protection of minority shareholders' rights is not prominent because the number of shareholders is small and relatively concentrated. In mixed-ownership FHCs, when state-owned capital is the controlling shareholder, nonstate-owned shares, as minority shareholders, are in a vulnerable position in the protection of rights [17]. Therefore, what is the role of the CPC in a state-owned FHC? As such, it provides a special channel of redress for the protection of minority shareholders' rights: discipline inspection and supervision. The Chinese corporate governance system is a special channel belonging to state-owned enterprises, and it is a form of expression of the party's organisation performing its monitoring function. According to the Chinese Supervision Law enacted in 2018, discipline inspection and supervision mainly target the corruption of party members and public officials, which includes managers of SOEs.[44] This means that minority shareholders can protect their rights by reporting directors, executives, and shareholders to the Discipline Inspection Commission of the state-owned FHC and the State Supervision Commission.

The advantage of such a system for minority shareholders is that it significantly reduces the cost of protecting minority shareholders' rights. In the case of state-owned FHCs, whistleblowing by minority shareholders is convenient and saves a few costs, including legal fees. It is the job of the disciplinary and inspection authorities to investigate and collect evidence from those who have been reported. However, from the perspective of minority shareholder rights protection, there are some shortcomings in this system. It is manifested in two specific ways. First, the responsibilities of the CPC are not clear. In Chinese law, the protection of minority shareholders' rights involves the duty of fidelity and diligence imposed by the Chinese Company Law and the Code of Governance of Listed Companies on Directors, Supervisors, and

[44] See Article 15, Supervision Law of the People's Republic of China (中华人民共和国监察法). According to this article, the supervisory authority supervises the managers of SOEs.

Managers.[45] Therefore, do the CPC have a duty and responsibility for the protection of minority shareholders' rights? If so, what should the duties and obligations be? This is not reflected in the company law and corporate governance codes. Second, there is a lack of disclosure on the protection of minority shareholders' rights. At present, from the perspective of disciplinary supervision, the disclosure of disciplinary supervision of state-owned FHCs is general and lacks specific disclosure. For example, how many cases are there each year regarding the protection of minority shareholders' rights? How many cases have been properly dealt with? These will need to be further reformed later.

However, the position of the CPC in a nonstate-owned FHC is different from its position in a state-owned FHC. In a state-owned FHC, the CPC is more inclined to be perceived in the role of a leader [11]. In contrast, in nonstate-owned FHCs, the CPC is the role of a general participant. This difference is also reflected in the protection of minority shareholders' rights. In state-owned FHCs, the CPC provides a special form of protection for minority shareholder rights, although this still needs to be improved. In the case of nonstate FHCs,[46] regulatory pilots do not have a corporate governance design, such as a disciplinary committee, to monitor them. Therefore, how can the CPC play a role in protecting the rights of minority shareholders? Indeed, it is difficult to provide effective experience in Chinese judicial practice at the moment. However, in 2019, the Chinese government issued a notice hoping to improve the building of party organisations in nonstate enterprises.[47] Moreover, a specific institutional design for how the CPC can play a role in nonstate-owned enterprises is lacking. In addition, in nonstate-owned FHCs, if the building of a party organisation [11] is inevitable in future, then the CPC can play an active role in the supervision of corporate governance. The reason is that although the CPC is not at the heart of corporate governance in a nonstate-owned FHC, it still has a constraining and supervisory role over the party members in the company. Therefore, if there are members of the CPC among the controlling shareholders, directors, or senior management of the company, they are likewise subject to disciplinary supervision by the CPC. Therefore, minority shareholders can use the CPC to constrain party members in the governance of the company.

[45] See Article 147, Chinese Company Law; Article 4, the Code of Governance for Listed Companies in China. According to the articles, shareholders, actual controllers, directors, supervisors, and senior management of listed companies should safeguard the interests of listed companies in accordance with regulatory requirements. Directors, supervisors, and senior management should continue to learn and improve their ability to perform their duties faithfully, diligently, and prudently.

[46] Such as Ping An Insurance, Ant Group and Suning.com.

[47] See Opinions of the Central Committee of the Communist Party of China and the State Council on Creating a Better Development Environment to Support the Reform and Development of Private Enterprises (中共中央、国务院关于营造更好发展环境支持民营企业改革发展的意见).

8.2.2 Rethinking the Optimisation of Governance Structures for the Engagement of Minority Shareholders

The governance structure of FHCs in China differs from that of other jurisdictions. There is no conflict between the existence of a supervisory board and independent directors in the governance of a Chinese FHC. Instead, the most important purpose in Chinese corporate governance is to properly manage the relationship between controlling and minority shareholders and between shareholders and management. To justify the analysis, this book addresses the Board of Directors and the supervisory board separately. In the optimisation of the Board of Directors, the evaluation mechanism is an important reference. In the case of the supervisory board, the most important objective in the governance of Chinese FHCs is to enable the supervisory board to perform its supervisory function. However, the problem with the supervisory board is that it is not sufficiently supervised, so the necessary reforms are advocated.

8.2.2.1 Rethinking the Optimisation of the Evaluation of the Board of Directors

Board evaluation is an important tool for addressing the long-standing issue of trust between shareholders and management in proxy problems, but board evaluation is also a very ambitious project. The book focuses on just two of the more salient issues. One aspect concerns the assessment of the independence of independent directors, and the other concerns the assessment of directors' duty of loyalty and diligence.

Through the analysis of corporate governance codes in other jurisdictions, the independence of independent directors and the assessment are very important elements.[48] In 2020, the People's Bank of China issued a regulatory scheme for FHCs, followed by regulations on the supervision and management of directors, supervisors, and senior management of FHCs in 2021.[49] However, the assessment of directors is dependent on the PBOC and its branches.[50] As a result, supervision is the main way in which independent directors of FHCs are assessed. At this point, another question arises as to what role the internal mechanisms of corporate governance play in the assessment of independent directors of FHCs. In Chinese law, there still seems to be a research gap. With respect to the experience of other jurisdictions, there are two main models for evaluating the independence of independent

---

[48] See Chap. 6.

[49] See Interim Regulations on the Administration of Filing of Director, Supervisor and Senior Management Positions in Financial Holding Companies (金融控股公司董事、监事、高级管理人员任职备案管理暂行规定). It proves the point as a whole, and it covers all the articles.

[50] See Article 21, Interim Regulations on the Administration of Filing of Director, Supervisor and Senior Management Positions in Financial Holding Companies. Under this provision, the PBOC and its branches assess and provide guidance on the management system for the appointment of directors, supervisors and senior management established by FHCs, and check whether the said system is effectively implemented.

directors in terms of corporate governance codes: first, the European model. They have adopted very detailed evaluation criteria for the independence of independent directors, which include France and the UK. It is considered to be a very rigorous evaluation model. Second, the U.S. model is used. For the evaluation of the independence of independent directors, this model does not provide detailed criteria in the corporate governance code but rather general descriptions and recommendations.

Therefore, which model should be adopted for the evaluation of independent directors in Chinese FHCs? The European model may be a trend. China has adopted the U.S. model for evaluating the independence of independent directors, as evidenced by the governance codes of listed companies and commercial banks in China.[51] However, in the recent code of governance for banks and insurance institutions, independent directorship is explained in a special section, and the requirements for independent directors are carefully defined.[52] It is even though it is still in draft form and has not yet come into force. However, this already indicates that Chinese regulators adopt more stringent standards for evaluating the independence of independent directors in prudential institutions, which is already very similar to the European model. In addition, the newly published regulations for directors, supervisors and officers of FHCs have adopted the European model. The independence of independent directors is regulated in two main areas: first, independent directors are regulated in terms of kinship and affiliation; second, independent directors cannot serve for more than six years and cannot serve in more than two FHCs.[53] Nevertheless, the evaluation of independent directorship in FHCs has been given stricter rules at the regulatory level, which should also be given more innovation in the internal governance mechanism of the company, which relies on the disclosure of the evaluation system.

In addition, there is some confusion in the current Chinese law regarding the duty of loyalty and diligence of the directors of FHCs. According to the FHC regulations

---

[51] See Article 56, the Code of Governance for Listed Companies in China. Under this provision, the performance evaluation of directors and senior management is organised by the Board of Directors or its Remuneration and Evaluation Committee. Listed companies may entrust a third party to conduct performance evaluation. The performance evaluation of independent directors and supervisors is carried out by way of self-evaluation and mutual evaluation.

See Article 23, Measures for the Evaluation of the Performance of Directors of Commercial Banks (for Trial Implementation). Under this provision, independent directors should express an objective and impartial independent opinion on matters discussed by the board of directors and focus on safeguarding the rights of depositors and minority shareholders.

[52] See Article 33, Code of Corporate Governance for Bancassurance Institutions. According to this provision, an independent director is a director who does not hold a position other than director in the bancassurance institution in which he or she works and does not have a relationship with the bancassurance institution, its shareholders or the person in effective control that may influence his or her independent and objective judgment of the company's affairs.

[53] See Article 13, Interim Regulations on the Administration of Filing of Director, Supervisor and Senior Management Positions in Financial Holding Companies. Under this provision, an independent director may not serve for more than six years in aggregate in the same FHC and may serve as an independent director in at most two FHCs at the same time.

that have just come into force in China,[54] they do not contain a description of the directors' duties of diligence and loyalty. However, a review of the overall Chinese commercial legal system shows that directors' duties of loyalty and diligence are reflected in various legal systems.[55] Thus, are directors of Chinese FHCs not required to fulfil their duties of loyalty and diligence? Not truly. Chinese FHC pilots include both listed and unlisted companies; banking and insurance institutions; and internet companies. From this perspective, all FHCs that meet certain conditions should follow the appropriate regulations and governance requirements. The reason why there is no provision for the duty of loyalty and diligence for directors of FHCs is likely because the governance code on FHCs is still in its infancy, and this still needs to be supported by more business practices.

However, in terms of the overall corporate governance system in China, the director evaluation mechanism is still very weak. In the code of governance for listed companies, the evaluation of director performance is encouraged in the hope that listed companies will be transparent in the evaluation of directors and report to shareholders' meeting on the performance of directors.[56] However, specific guidance is lacking. In terms of director evaluation mechanisms for state-owned enterprises, director evaluation in China relies on the regulations of the SASAC in different provinces. However, thus far, among the 34 local provinces in China, only five provinces have published evaluation programmes for directors of state-owned enterprises.[57] Thus, for both listed and unlisted SOEs and nonSOEs, in the case of FHCs, China currently lacks an effective evaluation mechanism for director loyalty and diligence, which may be one of the reasons for the criticism of corporate governance in China [21].

In future, the evaluation of the duty of loyalty and diligence of executive directors should be optimised in the following ways. First, the specific content of the duty of loyalty and diligence should be clarified. These two duties of directors are widespread

[54] Such as "Interim Provisions on the Administration of Filing of Appointment of Directors, Supervisors and Senior Management of Financial Holding Companies" and "TMSAFHC".

[55] These include Article 147, the Chinese Company Law; Article 4, the Code of Governance for Listed Companies in China.

[56] See Article 55, Code of Governance for Listed Companies in China. Under this provision, listed companies shall establish fair and transparent criteria and procedures for evaluating the performance and performance of directors, supervisors, and senior management.

[57] These include the Interim Measures for the Evaluation of External Directors of Enterprises under the Control of Beijing Municipality (北京市管企业外部董事评价暂行办法), the Measures for the Evaluation of the Board of Directors and Directors of Pilot Enterprises of the Board of Directors of Henan Province (for Trial Implementation) (河南省董事会试点企业董事会、董事评价办法(试行)), the Measures for the Evaluation of the Board of Directors and Directors of Enterprises under the Direct Control of the Shenzhen State-owned Assets Supervision and Administration Bureau (for Trial Implementation) (深圳市国有资产监督管理局直管企业董事会及董事评价办法(试行)), the Work Plan for the Evaluation of External Directors and the Assessment of External Supervisors of Enterprises under the Control of Shandong Province in 2008 (2008年度山东省管企业外部董事评价及外派监事考核工作方案), the Measures for the Evaluation of the Board of Directors and Director Evaluation Measures (for Trial Implementation) (江苏省属国有独资公司董事会及董事评价办法(试行)). They prove the points as a whole, and they cover all the articles.

in Chinese law. However, what do they mean in concrete terms? This lacks detailed guidance. This can lead to a dilemma in the evaluation mechanism. Second, China should establish a soft law mechanism for corporate governance codes. "Comply or explain" is a good disclosure principle that allows for widespread scrutiny of the transparency of directors' performance, and China should explore the soft law route in its corporate governance regime to implement this principle in future.

8.2.2.2 Rethinking the Optimisation of the Supervisory Board

In the Chinese corporate governance structure, unlike in other jurisdictions, the supervisory board is jointly responsible for the supervisory function of a company with a system of independent directors. It is a break from the traditional "one tyre" and "two tyres" structure design. The legislative intent was to strengthen the oversight of corporate governance and thereby protect the rights of minority shareholders. However, since the introduction of this system in Chinese company law in 1993, its role in corporate governance has not been reflected, and this role has remained virtually unchanged in successive amendments to the company law [13]. This has led to several embarrassing phenomena. For example, in commercial banks, the supervisory board is ultimately responsible for the evaluation of the directors.[58] However, if the role of the supervisory board is a sham, how can the impartiality of the directors' evaluation be ensured? How can the rights of minority shareholders be protected? In the current regulatory scheme for the governance of FHCs in China, there is little provision for a supervisory board. Thus, in the absence of regulation and the lack of a disciplinary mechanism for corporate governance, the protection of minority shareholders' rights in Chinese FHCs is already facing a very dangerous situation. Along with the reform of the governance of FHCs in China, the reform of the supervisory board system is a very important topic. In exploring this aspect, it is important to focus on two aspects, namely the independence of the supervisory board and the monitoring of the supervisory board.

There is a lack of safeguards for the independence of the members of the supervisory board in Chinese corporate governance. The coexistence of a supervisory board and independent directors in Chinese corporate governance is an important Chinese characteristic. Why is the independence regime of the supervisory board not regulated in detail in Chinese corporate governance? Many existing studies in the literature support the idea that supervisory boards should remain independent, but no explanation is given for these designs by Chinese legislators in the first place. There are perhaps too many subjective and historical reasons for this. Therefore, after

[58] See Article 5, Measures for Evaluating the Performance of Directors of Commercial Banks (for Trial Implementation). Under this provision, the supervisory board of a commercial bank is ultimately responsible for the evaluation of the performance of directors, and the banking supervisory authority supervises the evaluation of the performance of directors of commercial banks.

being revised in 2018, the Chinese code of governance for listed companies encouraged the independence of supervisory boards but did not provide detailed guidance.[59] However, a shift in the attitudes of Chinese legislators towards this regime has also been noted. For example, the corporate governance codes for banks and insurance institutions, which are still in draft form, already contain some detailed requirements for the independence of supervisors. For example, external supervisors may not serve for more than six years cumulatively in a bank or insurance institution.[60] It is a solution that considers the impact of the length of service on independence.

In the current absence of detailed guidance at the corporate governance level on the independence of supervisors of FHCs, Chinese legislators can work on two fronts. First, the factors that affect the independence of the supervisory board should be described in the future governance code for FHCs. These are also factors that affect the independence of independent directors. China has already made new attempts to address the independence of independent directors in banking and insurance institutions, so legislators could also make more progress in the design of the independence of supervisory directors in FHCs. Second, the independence of the supervisory board is designed to absorb the current FHC regulatory pilots. Six FHC pilots have established supervisory boards. An examination of the design of the supervisory boards of these six FHCs reveals that Ping An Insurance's actions in relation to the independence of its supervisory board are recommendable. According to its 2020 annual report, it discloses the report of the supervisory board and provides a description of the independence of the supervisory board, covering matters such as the company's compliance, the authenticity of financial reports, the use of funds raised, connected transactions, the internal control system, the implementation of the shareholders' meeting, the evaluation of the performance of directors and the shareholders' dividend policy.[61]

From the perspective of the governance of FHCs in China, the supervisory board assumes a monitoring function over management and is an important institution for the protection of shareholders' rights. However, supervisory board oversight failures are not uncommon, and there is currently no mention of the design of supervisory board independence in the governance regulation of FHCs, which means that supervisory board corruption is not entirely avoidable. A question that arises at this point, then, that is worth discussing is who will monitor the supervisory board. In the context of Chinese law, there are two main routes: regulation and disclosure. For

---

[59] See Article 45, Code of Governance for Listed Companies in China. According to this article, the supervisory board should be staffed and structured in such a way as to ensure that the supervisory board is able to perform its duties independently and effectively. Supervisors should have appropriate professional knowledge or work experience and be able to perform their duties effectively. Directors and senior management of listed companies shall not also serve as supervisors.

[60] See Article 59, the Code of Corporate Governance for Bancassurance Institutions. According to this provision, the term of office of a supervisor shall not exceed three years and he/she may be re-elected at the end of the term. External supervisors may not serve for more than six years in aggregate at a bank or insurance institution.

[61] See Ping An Insurance Annual Report 2020.

regulation, the People's Bank of China and its branches are responsible for supervising the conduct of supervisors under the latest regulations in force regarding supervisors of FHCs in China.[62] From a disclosure perspective, the code of governance for listed companies in China requires the supervisory committee to report to the AGM of shareholders on the performance of directors' duties and for disclosure by listed companies.[63] These circumstances indicate that there is little effective design in terms of internal corporate governance mechanisms for the monitoring of supervisory boards. The absence of monitoring can lead to corruption.

For future reforms, third-party enforcement strategies may be the recommended corporate governance solution in situations where supervisory board oversight is ineffective. With respect to these strategies, legal economists offer three options, namely the gatekeeper strategy, the whistleblower strategy, and private incentives, including reputational concerns or contractual arrangements [12]. Certainly, the use of these strategies or some of them in a particular FHC depends on the circumstances of the company. An FHC may consider a specific evaluation by criteria such as efficiency, cost, and comparative advantage [19]. In retrospect, it may take some time for these three strategies to be applied to FHCs under Chinese law. For example, in terms of the gatekeeper strategy, the 2019 Chinese Securities Law takes a very important step in this regard by requiring all financial and accounting documents of listed companies for the last three years to be audited.[64] This gives accountants the role of the gatekeeper in corporate governance, but such a strategy is not currently being introduced in terms of monitoring by the supervisory board. In Chinese law, accounting firms are currently primarily responsible for the audit of financial reports. Therefore, is it possible in future to audit corporate governance reports or supervisory board reports? This is a strategy that we look forward to.

References

1. Barker RM (2010) Corporate governance, competition, and political parties: explaining corporate governance change in Europe. Oxford University Press, Oxford

[62] See Article 21, the Interim Provisions on the Administration of Filing of Appointment of Directors, Supervisors and Senior Management of Financial Holding Companies. Under this provision, the PBOC and its branches assess and provide guidance on the management system for the appointment of directors, supervisors and senior management established by FHCs, and check whether the said system is effectively implemented.

[63] See Article 57, Code of Governance for Listed Companies in China. According to this article, the Board of Directors and the supervisory committee shall report to the general meeting of shareholders on the performance of their duties, the results of their performance evaluation and their remuneration, and the listed company shall disclose the results of the evaluation.

[64] See Article 59, Chinese Securities Law. Under this provision, the regulator is required to review a company's initial public offering of new shares for which an unqualified audit report has been issued on its financial accounting report for the last three years. Prior to the amendment to the Securities Law, this provision did not include a reference to an "unqualified audit report".

2. Carreau D, Letréguilly H (2012) Offres publiques: OPA, OPE, OPR. Répertoire de droit commercial 133–135
3. Castres Saint-martin-drummond F (1993) Les sociétés dites "holdings". Dissertation, Université Panthéon-Assas Paris II
4. Coates IV JC (2018) Mergers, acquisitions, and restructuring: types, regulation, and patterns of practice. In: Gordon JN, Ringe W (ed) The oxford handbook of corporate law and governance, Oxford University Press, Oxford
5. Coleman JL (1995) Truth and objectivity in law. Leg Theory 1(1):33–68
6. Guan E (2012) Research on the construction of party organisations in nonpublic enterprises. Dissertation, Dalian Maritime University. (管恩琦,《非公有制企业党的组织建设研究》,大连海事大学法学博士论文,2012年,第83页)
7. Guyon Y (2002) Assemblées d'actionnaires—Tenue de l'assemblée (Shareholders' meetings - Holding the meeting). Répertoire des sociétés (Company directory) 185–191
8. Huang F (2017) Dual class shares around the top global financial centres. J Bus Law 2:154
9. Ishiyama J (2015) Political parties, democracy, and good governance. In: Asefa S, Huang W(ed) The political economy of good governance, W.E. Upjohn Institute, Michigan
10. Ji X (2020) Correctly understood the positioning of the responsibilities of party organisations in mixed-ownership enterprises. China Party and Government Cadre Forum 9: 53. (姬旭辉:|正确认识混合所有制企业党组织的职责定位》,中国党政干部论坛,2020年第9期,第53页)
11. Jiang D (2017) Towards political corporate law: how party organisations can participate in corporate governance. Journal of Central South University (Social Science Edition) 3: 29. (蒋大兴:《走向"政治性公司法"—党组织如何参与公司治理》,中南大学学报(社会科学版),2017年第3期,第29页。)
12. Kraakman RH (1986) Gatekeepers: the anatomy of a third-party enforcement strategy. J Law Econ Organ 1:56
13. Ma G (2021) An exploration of the change in the institutional structure of the supervisory board in the context of the revision of the company law. Journal of Shanghai Law School of Politics and Law (Rule of Law Series) 1. (马更新:《公司法》修订语境下的监事会制度架构变革探析》,上海政法学院学报(法治论丛),2021,第1页)
14. Nolan RC (2006) The continuing evolution of shareholder governance. Cambridge Law J 65(1):113
15. OECD (2015) Recommendation of the council on principles of corporate governance, OECD. https://legalinstruments.oecd.org/en/instruments/OECD-LEGAL-0413. Accessed 21 Sept 2020
16. Pluchart JJ (2009) Management stratégique et gouvernance d'entreprise–Management par la valeur (Strategic management and corporate governance - Value management). Editions T.I, Saint-Denis
17. Wang X (2015) Study on the legal system of state-owned enterprises. Central Compilation and Publishing House, Beijing. (王新红:《国有企业法律制度研究》,北京:中央编译出版社,2015年)
18. Wu T, Long Y (2019) European listings of Chinese companies. China Economic Press, Beijing. (吴亭亭和龙跃林:《中国企业欧洲上市》,北京,中国经济出版社,2019年)
19. Yao Y (2019) Equity capital: practical solutions for corporate equity design and operation. China Economic Press, Beijing. (姚宇峰:《股权资本:企业股权设计与运作实战方案》,北京,中国经济出版社,2019,第21页)
20. Zhang W (2015) Corporate governance and corporate performance of mixed ownership. Tsinghua University Press, Beijing. (张文魁:《混合所有制的公司治理与公司业绩》,清华大学出版社,2015年,第15页。)
21. Zhao X (2020) Controlling shareholders in corporate governance and their legal regulation. Chinese J Law 4:93

Chapter 9
Rethinking the Shareholders' Rights Protection in Chinese Financial Holding Companies Governance in the Context of New Technologies

Abstract This chapter looks at the relationship between new technologies and the protection of shareholders' rights in Chinese law. It also responds to the situation in other jurisdictions. Overall, Chinese law needs to reflect on this relationship, as it has been argued for some of the theoretical and practical conflicts. In terms of new technologies, Chinese FHC pilots can be divided into two types: traditional FHCs and internet FHCs. They focus on different issues in the face of the impact of new technologies on the protection of shareholders' rights. The digital transformation of traditional FHCs is necessary because it responds to the current policy requirements of digital corporate governance in China. It also faces competition from both domestic and international sources. Internet FHCs have an inherent advantage in terms of new technology and shareholder rights protection. At this point, they need to focus on issues beyond technology.

Keywords Digital transformation · Competitiveness · Fintech infrastructure · Technology compliance · State-owned enterprises

Among the eight FHCs pilots currently announced in China, multiple classifications have been made. For example, on the basis of whether they are listed or not, they can be classified as listed FHCs and unlisted FHCs; on the basis of the type of shareholders, they can be classified as wholly state-owned FHCs, nonstate-owned mixed-own FHCs and state-owned FHCs by shares.[1] When the book analyses the impact of new technologies on FHCs, current pilot companies can be divided into traditional FHCs and internet FHCs.[2] The typical representatives of internet FHCs are Ant Group and Suning.com, whereas the remaining six companies are all traditional FHCs. Comparatively speaking, internet FHCs are more aggressive in their application of new technologies, whereas traditional FHCs are meeting the challenges in their transformation in the face of new technologies reforming the governance of

---

[1] See Chap. 8.

[2] Based on different classification bases, it can be classified for the existing Chinese FHC regulatory pilots in different ways.

K. Ma, *Shareholder Rights Protection Mechanisms for Chinese Financial Holding Companies*, International and Comparative Law in the Asia Pacific,
https://doi.org/10.1007/978-981-97-9731-8_9

FHCs. According to the financial stability report released by the People's Bank of China in 2018, internet FHCs are an essential component of Chinese FHCs in future, and their number will grow.[3] Therefore, for classification criteria, there will be correspondingly different findings. This chapter analyses the relationship between new technologies and the protection of shareholders' rights in terms of the responses of traditional FHCs and internet FHCs to new technologies. In the face of the impact of new technologies on corporate governance, traditional FHCs and internet FHCs have different coping strategies. While traditional FHCs should achieve digital transformation, internet FHCs need to pay more attention to other stakeholders in corporate governance.

9.1 Rethinking the Digital Transformation in Chinese Traditional Financial Holding Company Governance

"Digital transformation" is a term that has received much attention, but it is not a specific legal term. However, it can often be found in legal documents in different jurisdictions. For example, in France, a regulation was passed in 2019 to create a special organisation responsible for digital transformation, namely, *la Direction interministérielle du numérique*.[4] A U.S. jurisprudence in 2012 linked the digital transformation of companies to intellectual property and financial statements.[5] The Chinese SASAC published a typical case on the digital transformation of state-owned enterprises in 2021.[6] However, there is no definition of this term by legislators. In addition, digital transformation can be understood as the introduction of digital technologies in traditional companies and the gradual reform of corporate governance and business operations. It represents a process of governance reform.

With respect to the relationship between digital transformation and the protection of shareholders' rights, digital transformation is an important way to protect shareholder rights. For Chinese FHCs in which the government is the controlling or sole shareholder, digital transformation is not only an important way to protect shareholder rights but also a national strategy. In 2020, the Chinese SASAC started

[3] See China Financial Stability Report 2018.

[4] Décret n° 2019–1088 du 25 octobre 2019 relatif au système d'information et de communication de l'Etat et à la direction interministérielle du numérique. It proves the point as a whole, and it covers all the articles.

[5] Hutchinson *v.* Perez, 2013 WL 1,775,374, 1–4 (United States District Court, S.D. New York, 2013).

[6] Notice on the Release of Typical Cases of Digital Transformation of State-owned Enterprises in 2020 (关于发布2020年国有企业数字化转型典型案例的通知). It proves the point as a whole, and it covers all the articles.

to promote the digital transformation of state-owned enterprises by means of administrative legislation.[7] The book will detail the reasons for the transformation of traditional FHCs in the context of new technologies as well as the ways in which the transformation takes place.

9.1.1 *Reasons for Digital Transformation*

There are many reasons for digital transformation, and here, the book will focus the arguments only on the protection of shareholder rights and corporate governance in FHCs. The digital transformation of FHCs is an important way to protect shareholder rights in the technological age. To realise shareholder rights, traditional Chinese FHCs should focus on improving their competitiveness to ensure long-term shareholder engagement and realise their rights to dividends. The reason why the book advocates the digital transformation of governance for traditional FHCs is that, in addition to competitive considerations, it is also a way to cater to the trend of digitalisation of corporate governance in China. This helps to provide a better understanding of the relationship between the digital transformation of corporate governance and the protection of shareholders' rights, thus demonstrating that digitalisation is a key strategy in the internal governance mechanism for the protection of shareholders' rights in future FHCs. Starting from the internal protection mechanism, the book explains the transition in two ways: the first is to respond to the policy on the protection of shareholders' rights in Chinese digital corporate governance; the second is to enhance the competitiveness of traditional Chinese FHCs.

9.1.1.1 Responding to Policies on Shareholders' Rights Protection in Chinese Digital Corporate Governance

The year 2020 is an important turning point for the digitalisation of corporate governance in China because Chinese economic policy in 2020 explicitly calls for digital transformation.[8] This is reflected in the digitalisation of corporate governance.[9] In this context, the relationship between digital corporate governance and shareholder rights in China will be further improved, mainly in the form of a redefinition of the

[7] Notice on Accelerating the Digital Transformation of State-owned Enterprises (关于加快推进国有企业数字化转型工作的通知). It proves the point as a whole, and it covers all the articles.

[8] The China Development and Reform Commission has released "Digital Transformation Partnership Action Initiative (数字化转型伙伴行动倡议)". It proves the point as a whole, and it covers all the articles.

[9] In "Notice on the Release of Typical Cases of Digital Transformation of State-owned Enterprises in 2020" the Chinese government released 100 typical cases in 8 categories including product and service innovation, intelligent production and operation, digital marketing services, digital ecology, new-generation information technology, industrial control security, integrated management system of industrialisation, and comprehensive services.

content and realisation of shareholder rights. With respect to the governance of FHCs, the regulation of FHCs in China is just on the right track, and corporate governance is still in the exploratory stage. In the face of the trend towards digital governance, FHCs cannot avoid it. Chinese digital governance policy provides a good competitive environment in which FHCs can use new technologies to achieve governance.[10] An analysis of Chinese corporate governance digitisation policies reveals two types: government-led and company-led.

In Chinese FHC pilots, government-led digital transformation is aimed mainly at wholly state-owned companies and state-owned companies by shares.[11] The main role of the government in the digital transformation of state-owned enterprises consists of six aspects.[12] First, the SASAC provides guidance. Owing to the special nature of wholly state-owned companies and state-owned companies by shares,[13] this guidance may take the form of administrative intervention in business decisions. Government intervention in this case involves the engagement of shareholders. Second, an online assessment of the organisation's digital transformation is needed. China has now launched a digital transformation service platform for SOEs, which will provide advice on transformation [9]. In 2021, the SASAC selected a total of 100 typical cases for other SOEs to follow.[14] Fourth, it promotes the construction of a collaborative innovation platform for digital transformation. This promotes cooperation between different enterprises. Fifth, it will promote a system of responsibility for the digital transformation of SOEs by the "one hand". In Chinese law, the head of an SOE is usually the Secretary-General of the Party Committee (Party group), the chairperson of the Board of Directors, and the general manager of an enterprise without a Board of Directors.[15] Sixth, exchanges and seminars on digital transformation are organised. All these measures will directly or indirectly safeguard the rights of shareholders.

---

[10] See Article 5, Digital Transformation Partnership Action Initiative. According to this provision, in order to create a fair, healthy and healthy competition mechanism, it is necessary to effectively comply with the cybersecurity law, protect data security and user privacy, and improve the work related to the transfer of training and re-employment of disadvantaged groups in the digital transformation of enterprises.

[11] See Chap. 8. Currently, there are only five, including Everbright Group, CITIC Group, China Merchants Group, Shanghai International Group, and Beijing Financial Holdings Group.

[12] See "Notice on Accelerating the Digital Transformation of State-owned Enterprises" and refer to all six points.

[13] See Chap. 8.

[14] See Notice on the Release of Typical Cases of Digital Transformation of State-owned Enterprises in 2020 (关于发布2020年国有企业数字化转型典型案例的通知). It proves the point as a whole, and it covers all the articles.

[15] See Notice of the General Office of the CPC Hubei Provincial Committee and the General Office of the Hubei Provincial People's Government on the Issuance of the Opinions on the Prevention and Control of Integrity Risks in State-owned Enterprises in Hubei Province and Five Supporting Systems (中共湖北省委办公厅、湖北省人民政府办公厅关于印发《湖北省国有企业开展廉洁风险防控工作的意见》及五个配套制度的通知). It proves the point as a whole, and it covers all the articles.

In nonstate-owned mixed FHCs, the trend towards the digitalisation of corporate governance differs somewhat from that of the government-led model. First, regulators have not issued specific guidance on the digitalisation of corporate governance in nonstate FHCs. Second, the digitalisation of corporate governance by nonstate FHCs is more likely to be perceived as a business decision. Therefore, in nonstate mixed-ownership FHCs, government policy on digital transformation is encouraging and supportive only, without much intervention.[16] The process relies more on business decisions in the governance of the FHC.

For Chinese FHCs, which are more effective at protecting shareholder rights, is the government-led or company-led drive used to digitise corporate governance? This is a complex question, as the types of shareholders are not the same. When the government is a shareholder, it is more focused on long-term interests; however, natural minority shareholders are more concerned with short-term returns. Therefore, if you look at the rights to dividend, the company-led model is more quickly validated, as evidenced in the case of Ping An Insurance. The government-led model, on the other hand, has difficulty directly observing returns to government shareholders from digital transformation, as many SOEs do not currently disclose their annual reports to the community. Therefore, it cannot be judged. However, in terms of results thus far, the company-led model has produced convincing results, whereas the government-led model has made slow progress.

9.1.1.2 Improving the Competitiveness of Traditional Chinese Financial Holding Companies

In addition to responding to the trend towards digital corporate governance in China, traditional Chinese FHCs are embracing digitalisation in terms of shareholder rights protection, which is also intended to increase their overall competitiveness. Therefore, what is competitiveness? The term is explained by the French Ministère de l'Économie, des Finances et de la Relance. From a company's point of view, it refers to a company's ability to face competition, focusing not only on the price of the products it offers but also on their quality; in addition, it reflects a company's ability to face international competition [19]. This definition is also shared by scholars [25].

Moreover, competitiveness may not be a legal term, but jurisprudence has explained its application. As an example, in a decision from Cour de Cassation in 2019, the judge in France considered that maintaining competitiveness was a different concept to improve the outcome of competition and that the existence of competition was not a reason to dismiss an employee in a competitive economy.[17] Thus, although there is no fixed legal concept of competitiveness, its application is limited by the law. For traditional FHCs in China, the competitive pressure they face stems mainly from international competition and competition from domestic internet FHCs.

---

[16] See Outline of the Fourteenth Five-Year Plan for National Economic and Social Development of the People's Republic of China and Vision 2035.

[17] Cour de cassation, civile, Chambre sociale, 10 juillet 2019, n° 17–23.274.

An explanation of the concept of competitiveness reveals that international competitiveness is a specific manifestation of competitiveness. With respect to the pilot FHCs in China, whether they are wholly state-owned FHCs, state-owned FHCs by shares or nonstate-owned mixed-ownership FHCs, the same applies to traditional Chinese FHCs. In all of them, government shareholders are actively engaged in the governance of the company. From a legal perspective, digital transformation has a positive effect on the protection of shareholders' rights, which is more evident in terms of shareholders' right to dividend. The book can use Ping An Insurance as an example for this argument, as it is the most active of the Chinese traditional FHC pilots in terms of digital transformation. The positive effect of digital transformation on the protection of shareholders' rights is reflected in two main areas. First, sustainable competitiveness delivers long-term returns for shareholders. Finance is an important core competency for the country. This view is rooted mainly in the face of international competition. Ping An Insurance released the Xinhua CN-ESG evaluation system in 2020 through AI technology.[18] It is the Chinese standard for ESG issues, and Ping An Insurance is at the forefront of China in terms of investing in and competing for the future of ESG. Moreover, it is in response to international competition, as proven by the three FHCs in other jurisdictions, including France, the U.S., and the UK, that have already made significant investments in ESG.[19] In the context of economic globalisation, a digital transformation approach to sustainability competitiveness is an accepted approach for FHCs. Second, competitive barriers can generate substantial and stable returns for shareholders. The concept of "competitive barriers" is controversial. Companies want to overcome barriers to competition to be competitive and generate substantial returns, and intellectual property can often be an effective tool in this regard. However, competition and antitrust laws restrict barriers to competition. For example, in a CJEU case in 2014,[20] it was noted that whether a "Gentlemen's Agreement" constitutes a barrier to competition and thus restricts and undermines competition in a market depends not only on the content of the agreement but also on the economic context. In the end, the judge found that "barriers to entry were not insurmountable" [22]. However, not all barriers to competition are restricted by law. From the perspective of the Chinese Anti-Monopoly Law, the regulator has provided seven exceptions to monopoly agreements, one of which is for companies to improve new technologies and develop new products.[21] Therefore, Chinese law is supportive of corporate governance to improve competitiveness through technological improvements. Ping Insurance is committed to becoming the largest internet insurance service group in China through digital transformation and

---

[18] See Ping An Insurance Annual Report 2020.

[19] See their annual reports in 2020.

[20] Case C-180/16 P Toshiba Corp. v European Commission [2017] ECLI: EU: C: 2017: 520.

[21] See Article 15, Chinese Anti-Monopoly Law. According to this provision, the circumstances that do not constitute regulated monopoly agreements include seven types, among which monopoly agreements for the improvement of technology, research and development of new products will not violate China's anti-monopoly law.

the development of a healthcare service ecosystem.[22] This could lead to substantial and stable returns for shareholders' future investments.

From the perspective of domestic competition, traditional FHCs face competitive pressure from internet FHCs. This is mainly because internet FHCs have an inherent advantage in terms of digitalisation. Therefore, traditional FHCs must accelerate the digitalisation process via transformation. This is a new requirement for competition in the internet era, which means that traditional companies must connect to digitalisation. In the case of the Chinese internet FHC pilot Ant Group, the most typical impact on traditional FHCs is mobile payments. According to a report published by a leading Chinese third-party consultancy, Ant Group's Alipay business accounted for 54.4% of the Chinese market in terms of mobile payments in 2020 [12]. However, the payments business has traditionally belonged to banks. Therefore, the competitive pressure of internet FHCs on the subsidiaries of traditional FHCs is obvious.

9.1.2 *Paths to Digital Transformation*

"Path dependence" is a concept developed in the field of political science in the 1990s that emphasises the influence of past policies on modern decision-making [20]. This theory has also been applied to corporate governance, where a company's governance structure is dependent on its earlier model [3]. This is also evident in the corporate governance of Chinese SOEs. Chinese corporate law scholars believe that the future of corporate governance in China should be free from current laws and overcome path dependence [30]. Having confirmed the importance of the transformation, it is also necessary to analyse dialectically the measures taken by these traditional FHCs in the process of digitising their governance. In addition, it is aimed at two main areas: first, with respect to the innovation of corporate governance structures. Second, we address the development of financial infrastructure.

9.1.2.1 Innovating the Governance Structures

Whether it is the company law or the code of corporate governance, there is already a basic framework for the governance structure of companies in China, which includes the board of directors, the supervisory board, and the shareholders' meeting.[23] With respect to the historical development of corporate governance worldwide, two main

[22] See Ping An Insurance Annual Report 2020.

[23] See Article 37, China Company Law. Article 17, Code of Governance for Listed Companies in China. According to this article, the election of directors and supervisors shall fully reflect the views of small and medium-sized shareholders. The cumulative voting system shall be actively implemented in the election of directors and supervisors at general meetings. Listed companies in which a single shareholder and persons acting in concert with him own 30% or more of the shares shall adopt the cumulative voting system. Listed companies that adopt the cumulative voting system shall stipulate the implementation rules in their articles of association.

models of corporate governance structures have been developed: the one-tier system and the two-tier system. Although the Chinese corporate governance structure does not strictly follow these two models,[24] it has been developed on the basis of them. In a way, this may be an innovation in Chinese law, or at least it provides an alternative model of practice. Specifically, from the perspective of shareholder rights protection, this research focuses on two improvements to the challenges posed by digitalisation to traditional FHCs: focusing on independent directors and special committees.

The supervisory role of independent directors in protecting the shareholders of FHCs has been repeatedly discussed. The composition of independent directors is a key design for their independence. Therefore, for a traditional FHC's independent directors, the company should add people with mastery of technology and FHC operations to the independent directors, which places a requirement on the background of the independent directors. Therefore, the composition is relatively reasonable from the perspective of independent directors' supervisory responsibilities.

In addition to independent directors, a recommended approach is the reform of specialised committees, a design widely found in corporate governance codes in different jurisdictions. Therefore, what is the place of specialised committees in corporate governance? Examining jurisdictions outside of China and using the corporate governance codes analysed as an example. In one-tier systems such as France, the U.S., and the UK, the specialised committee is a department under the board of directors and is responsible for assisting the board of directors in its work.[25]

Under Chinese law, specialised committees are subordinate bodies of the board of directors, as reflected in the five current corporate governance codes in China.[26] There are different requirements in different companies as to whether a specialised committee must be established. For listed companies, an audit committee is mandatory, whereas other committees are free to establish.[27] Banking and insurance institutions and securities companies are required to set up specialised

---

[24] The reason is that in Chinese listed companies, the supervisory board and the independent directors coexist. However, according to traditional theory, independent directors exist in the one-tier system, while in the two-tier system, the supervisory board performs the supervisory function of independent directors.

[25] It is reflected in the corporate governance codes of France, the U.S., and the UK.

[26] See Article 59, the Code of Governance for Securities Investment Fund Management Companies (for Trial Implementation). Article 41, the Code of Governance for Securities Companies (2020 Amendment). Article 38, the Code of Governance for Listed Companies (2018 Amendment). Article 31, the Governance Rules for Companies Listed on the National Small and Medium Enterprises Stock Transfer System. Article 55, the Code of Corporate Governance for Bancassurance Institutions. These articles all refer to the system of specialised committees.

[27] See Article 38, Code of Governance for Listed Companies in China. According to this provision, the board of directors of a listed company shall establish an audit committee and may establish relevant special committees such as strategy, nomination, remuneration and appraisal as necessary. The members of the special committees shall be composed of all directors, of which the audit committee, nomination committee and remuneration and evaluation committee shall have a majority of independent directors and shall be the convenors, and the convenor of the audit committee shall be an accounting professional.

committees.[28] Securities investment fund management companies and companies listed on the National Small and Medium-sized Enterprises (SMEs) Stock Transfer System can choose to set up one or not according to their actual needs.[29] These provisions are legally binding, as the Chinese corporate governance code is divided into a hard law model.

In the case of FHCs, the Chinese pilots have both listed companies and banking and insurance institutions for corporate governance codes. Thus, if the corresponding regulations are considered, they may appear to be designed differently for different companies. Thus, the development of a governance code for FHCs may be prompted. Among the traditional Chinese FHC pilots, the one with the most representative specialised committee in terms of digital transformation is Ping An Insurance. According to the disclosure in Ping An Insurance's 2020 annual report, its corporate governance structure consists of a general meeting of shareholders, a board of directors, a supervisory board, and an executive committee. The executive committee is the highest executive body under the board of directors. The technology development committee is set up in the executive committee, so it is in line with the provisions of the governance code for listed companies in China. In addition, there are many specialised committees within the executive committee.[30] This shows that specialised committees play a very important role in the corporate governance of Ping An Insurance. It should be a role model for the future digital transformation of traditional FHCs in China.

Therefore, in the governance of FHCs in China, specialised committees can play a positive role in helping traditional FHCs achieve digital transformation and protect shareholders' rights, and some FHCs have already made useful explorations and proven themselves in this regard. However, different types of traditional FHCs should be treated differently as to whether to establish a specialised committee on digitalisation. A one-size-fits-all approach is not necessarily conducive to shareholder rights protection.

9.1.2.2 Improving the Fintech Infrastructure

In the process of digitalisation, traditional FHCs lack adequate fintech infrastructure compared with internet FHCs.[31] While there does not seem to be a uniform legal definition of the concept of fintech infrastructure, there has been some exploration of the concept, both at a theoretical and practical level. From a theoretical perspective, in 2017, the governor of the Bank of England, Mark Carney, proposed

---

[28] See Article 55, the Code of Corporate Governance for Banking and Insurance Institutions; Article 41, the Code of Corporate Governance for Securities Firms (2020).

[29] See Article 31, the Governance Rules for Companies Listed on the National SMEs Stock Transfer System. This paragraph explains the content of this article very well.

[30] See Ping An Insurance Annual Report 2020.

[31] See Article 2, Notice on Accelerating the Digital Transformation of State-owned Enterprises (关于加快推进国有企业数字化转型工作的通知).

two concepts for fintech infrastructure, namely, the right soft infrastructure and the right hard infrastructure, and raised several questions in response to this issue. For example, it is important to consider the impact of fintech infrastructure on systemically important markets and how it differs from traditional financial infrastructure [5]. French commercial law scholars argue that AI will be an important tool for achieving corporate social responsibility and suggest that the EU's efforts in infrastructure [7]. However, there is no direct description of fintech infrastructure. From the perspective of Chinese law, in 2019, the People's Bank of China published a plan on fintech, which referred to the development of fintech infrastructure.[32] Through a generalised analysis, three main categories of fintech infrastructure are mentioned: laws and standards, information technology facilities, and telecommunications infrastructure. Therefore, legal scholars play an important role in this process.

To demonstrate the importance of this point, this book will be discussed separately from the perspective of both a case study and a theoretical analysis. More specifically, this section explores mainly traditional FHCs in a nonstate mixed-ownership model. The reasons for this are several: first, in the construction of the internal governance mechanism of an FHC, it does not focus on the wholly state-owned FHC because it is more in need of regulation. Second, among nonstate-owned mixed-ownership FHCs, traditional FHCs, represented by Ping An Insurance, have made good attempts.

Fintech infrastructure is a novel concept, and it may depend more on practical exploration as to what exactly it encompasses. The law should play an adequate role in the development of infrastructure for FHCs, as evidenced by the definition of fintech infrastructure in Chinese policies. It has also been identified from the 2019 UK jurisprudence that fintech infrastructure may be controversial in commercial practice. However, from a company law or corporate governance perspective, these are not yet sufficient to justify legislative concerns. In addition, it is important to consider society rather than a particular interest group when making rules [22]. Therefore, with laws and standards as part of the fintech infrastructure, more cases will be needed to inform the development and improvement of laws and corporate governance codes. Ping An Insurance is a very typical case in current Chinese regulatory pilots of traditional FHCs in terms of fintech infrastructure development. Moreover, it serves as a mixed-ownership FHC, which is a reference for the future transformation of Chinese wholly state-owned companies and state-owned companies by shares.[33] In 2020, Ping An Insurance defined itself as "a leading international technology-based personal financial and lifestyle services group".[34] It is the recognition of digital transformation. The case of Ping An Insurance can be used to explain the relationship between fintech infrastructure and shareholder rights protection well. Fintech infrastructure protects shareholders' rights to dividends very well. In the book, Ping An Insurance is categorised as a traditional FHC because it did not develop from an internet company.

---

[32] See Chaps. 2, 3, the Financial Technology (FinTech) Development Plan (2019–2021) (金融科技(FinTech)发展规划(2019-2021年)).

[33] See Chap. 8.

[34] See Ping An Insurance Annual Report 2020.

However, it also differs from Chinese SOEs in that it has a very decentralised shareholding structure, with no controlling shareholders and no effective controllers, and it has a global shareholder base of 938,606.[35] The combined government shareholding rate is 9.33%.[36] Dividends to shareholders for the year 2020 amounted to approximately RMB 40 billion, an increase of 7.3% year-over-year.[37] Although the role of fintech cannot be judged through its disclosures, it should be acknowledged for its positive role as an infrastructure that has helped Ping An Insurance achieve digital transformation and continuously protects shareholders' rights to dividends.

Ping An Insurance is a representative mixed-ownership FHC among the current FHCs in China and a role model for traditional Chinese FHCs in terms of digital transformation. Its corporate governance practices in relation to fintech infrastructure have also led to deeper thinking. Thus, how should traditional FHCs respond to the development of fintech infrastructure in the context of Chinese mixed-ownership reform?

While Ping An Insurance provides a good case study, it is not necessarily appropriate for all traditional FHCs in China. The main reason is that in other traditional FHC pilots in China, the shareholding structure is highly concentrated, including wholly state-owned companies and state-owned companies by shares.[38] Their development in terms of fintech infrastructure differs from that of Ping An Insurance, which has decentralised shareholding, with government shareholders playing an important role. Therefore, it is necessary to analyse the situation in the context of the current traditional FHC pilots in China.

9.2 Rethinking Digital Governance in Chinese Internet Financial Holding Companies

Traditional FHCs and internet FHCs adopt different strategies in the face of the impact of new technologies on FHCs. A traditional FHC should consider how to digitalise itself through transformation. The internet FHC is different because it has developed from a digital base, so digitalisation is in its "DNA". With the growth of internet companies, their own path-dependency model has gradually developed. However, unlike traditional FHCs, the impact of path dependency is limited in internet FHCs. The technology of internet FHCs is rapidly updated, and the inheritance model is quickly subverted by new models. The example of Ant Group, a representative of Chinese internet FHCs, is a full application of internet technology to provide financial services. Before the development of the Alibaba Group's cloud computing services,

[35] This figure is on 31 January 2021, according to page 109 of the 2020 Annual Report.

[36] Analysis based on its disclosure of the top 10 shareholders.

[37] See Ping An Insurance Annual Report 2020.

[38] See Chap. 8.

for China's large population,[39] it would have been difficult to develop data analysis of the large population without the power of the state apparatus, and website crashes used to occur due to the sheer number of visitors. This places a high demand on compliance, as when there are problems with websites, they can be accompanied by many complaints and disputed cases. However, when cloud computing was developed, these feared issues were addressed. Therefore, it is very flexible, and the path dependency is short-lived. However, the issue raised by its rapid development is how to manage relationships with other stakeholders, which is not a problem that can be solved by technology alone. From a corporate governance perspective, it is partly about achieving effective governance and partly about achieving sustainable success.

Specifically, internet FHCs need to focus on the following two issues when dealing with other stakeholders: first, how to address the relationship between shareholders and the Communist Party of China (CPC). Second, how can the technical compliance system be improved?

9.2.1 Rethinking the Relationship Between Shareholders and the Communist Party of China

Internet FHCs are very important and innovative components of Chinese FHCs, but most of them are nonstate FHCs in which the government may enter as a participant in their development but will not take a controlling stake. Among the current pilot FHCs, Ant Technology and Suning.com are such cases. Why do they still need to address the relationship with the CPC in the case of internet FHCs? One of the root causes of this problem lies in the provisions of the Chinese Company Law. Under Chinese Company Law, companies should provide conditions for the CPC to carry out their activities when the requirements of the CPC's constitution are met.[40] In addition, according to the constitution of the CPC, a party organisation should be established whenever there are three party members in the company.[41] This means that the CPC has become an almost unavoidable topic in internet FHCs. However, how is the CPC involved in corporate governance? According to Chinese company law scholars, this topic is controversial [14]. Therefore, from a practical point of view, internet FHCs need to be flexible in dealing with the relationship between shareholders and the CPC. To better explain these points, two key issues are analysed: the ways in which the CPC is involved in corporate governance and the liability of the CPC in business decision-making.

---

[39] According to the National Bureau of Statistics of China 2021 Census, the current total is 141.78 million people.

[40] See Article 19, Chinese Company Law. According to this article, in companies, organisations of the CPC shall be established, and party activities shall be carried out in accordance with the provisions of the CPC Constitution. The company shall provide the necessary conditions for the activities of the Party organisation.

[41] See Article 30, Constitution of the Communist Party of China.

9.2.1.1 Rethinking Two Fundamental Issues on the Participation of the Communist Party of China

Whether and how the CPC should be involved in corporate governance in nonpublicly owned companies is a long-standing controversial issue in Chinese company law. According to a survey conducted by Chinese researchers, as of 2018, only 48.31% of Chinese nonstate-owned enterprises had established a party organisation, compared with 27.42% in 2002 [11]. Therefore, does this mean that nonstate-owned enterprises that do not have a party organisation are in breach of company law? If viewed purely from the perspective of textual analysis, it would indeed be inconsistent with company law. However, in reality, these enterprises have not been penalised for this. Therefore, the participation of the CPC in nonstate-owned enterprises is ambiguous in real life. In the case of internet FHCs, these same issues need to be addressed. Specifically, the book needs to clarify two questions: is the CPC a political intervention or an economic intervention in the face of the application of new technologies in corporate governance, and should the participation of the CPC in an internet FHC be based on the party's constitution or the company's articles of association?

There is continuing controversy in Chinese legal circles regarding whether the participation of the CPC in corporate governance is a form of political intervention or economic participation. For example, Daxing Jiang, a leading Chinese legal scholar, argues that if the CPC is participating in corporate governance, then political interference is inevitable [14]. He also highlights some of the views of other scholars, such as that the integration of the CPC into corporate governance is a step backwards for Chinese company law.[42] However, others argue that the participation of the CPC in nonstate enterprises is different from that in state-owned enterprises. In nonstate enterprises, the CPC does not directly manage the company's employees, property, or possessions. Its role is mainly in guiding, supervising, defending rights, coordinating, and building corporate culture in the company [29]. Therefore, by summarising these points, the book can reinterpret the core questions explored here: first, can political interference be avoided when the CPC is engaged in the governance of internet FHCs? Second, if it cannot be avoided, how does one come to view its role in corporate governance?

In the case of internet FHCs, political interference by the CPC is perhaps inevitable, even though the government's shareholding ratio is not very high. The main reason for this consists of two aspects. First, nonstate enterprises may, in some cases, want political intervention by the CPC. This can be demonstrated by Chinese jurisprudence in 2019. This jurisprudence is an administrative lawsuit brought by a private enterprise against the government.[43] The court's judgement revealed that the enterprise argued that the government had no basis for imposing an administrative penalty on it. It argued that the commercial bank had been inspected by the CPC and

[42] *Ibid*.

[43] Hainan Shuanglin Gravel Processing Co., Ltd. v. People's Government of Xiuying District, Haikou City (海南双林碎石加工有限公司诉海口市秀英区人民政府,海南省海口市中级人民法院(2019)琼01行初260号行政判决书).

had not violated the government's administrative regulations. Therefore, the enterprise wanted the administrative intervention of the CPC in the commercial decision, which would have saved them from the risk of being penalised. Therefore, is this the same situation in internet FHCs? Although there is a lack of additional jurisprudential support, it is believed that such support is inevitable in the long-term future. This might be considered a path dependency of the CPC's participation in corporate governance. Second, in nonstate enterprises, membership in the CPC intersects with the management of the company. This combines the participation of the CPC with the management's administration. According to a related study, 56% of the chairpersons of private listed companies in China during the period of 2004–2014 were members of the CPC [8]. This means that the chairperson will also be a member of the CPC. Therefore, in this case, there is a mixture of political intervention by the CPC and the management of the company. Returning to the internet FHC pilot studied. According to their disclosures, the CPC is not included in the corporate governance structure, as evidenced by the prospectus of Ant Group [28] and the annual report of Sunning.com.[44] However, they both have established party organisations and many party members among their staff [25]. Therefore, political interference by the CPC is inevitable in internet FHCs, especially in regard to compliance with basic state policies.

In addition, the article of association is an important basis for the participation of various stakeholders in the governance of a company [17]. It provides a detailed explanation of the company's governance structure, which is an important way of reflecting shareholder freedom and democracy. Therefore, if the CPC is engaged in corporate governance, then it should be reflected in the company's articles of association. As Ant Group is not yet listed and its articles of association are not disclosed to the public, the book has chosen another internet FHC, Suning.com, for analysis. According to the articles of association disclosed by Suning.com, the CPC is not described or explained. Therefore, what is the CPC participating in governance according to Suning.com? According to the documents disclosed by Suning.com in 2018 [24], it is mainly in accordance with the Constitution of the CPC. Moreover, in terms of Chinese company law, the company also performs the activities of the CPC on the basis of the Constitution of the CPC.[45] Therefore, at present, the participation of the CPC in corporate governance is mainly based on the Constitution of the CPC.

At this point, the party constitution and the articles of association coexist in the governance of an internet FHC. How, then, can their relationship be understood? Theoretically, they are bound by different objects. The party constitution binds members of the CPC.[46] Specifically, in the case of an internet FHC, it is supposed to bind the party members in the company. In contrast, the articles of association bind

[44] See Suning.com Annual Report 2020.

[45] See Article 19, Chinese Company Law.

[46] See Constitution of the Communist Party of China.

the company, its shareholders, directors, supervisors, and senior management.[47] This has been confirmed by the jurisprudence of the Chinese Supreme Court and affirms that the articles of association are the most important rule of autonomy for a company [17]. According to the Supreme Court's interpretation, the articles of association then take precedence over the Party's constitution in corporate governance. It returns to the contractual attributes of a company, as French jurists have noted [10]. It is in line with the definition of the foundations of a company.

From a practical point of view, regarding the issue of corporate governance, if there is a conflict between the articles of association and the party constitution or between the articles of association and a resolution made in accordance with the party constitution, which should take precedence? In the case of Suning.com [26], neither its articles of association nor the party constitution explains the issue. However, theoretically, the articles of association are the most important autonomy rule of the company, and in the event of a dispute [10], the articles of association should take precedence within the scope of autonomy. In addition, a Chinese case law in 2020 supported this view.[48] Although the parties to the dispute in this case did not involve an internet FHC, it involved a nonstate-owned enterprise,[49] so it may provide a reference for the governance of internet FHCs in future. This case law establishes that in corporate governance, the CPC is not free to infringe on the rights of stakeholders in corporate governance through resolutions adopted by the party constitution.

9.2.1.2 Rethinking the Participation of the Communist Party of China in Developing Business Decisions

Apart from the way in which the CPC is involved in FHCs, another controversial issue is what the relationship between the CPC and shareholders looks like in business decisions. Why is it important for companies to manage this relationship? In addition, it has a dynamic relationship. The CPC in internet FHCs may intervene in business decisions through their resolutions, which may pose a threat to the protection of shareholders' rights. To explain the relationship between the CPC and shareholders in business decisions, the book analyses the CPC in terms of their sources of rights and liabilities.

It is argued that there is a legal basis for the participation of the CPC in the governance of internet FHCs but that the provisions of company law are very general. It is not clear what the activities of the CPC are, but do they include the business decisions of the internet FHC? It may appear differently in different companies. In

[47] See Article 11, Chinese Company Law. Under this provision, the articles of association must be drawn up in accordance with the law to establish a company. The articles of association are binding on the company, its shareholders, directors, supervisors and senior management.

[48] Liuzhou Guosheng Real Estate Development Co. v. Bian Liming (柳州市国盛房地产开发有限公司诉边利明,广西壮族自治区柳州市中级人民法院(2020)桂02民终2113号民事判决书).

[49] It refers mainly to wholly state-owned enterprises and state-owned joint stock companies.

the case of Suning.com's articles of association, there is no provision for the role and status of the CPC in corporate governance. It is believed that the CPC has no right to participate in the company's decision-making.

However, a different view is shown in the 2020 case.[50] Although the decision did not concern an FHC, it also shows that the CPC in nonstate enterprises may have the right to participate in business decisions. Since it is agreed upon in its articles of association that the CPC can make decisions on important matters before the company, the CPC may at this point be engaged in the commercial decisions of the company. Therefore, in the absence of explicit provisions in the law on the participation of the CPC in business decisions, a company may agree through its articles regarding whether the CPC can participate in the company's business decisions. Its rights also derive from the joint resolution of shareholders. This view is also recognised by business practice. For example, in 2017, a listed company in China wanted to include a provision for the CPC in its articles of association, but this proposal was rejected at the shareholders' meeting [28]. This means that corporate governance mechanisms should respect the wishes of shareholders when shareholders of nonstate enterprises do not want the CPC to be involved in business decisions.

When confronted with the participation of the CPC in internet FHCs, there are three confusing issues: the establishment of party organisations in internet FHCs; the participation of the CPC in the governance of internet FHCs; and the participation of the CPC in the business decisions of internet FHCs. First, the establishment of a party organisation in an internet FHC is provided with a legal basis by the Chinese Company Law, whereas the right of the CPC to participate in corporate governance and business decision-making is derived from the resolutions and articles of associations of the general meeting of shareholders. However, the participation of the CPC in corporate governance does not necessarily mean that they can participate in business decision-making. The CPC has an active role in risk management, and internet FHCs can limit the scope for the CPC to participate in corporate governance through their articles of association. However, in regard to business decisions, especially those involving internet technology, the source of their right to participate should be the common will of shareholders.

With respect to the liabilities of the Communist Party of China, it is understood that in Chinese internet FHCs, the participation of the CPC in corporate governance or business decisions is dependent on shareholder resolutions or articles of association. However, it is important to note that from the current pilot internet FHCs, the participation of the CPC in corporate governance is not provided for in the company's articles of association. Naturally, several other types of companies whose articles of association provide clarity from a jurisprudential perspective have been identified. However, from the perspective of the future long-term development of internet FHCs, if the CPC is to be engaged in the business decisions of the company, then the corresponding liabilities of the CPC should also be defined. The Chinese legal system is heavily influenced by Marx. The Marxist proposition that there are no rights without

[50] Liuzhou Guosheng Real Estate Development Co. v. Bian Liming (柳州市国盛房地产开发有限公司诉边利明,广西壮族自治区柳州市中级人民法院(2020)桂02民终2113号民事判决书).

obligations and no obligations without rights [23]. It has also been advocated in the study of Chinese law [15]. The same is true for the CPC. Once the CPC has the right to participate in an internet FHC through its articles of association, its corresponding obligations and responsibilities should also be stated at the same time. This view is also recognised by Chinese jurisprudence researchers. Some scholars have studied the status of the CPC in SOEs and reported that the responsibilities of the CPC are often not sufficiently explained [15]. The Chinese government also seems to be aware of the importance of the issue. A 2017 Chinese State Council on governance in SOEs clearly stated the legal status of the CPC in the governance of SOEs and clarified their rights and obligations.[51] However, there is no detailed guidance or explanation of the responsibilities of the CPC in nonstate-owned enterprises.

If the CPC is to be held accountable in the business decisions of an internet FHC, what liabilities should it assume? There is some controversy here. The main issue is whether the articles of association can bind the CPC. The reason is that, according to the Chinese Company Law, the articles of association are binding on the company, its shareholders, directors, supervisors, and senior management.[52] Some scholars have argued that it is possible to make the liability of the CPC explicit in the company's articles of association [15]. However, the conflict here is that if it is stated in the articles of association, it would conflict with the provisions of the Chinese Company Law, as it would be contrary to the provisions of the company law on the objects of binding on the articles of association.

The binding nature of the statute contains both natural and legal persons under the provisions of company law. However, the legal person is a company, and the others are liable in the form of a natural person. Does the CPC, as a kind of institutional design in a company, need to be independently liable? Or is it the party members who are liable? If the CPC needs to be independently liable, then this will also lead to a change in company law. However, if the liability is to be borne by party members, then it should be based on the party constitution, party rules and other civil, criminal, and administrative regulations. At this point, it can be found that this goes beyond the internal governance of the company and resorts to regulation. This means that there is a lack of appropriate mechanisms in corporate governance for the liability of the CPC. If there is a lack of mechanisms of checks and balances in internal governance, this can easily lead to infringement by the CPC on shareholders, as has been demonstrated in the preceding jurisprudence.[53] Therefore, from the perspective of protecting shareholders' rights, the participation of the CPC in business decisions should be carefully decided in internet FHCs. In the absence of a well-developed internal liability mechanism, it may be an appropriate option under Chinese law for the CPC not to participate in business decisions.

---

[51] See Guidance from the General Office of the State Council on Further Improving the Corporate Governance Structure of State-owned Enterprises (国务院办公厅关于进一步完善国有企业法人治理结构的指导意见). It proves the point as a whole, and it covers all the articles.

[52] See Article 11, Chinese Company Law.

[53] Liuzhou Guosheng Real Estate Development Co. v. Bian Liming (柳州市国盛房地产开发有限公司诉边利明,广西壮族自治区柳州市中级人民法院(2020)桂02民终2113号民事判决书).

9.2.2 Rethinking the Technology Compliance System

In an internet FHC, despite its advantages in the face of new technologies, it should avoid the misuse of technology in corporate governance when technology compliance is important. Therefore, what is technology compliance? Over the past few years, Chinese law has paid attention to this issue. Throughout the Chinese legal system, there are three main areas where technology compliance is regulated: the operation of securities funds,[54] the import and export of technology,[55] and the transport of goods by road on online platforms.[56] In the area of securities fund operation, Chinese law explains that in relation to technical compliance, the process design, function setting, parameter configuration and technical implementation of the securities fund operation system should follow the principle of business compliance and should not violate the laws and regulations of the CSRC.[57] Moreover, technical compliance and risk management are in conjunction with each other. In addition, in road cargo transportation on online platforms, Chinese law provides a detailed explanation of technical compliance standards.[58]

In addition, technical compliance is an internationally recognised trend. In the jurisdictions studied, technology compliance has received similar attention in recent years. For example, the EU's regulatory proposal in 2021 suggests that some Member States, such as France, are already considering national legal tools to ensure compliance with the fundamental rights and duties regime for AI. The UK also updated its "Technology Code of Practice" in 2021, with "Public Services Network (PSN) compliance' for compliance" [4]. North Dakota has a direct provision on technology compliance in the U.S. law, which states that technology compliance should be

[54] Information Technology Management Measures for Securities and Fund Operators (Amendment 2021) (证券基金经营机构信息技术管理办法(2021修正)). It proves the point as a whole, and it covers all the articles.

[55] Ministry of Commerce and General Administration of Customs Announcement No. 66 of 2020–Announcement of Matters Relating to the Application for Import and Export Licences for Dual-Use Items and Technologies and Paperless Customs Clearance (商务部、海关总署公告2020年第66号——公布两用物项和技术进出口许可证申领和通关无纸化有关事项). It proves the point as a whole, and it covers all the articles.

[56] See Notice of the General Office of the Ministry of Transport on Further Improving the Monitoring of Road Cargo Transport Information on the Network Platform (交通运输部办公厅关于进一步做好网络平台道路货物运输信息化监测工作的通知). It proves the point as a whole, and it covers all the articles.

[57] See Article 14, Measures for the Administration of Information Technology of Securities and Fund Operators (amended 2021) (证券基金经营机构信息技术管理办法(2021修正)). According to this provision, before engaging in securities and fund business activities by means of information technology, securities, and fund operators shall carry out internal reviews to ensure compliance with the law in terms of parameters, technology, and establish archival records.

[58] See Annex I, Notice from the General Office of the Ministry of Transport on Further Improving the Monitoring of Road Cargo Transport Information on the Network Platform (交通运输部办公厅关于进一步做好网络平台道路货物运输信息化监测工作的通知).

conducted by the information technology committee and that compliance should address information technology plans, standards, and policies, etc.[59]

Therefore, to better protect shareholders' rights, internet FHCs should have a newer understanding of technical compliance. This is manifested in two ways. First, Chinese internet FHCs should clarify the standards for technology compliance. Second, Chinese internet FHCs should innovate their monitoring mechanisms for technology compliance.

9.2.2.1 Rethinking the Standards for Technology Compliance

Corporate compliance has a long history of development [6]. However, there is much debate about compliance standards. In the case of Chinese law, there is thus far no uniform corporate compliance standard in China, and the current corporate governance code does not incorporate a compliance regime [6]. As a more specific area of corporate compliance, there are even fewer technical compliance standards. The history of corporate compliance in China is not long, and there are a variety of corporate compliance standards. At the international level, there is a set of guideline standards for compliance. For example, in April 2021, the International Organisation for Standardisation published the corporate compliance standard ISO 37301, which replaced the ISO 19600 standard published in 2014. This standard is considered to incorporate compliance in the internet sector. Therefore, the book can consider this to be a recommended standard for technical compliance in future. However, after the release of the ISO 19600 standard in 2014, China did not establish a specific corporate compliance system as a result. Therefore, how should China apply the newly released ISO 37301 to the practice of internet FHCs? To address this point, this book presents two aspects related to the selection and implementation of technology compliance standards.

For the corporate compliance system in Chinese law, since the 1980s, a corporate compliance regime has been gradually introduced into Chinese law [24]. The earliest compliance standards in China were promulgated in 1989 for auditing.[60] It was followed by the Bank of Chinese publication of compliance standards in 1989, which was the earliest industry standard for corporate compliance in China.[61] Thereafter, in 2006, Chinese banking regulators lay down and interpreted compliance risk standards for commercial banks, which was also the earliest compliance

---

[59] See § 54-10-28, North Dakota Century Code. According to this provision, the State Auditor may conduct IT compliance reviews through individual agency audits of IT management, IT plan compliance, and IT standards and son on.

[60] Including "Interim Regulations on Auditing by the Ministry of Home Affairs" (民政部审计工作暂行规定), Auditing Regulations of the Ministry of Home Affairs on Breaches of Financial Discipline" (民政部关于违反财经纪律的审计规定), "Compliance Standards for Auditing the Financial and Accounting Work of Ministry of Home Affairs" (民政部单位财会工作审计合规标准). In addition, they prove the points as a whole, and they cover all the articles.

[61] The Bank of China Accountability for Compliance with the Law (中国银行依法合规经营责任制). It proves the point as a whole, and it covers all the articles.

regulation in China around corporate governance. Therefore, compliance in the banking sector has always been a major focus of the Chinese economic market. The real close attention to compliance in China started mainly after 2012, when China enacted specific compliance regulations for securities companies, insurance companies, enterprises operating abroad, central enterprises, banks' foreign exchange business, anti-monopoly compliance, securities companies, and securities investment fund management companies.[62]

An analysis of the Chinese corporate compliance regime and development history reveals that although China does not have a specific compliance standard for FHCs, a system of compliance standards for subsidiaries of FHCs has been built under Chinese law. Therefore, at this point, for the technical compliance standards for internet FHCs, there are two main questions: first, is it better to use the existing compliance standards directly or to specifically develop technical compliance standards for internet FHCs? Second, can an internet FHC develop its own technical compliance standards through its internal corporate governance mechanisms?

In relation to the first issue, there is a need to develop a dedicated technical compliance standard. When a dedicated technical compliance standard is developed, that standard is no longer limited to internet FHCs, as traditional FHCs face technical compliance issues. The book advocates the development of a dedicated technology compliance standard because there is still a lack of technology compliance standards suitable for FHCs from the current Chinese corporate compliance regime. Furthermore, the development of technical compliance standards is an international trend, which has been evidenced in the jurisdictions studied, such as the EU, the U.S., and the UK. Therefore, if China lacks focus in this area, then this does not bode well for the international competition of Chinese FHCs in future. In this context, the importance of compliance was demonstrated in 2017 when the Chinese technology company ZTE penalised compliance issues in its investments in the U.S. [6]. For the second question, internet FHCs can develop technical compliance standards through internal corporate governance mechanisms. There are already precedents for this in the context of Chinese law; for example, the Bank of China already developed

[62] They include "Guidelines for Assessing the Effectiveness of Compliance Management of Securities Companies (证券公司合规管理有效性评估指引)", "Circular of the General Office of the State Council on Further Strengthening Trade Policy Compliance (国务院办公厅关于进一步加强贸易政策合规工作的通知)", "Measures for Compliance Management of Insurance Companies (保险公司合规管理办法) ", "Implementation Guidelines for Compliance Management of Securities Companies (证券公司合规管理实施指引)", "Compliance Management of Enterprises' Overseas Operations(企业境外经营合规管理指引)", "Guidelines on Compliance Management of Enterprises' Overseas Operations and Guidelines on Compliance Management of Central Enterprises (for Trial Implementation) (中央企业合规管理指引(试行))", "Measures on Compliance and Prudent Operation Assessment of Banks' Foreign Exchange Business (银行外汇业务合规与审慎经营评估办法)", "Guidelines on Anti-monopoly Compliance of Operators (经营者反垄断合规指南)", "Measures on Compliance Management of Securities Companies and Securities Investment Fund Management Companies (证券公司和证券投资基金管理公司合规管理办法)". In addition, they prove the points as a whole, and they cover all the articles.

corporate compliance standards from a corporate governance perspective in 1999.[63] Therefore, in the absence of specific provisions on technical compliance standards in current Chinese law, internet FHCs can refer to ISO 37301 in their corporate governance to improve the internal governance of technology compliance and to protect the rights of shareholders.

With respect to the implementation of technology compliance standards, the binding nature of a technical compliance standard is an issue that can be confusing. European scholars consider it to be similar to soft law at this stage, but in the course of its development, it is gradually converted from national law to European directives, at which point it becomes hard law and businesses need to pay sufficient attention to it [2]. Indeed, if the book looks at the content of compliance, it is usually understood that it should comply with the law, as evidenced by corporate governance codes in other jurisdictions.[64] Therefore, internet FHCs are obliged to comply with these provisions, as the legal requirements for technical compliance standards are legally binding.

In accordance with the principle of "complying or explaining", compliance with the corporate governance code is not legally binding. Therefore, are compliance statements with the code also subject to soft law effects? This requires a look again at the binding nature of corporate governance codes. Most corporate governance codes are "recommendations", which are soft laws in nature. Some jurisdictions, such as France and the UK, have corporate governance codes that explicitly state that all provisions are soft law. Therefore, for technical compliance standards, if there are already national laws and regulations governing this, then it is undoubtedly legally binding. However, if it is not specifically regulated by national laws or regulations or if it is a corporate governance code or a company-designed compliance standard, then it is not legally enforceable.

Therefore, how binding are the technical compliance standards in Chinese law? First, those technical compliance standards that have been or will be explicitly set out in laws and regulations fall under the binding category of hard law; second, the technical compliance standards set out in corporate governance codes are also hard law. Second, the technical compliance standards stipulated in the code of corporate governance are also legally binding, as the code of corporate governance in China is recognised more as hard law than soft law. The articles of association may be used as a basis for judges' decisions [21].

9.2.2.2 Rethinking the Monitoring of Technology Compliance

Compliance is not a new thing for corporate governance. Although there is no specific institutional design for technical compliance, some clues can be found in the design of past corporate compliance oversight. Monitoring is necessary, as there are many

[63] See Legal Compliance Responsibility System of Bank of China 1999 (中国银行依法合规经营责任制1999). It proves the point as a whole, and it covers all the articles.

[64] See the corporate governance codes in France, the USA, and the UK.

cases of compliance corruption. For example, in a UK jurisprudence in 2019,[65] the decision confirmed the failure of the audit committee in corporate governance for compliance monitoring. This failure may be due to auditor negligence. In companies that rely on the audit committee for compliance monitoring, the key to successful corporate governance is whether "reliance" can be achieved. Although the interpretation of "reliance" in the law can be influenced by "legal causation", as in this case law, judges distinguish between the true legal cause of loss and "merely the occasion". This distinction can have an impact on the court's judgement on compliance monitoring, which ultimately affects whether "reliance" is achieved. The financial crisis, including the cases of Lehman Brothers and Enron, has shown that compliance without monitoring is not immune to fraud and corruption. There are many regulatory efforts in this area, such as "La loi Sapin II", which came into force in France in 2017 and imposes higher requirements for compliance as an obligation for companies [16].

Thus, in an internet FHC, technical compliance is about avoiding systemic risks due to technical corruption and thus avoiding damage to shareholders' rights, which has been proven historically and should be considered in the future development of the company. Specifically, a detailed analysis of technical compliance in terms of disclosure and whistleblower protection systems is presented here.

There is currently no specific explanation for technical compliance disclosures. The corresponding system for such disclosure is still under construction and improvement. However, the Chinese law on the regulation of technology compliance in securities and fund operators provides a description of the matters that need to be disclosed, and it requires securities and fund operators to disclose contingency plans for information system failures.[66] However, from a corporate governance perspective, the transparency of technology compliance should not stop there. In theory, compliance disclosure should fall under the category of a way to improve the transparency of corporate governance, so it is similar to matters such as financial disclosure and executive compensation disclosure, which are a means of regulating corporate governance.

Currently, there is a lack of effective guidance and recommendations in corporate governance codes for technology compliance disclosures. From a practical perspective, it can be found for the practices of three FHCs in the other jurisdictions studied, as well as the Chinese internet FHC pilots Ant Group and Suning.com, in relation to technology compliance disclosures. The survey revealed that there are currently no representative cases in this regard. Overall, FHCs are beginning to explore the use of new technologies to improve compliance, such as the smart compliance programme launched by Crédit Agricole S.A. in France, which hopes to improve compliance

[65] AssetCo plc v Grant Thornton UK LLP [2019] EWHC 150 (Comm).

[66] See Article 38, Measures for the Administration of Information Technology of Securities and Fund Operators (amended 2021) (证券基金经营机构信息技术管理办法(2021修正)). According to this provision, securities fund operators should formulate and continuously improve emergency response plans, including emergency management construction objectives, backup information system construction and recovery mechanisms, backup data recovery mechanisms, and should provide explanations on emergency response plan disclosure.

disclosure and experience through internet technology over the next three years.[67] However, compliance with technology itself may still be in the exploratory stage. FHCs are currently concerned with the risks that technology may pose through risk management disclosures.

Notably, in relation to technology compliance disclosures, legal academics noted in 2010 that technology often lacks transparency. This creates considerable ambiguity for those seeking to monitor compliance with the internal and external operations of companies, which can easily lead to some significant risks. As a result, there is still a long way to go in terms of relevant disclosure [1]. The practice of internet FHCs still needs time to be explored in relation to technology compliance disclosures.

In addition, the whistleblowing system assumes an important monitoring function and is one of the reference criteria for the evaluation of corporate governance. At the same time, it is an important way of protecting the rights of shareholders. The definition of a whistleblower needs to be interpreted in a specific context. In corporate governance, it usually refers to the employees of the company [18]. This can be confirmed in the whistleblowing policies disclosed by Crédit Agricole S.A. and HSBC in their annual reports.[68] However, in business practice, companies can define whistleblowers according to the actual circumstances. For example, HSBC considers whistleblowers to include not only current employees but also past employees.[69]

Furthermore, there is some controversy over the connotations of whistleblowers. For example, in the context of the EU's Directive on whistleblower protection in 2019, researchers have argued that whistleblowers include those who report through both internal and external reporting channels [27]. However, some scholars argue that whistleblowers refer mainly to those who report to regulators.[70] Therefore, the definition of whistleblower in the book adopts a broader interpretation to include reporters from both internal and external reporting.

In terms of international standards for compliance, whistleblowing tools and processes are encouraged as a way of managing compliance in the newly published ISO 37301 [13]. In addition, Europe enacted a directive on whistleblower systems in 2019, which benefits from the French la loi Sapin II and builds on French law to establish protection for whistleblowers at the European level [18]. In U.S. law, in 2015, the federal investigation process for complaints was further refined on the basis of the Sarbanes–Oxley Act, reducing the burden and cost for whistleblowers.[71] In UK law, there was even specific legislation for employee whistleblowing as early as 1998.[72]

---

[67] See Crédit Agricole S.A. Annual Report 2020.

[68] See their 2020 annual reports.

[69] See HSBC Annual Report 2020.

[70] For example, Professor Jennifer Arlen endorses this view in the course "Economic Analysis of Corporate Misconduct" organised by the Norwegian School of Economics in May 2021.

[71] See § 1980.104, Code of Federal Regulations. This provision sets out the whistleblowing procedure and the process by which the regulator will deal with whistleblowing matters.

[72] See Public Interest Disclosure Act 1998 (PIDA). It proves the point as a whole, and it covers all the articles.

Chinese law currently lacks specific provisions on the protection of whistleblowers in corporate governance. The provisions of Chinese law on the whistleblower system can be divided into two categories. The first category focuses on reporting illegal and criminal activities to state authorities or industry associations. For example, the provisions of the Chinese Criminal Procedure Law and the report on the illegal and irregular behaviour of internet financial institutions issued by the China internet Finance Association in 2016.[73] The second category focuses on the reporting of corruption by state officials. For example, in 2016, the Supreme People's Procuratorate and other authorities jointly issued regulations on the protection system for whistleblowers of official crimes.[74] Therefore, there is a lack of special provisions in Chinese law for a whistleblower protection system for employees in corporate governance.

The protection system for employee whistleblowers in Chinese law is not well developed, and in the future governance of internet FHCs, it will require them to actively innovate their corporate governance mechanisms. Internet FHCs are more likely to be disruptors of fixed models than traditional FHCs are. The employee whistleblowing case of China Life Insurance Company in 2021 has attracted much attention from Chinese people. This situation may lead to progress in future regulation. However, as far as current governance is concerned, better and more innovative models from internet FHCs can be expected. This has already been demonstrated in the many disruptive models brought about by internet technology. In addition, it will be expected for the whistleblower protection system!

References

1. Bamberger KA (2010) Technologies of compliance: risk and regulation in a digital age. Texas Law Review 4:732
2. Boursier ME et al (2020) Code de la compliance. Dalloz, Paris
3. Branson DM (2012) Global convergence in corporate governance? What a difference 10 years make. In: Thomas C, Branson D (ed) The SAGE handbook of corporate governance, SAGE Publications Ltd, London
4. Cabinet office (2015) Public services network (PSN) compliance, Cabinet Office. https://www.gov.uk/guidance/public-services-network-psn-compliance. Accessed 21 Sept 2020
5. Carney M (2017) Building the infrastructure to realise fintech's promise, Bank of England. https://www.bankofengland.co.uk/speech/2017/building-the-infrastructure-to-realise-FinTechs-promise. Accessed 21 Sept 2021
6. Chen R (2020) Basic issues of corporate compliance. China Law Review 1:180. (陈瑞华:《企业合规的基本问题》,中国法律评论,2020年第1期,第180页)

[73] See Announcement on the Opening of the internet Financial Reporting Information Platform (关于开通互联网金融举报信息平台的公告). It proves the point as a whole, and it covers all the articles.

[74] See Several Provisions of the Supreme People's Procuratorate, the Ministry of Public Security and the Ministry of Finance on the Protection and Reward of Whistleblowers for Official Offences (最高人民检察院、公安部、财政部关于保护、奖励职务犯罪举报人的若干规定). It proves the point as a whole, and it covers all the articles.

7. Council of Europe (2020) SDG 9: Build resilient infrastructure, promote sustainable industrialization and foster innovation, Council of Europe. https://www.coe.int/fr/web/un-agenda-2030/goal 9. Accessed 21 Sept 2021
8. Dai Y et al (2017) Party membership of private enterprise chairpersons and corporate financial irregularities. Accounting Research 6:75. (戴亦一(等):《民营企业董事长的党员身份与公司财务违规》,会计研究,2017年第6期,第75页)
9. Digital Transformation Service Platform (2022) Digital transformation in state-owned enterprises (国有企业数字化转型专题), Digital transformation service platform. http://gq.dlttx.com/. Accessed 21 Sept 2020
10. Germain M, Magnier V (2017) Traité de droit des affaires. Tome 2, Les sociétés commerciales. LGDJ, Paris
11. He X et al. (2019) Analysed the current situation of party organisation construction in Chinese private enterprises. 3rd Edn. China Business Times. (何轩 等:《我国民营企业党组织建设现状分析报告》,中华工商时报,2019年第3版)
12. Iresearch (2020) Chinese third party payment industry research report 2020 (2020年中国第三方支付行业研究报告), Iresearch. http://report.iresearch.cn/report/202004/3552.shtml. Accessed 21 Sept 2021
13. Jaric A, Loewenthal H (2021) Notable developments in the new ISO standard for compliance management systems, Deloitte. https://www2.deloitte.com/au/en/blog/risk-advisory-blog/2021/notable-developments-new-iso-standard-compliance-management-systems.html. Accessed 21 Sept 2021
14. Jiang D (2017) Towards "Political corporate law": how party organisations can participate in corporate governance. J Cent South Univ (Social Science Edition) 3: 29. (蒋大兴:《走向"政治性公司法"——党组织如何参与公司治理》,中南大学学报(社会科学版),2017年第3期,第29页)
15. Jiang J, LI Y (2017) On the role of company articles of association in the participation of party organisations in the governance of state-owned enterprises. J Cent South Univ (Social Science Edition) 3: 38. (蒋建湘和李依伦:《论公司章程在党组织参与国企治理中的作用》,中南大学学报(社会科学版),2017年第3期,第38页)
16. LexisNexis (2017) Sapin 2: Quand la conformité devient une exigence légale, LexisNexis. https://bis.lexisnexis.fr/blog/article/sapin2-obligations. Accessed 21 Sept 2020
17. Liu B (2021) A review of corporate ideation mechanisms in the context of corporate governance. J China Univ Polit Sci Law 2:141. (刘斌:《公司治理视域下公司表意机制之检讨》,中国政法大学学报,2021年第2期,第141页)
18. Magnier V (2020) Le lanceur d'alerte-actionnaire ou mandataire social, un acteur "stratégique" de la gouvernance des sociétés (The whistleblower-shareholder or corporate officer: a "strategic" player in corporate governance). Recueil Dalloz 1307
19. Minister for the Economy, Finance and Economic Recovery (2019) La compétitivité (The competitiveness), Minister for the Economy, Finance and Economic Recovery. https://www.economie.gouv.fr/facileco/competitivite. Accessed 21 Sept 2020
20. Palier B (2010) Path dependence. Dictionnaire des politiques publiques (Dictionary of Public Policy) 411
21. Qian Y (2021) The reconstruction of China's company law system: an interpretivist perspective. Political Science and Law 2:2. (钱玉林:《我国《公司法》体系的重构:一种解释论的观点》,《政治与法律》2021年第2期,第2页)
22. Rousseau S (2009) L'analyse économique du droit (Economic analysis of law). In: Lienhard A (ed) Recueil dalloz. Dalloz, Paris. Schmuck R (2008) Measuring company competitiveness. In: Proceedings papers of business sciences: symposium for young researchers (FIKUSZ) 2008, Budapest, 2008
23. Shu G (2012) Introduction to jurisprudence. Peking University Press, Peking. (舒国滢:《法理学导论》,北京:北京大学出版社,2012年)
24. Sun C (2021) On corporate compliance as a regulatory incentive. Administrative Reform 4:84. (孙春蕾:《论作为监管激励机制的企业合规》,行政管理改革,2021年第4期,第84页)

25. Suning.com (2018) Management of the restructuring of the party organisation and the re-election of members of suning holdings group (苏宁控股集团党组织架构调整及委员改选管理办法), Suning.com. http://www.suning.cn/cms/partyPolicy2018/22944.htm. Accessed 21 Sept 2020
26. Suning.com (2018) Party building five-year development outline (2018–2022) (苏宁党建五年发展纲要(2018–2022), Suning.com. http://www.suning.cn/cms/partyPolicy2018/22937.htm. Accessed 21 Sept 2020
27. Vandekerckhove W (2021) Is it freedom? The coming about of the EU directive on whistleblower protection. J Bus Ethics 6
28. Wang Y (2017) Party-enterprise integration: Chinese wisdom and paths for corporate governance. Board of Directors 11:59. (王勇华:《"党企融合":公司治理的中国智慧与路径》,董事会,2017年第11期,第59页)
29. Yang D (2018) The reinvention of the firm: financial markets and the modern transformation of Chinese enterprises. Social Science Literature Press, Beijing. (杨典:《公司的再造:金融市场与中国企业的现代转型》,北京:社会科学文献出版社,2018年,第240页)
30. Zhao X (2021) Dilemmas and pathways of Chinese corporate governance system, Modern Law Science, 2, p 89. (赵旭东:《中国公司治理制度的困境与出路》,现代法学,2021年第2期,第89页)

Appendix A

Survey on the Financial Supervision of 192 Member States of the United Nations (China Excluded)

K. Ma, *Shareholder Rights Protection Mechanisms for Chinese Financial Holding Companies*, International and Comparative Law in the Asia Pacific,
https://doi.org/10.1007/978-981-97-9731-8

Serial number	Member States of UN	Continent	Is there a central bank? If yes, please directly specify it and the reference	Is there a banking regulatory authority? If so, please describe directly it or them and the reference	Is there an insurance regulatory authority? If so, please describe directly it or them and the reference	Is there a securities market regulatory authority? If so, please describe directly it and the reference	Is there a financial holding company? If so, please directly show references
1	Benin	Africa	The Central Bank of West African States (https://www.bceao.int/en/content/presentation-bceao)	The Central Bank of West African States (https://books.google.fr/books?id=YAcJWep3Lk0C&pg=PA22&lpg=PA22&dq=benin+commercial+bank+regulation+authority&source=bl&ots=JpQEgEHNPB&sig=ACfU3U3CGw1EkpaM85lvBNely7X8feY5aw&hl=fr&sa=X&ved=2ahUKEwjQtYSa38TqAhVBxhoKHUGjC8YQ6AEwAXoECAoQAQ#v=onepage&q=benin%20commercial%20bank%20regulation%20authority&f=false)	Commission Régionale de Contrôle des Assurances (https://cima-afrique.org/crca-membres-2/)	The Central Bank of West African States (https://books.google.fr/books?id=KHFZg5ORFSYC&pg=RA1-PA34&lpg=RA1-PA34&dq=benin+securities+market+regulatory+authority&source=bl&ots=K3J94mGmub&sig=ACfU3U1x9kaEOtbwgasLyCd7YqPt_uJP5A&hl=fr&sa=X&ved=2ahUKEwiCr9mX6sTqAhWF2uAKHdznCUIQ6AEwAXoECAgQAQ#v=onepage&q=benin%20securities%20market%20regulatory%20authority&f=false)	https://en.wikipedia.org/wiki/Bank_of_Africa_Group

(continued)

(continued)

Serial number	Member States of UN	Continent	Is there a central bank? If yes, please directly specify it and the reference	Is there a banking regulatory authority? If so, please describe directly it or them and the reference	Is there an insurance regulatory authority? If so, please describe directly it or them and the reference	Is there a securities market regulatory authority? If so, please describe directly it and the reference	Is there a financial holding company? If so, please directly show references
2	Algeria	Africa	The Bank of Algeria (https://www.bank-of-algeria.dz/)	Bank of Algeria, The Money and Credit Council, The Banking Commission (https://www.imf.org/external/np/rosc/dza/index.htm#:~:text=Regulation%20and%20supervision%20of%20the,role%20played%20by%20the%20governor.&text=The%20Money%20and%20Credit%20Council,for%20licensing%20and%20regulation%20(Arts.)	The Ministry of Finance's Insurance Supervision Commission (https://oxfordbusinessgroup.com/overview/encouraging-coverage-improved-regulation-and-services-should-help-sector-expand)	The Securities and Investments Organization and Monitoring Commission (http://www.sgbv.dz/?page=rubrique&lang=eng&mod=131)	Unknown
3	Angola	Africa	The National Bank of Angola (https://www.bna.ao/Conteudos/Artigos/detalhe_artigo.aspx?idc=139&idsc=168&idl=2)	The National Bank of Angola (https://www.globallegalinsights.com/practice-areas/banking-and-finance-laws-and-regulations/angola#:~:text=BNA%20is%20the%20banking%20supervisory,set%20out%20in%20Law%20no.)	The Angolan Agency for Insurance Regulation and Supervision (http://www.angop.ao/angola/en_us/noticias/economia/2017/8/39/Angola-Creation-import-insurance-ARSEG-priority,c8eeb3bf-5c8b-4de8-8084-5839dcfcef5d.html)	Capital Market Commission (https://www.cosse.africa/wp-content/uploads/2017/03/cosse_exchange-information_angola-1.pdf)	Unknown

(continued)

(continued)

Serial number	Member States of UN	Continent	Is there a central bank? If yes, please directly specify it and the reference	Is there a banking regulatory authority? If so, please describe directly it or them and the reference	Is there an insurance regulatory authority? If so, please describe directly it or them and the reference	Is there a securities market regulatory authority? If so, please describe directly it and the reference	Is there a financial holding company? If so, please directly show references
4	Botswana	Africa	The Bank of Botswana (https://www.bankofbotswana.bw/)	The Bank of Botswana (https://www.bankofbotswana.bw/content/regulations)	Non-Bank Financial Institutions Regulatory Authority (https://www.insurancegateway.co.za/Botswana/Directory/ViewCategory/Irn=971&URL=Regulators#.Xwq8KpNLhhE)	The Central Securities Depository Company of Botswana (https://www.rmb.co.bw/page/regulatory-framework#:~:text=NBFIRA%20is%20an%20independent%20regulatory,in%20conjunction%20with%20the%20BSE.)	https://www.bihl.co.bw/about-us

(continued)

(continued)

Serial number	Member States of UN	Continent	Is there a central bank? If yes, please directly specify it and the reference	Is there a banking regulatory authority? If so, please describe directly it or them and the reference	Is there an insurance regulatory authority? If so, please describe directly it or them and the reference	Is there a securities market regulatory authority? If so, please describe directly it and the reference	Is there a financial holding company? If so, please directly show references
5	Burkina Faso	Africa	Central Bank of West African States (https://www.bceao.int/en/etats-membres/burkina-faso)	Central Bank of West African States (https://books.google.fr/books?id=a0IuF5RmrbEC&pg=PA424&lpg=PA424&dq=Burkina+Faso+commercial+bank+regulation+authority+Central+Bank+of+West+African+States&source=bl&ots=ntvgAtPhlf&sig=ACfU3U2tPXWZslimRPQr2lsYXC-Wx8yrVQ&hl=fr&sa=X&ved=2ahUKEwi6_ZTGp8fqAhWHy4UKHQjFADIQ6AEwA3oECAYQAQ#v=onepage&q=Burkina%20Faso%20commercial%20bank%20regulation%20authority%20Central%20Bank%20of%20West%20African%20States&f=false)	Commission Régionale de Contrôle des Assurances (CRCA) (https://www.africa-re.com/dashboards/BF)	Central Bank of West African States (https://books.google.fr/books?id=0dYVBgAAQBAJ&pg=PA64&lpg=PA64&dq=Burkina+Faso++securities+market+regulation+authority+Central+Bank+of+West+African+States&source=bl&ots=rf2Fvq8dsu&sig=ACfU3U3hsLmFjxHLV8GXiDp_QEHyZIMLuw&hl=fr&sa=X&ved=2ahUKEwiUnv33p8fqAhURzhoKHQJ1BcoQ6AEwBnoECAYQAQ#v=onepage&q=Burkina%20Faso%20%20securities%20market%20regulation%20authority%20Central%20Bank%20of%20West%20African%20States&f=false)	https://burkinafaso.desertcart.com/products/71976059-how-to-start-a-financial-holding-company-plus-business-plan

(continued)

(continued)

Serial number	Member States of UN	Continent	Is there a central bank? If yes, please directly specify it and the reference	Is there a banking regulatory authority? If so, please describe directly it or them and the reference	Is there an insurance regulatory authority? If so, please describe directly it or them and the reference	Is there a securities market regulatory authority? If so, please describe directly it and the reference	Is there a financial holding company? If so, please directly show references
6	Cameroon	Africa	Bank of Central African States (https://www.sesric.org/central-bank-detail.php?c_code=12)	Bank of Central African States (https://www.econrsa.org/system/files/workshops/papers/2012/akon-banking-sector.pdf)	The Regional Insurance Monitoring Commission (CRCA) of the CIMA (Inter-African Conference of Insurance Markets) (https://www.businessincameroon.com/law/2405-7149-the-regulatory-body-in-the-western-and-central-african-insurance-sector-suspends-the-activities-of-cameroonian-insurer-samaritan)	Financial Markets Commission (https://www.businessincameroon.com/bank/2310-8493-cameroon-financial-markets-commission-gives-green-light-for-new-bond-issuance-on-douala-stock-exchange)	https://ec.europa.eu/commission/presscorner/detail/en/BEI_07_134

(continued)

(continued)

Serial number	Member States of UN	Continent	Is there a central bank? If yes, please directly specify it and the reference	Is there a banking regulatory authority? If so, please describe directly it or them and the reference	Is there an insurance regulatory authority? If so, please describe directly it or them and the reference	Is there a securities market regulatory authority? If so, please describe directly it and the reference	Is there a financial holding company? If so, please directly show references
7	Central African Republic	Africa	The Bank of Central African States (https://en.wikipedia.org/wiki/Bank_of_Central_African_States)	The Bank of Central African States (https://books.google.fr/books?id=UdUaDgAAQBAJ&pg=PA8&lpg=PA8&dq=Central+African+Republic+commercial+bank+regulation+authority&source=bl&ots=X9_Q2su5X2&sig=ACfU3U3vArYWPzfZ_1V_4Lo94oocfuvm9Q&hl=fr&sa=X&ved=2ahUKEwjRq8v858nqAhWq4YUKHXUBARcQ6AEwCHoECAkQAQ#v=onepage&q=Central%20African%20Republic%20commercial%20bank%20regulation%20authority&f=false)	The Commission Regional des Assurances (CRCA) (https://www.marketresearch.com/GlobalData-v3648/Governance-Risk-Compliance-Central-African-12727936/)	The Central African Securities Exchange (https://books.google.fr/books?id=1OEepKsBc1YC&pg=PA155&lpg=PA155&dq=Central+African+Republic+securities+company+regulation+authority&source=bl&ots=PCqx1RM9BZ&sig=ACfU3U3jtsZzN7Wakg6zr3M8BFDhPnPg_g&hl=fr&sa=X&ved=2ahUKEwiRyMHx6snqAhVX9IUKHUKzBAMQ6AEwCXoECAoQAQ#v=onepage&q=Central%20African%20Republic%20securities%20company%20regulation%20authority&f=false)	https://rfhl.com/

(continued)

(continued)

Serial number	Member States of UN	Continent	Is there a central bank? If yes, please directly specify it and the reference	Is there a banking regulatory authority? If so, please describe directly it or them and the reference	Is there an insurance regulatory authority? If so, please describe directly it or them and the reference	Is there a securities market regulatory authority? If so, please describe directly it and the reference	Is there a financial holding company? If so, please directly show references
8	Côte D'Ivoire	Africa	La Banque Centrale des États de l'Afrique de l'Ouest (BCEAO) (https://www.bceao.int/fr/etats-membres/cote-divoire)	La Banque Centrale des États de l'Afrique de l'Ouest (BCEAO) (https://books.google.fr/books?id=ZzezDwAAQBAJ&pg=PA173&lpg=PA173&dq=C%C3%B4te+D%27Ivoire+commercial+bank+regulation+authority&source=bl&ots=AzF7XVTbhH&sig=ACfU3U2wzn58iB7_5Q0oQlCFBSWI1smeYQ&hl=fr&sa=X&ved=2ahUKEwiloqDm-8vqAhUNy4UKHXv1A-MQ6AEwAHoECAgQAQ#v=onepage&q=C%C3%B4te%20D'Ivoire%20commercial%20bank%20regulation%20authority&f=false)	The Ministry of Economy and Finance (MoEF) of CIMA (https://oxfordbusinessgroup.com/overview/gaining-ground-healthy-premium-growth-new-products-and-regulatory-reform-look-set-drive-sector)	Conseil Régional de l'Epargne Publique et des Marchés Financiers (https://books.google.fr/books?id=0dYVBgAAQBAJ&pg=PA64&lpg=PA64&dq=C%C3%B4te+D%27Ivoire+securities+company+regulation+authority&source=bl&ots=rf2Fxm8dpq&sig=ACfU3U35jVNgSw5DaWbJDVWdd_s8uFcnpg&hl=fr&sa=X&ved=2ahUKEwi_1e_t-8vqAhWFy4UKHY3TDNsQ6AEwA3oECAgQAQ#v=onepage&q=C%C3%B4te%20D'Ivoire%20securities%20company%20regulation%20authority&f=false)	https://books.google.fr/books?id=0dYVBgAAQBAJ&pg=PA45&lpg=PA45&dq=C%C3%B4te+D%27Ivoire+financial+holding+company&source=bl&ots=rf2Fxm8dqm&sig=ACfU3U0eHkgZ2Rsbw1JfxWyAW9FUZsxChw&hl=fr&sa=X&ved=2ahUKEwiI9sLw-8vqAhWEzYUKHc8zC9kQ6AEwA3oECAgQAQ#v=onepage&q=C%C3%B4te%20D'Ivoire%20financial%20holding%20company&f=false

(continued)

(continued)

Serial number	Member States of UN	Continent	Is there a central bank? If yes, please directly specify it and the reference	Is there a banking regulatory authority? If so, please describe directly it or them and the reference	Is there an insurance regulatory authority? If so, please describe directly it or them and the reference	Is there a securities market regulatory authority? If so, please describe directly it and the reference	Is there a financial holding company? If so, please directly show references
9	Egypt	Africa	The Central Bank of Egypt (https://www.cbe.org.eg/en/Pages/default.aspx)	The Central Bank of Egypt (https://www.pwc.com/m1/en/services/tax/me-tax-legal-news/2019/egypt-exported-services-new-guidance-issued-egyptian-tax-authority.html)	The Financial Regulatory Authority (http://www.fra.gov.eg/content/efsa_en/efsa_pages_en/main_efsa_page_en.htm)	The Financial Regulatory Authority (http://www.fra.gov.eg/content/efsa_en/efsa_pages_en/main_efsa_page_en.htm)	https://www.zonebourse.com/EFG-HERMES-HOLDING-S-A-E-64[illegible]3[illegible]48/societe/
10	Ghana	Africa	The Bank of Ghana (https://www.bog.gov.gh/)	The Bank of Ghana (https://www.bog.gov.gh/supervision-regulation/regulatory-framework/)	The National Insurance Commission (https://nicgh.org/)	The Securities and Exchange Commission (https://sec.gov.gh/overview/)	https://www.bog.gov.gh/wp-content/uploads/2019/09/Financial-Holding-Companies-Directive-Exposure.pdf
11	Liberia	Africa	Central Bank of Liberia (https://www.cbl.org.lr/)	Central Bank of Liberia (https://www.privacyshield.gov/article?id=Liberia-Banking-Systems#:~:text=The%20CBL%20is%20responsible%20for,the%20financial%20sector%20in%20Liberia.&text=Foreign%20banks%20or%20branches%20can,regulations%20required%20by%20the%20CBL.)	Central Bank of Liberia (https://www.cbl.org.lr/2content.php?sub=229&related=28&third=229&pg=sp&pt=Insurance)	Central Bank of Liberia (https://cbl.org.lr/doc/Securities%20Market%20Act%20-%202016.pdf)	http://ibliberia.com/doc/IBLL_2014_Audit_FINAL[illegible]52015.pdf

(continued)

(continued)

Serial number	Member States of UN	Continent	Is there a central bank? If yes, please directly specify it and the reference	Is there a banking regulatory authority? If so, please describe directly it or them and the reference	Is there an insurance regulatory authority? If so, please describe directly it or them and the reference	Is there a securities market regulatory authority? If so, please describe directly it and the reference	Is there a financial holding company? If so, please directly show references
12	Madagascar	Africa	Central Bank of Madagascar (https://www.banky-foibe.mg/)	Banking and Financial Supervision Commission (CSBF) (http://www.imf.org/external/np/seminars/eng/2008/afrfin/pdf/andrianasolo.pdf)	The Committee of Insurance Companies (https://www.africa-re.com/blogs/3-market-reports/articles/41-the-insurance-market-of-madagascar)	Central Bank of Madagascar (https://comparebrokers.co/compare/madagascar-brokers/)	http://www.careratingsafrica.com/downloads/CIEL%20FINANCE%20LTD%20-%20Final%20rationale.pdf
13	Malawi	Africa	Reserve Bank of Malawi (https://en.wikipedia.org/wiki/Reserve_Bank_of_Malawi)	Reserve Bank of Malawi (https://www.rbm.mw/Supervision/BankSupervision/?activeTab=BASUGuidelines)	Reserve Bank of Malawi (https://www.rbm.mw/Supervision/PensionsandInsurance/?activeTab=PISUAbout)	Malawi Stock Exchange (https://mse.co.mw/index.php?route=common/about)	https://www.fdh.co.mw/
14	Mauritius	Africa	Bank of Mauritius (https://www.bom.mu/)	Bank of Mauritius (https://en.wikipedia.org/wiki/Mauritius_Commercial_Bank)	Financial Services Commission (https://www.fscmauritius.org/en/statistics/insurance-and-pensions)	Financial Services Commission (https://www.fscmauritius.org/en/statistics/securities)	http://www.the-businessreport.com/article/sophisticated-secure-financial-platform-africa-central-bank/
15	Morocco	Africa	Bank Al-Maghrib (https://en.wikipedia.org/wiki/Bank_Al-Maghrib)	Bank Al-Maghrib (https://www.globallegalinsights.com/practice-areas/banking-and-finance-laws-and-regulations/morocco)	The Supervisory Authority of Insurance and Social Welfare (ACAPS) (https://www.acaps.ma/en/who-are-we)	The Moroccan Capital Market Authority (http://www.casablanca-bourse.com/bourseweb/en/content.aspx?IdLink=231&Cat=4)	https://en.wikipedia.org/wiki/Compagnie_g%C3%A9n%C3%A9rale_du_Maroc

(continued)

(continued)

Serial number	Member States of UN	Continent	Is there a central bank? If yes, please directly specify it and the reference	Is there a banking regulatory authority? If so, please describe directly it or them and the reference	Is there an insurance regulatory authority? If so, please describe directly it or them and the reference	Is there a securities market regulatory authority? If so, please describe directly it and the reference	Is there a financial holding company? If so, please directly show references
16	Namibia	Africa	Bank of Namibia (https://en.wikipedia.org/wiki/Bank_of_Namibia)	Bank of Namibia (https://www.bon.com.na/Bank/Banking-Supervision.aspx)	Namibia Financial Institutions Supervisory Authority (https://www.namfisa.com.na/pension-funds-friendly-societies/)	Namibia Financial Institutions Supervisory Authority (https://www.namfisa.com.na/)	https://www.intelligentcio.com/africa/2019/10/30/namibian-financial-holdings-company-improves-infrastructure-thanks-to-nutanix/
17	Burundi	Africa	The Bank of the Republic of Burundi (https://en.wikipedia.org/wiki/Bank_of_the_Republic_of_Burundi)	The Bank of the Republic of Burundi (https://www.brb.bi/en/content/commercial-banks)	L'Agence de Régulation et de Contrôle des Assurances (ARCA) (https://www.businesswire.com/news/home/20180307006348/en/Burundian-Insurance-Industry-Governance-Risk-Compliance-Report)	The East African Securities Regulatory Authority (https://regionweek.com/burundis-capital-market-to-be-operational-before-the-end-of-november-2018/)	Unknown
18	Cabo Verde	Africa	The Bank of Cape Verde (https://en.wikipedia.org/wiki/Bank_of_Cape_Verde)	The Bank of Cape Verde (https://www.state.gov/reports/2019-investment-climate-statements/cabo-verde/)	The Bank of Cape Verde (https://www.state.gov/reports/2019-investment-climate-statements/cabo-verde/)	The General Auditor of the Securities Market (https://www.anna-web.org/wp-content/uploads/2015/12/CV_Company_Profile_0818.pdf)	Unknown

(continued)

(continued)

Serial number	Member States of UN	Continent	Is there a central bank? If yes, please directly specify it and the reference	Is there a banking regulatory authority? If so, please describe directly it or them and the reference	Is there an insurance regulatory authority? If so, please describe directly it or them and the reference	Is there a securities market regulatory authority? If so, please describe directly it and the reference	Is there a financial holding company? If so, please directly show references
19	Nigeria	Africa	Central Bank of Nigeria (https://www.cbn.gov.ng/)	Central Bank of Nigeria (https://uk-practicallaw-thomsonreuters-com.proxy.scd.u-psud.fr/w-007-9148?transitionType=Default&contextData=(sc.Default)&firstPage=true)	The National Insurance Commission (https://www.naicom.gov.ng/)	The Securities and Exchange Commission (https://sec.gov.ng/)	https://www.cbn.gov.ng/out/2014/fprd/combineddocument-holdco%20regulations%20draft%20guidelines.pdf
20	Rwanda	Africa	The National Bank of Rwanda (https://www.bnr.rw/home/)	The National Bank of Rwanda (https://www.bnr.rw/financial-stability/bank-supervision/)	The National Bank of Rwanda (https://www.businesswire.com/news/home/20190307005845/en/Rwanda-Insurance-Industry-Governance-Risk-Compliance-Report)	Rwanda's Capital Market Authority (http://www.cma.rw/index.php?id=118)	https://www.swfinstitute.org/profile/5cddf33bd7b0da24d2abce8e
21	Sierra Leone	Africa	The Bank of Sierra Leone (http://www.bsl.gov.sl/)	The Bank of Sierra Leone (http://www.bsl.gov.sl/Banking_Supervision.html)	Sierra Leone Insurance Commission (SLICOM) (https://www.africa-re.com/dashboards/SL)	The Bank of Sierra Leone (http://www.bsl.gov.sl/pdf/guide-capmkt.pdf)	http://bsl.gov.sl/The_Banking_Act2019.pdf

(continued)

(continued)

Serial number	Member States of UN	Continent	Is there a central bank? If yes, please directly specify it and the reference	Is there a banking regulatory authority? If so, please describe directly it or them and the reference	Is there an insurance regulatory authority? If so, please describe directly it or them and the reference	Is there a securities market regulatory authority? If so, please describe directly it and the reference	Is there a financial holding company? If so, please directly show references
22	Somalia	Africa	Central Bank of Somalia (https://centralbank.gov.so/)	Central Bank of Somalia (https://centralbank.gov.so/overview/)	Insurance Supreme Committee (http://somalilandlaw.net/insurance_companies_bill.htm)	Somali Stock Exchange (https://sseinitiative.org/stock-exchange/somalia/)	https://www.mas.gov.sg/regulation/regulations/mas-sanctions-and-freezing-of-assets-of-persons-somalia-regulations-2010
23	Chad	Africa	The Bank of Central African States (https://en.wikipedia.org/wiki/Bank_of_Central_African_States)	Commission de Banque de l'Afrique Centrale (COBAC) (https://www.export.gov/apex/article2?id=Chad-Banking-Systems)	Commission Régionale de Contrôle des Assurances (CRCA) (https://www.africa-re.com/dashboards/TD)	La Communauté économique et monétaire de l'Afrique centrale (CEMAC) (https://www.africanbondmarkets.org/en/country-profiles/central-africa/chad/)	Unknown

(continued)

(continued)

Serial number	Member States of UN	Continent	Is there a central bank? If yes, please directly specify it and the reference	Is there a banking regulatory authority? If so, please describe directly it or them and the reference	Is there an insurance regulatory authority? If so, please describe directly it or them and the reference	Is there a securities market regulatory authority? If so, please describe directly it and the reference	Is there a financial holding company? If so, please directly show references
24	South Africa	Africa	South African Reserve Bank (https://www.resbank.co.za/Pages/default.aspx)	South African Reserve Bank (https://uk-practicallaw-thomsonreuters-com.proxy.scd.u-psud.fr/w-007-6934?transitionType=Default&contextData=(sc.Default)&firstPage=true)	The Prudential Authority (https://content-next-westlaw-com.proxy.scd.u-psud.fr/1-505-2026?transitionType=Default&contextData=(sc.Default)&__lrTS=20170518190936763&firstPage=true&bhab=0&bhav=&bhqs=1)	Financial Services Board (FSB) (https://en.wikipedia.org/wiki/Financial_Services_Board_(South_Africa))	https://www.resbank.co.za/AboutUs/Departments/Pages/Prudential-Authority.aspx
25	Uganda	Africa	Bank of Uganda (https://www.bou.or.ug/bou/bouwebsite/BOU-HOME)	Bank of Uganda (https://www.bou.or.ug/bou/bouwebsite/Supervision/actsandregulations.html)	The Insurance Regulatory Authority of Uganda (https://en.wikipedia.org/wiki/Insurance_Regulatory_Authority_of_Uganda#:~:text=The%20Insurance%20Regulatory%20Authority%20of,business%20of%20Insurance%20in%20Uganda%22.)	Capital Markets Authority (https://cmauganda.co.ug/)	https://www.monitor.co.ug/Business/Finance/Stanbic-Bank-becomes-holding-company/688608-4881288-llnov7z/index.html

(continued)

(continued)

Serial number	Member States of UN	Continent	Is there a central bank? If yes, please directly specify it and the reference	Is there a banking regulatory authority? If so, please describe directly it or them and the reference	Is there an insurance regulatory authority? If so, please describe directly it or them and the reference	Is there a securities market regulatory authority? If so, please describe directly it and the reference	Is there a financial holding company? If so, please directly show references
26	Comoros	Africa	The Central Bank of the Comros (https://en.wikipedia.org/wiki/Central_Bank_of_the_Comoros)	The Central Bank of the Comros (https://2009-2017.state.gov/documents/organization/82217.pdf)	The Central Bank of the Comros (https://www.africa-re.com/dashboards/KM)	Unknown	Unknown
27	Congo	Africa	The Bank of the Central African States (BEAC) (https://www.privacyshield.gov/article?id=Republic-of-Congo-Banking-Systems)	Commission de Banque de l'Afrique Centrale (COBAC) (https://www.export.gov/apex/article2?id=Chad-Banking-Systems)	Commission Régionale de Contrôle des Assurances (CRCA) (https://www.africa-re.com/dashboards/TD)	La Communauté économique et monétaire de l'Afrique centrale (CEMAC) (https://www.africanbondmarkets.org/en/country-profiles/central-africa/chad/)	Unknown
28	United Republic of Tanzania	Africa	Bank of Tanzania (https://en.wikipedia.org/wiki/Bank_of_Tanzania)	Bank of Tanzania (https://www.bot.go.tz/Currency/Bankingservices)	Tanzania Insurance Regulatory Authority (http://www.tira.go.tz/)	Capital Markets and Securities Authority (https://www.cmsa.go.tz/index.php/2015-03-01-17-53-30/supervised-entities)	https://www.imf.org/~/media/Files/Publications/CR/2018/cr18346.ashx

(continued)

(continued)

Serial number	Member States of UN	Continent	Is there a central bank? If yes, please directly specify it and the reference	Is there a banking regulatory authority? If so, please describe directly it or them and the reference	Is there an insurance regulatory authority? If so, please describe directly it or them and the reference	Is there a securities market regulatory authority? If so, please describe directly it and the reference	Is there a financial holding company? If so, please directly show references
29	Zimbabwe	Africa	Reserve Bank of Zimbabwe (https://www.rbz.co.zw/)	Reserve Bank of Zimbabwe (https://www.rbz.co.zw/index.php/about-us/departments/bank-supervision)	The Insurance and Pensions Commission (IPEC) (https://www.ibanet.org/Article/NewDetail.aspx?ArticleUid=4fdec4bd-cc58-4cb9-975d-22302f076e2a)	The Securities and Exchange Commission of Zimbabwe (http://www.seczim.co.zw/about-secz/who-is-secz)	https://www.marketscreener.com/ZB-FINANCIAL-HOLDINGS-LIM-20701945/company/
30	Democratic Republic of the Congo	Africa	The Central Bank of the Congo (http://www.bcc.cd/)	The Central Bank of the Congo (https://www.cliffordchance.com/content/dam/cliffordchance/briefings/2019/10/guide-to-financial-regulation-in-africa.pdf)	Insurance Regulatory and Supervisory Authority (ARCA) (https://juriafrique.com/eng/2019/10/21/arca-for-the-regulation-of-the-insurance-sector-in-drc/)	Unknown	Unknown

(continued)

(continued)

Serial number	Member States of UN	Continent	Is there a central bank? If yes, please directly specify it and the reference	Is there a banking regulatory authority? If so, please describe directly it or them and the reference	Is there an insurance regulatory authority? If so, please describe directly it or them and the reference	Is there a securities market regulatory authority? If so, please describe directly it and the reference	Is there a financial holding company? If so, please directly show references
31	Djibouti	Africa	Banque Centrale de Djibouti (https://banque-centrale.dj/)	Banque Centrale de Djibouti (http://firstforum.org/DownloadSpecialReportDetail.3519.ashx)	The insurance directorate at the Ministry of Economy and Finance (https://www.businesswire.com/news/home/20200508005294/en/Djibouti-Insurance-Market-Industry-Trends-Share-Size)	The East African Securities Regulatory Authority (https://books.google.fr/books?id=HnGGEqGukvgC&pg=PA33&lpg=PA33&dq=Djibouti+securities+regulation+authority&source=bl&ots=3NWlKdw5gS&sig=ACfU3U2bzxBwbuxq7FFXRe-NrdJwbARaIQ&hl=fr&sa=X&ved=2ahUKEwjl1MO3rMzqAhXk6eAKHfmkDCkQ6AEwBnoECAcQAQ#v=onepage&q=Djibouti%20securities%20regulation%20authority&f=false)	Unknown
32	Equatorial Guinea	Africa	La Banque des États de l'Afrique centrale (https://www.bankersalmanac.com/demographix.aspx?cid=GNQ)	La Commission Bancaire de l'Afrique Centrale (COBAC) (https://www.imf.org/external/pubs/ft/scr/2016/cr16358.pdf)	National Directorate of Banking and Insurance (https://www.imf.org/external/pubs/ft/scr/2016/cr16358.pdf)	Central African Securities Exchange (BVMAC) (https://www.doingbusiness.org/content/dam/doingBusiness/country/e/equatorial-guinea/GNQ.pdf)	Unknown

(continued)

(continued)

Serial number	Member States of UN	Continent	Is there a central bank? If yes, please directly specify it and the reference	Is there a banking regulatory authority? If so, please describe directly it or them and the reference	Is there an insurance regulatory authority? If so, please describe directly it or them and the reference	Is there a securities market regulatory authority? If so, please describe directly it and the reference	Is there a financial holding company? If so, please directly show references
33	Eritrea	Africa	The Bank of Eritrea (https://en.wikipedia.org/wiki/Bank_of_Eritrea)	The Bank of Eritrea (https://www.tesfanews.net/eritrea-issued-legal-notice-to-regulate-new-currency/)	Unknown	Unknown	Unknown
34	Eswatini	Africa	Central Bank of Eswatini (https://www.centralbank.org.sz/)	Central Bank of Eswatini (https://www.centralbank.org.sz/about/departments/regulation/index.php)	Financial Services Regulatory Authority (https://www.fsra.co.sz/)	Eswatini Stock Exchange (https://www.fsra.co.sz/sectors/cm/licensed/buka.php?yiphi=391)	Unknown

(continued)

(continued)

Serial number	Member States of UN	Continent	Is there a central bank? If yes, please directly specify it and the reference	Is there a banking regulatory authority? If so, please describe directly it or them and the reference	Is there an insurance regulatory authority? If so, please describe directly it or them and the reference	Is there a securities market regulatory authority? If so, please describe directly it and the reference	Is there a financial holding company? If so, please directly show references
35	Ethiopia	Africa	National Bank of Ethiopia (https://nbebank.com/)	National Bank of Ethiopia (https://www.2merkato.com/articles/industry/869-banking-in-ethiopia-regulations-and-procedures)	National Bank of Ethiopia (https://www.businesswire.com/news/home/20190716005803/en/Governance-Risk-Compliance-Ethiopian-Insurance-Industry-2018-2019#:~:text=The%20Ethiopian%20insurance%20industry%20is%20regulated%20by%20the%20NBE.&text=The%20government%20does%20not%20permit,on%20a%20cross%2Dborder%20basis.)	No regulators (https://www.bloomberg.com/news/articles/2020-06-30/ethiopia-to-set-up-regulator-for-first-stock-exchange-this-year) (https://chilot.me/wp-content/uploads/2013/05/regulation-of-initial-public-offering-of-shares-in-ethiopia-critical-issues-and-challenges1.pdf)	Unknown
36	Gabon	Africa	Bank of Central African States (https://www.beac.int/)	The Bank of the Central African States (BEAC) (https://www.privacyshield.gov/article?id=Gabon-Banking-Systems)	National Insurance Directorate (https://www.atlas-mag.net/en/article/the-gabonese-insurance-industry-2013-2017-turnover)	The Bank of the Central African States (BEAC) (https://www.elibrary.imf.org/view/IMF002/02699-9781451813920/02699-9781451813920/02699-9781451813920_A001.xml?redirect=true)	Unknown

(continued)

(continued)

Serial number	Member States of UN	Continent	Is there a central bank? If yes, please directly specify it and the reference	Is there a banking regulatory authority? If so, please describe directly it or them and the reference	Is there an insurance regulatory authority? If so, please describe directly it or them and the reference	Is there a securities market regulatory authority? If so, please describe directly it and the reference	Is there a financial holding company? If so, please directly show references
37	Gambia (Republic of The)	Africa	The Central Bank of The Gambia (https://www.cbg.gm/)	The Central Bank of The Gambia (https://www.cbg.gm/banking-supervision)	The Central Bank of The Gambia (https://www.africa-re.com/dashboards/GM)	The Central Bank of The Gambia (https://www.cbg.gm/monetory-policy-committee)	Unknown
38	Guinea	Africa	The Central Bank of the Republic of Guinea (https://www.bcrg-guinee.org/)	The Central Bank of the Republic of Guinea (https://ecobank.com/gn/personal-banking/countries)	The Central Bank of the Republic of Guinea (https://www.businesswire.com/news/home/20171018006151/en/Guinean-Insurance-Industry-Governance-Risk-Compliance-Report)	The Central Bank of the Republic of Guinea (https://www.imf.org/~/media/Files/Publications/CR/2020/English/1GINEA2020001.ashx)	Unknown
39	Guinea Bissau	Africa	Central Bank of West African States (https://www.bceao.int/fr/etats-membres/guinee-bissau)	The Central Bank of West African States (BCEAO) (https://www.afdb.org/fileadmin/uploads/afdb/Documents/Publications/24108386-FR-GUINEA-BISSAU.PDF)	Conférence Interafricaine des Marchés d'Assurances (CIMA) (https://www.aig.com/knowledge-and-insights/k-and--article-insurance-regulation-in-cima-africa)	The Savings and Financial Markets Regional Council (CREPMF) (https://www.afdb.org/fileadmin/uploads/afdb/Documents/Publications/24108386-FR-GUINEA-BISSAU.PDF)	Unknown

(continued)

(continued)

Serial number	Member States of UN	Continent	Is there a central bank? If yes, please directly specify it and the reference	Is there a banking regulatory authority? If so, please describe directly it or them and the reference	Is there an insurance regulatory authority? If so, please describe directly it or them and the reference	Is there a securities market regulatory authority? If so, please describe directly it and the reference	Is there a financial holding company? If so, please directly show references
40	Kenya	Africa	Central Bank of Kenya (https://www.centralbank.go.ke/)	Central Bank of Kenya (https://www.centralbank.go.ke/bank-supervision/)	The Insurance Regulatory Authority (https://www.ira.go.ke/)	The Capital Markets Authority (CMA) and the Nairobi Securities Exchange (NSE) (http://www.ijhssnet.com/journals/Vol_2_No_20_Special_Issue_October_2012/25.pdf)	Unknown
41	Lesotho	Africa	Central Bank of Lesotho (https://www.centralbank.org.ls/)	Central Bank of Lesotho (https://www.centralbank.org.ls/index.php/legislation/122-supervision/540-regulations)	Central Bank of Lesotho (https://www.businesswire.com/news/home/20190219005473/en/Lesotho-Insurance-Industry-Governance-Risk-Compliance-Report)	Maseru Securities Market (MSM) (https://www.msm.org.ls/)	Unknown
42	Libya	Africa	Central Bank of Libya (https://en.wikipedia.org/wiki/Central_Bank_of_Libya)	Central Bank of Libya (https://cbl.gov.ly/en/banking-supervision/)	Ministry of economy and trade (https://www.atlas-mag.net/en/article/the-libyan-insurance-market)	Libyan Capital Market Authority (https://lcma.gov.ly/en/?s=securities)	Unknown

(continued)

(continued)

Serial number	Member States of UN	Continent	Is there a central bank? If yes, please directly specify it and the reference	Is there a banking regulatory authority? If so, please describe directly it or them and the reference	Is there an insurance regulatory authority? If so, please describe directly it or them and the reference	Is there a securities market regulatory authority? If so, please describe directly it and the reference	Is there a financial holding company? If so, please directly show references
43	Mali	Africa	Central Bank of West African States (https://www.bceao.int/en/etats-membres/mali)	Central Bank of West African States (https://www.bceao.int/en/content/legal-notices)	Commission Régionale de Contrôle des Assurances (CRCA) (https://www.africa-re.com/dashboards/ML)	Bourse Regionale des Valeurs (https://www.doingbusiness.org/content/dam/doingBusiness/country/m/mali/MLI.pdf)	Unknown
44	Mauritania	Africa	Banque Centrale de Mauritanie (https://www.bcm.mr/)	Banque Centrale de Mauritanie (http://www.menafatf.org/sites/default/files/MutulalEvaluationReportMauritaniaEng.pdf)	The Ministry of Commerce (http://www.menafatf.org/sites/default/files/MutulalEvaluationReportMauritaniaEng.pdf)	No securities exchange (http://www.menafatf.org/sites/default/files/MutulalEvaluationReportMauritaniaEng.pdf)	Unknown
45	Mozambique	Africa	Bank of Mozambique (https://en.wikipedia.org/wiki/Bank_of_Mozambique)	Bank of Mozambique (https://www.globallegalinsights.com/practice-areas/banking-and-finance-laws-and-regulations/mozambique#:~:text=The%20Bank%20of%20Mozambique%20is,92%2C%20of%203%20January%201992.)	Mozambique Supervisory Institute of Insurance (https://www.africa-re.com/dashboards/MZ)	Minister of Finance (http://african-exchanges.org/en/membership/members/mozambique-stock-exchange-mse)	Unknown

(continued)

(continued)

Serial number	Member States of UN	Continent	Is there a central bank? If yes, please directly specify it and the reference	Is there a banking regulatory authority? If so, please describe directly it or them and the reference	Is there an insurance regulatory authority? If so, please describe directly it or them and the reference	Is there a securities market regulatory authority? If so, please describe directly it and the reference	Is there a financial holding company? If so, please directly show references
46	Niger	Africa	Central Bank of West African States (BCEAO) (https://www.bceao.int/en/etats-membres/niger)	Central Bank of West African States (BCEAO) (https://www.bis.org/country/ne.htm)	Commission Régionale de Contrôle des Assurances (https://cima-afrique.org/les-etats-membres/)	The Conseil Régional de l'Epargne Publique et des Marchés Financiers (http://www.crepmf.org/Wwwcrepmf/CREPMF/Mission.aspx)	Unknown
47	Sao Tome and Principe	Africa	The Central Bank of São Tomé and Príncipe (https://en.wikipedia.org/wiki/Central_Bank_of_S%C3%A3o_Tom%C3%A9_and_Pr%C3%ADncipe)	The Central Bank of São Tomé and Príncipe (http://www.bcstp.st/)	The Central Bank of São Tomé and Príncipe (http://www.bcstp.st/)	Central Africa Regional Stock Exchange (BVMAC) (https://www.africanbondmarkets.org/en/country-profiles/central-africa/)	Unknown
48	Senegal	Africa	The Central Bank of West African States (BCEAO) (https://www.bceao.int/en/etats-membres/senegal)	The Central Bank of West African States (BCEAO) (https://www.bceao.int/en/content/legal-notices)	Commission Régionale de Contrôle des Assurances (CRCA) (https://www.africa-re.com/dashboards/SN)	The Conseil Régional de l'Epargne Publique et des Marchés Financiers (https://www.elibrary.imf.org/view/IMF002/06160-9781451833942/06160-9781451833942/06160-9781451833942_A001.xml?redirect=true)	Unknown

(continued)

(continued)

Serial number	Member States of UN	Continent	Is there a central bank? If yes, please directly specify it and the reference	Is there a banking regulatory authority? If so, please describe directly it or them and the reference	Is there an insurance regulatory authority? If so, please describe directly it or them and the reference	Is there a securities market regulatory authority? If so, please describe directly it and the reference	Is there a financial holding company? If so, please directly show references
49	Seychelles	Africa	Central Bank Of Seychelles (https://www.cbs.sc/)	Central Bank Of Seychelles (https://www.imf.org/external/pubs/ft/scr/2004/cr04381.pdf)	The Seychelles Financial Services Authority (https://www.fsaseychelles.sc/insurance-regulated-entities/)	The Seychelles Financial Services Authority (https://www.fsaseychelles.sc/)	Unknown
50	South Sudan	Africa	Bank of South Sudan (https://www.bankofsouthsudan.org/)	Bank of South Sudan (http://www.gurtong.net/Business/Finance/tabid/68/Default.aspx)	Insurance Regulatory Authority (http://www.gurtong.net/Business/Insurance/tabid/464/Default.aspx)	stock market or related regulatory system (https://www.state.gov/reports/2019-investment-climate-statements/south-sudan/)	Unknown
51	Sudan	Africa	Central Bank of Sudan (https://cbos.gov.sd/en)	Central Bank of Sudan (https://en.wikipedia.org/wiki/Central_Bank_of_Sudan)	The Insurance Supervisory Authority of Sudan (https://www.ifsb.org/press_full.php?id=248&submit=more)	Khartoum Stock Exchange (https://sudantribune.com/Khartoum-Stock-Exchange-Who-should,22507)	Unknown

(continued)

(continued)

Serial number	Member States of UN	Continent	Is there a central bank? If yes, please directly specify it and the reference	Is there a banking regulatory authority? If so, please describe directly it or them and the reference	Is there an insurance regulatory authority? If so, please describe directly it or them and the reference	Is there a securities market regulatory authority? If so, please describe directly it and the reference	Is there a financial holding company? If so, please directly show reference
52	Togo	Africa	The Central Bank of West African States (https://www.bceao.int/en/etats-membres/togo)	The Central Bank of West African States (https://www.bceao.int/en/content/decentralized-financial-systems)	Commission Régionale de Contrôle des Assurances (CRCA) (https://www.africa-re.com/dashboards/TG)	The Bourse Regionale des Valeurs Mobilieres (BRVM) (https://sseinitiative.org/stock-exchange/brvm/#:~:text=About%20the%20stock%20exchange,Togo%2C%20Burkina%20Faso%20et%20Niger.)	Unknown
53	Tunisia	Africa	Central Bank of Tunisia (https://en.wikipedia.org/wiki/Central_Bank_of_Tunisia)	Central Bank of Tunisia (https://www.bct.gov.tn/bct/siteprod/page.jsp?id=59&la=AN)	General Insurance Committee (https://www.businesswire.com/news/home/20171018006069/en/Tunisian-Insurance-Industry-Governance-Risk-Compliance-Report)	Central Bank of Tunisia (https://www.bct.gov.tn/bct/siteprod/page.jsp?id=67&la=AN)	Unknown

(continued)

(continued)

Serial number	Member States of UN	Continent	Is there a central bank? If yes, please directly specify it and the reference	Is there a banking regulatory authority? If so, please describe directly it or them and the reference	Is there an insurance regulatory authority? If so, please describe directly it or them and the reference	Is there a securities market regulatory authority? If so, please describe directly it and the reference	Is there a financial holding company? If so, please directly show references
54	Zambia	Africa	Bank of Zambia (https://www.boz.zm/)	Bank of Zambia (https://www.boz.zm/financial-sector-development.htm#:~:text=In%20terms%20of%20regulation%2C%20there,regulators%20of%20the%20financial%20sector.&text=The%20Bank%20of%20Zambia%20(BoZ,of%20the%20Laws%20of%20Zambia.)	The Pensions and Insurance Authority (https://www.pia.org.zm/)	Securities & Exchange Commission Zambia (https://www.seczambia.org.zm/)	Unknown
55	Armenia	Asia	The Central Bank of Armenia (https://www.cba.am/en/sitepages/default.aspx)	Central Bank of Armenia (https://www.imf.org/external/pubs/ft/scr/2013/cr1310.pdf)	The Board of the Central Bank (http://www.parliament.am/law_docs/220507HO177eng.pdf?lang=eng)	Central Bank of Armenia (https://amx.am/en/4/about-us)	Unknown
56	Bangladesh	Asia	Bangladesh Bank (https://www.bb.org.bd/)	Bangladesh Bank (https://www.bb.org.bd/aboutus/regulationguideline/guidelist.php)	Insurance Development and Regulatory Authority of Bangladesh (http://www.idra.org.bd/)	Bangladesh Securities and Exchange Commission (https://www.sec.gov.bd/)	Unknown

(continued)

(continued)

Serial number	Member States of UN	Continent	Is there a central bank? If yes, please directly specify it and the reference	Is there a banking regulatory authority? If so, please describe directly it or them and the reference	Is there an insurance regulatory authority? If so, please describe directly it or them and the reference	Is there a securities market regulatory authority? If so, please describe directly it and the reference	Is there a financial holding company? If so, please directly show references
57	Bhutan	Asia	The Royal Monetary Authority of Bhutan (https://www.rma.org.bt/)	The Royal Monetary Authority of Bhutan (https://www.rma.org.bt/EXTERNALWEB/searchResult.jsp)	The Royal Monetary Authority of Bhutan (https://www.rma.org.bt/SAIRFprofile.jsp)	The Royal Monetary Authority of Bhutan (https://www.rma.org.bt/EXTERNALWEB/DownloadImage?FILENAME=THIRDFILENAME&IDCOLNAME=LAWID&ID=34&TABLE=TBLWEB_LAWSBYLAW&IMAGECOL=THIRDFILE)	Unknown
58	Brunei Darussalam	Asia	The Monetary Authority of Brunei Darussalam (https://en.wikipedia.org/wiki/Monetary_Authority_of_Brunei_Darussalam)	The Monetary Authority of Brunei Darussalam (https://www.ambd.gov.bn/about-ambd)	The Monetary Authority of Brunei Darussalam (https://www.businesswire.com/news/home/20190222005132/en/Brunei-Insurance-Industry-Governance-Risk-Compliance-Report)	The Monetary Authority of Brunei Darussalam (https://ambd.gov.bn/regulatory/capital-market-unit)	Unknown
59	Afghanistan	Asia	Da Afghanistan Bank (https://dab.gov.af/)	Da Afghanistan Bank (https://dab.gov.af/Licensed-Finacial-Institutions)	Insurance Commission of Afghanistan (http://old.mof.gov.af/en/page/14369/dm-amin/insurance-department)	Kabul Stock Exchange	https://www.lexadin.nl/wlg/legis/nofr/oeur/arch/afg/banking_legislation.pdf

(continued)

(continued)

Serial number	Member States of UN	Continent	Is there a central bank? If yes, please directly specify it and the reference	Is there a banking regulatory authority? If so, please describe directly it or them and the reference	Is there an insurance regulatory authority? If so, please describe directly it or them and the reference	Is there a securities market regulatory authority? If so, please describe directly it and the reference	Is there a financial holding company? If so, please directly show references
60	Azerbaijan	Asia	The Central Bank of Azerbaijan (https://www.cbar.az/home?language=en)	The Central Bank of Azerbaijan; the Financial Market Supervisory Authority (https://bakuresearchinstitute.org/azerbaijani-2018-ci-ild%C9%99-az%C9%99rbaycanin-bank-sektoru/)	Financial Market Supervisory Authority (https://en.wikipedia.org/wiki/Financial_Market_Supervisory_Authority_of_Azerbaijan)	Financial Market Supervisory Authority (https://fcpablog.com/2019/12/26/azerbaijan-financial-market-regulator-succeeds-globally-falls-short-locally/)	https://cyberleninka.ru/article/n/azerbaijan-banking-system-challenges-and-prospects-of-globalization
61	Bahrain	Asia	The Central Bank of Bahrain (https://www.cbb.gov.bh/)	The Central Bank of Bahrain (https://www.cbb.gov.bh/)	The Central Bank of Bahrain (https://www.cbb.gov.bh/)	The Central Bank of Bahrain (https://www.cbb.gov.bh/)	https://www.swfinstitute.org/profile/5b60b726d857bc771014e13c

(continued)

(continued)

Serial number	Member States of UN	Continent	Is there a central bank? If yes, please directly specify it and the reference	Is there a banking regulatory authority? If so, please describe directly it or them and the reference	Is there an insurance regulatory authority? If so, please describe directly it or them and the reference	Is there a securities market regulatory authority? If so, please describe directly it and the reference	Is there a financial holding company? If so please directly show references
62	Democratic People's Republic of Korea	Asia	The Central Bank of the Democratic People's Republic of Korea (https://en.wikipedia.org/wiki/Central_Bank_of_the_Democratic_People%27s_Republic_of_Korea)	The Central Bank of the Democratic People's Republic of Korea (https://namu.wiki/w/%EC%A1%B0%EC%84%A0%EB%AF%BC%EC%A3%BC%EC%A3%BC%EC%9D%98%EC%9D%B8%EB%AF%BC%EA%B3%B5%ED%99%94%EA%B5%AD%20%EC%A4%91%EC%95%99%EC%9D%80%ED%96%89)	The Central Bank of the Democratic People's Republic of Korea (https://namu.wiki/w/%EC%A1%B0%EC%84%A0%EB%AF%BC%EC%A3%BC%EC%A3%BC%EC%9D%98%EC%9D%B8%EB%AF%BC%EA%B3%B5%ED%99%94%EA%B5%AD%20%EC%A4%91%EC%95%99%EC%9D%80%ED%96%89)	No stock exchange (https://www.marketwatch.com/story/how-to-invest-in-north-korean-denuclearization-2019-02-27-101034024)	Unknown
63	Cambodia	Asia	The National Bank of Cambodia (https://www.nbc.org.kh/english/)	The National Bank of Cambodia (http://www.cambodiainvestment.gov.kh/law-on-banking-and-financial-institutions_991118.html)	Ministry of Economy and Finance (https://uk-practicallaw-thomsonreuters-com.proxy.scd.u-psud.fr/w-012-6781?transitionType=Default&contextData=(sc.Default)&firstPage=true)	Securities and Exchange Commission of Cambodia (http://www.secc.gov.kh/english/)	https://opendevelopmentcambodia.net/tag/financial-holding-company/

(continued)

(continued)

Serial number	Member States of UN	Continent	Is there a central bank? If yes, please directly specify it and the reference	Is there a banking regulatory authority? If so, please describe directly it or them and the reference	Is there an insurance regulatory authority? If so, please describe directly it or them and the reference	Is there a securities market regulatory authority? If so, please describe directly it and the reference	Is there a financial holding company? If so, please directly show references
65	Georgia	Asia	National Bank Of Georgia (https://www.nbg.gov.ge/index.php?m=2)	The Bank Supervision Agency (https://www.nbg.gov.ge/index.php?m=523&lng=eng)	The Insurance and Financial Oversight Division (https://www.oci.ga.gov/Insurers/Home.aspx)	The Georgia Secretary of State (https://dbf.georgia.gov/securities-investments#:~:text=State%20Securities%20Regulator,from%20the%20state%20of%20Georgia.)	https://dbf.georgia.gov/banks-holding-companies
66	India	Asia	Reserve Bank of India (https://www.rbi.org.in/)	Reserve Bank of India (RBI) (https://uk-practicallaw-thomsonreuters-com.proxy.scd.u-psud.fr/w-007-9424?transitionType=Default&contextData=(sc.Default)&firstPage=true)	The Insurance Regulatory and Development Authority of India (https://en.wikipedia.org/wiki/Insurance_Regulatory_and_Development_Authority)	Securities Exchange Board of India (SEBI) (https://www.karvyonline.com/knowledge-center/beginner/financial-regulators-in-india)	https://papers.ssrn.com/sol3/Delivery.cfm?abstractid=2136365#:~:text=Banks%2C%20at%20present%2C%20in%20India,from%20the%20global%20financial%20crisis

(continued)

(continued)

Serial number	Member States of UN	Continent	Is there a central bank? If yes, please directly specify it and the reference	Is there a banking regulatory authority? If so, please describe directly it or them and the reference	Is there an insurance regulatory authority? If so, please describe directly it or them and the reference	Is there a securities market regulatory authority? If so, please describe directly it and the reference	Is there a financial holding company? If so, please directly show references
67	Indonesia	Asia	Central Bank of Indonesia (https://www.bi.go.id/en/Default.aspx)	Financial Services Authority (Indonesia) (https://en.wikipedia.org/wiki/Financial_Services_Authority_(Indonesia))	Financial Services Authority (Indonesia) (https://uk-practicallaw-thomsonreuters-com.proxy.scd.u-psud.fr/3-524-2907?transitionType=Default&contextData=(sc.Default)&firstPage=true)	Financial Services Authority (Indonesia) (https://en.wikipedia.org/wiki/Financial_Services_Authority_(Indonesia))	https://jakartaglobe.id/news/ojk-tells-financial-conglomerates-form-holding-companies-jan 1-2019
68	Iraq	Asia	Central Bank of Iraq (https://cbiraq.org/)	Central Bank of Iraq (https://law.stanford.edu/wp-content/uploads/2018/04/ILEI-Commercial-Law-II-2013.pdf)	The Iraqi Insurance Diwan (IID) (https://www.businesswire.com/news/home/20190715005299/en/Iraqi-Insurance-Industry-2019-Governance-Risk-Compliance)	Iraq Securities Commission (https://en.wikipedia.org/wiki/Iraq_Securities_Commission)	https://www.cbi.iq/documents/banking_law_f.pdf
69	Israel	Asia	The Bank of Israel (https://www.boi.org.il/en)	The Bank of Israel (https://www.boi.org.il/en/BankingSupervision/Pages/Default.aspx)	The Capital Market, Insurance and Savings Authority (https://www.gov.il/en/departments/Units/department_cma)	The Israel Securities Authority (http://www.isa.gov.il/sites/ISAEng/Pages/default.aspx)	https://www.swfinstitute.org/profile/5c0608d2286f6c539f371f30

(continued)

(continued)

Serial number	Member States of UN	Continent	Is there a central bank? If yes, please directly specify it and the reference	Is there a banking regulatory authority? If so, please describe directly it or them and the reference	Is there an insurance regulatory authority? If so, please describe directly it or them and the reference	Is there a securities market regulatory authority? If so, please describe directly it and the reference	Is there a financial holding company? If so, please directly show references
70	Japan	Asia	Bank of Japan (https://www.boj.or.jp/en/)	Financial Services Agency (https://en.wikipedia.org/wiki/Financial_Services_Agency)	Financial Services Agency (https://uk-practicallaw-thomsonreuters-com.proxy.scd.u-psud.fr/0-501-3163?transitionType=Default&contextData=(sc.Default)&firstPage=true)	The Securities and Exchange Surveillance Commission (https://en.wikipedia.org/wiki/Securities_and_Exchange_Surveillance_Commission)	https://www.fsa.go.jp/en/refer/guide/conglomerate/01.html
71	Jordan	Asia	Central Bank of Jordan (https://www.cbj.gov.jo/Pages/viewpage.aspx?pageID=176)	Central Bank of Jordan (https://www.cbj.gov.jo/Pages/viewpage.aspx?pageID=190)	Jordan Insurance Federation (http://www.joif.org/)	Jordan Securities Commission (https://en.wikipedia.org/wiki/Jordan_Securities_Commission)	https://www.thejordancompany.com/investments/rfour
72	Kazakhstan	Asia	The National Bank of Kazakhstan (https://nationalbank.kz/?switch=english)	The National Bank of Kazakhstan (http://images.mofcom.gov.cn/ozs/table/kaza/banking.pdf)	Financial Supervisory Agency (https://www.firstinitiative.org/stories/kazakhstan-reinsurance-regulation-0)	The National Bank of Kazakhstan (https://content-next-westlaw-com.proxy.scd.u-psud.fr/Document/Ib9100994606f11e598dc8b09b4f043e0/View/FullText.html?contextData=(sc.Default)&transitionType=Default&firstPage=true&bhab=0&bhav=&bhqs=1)	http://www.kng.kz/about-the-company/#:~:text=KNG%20Finance%20is%20a%20Kazakhstani,the%20residents%20of%20the%20country

(continued)

(continued)

Serial number	Member States of UN	Continent	Is there a central bank? If yes, please directly specify it and the reference	Is there a banking regulatory authority? If so, please describe directly it or them and the reference	Is there an insurance regulatory authority? If so, please describe directly it or them and the reference	Is there a securities market regulatory authority? If so, please describe directly it and the reference	Is there a financial holding company? If so, please directly show references
73	Kuwait	Asia	Central Bank of Kuwait (https://www.cbk.gov.kw/en)	Central Bank of Kuwait (https://www.cbk.gov.kw/en/supervision/cbk-regulations-and-instructions/instructions-for-conventional-banks)	The Insurance Regulation Unit (IRU) (https://uk-practicallaw-thomsonreuters-com.proxy.scd.u-psud.fr/8-629-5351?__lrTS=20180311234448235&transitionType=Default&contextData=(sc.Default)&firstPage=true)	Capital Markets Authority (Kuwait) (https://www.cma.gov.kw/en/web/cma/search-results?searchKeyword=securities&dateFilter=any_date&announcementTag=&announcementTagAdv=&specific_date=&specific_month=1&specific_year=2020&specific_month_year=2020&date_from=&date_to =)	https://www.zawya.com/mena/en/company/Financial_Group_of_Kuwait_Holding_Company-40483/
74	Kyrgyzstan	Asia	National Bank of the Kyrgyz Republic (https://www.nbkr.kg/index.jsp?lang=ENG)	National Bank of the Kyrgyz Republic (https://www.nbkr.kg/index1.jsp?item=42&lang=ENG)	Financial Market Supervisory and Regulatory Service (GOSFINNADZOR) (https://eurasiangroup.org/en/kyrgyzskaya-respublika)	Kyrgyz Stock Exchange (https://www.ibanet.org/LPD/Financial_Services_Section/Securities_Law_Committee/Related_Links.aspx)	https://www.nbkr.kg/index1.jsp?item=42&lang=ENG

(continued)

(continued)

Serial number	Member States of UN	Continent	Is there a central bank? If yes, please directly specify it and the reference	Is there a banking regulatory authority? If so, please describe directly it or them and the reference	Is there an insurance regulatory authority? If so, please describe directly it or them and the reference	Is there a securities market regulatory authority? If so, please describe directly it and the reference	Is there a financial holding company? If so, please directly show references
75	Lebanon	Asia	Banque Du Liban (https://www.bdl.gov.lb/)	Banque Du Liban (https://www.lexology.com/library/detail.aspx?g=2d4ae30a-184e-4ac5-8e42-6b36dbfbe0fc#:~:text=Which%20regulatory%20authorities%20are%20primarily,for%20overseeing%20banks%20in%20Lebanon.)	Insurance Control Commission (ICC) (https://uk-practicallaw-thomsonreuters-com.proxy.scd.u-psud.fr/w-009-0051?transitionType=Default&contextData=(sc.Default)&firstPage=true)	The Capital Markets Authority (CMA) (https://www.cma.gov.lb/?s=securities)	https://www.iosco.org/library/resolutions/pdf/IOSCORES7.pdf
76	Malaysia	Asia	Central Bank of Malaysia (https://en.wikipedia.org/wiki/Central_Bank_of_Malaysia)	Labuan Financial Services Authority (https://uk-practicallaw-thomsonreuters-com.proxy.scd.u-psud.fr/w-008-0538?transitionType=Default&contextData=(sc.Default)&firstPage=true)	Bank Negara Malaysia (http://aitri.org/aitri/media/attachments/2020/02/21/insurance-laws-regulation-of-selected-asean-countries-a-comparative-analysis.pdf)	Securities Commission Malaysia (https://www.sc.com.my/regulation)	https://www.straitstimes.com/business/companies-markets/new-rules-for-financial-holding-companies-in-malaysia#:~:text=Malaysia's%20new%20Basel%20III%20capital,starting%20from%20Jan%201%2C%202019

(continued)

(continued)

Serial number	Member States of UN	Continent	Is there a central bank? If yes, please directly specify it and the reference	Is there a banking regulatory authority? If so, please describe directly it or them and the reference	Is there an insurance regulatory authority? If so, please describe directly it or them and the reference	Is there a securities market regulatory authority? If so, please describe directly it and the reference	Is there a financial holding company? If so, please directly show references
77	Maldives	Asia	Maldives Monetary Authority (http://www.mma.gov.mv/#/)	Maldives Monetary Authority (http://knowyourcountry.info/files/maldivesamlaug14_3.pdf)	Maldives Monetary Authority (https://www.fsa.go.jp/en/glopac/Presentation_14/Maldives.pdf)	The Capital Market Development Authority (https://en.wikipedia.org/wiki/Capital_Market_Development_Authority_Maldives#:~:text=The%20Capital%20Market%20Development%20Authority,the%20capital%20market%20of%20Maldives.&text=CMDA%20is%20governed%20by%20a,Chief%20Executive%20Officer%20(CEO).)	https://asia.nikkei.com/Companies/Mega-Financial-Holding-Co.-Ltd2
78	Mongolia	Asia	Bank of Mongolia (https://www.mongolbank.mn/eng/)	Bank of Mongolia (http://documents.worldbank.org/curated/en/438681468053942906/pdf/704190ESW0P0850ber0on000secured0doc.pdf)	Financial Regulatory Commission (FRC) (https://www.businesswire.com/news/home/20190412005293/en/Mongolia-Insurance-Industry-Governance-Risk-Compliance-Report)	Financial Regulatory Commission of Mongolia (https://sseinitiative.org/stock-exchange/msx/)	http://www.ardcredit.com/en/about

(continued)

(continued)

Serial number	Member States of UN	Continent	Is there a central bank? If yes, please directly specify it and the reference	Is there a banking regulatory authority? If so, please describe directly it or them and the reference	Is there an insurance regulatory authority? If so, please describe directly it or them and the reference	Is there a securities market regulatory authority? If so, please describe directly it and the reference	Is there a financial holding company? If so, please directly show references
79	Myanmar	Asia	Central Bank of Myanmar (https://en.wikipedia.org/wiki/Central_Bank_of_Myanmar)	Central Bank of Myanmar (https://www.cbm.gov.mm/content/banking-regulation-department)	The Insurance Business Regulatory Board (https://practiceguides.chambers.com/practice-guides/insurance-reinsurance-2020/myanmar)	The Securities Exchange Commission of Myanmar (SECM) (http://www.capital-markets-intelligence.com/wp-content/uploads/2015/02/MORI_H_MYANMAR_ECM_2015.pdf)	https://fullertonmyanmar.com/about-us/shareholders/
80	Iran (Islamic Republic of)	Asia	The Central Bank of Iran (https://en.wikipedia.org/wiki/Central_Bank_of_Iran#:~:text=The%20Central%20Bank%20of%20Iran,the%20central%20bank%20of%20Iran.)	The Central Bank of Iran (https://www.tamimi.com/law-update-articles/overview-of-the-iranian-banking-system/)	The Central Insurance of Iran (https://goirantours.com/all-the-details-about-iran-insurance-companies/)	The Tehran Stock Exchange (https://www.asiasecuritiesforum.org/pdf/2017/10_Report_SEBA.pdf)	Unknown
81	Oman	Asia	Central Bank of Oman (https://www.cbo.gov.om/)	Central Bank of Oman (https://www.cbo.gov.om/Pages/RegulatoryFramework.aspx)	Capital Market Authority (https://www.cma.gov.om/)	Capital Market Authority (https://sseinitiative.org/stock-exchange/msm/)	https://www.iosco.org/library/resolutions/pdf/IOSCORES7.pdf

(continued)

(continued)

Serial number	Member States of UN	Continent	Is there a central bank? If yes, please directly specify it and the reference	Is there a banking regulatory authority? If so, please describe directly it or them and the reference	Is there an insurance regulatory authority? If so, please describe directly it or them and the reference	Is there a securities market regulatory authority? If so, please describe directly it and the reference	Is there a financial holding company? If so, please directly show references
82	Pakistan	Asia	State Bank of Pakistan (http://www.sbp.org.pk/)	State Bank of Pakistan (https://en.wikipedia.org/wiki/State_Bank_of_Pakistan)	Securities & Exchange Commission of Pakistan (https://jamapunji.pk/about-secp)	The Securities & Exchange Commission of Pakistan (https://en.wikipedia.org/wiki/Securities_%26_Exchange_Commission_of_Pakistan#:~:text=The%20Securities%20%26%20Exchange%20Commission%20of,growth%20and%20prosperity%20in%20Pakistan.)	https://www.swfinstitute.org/profile/5c3[illegible]e3cc2c767608e1[illegible]482e5

(continued)

(continued)

Serial number	Member States of UN	Continent	Is there a central bank? If yes, please directly specify it and the reference	Is there a banking regulatory authority? If so, please describe directly it or them and the reference	Is there an insurance regulatory authority? If so, please describe directly it or them and the reference	Is there a securities market regulatory authority? If so, please describe directly it and the reference	Is there a financial holding company? If so, please directly show references
83	Philippines	Asia	The Bangko Sentral ng Pilipinas (BSP) (http://www.bsp.gov.ph/)	The Bangko Sentral ng Pilipinas (BSP) (http://www.lexmundi.com/images/lexmundi/PDF/PG/BankFinance/Phillipines.pdf)	Philippine Insurance Commissioner (PIC) (https://www.ibanet.org/Article/NewDetail.aspx?ArticleUid=47DFA919-DABC-4CE2-89E6-239CA0572FE8#:~:text=Current%20Philippine%20capital%20regime%20regulations&text=The%20RAP%20covered%20three%20major,'RBC%202')%20Framework.)	The Securities and Exchange Commission (SEC) (https://openknowledge.worldbank.org/handle/10986/15537#:~:text=The%20Securities%20and%20Exchange%20Commission,capital%20markets%20and%20their%20participants.&text=The%20Securities%20Regulation%20Code%20(SRC,the%20regulation%20of%20the%20markets.)	https://www.swfinstitute.org/profile/5cfeaa673ee00a3a9284d895

(continued)

(continued)

Serial number	Member States of UN	Continent	Is there a central bank? If yes, please directly specify it and the reference	Is there a banking regulatory authority? If so, please describe directly it or them and the reference	Is there an insurance regulatory authority? If so, please describe directly it or them and the reference	Is there a securities market regulatory authority? If so, please describe directly it and the reference	Is there a financial holding company? If so, please directly show references
84	Republic of Korea	Asia	The Bank of Korea (https://en.wikipedia.org/wiki/Bank_of_Korea#:~:text=The%20Bank%20of%20Korea%20(BOK,that%2C%20the%20bank%20targets%20inflation.)	The Financial Supervisory Service and Financial Services Commission (FSC) (https://www.globallegalinsights.com/practice-areas/banking-and-finance-laws-and-regulations/korea#:~:text=The%20two%20main%20regulators%20in,the%20Prime%20Minister%20of%20Korea.&text=The%20FSS%20is%20a%20financial,general%20oversight%20of%20the%20FSC.)	Financial Services Commission (http://www.fsc.go.kr/eng/lr/list.jsp?menu=0304&bbsid=BBS0057)	Financial Services Commission (http://meng.fsc.go.kr/)	http://koreanlii.or.kr/w/index.php/Financial_holding_companies?ckattempt=1
85	Saudi Arabia	Asia	The Saudi Arabian Monetary Authorit (https://en.wikipedia.org/wiki/Saudi_Arabian_Monetary_Authority)	The Saudi Arabian Monetary Authorit (https://www.saudilegal.com/banking#:~:text=The%20central%20bank%20of%20Saudi,SAMA%20Charter%2C%20Royal%20Decree%20No.&text=Banking%20in%20Saudi%20Arabia%20is,Control%20Regulation%2C%20Royal%20Decree%20No.)	Saudi Arabian Monetary Authority (https://uk-practicallaw-thomsonreuters-com.proxy.scd.u-psud.fr/3-577-5486?transitionType=Default&contextData=(sc.Default)&firstPage=true)	The Capital Market Authority (CMA) (https://content-next-westlaw-com.proxy.scd.u-psud.fr/Document/Ia1cf6dcec7f411e498db8b09b4f043e0/View/FullText.html?contextData=(sc.Default)&transitionType=Default&firstPage=true&bhab=0&bhav=&bhqs=1)	https://www.swfinstitute.org/profile/5b6f458def350e45039c8d04

(continued)

(continued)

Serial number	Member States of UN	Continent	Is there a central bank? If yes, please directly specify it and the reference	Is there a banking regulatory authority? If so, please describe directly it or them and the reference	Is there an insurance regulatory authority? If so, please describe directly it or them and the reference	Is there a securities market regulatory authority? If so, please describe directly it and the reference	Is there a financial holding company? If so, please directly show references
86	Singapore	Asia	Monetary Authority of Singapore (https://www.mas.gov.sg/)	Monetary Authority of Singapore (https://www.mas.gov.sg/regulation)	Monetary Authority of Singapore (https://www.mas.gov.sg/regulation/Insurance)	Monetary Authority of Singapore Singapore Exchange Regulation (https://uk-practicallaw-thomsonreuters-com.proxy.scd.u-psud.fr/7-634-7850?__lrTS=20200903161813745&transitionType=Default&contextData=%28sc.Default%29)	https://sso.agc.gov.sg/Act/FHCA2013/Uncommenced/
87	Thailand	Asia	Bank of Thailand (https://en.wikipedia.org/wiki/Bank_of_Thailand)	The Financial Institutions Policy Committee (https://www.fsa.go.jp/en/glopac/introductory/Presentation13/Thailand13.pdf)	The Office of Insurance Commission (https://en.wikipedia.org/wiki/Office_of_Insurance_Commission)	The Securities and Exchange Commission (SEC) (https://www.set.or.th/en/regulations/protection/protection_p1.html)	https://www.tradingview.com/markets/stocks-thailand/sectorandindustry-industry/financial-conglomerates/

(continued)

(continued)

Serial number	Member States of UN	Continent	Is there a central bank? If yes, please directly specify it and the reference	Is there a banking regulatory authority? If so, please describe directly it or them and the reference	Is there an insurance regulatory authority? If so, please describe directly it or them and the reference	Is there a securities market regulatory authority? If so, please describe directly it and the reference	Is there a financial holding company? If so, please directly show references
88	Turkey	Asia	Central Bank of the Republic of Turkey (https://www.tcmb.gov.tr/wps/wcm/connect/en/tcmb+en)	Banking Regulation and Supervision Agency (https://uk-practicallaw-thomsonreuters-com.proxy.scd.u-psud.fr/w-007-5596?transitionType=Default&contextData=(sc.Default)&firstPage=true)	Insurance Association of Turkey (https://www.tsb.org.tr/regulations.aspx?pageID=987)	Capital Markets Board of Turkey (CMB) (https://www.cmb.gov.tr/Sayfa/Index/0/0)	http://www.lawsturkey.com/regulation/26333-regulation-on-financial-holding-companies
89	United Arab Emirates	Asia	UAE Central Bank (https://www.centralbank.ae/en)	UAE Central Bank (https://www.centralbank.ae/en/laws-and-regulations/regulation)	Insurance Authority (https://u.ae/en/information-and-services/finance-and-investment/insurance#:~:text=from%20Insurance%20Authority-,Legal%20provisions,accordance%20with%20Federal%20Law%20No.&text=Liability%20insurance%20(third%20party%20liability,of%20trains%2C%20insurance%20of%20cash.)	Securities and Commodities Authority (https://en.wikipedia.org/wiki/Securities_and_Commodities_Authority#:~:text=Securities%20and%20Commodities%20Authority%20(SCA)%20is%20a%20UAE%20entity%20established,directly%20to%20the%20Economy%20Minister.)	https://www.tamiminvestments.com/

(continued)

(continued)

Serial number	Member States of UN	Continent	Is there a central bank? If yes, please directly specify it and the reference	Is there a banking regulatory authority? If so, please describe directly it or them and the reference	Is there an insurance regulatory authority? If so, please describe directly it or them and the reference	Is there a securities market regulatory authority? If so, please describe directly it and the reference	Is there a financial holding company? If so, please directly show references
90	Uzbekistan	Asia	Central Bank of Uzbekistan (https://en.wikipedia.org/wiki/Central_Bank_of_Uzbekistan)	Central Bank of Uzbekistan (https://cbu.uz/en/credit-organizations/)	State Insurance Supervisor (https://gratanet.com/laravel-filemanager/files/3/00Insurance%20_Uzbekistan.pdf)	Republican Stock Exchange Toshkent (https://uzse.uz/legislations/103?locale=en)	https://en.trend.az/business/finance/3165111.html
91	Lao People's Democratic Republic	Asia	Bank of the Lao P.D.R (https://en.wikipedia.org/wiki/Bank_of_the_Lao_P.D.R.)	The Bank of the Lao PDR (https://www.wto.org/english/thewto_e/acc_e/lao_e/WTACCLAO20A1_LEG_1.pdf)	The Ministry of Finance (https://uk-practicallaw-thomsonreuters-com.proxy.scd.u-psud.fr/w-012-6702?transitionType=Default&contextData=(sc.Default)&firstPage=true)	The Securities and Exchange Commission Office (https://www.waseda.jp/win-cls/CA_BMGS/ABMF%20Vol1%20Part%202%20Sec%206%20Lao%20PDR.pdf)	Unknown

(continued)

(continued)

Serial number	Member States of UN	Continent	Is there a central bank? If yes, please directly specify it and the reference	Is there a banking regulatory authority? If so, please describe directly it or them and the reference	Is there an insurance regulatory authority? If so, please describe directly it or them and the reference	Is there a securities market regulatory authority? If so, please describe directly it and the reference	Is there a financial holding company? If so, please directly show references
92	Viet Nam	Asia	The State Bank of Vietnam (https://www.sbv.gov.vn/webcenter/portal/en/home/sbv?_afrLoop=13248249933201326)	The State Bank of Vietnam (https://www.sbv.gov.vn/webcenter/portal/en/home/sbv/bsupervision/sventities?_afrLoop=13248290229390326#%40%3F_afrLoop%3D13248290229390326%26centerWidth%3D80%2525%26leftWidth%3D20%2525%26rightWidth%3D0%2525%26showFooter%3Dfalse%26showHeader%3Dfalse%26_adf.ctrl-state%3D11z9jhpg99_181)	The Insurance Supervisory Authority (https://uk-practicallaw-thomsonreuters-com.proxy.scd.u-psud.fr/2-568-9187?transitionType=Default&contextData=(sc.Default)&firstPage=true)	State Securities Commission of Vietnam (http://www.ssc.gov.vn/ubck/faces/en/enmenu/enpages_home;jsessionid=yXPcfnRGfpF3JQqkZRhhTT2fL65rSYQ6sLp424CDkhpQlXh7ztvV!-2084411581!2002739246?_afrLoop=32240838382000&_afrWindowMode=0&_afrWindowId=null)	https://www.shinhanfinance.com.vn/en/who-we-are pr [illegible]
93	Nepal	Asia	Nepal Rastra Bank (https://archive.nrb.org.np/)	Nepal Rastra Bank (Nepal - Banking Systems | export.govwww.export.gov › article › id = Nepal-Banking-Syst…)	Beema Samiti (https://www.businesswire.com/news/home/20180308005611/en/Nepalese-Insurance-Industry-Governance-Risk-Compliance-Report#:~:text=The%20Nepalese%20insurance%20industry%20is,a%20cross%2Dborder%20basis%20only.)	Securities Board of Nepal (SEBON) (https://www.sebon.gov.np/about-sebon#:~:text=Securities%20Board%20of%20Nepal%20(SEBON,under%20the%20Securities%20Act%2C%202006.)	Unknown

(continued)

(continued)

Serial number	Member States of UN	Continent	Is there a central bank? If yes, please directly specify it and the reference	Is there a banking regulatory authority? If so, please describe directly it or them and the reference	Is there an insurance regulatory authority? If so, please describe directly it or them and the reference	Is there a securities market regulatory authority? If so, please describe directly it and the reference	Is there a financial holding company? If so, please directly show references
94	Qatar	Asia	Qatar Central Bank (https://en.wikipedia.org/wiki/Qatar_Central_Bank)	Qatar Central Bank (http://www.cbq.qa/en/advice-and-information/information-library/policies-and-statements/pages/anti-money-laundering-and-terrorism-statement.aspx)	Qatar Financial Centre Regulatory Authority and the Qatar Central Bank (https://www.businesswire.com/news/home/20180312005947/en/Qatar-Insurance-Industry-Governance-Risk-Compliance-Report#:~:text=The%20insurance%20industry%20of%20Qatar,accident%20and%20health%20insurance%20business.)	Qatar Financial Markets Authority (QFMA) (https://www.qfma.org.qa/english/Pages/default.aspx)	Unknown
95	Sri Lanka	Asia	Central Bank of Sri Lanka (https://www.cbsl.gov.lk/)	Central Bank of Sri Lanka (https://www.cbsl.gov.lk/en/authorized-financial-institutions/licensed-commercial-banks)	Insurance Regulatory Commission of Sri Lanka (https://ircsl.gov.lk/)	The Securities and Exchange Commission of Sri Lanka (http://www.sec.gov.lk/?page_id=1434)	Unknown
96	Syrian Arab Republic	Asia	Central Bank of Syria (https://en.wikipedia.org/wiki/Central_Bank_of_Syria)	Central Bank of Syria (https://www.britannica.com/place/Syria/Finance)	Ministry of Finance (http://portal.egov.sy/services_guid.ar_guid/en/0/0/module.page.html)	Syrian Commission of financial markets and securities (http://www.dse.gov.sy/user/?page=law_show&id=1&pr=L)	Unknown

(continued)

(continued)

Serial number	Member States of UN	Continent	Is there a central bank? If yes, please directly specify it and the reference	Is there a banking regulatory authority? If so, please describe directly it or them and the reference	Is there an insurance regulatory authority? If so, please describe directly it or them and the reference	Is there a securities market regulatory authority? If so, please describe directly it and the reference	Is there a financial holding company? If so, please directly show references
97	Tajikistan	Asia	National Bank of Tajikistan (https://nbt.tj/en/)	National Bank of Tajikistan (https://nbt.tj/en/banking_system/overview_banking_system.php)	National Bank of Tajikistan (https://nbt.tj/en/sugurta/bozori-sugurtavi/2018/1-yanvari-soli-2018.php)	National Bank of Tajikistan and the Ministry of Finances (http://www.ebrd.com/downloads/legal/securities/tajsec.pdf)	Unknown
98	Timor-Leste	Asia	Central Bank of Timor-Leste (https://www.bancocentral.tl/en)	Central Bank of Timor-Leste (https://www.globallegalinsights.com/practice-areas/banking-and-finance-laws-and-regulations/timor-leste)	Central Bank of Timor-Leste (https://www.globallegalinsights.com/practice-areas/banking-and-finance-laws-and-regulations/timor-leste)	No stock exchange (https://www.ifrs.org/use-around-the-world/use-of-ifrs-standards-by-jurisdiction/timor-leste/)	Unknown
99	Turkmenistan	Asia	Central Bank of Turkmenistan (https://www.cbt.tm/en/)	Central Bank of Turkmenistan (https://www.cbt.tm/en/ulgam/sazlashdyrma.html)	The Ministry of Economy and Finance (https://silo.tips/download/insurance-law-of-turkmenistan-section-i-general-provisions-article-1-the-concept#:~:text=Insurance%20objects%20of%20legal%20entities,mandatory%20and%20voluntary%20insurance%20plans.)	No market for securities (https://www.pwc.com/uz/en/assets/pdf/doing-business-guide-in-turkmenistan-2012-2013.pdf)	Unknown

(continued)

(continued)

Serial number	Member States of UN	Continent	Is there a central bank? If yes, please directly specify it and the reference	Is there a banking regulatory authority? If so, please describe directly it or them and the reference	Is there an insurance regulatory authority? If so, please describe directly it or them and the reference	Is there a securities market regulatory authority? If so, please describe directly it and the reference	Is there a financial holding company? If so, please directly show references
100	Yemen	Asia	Central Bank of Yemen (http://centralbank.gov.ye/)	Central Bank of Yemen (http://centralbank.gov.ye/newslettar aspx?keyid=10&pid=8&lang=1&cattype=6)	Ministry of Trade and Industry (https://www.atlas-mag.net/en/article/the-yemenite-insurance-market)	No stock exchange (https://en.wikipedia.org/wiki/Economy_of_Yemen#:~:text=Yemen%20has%20no%20public%20stock,specialized%20state%2Downed%20development%20banks.)	Unknown
64	Cyprus	Europe	Central Bank of Cyprus (https://www.centralbank.cy/)	The European Central Bank (ECB) and the Central Bank of Cyprus (CBC) (https://uk-practicallaw-thomsonreuters-com.proxy.scd.u-psud.fr/w-007-5741?transitionType=Default&contextData=(sc.Default)&firstPage=true)	The Superintendent of Insurance (http://mof.gov.cy/en/directorates-units/insurance-companies-control-service)	The Cyprus Securities and Exchange Commission (https://en.wikipedia.org/wiki/Cyprus_Securities_and_Exchange_Commission#:~:text=The%20Cyprus%20Securities%20and%20Exchange,European%20MiFID%20financial%20harmonization%20law.)	https://www.internationaltaxreview.com/article/b1fbstd34jp0yj/why-cyprus-is-an-ideal-holding-company-location

(continued)

(continued)

Serial number	Member States of UN	Continent	Is there a central bank? If yes, please directly specify it and the reference	Is there a banking regulatory authority? If so, please describe directly it or them and the reference	Is there an insurance regulatory authority? If so, please describe directly it or them and the reference	Is there a securities market regulatory authority? If so, please describe directly it and the reference	Is there a financial holding company? If so, please directly show references
101	Albania	Europe	The Bank of Albania (https://www.bankofalbania.org/home/)	The Bank of Albania (https://aab.al/wp-content/uploads/2019/04/Bankieri-31-Anglisht-per-web.pdf)	The Financial Supervisory Authority (http://www.amf.gov.al/pdf/ligje/191_Law%20no.%2052%202014%20On%20the%20activity%20of%20insurance%20and%20reinsurance.pdf)	The Albanian Financial Supervisory Authority (https://www.alse.al/en/index.php/alse/regulatory-entities/financial-supervisory-authority/)	Unknown
102	Andorra	Europe	Unknown	Andorran Financial Authority (https://www.afa.ad/en/entitats-supervisades)	Andorran Financial Authority (https://www.afa.ad/en/entitats-supervisades)	No stock exchange (https://books.google.fr/books?id=ngfPVhiE1UsC&pg=PA17&lpg=PA17&dq=Andorra+securities+market+regulation&source=bl&ots=8Ap9kGwlse&sig=ACfU3U1WbDlnstRr1JHPrKoBvhUZP2cleg&hl=fr&sa=X&ved=2ahUKEwiEw4rsqbXqAhXaAGMBHRhtD8YQ6AEwDHoECAkQAQ#v=onepage&q=Andorra%20securities%20market%20regulation&f=false)	Unknown

(continued)

(continued)

Serial number	Member States of UN	Continent	Is there a central bank? If yes, please directly specify it and the reference	Is there a banking regulatory authority? If so, please describe directly it or them and the reference	Is there an insurance regulatory authority? If so, please describe directly it or them and the reference	Is there a securities market regulatory authority? If so, please describe directly it and the reference	Is there a financial holding company? If so, please directly show references
103	Bosnia and Herzegovina	Europe	The Central Bank of Bosnia and Herzegovina (https://www.cbbh.ba/?lang=en)	Banking Agency of the Federation of Bosnia and Herzegovina (https://www.bscee.org/members/BIH.html)	Insurance Supervisory Agency of Federation of Bosnia and Herzegovina (http://www.nados.ba/)	The Securities Commission of the Federation of Bosnia and Herzegovina (http://www.komvp.gov.ba/site/index.php/en/home)	Unknown
104	Bulgaria	Europe	The Bulgarian National Bank (https://en.wikipedia.org/wiki/Bulgarian_National_Bank)	Banking Supervision Department Bulgarian National Bank (https://www.bscee.org/members/BGR.html)	Financial Supervision Commission (https://www.fsc.bg/en/about-fsc/establishment/)	The Bulgaria Securities and Stock Exchanges Commission (https://silo.tips/download/republic-of-bulgaria-national-assembly-securities-stock-exchanges-and-investment)	Unknown
105	Iceland	Europe	Central Bank of Iceland (https://www.cb.is/)	Financial Supervisory Authority (https://en.fme.is/supervision/supervised-entities/)	Financial Supervisory Authority (https://en.fme.is/supervision/foreign-insurance-companies/)	Financial Supervisory Authority (https://en.wikipedia.org/wiki/Financial_Supervisory_Authority_(Iceland))	https://en.fme.is/published-material/rules/

(continued)

(continued)

Serial number	Member States of UN	Continent	Is there a central bank? If yes, please directly specify it and the reference	Is there a banking regulatory authority? If so, please describe directly it or them and the reference	Is there an insurance regulatory authority? If so, please describe directly it or them and the reference	Is there a securities market regulatory authority? If so, please describe directly it and the reference	Is there a financial holding company? If so, please directly show references
106	Austria	Europe	National Bank of Austria (https://www.centralbanking.com/central-banks/2480596/national-bank-of-austria)	European Central Bank (ECB);Financial Market Authority (FMA) (https://uk-practicallaw-thomsonreuters-com.proxy.scd.u-psud.fr/w-007-5098?transitionType=Default&contextData=(sc.Default)&firstPage=true)	The Austrian Financial Market Authority (FMA); European Insurance and Occupational Pensions Authority (EIOPA) (https://uk-practicallaw-thomsonreuters-com.proxy.scd.u-psud.fr/w-015-5489?transitionType=Default&contextData=(sc.Default))	The Austrian Stock Exchange (https://www.wienerborse.at/en/legal/legal-framework/)	Financial Market Holding Company of the Republic of Austria (https://www.bmf.gv.at/en/topics/financial-sector/austrian-financial-market-stability-package/institutions.html)

(continued)

(continued)

Serial number	Member States of UN	Continent	Is there a central bank? If yes, please directly specify it and the reference	Is there a banking regulatory authority? If so, please describe directly it or them and the reference	Is there an insurance regulatory authority? If so, please describe directly it or them and the reference	Is there a securities market regulatory authority? If so, please describe directly it and the reference	Is there a financial holding company? If so, please directly show references
107	Belarus	Europe	National Bank of the Republic of Belarus (https://www.nbrb.by/engl)	National Bank of the Republic of Belarus (https://www.nbrb.by/engl/legislation/banksupervision)	The Ministry of Finance (https://www.businesswire.com/news/home/20190307005848/en/Belarusian-Insurance-Industry-Governance-Risk-Compliance-Report)	The State Security Committee of the Republic of Belarus (https://books.google.fr/books?id=cY0-I4A_77QC&pg=PA10&lpg=PA10&dq=Belarus+securities+company+regulatory+authority&source=bl&ots=4rIIZ00-W5&sig=ACfU3U3IBD4vyCuFhv0gdScInrNsLnhKMQ&hl=fr&sa=X&ved=2ahUKEwing_X2oMLqAhVDxIUKHUyYABIQ6AEwCnoECAkQAQ#v=onepage&q=Belarus%20securities%20company%20regulatory%20authority&f=false)	https://www.eib.org/attachments/efs/republic_of_belarus_financial_sector_review_en.pdf
108	Belgium	Europe	The National Bank of Belgium (https://www.nbb.be/en)	National Bank of Belgium (https://www.nautadutilh.com/fr/file-download/download/public/1323)	Financial Services and Markets Authority (https://www.fsma.be/en/insurance)	Financial Services and Markets Authority (https://www.fsma.be/en/insurance)	https://www.swfinstitute.org/profile/598cdaa50124e9fd2d05b558

(continued)

(continued)

Serial number	Member States of UN	Continent	Is there a central bank? If yes, please directly specify it and the reference	Is there a banking regulatory authority? If so, please describe directly it or them and the reference	Is there an insurance regulatory authority? If so, please describe directly it or them and the reference	Is there a securities market regulatory authority? If so, please describe directly it and the reference	Is there a financial holding company? If so, please directly show references
109	Croatia	Europe	Croatian National Bank (https://www.hnb.hr/en/home)	Croatian Financial Services Supervisory Agency (https://www.hanfa.hr/en/)	Croatian Financial Services Supervisory Agency (https://www.hanfa.hr/insurance-market/)	Croatian Financial Services Supervisory Agency (https://www.hanfa.hr/about-us/)	https://www.investo.hr/en/faq-s/default.htm
110	Czech Republic	Europe	Czech National Bank (https://www.cnb.cz/en/)	Czech National Bank (https://www.cnb.cz/en/supervision-financial-market/financial-market-supervision/index.html)	Czech National Bank (https://www.cnb.cz/en/supervision-financial-market/conduct-of-supervision/status-of-supervision/supervision-of-the-insurance-industry/index.html)	The Prague Stock Exchange (https://www.imf.org/external/np/rosc/cze/securit.htm)	https://www.ppf.eu/en/companies
111	Denmark	Europe	Danmarks Nationalbank (https://www.nationalbanken.dk/en)	The Financial Supervisory Authority (https://uk-practicallaw-thomsonreuters-com.proxy.scd.u-psud.fr/w-007-8508?transitionType=Default&contextData=(sc.Default)&firstPage=true)	Financial Supervisory Authority (https://en.wikipedia.org/wiki/Financial_Supervisory_Authority_(Denmark))	Financial Supervisory Authority (https://en.wikipedia.org/wiki/Financial_Supervisory_Authority_(Denmark))	https://www.swfinstitute.org/profile/5c9253877ba26c5308ba2ab1

(continued)

(continued)

Serial number	Member States of UN	Continent	Is there a central bank? If yes, please directly specify it and the reference	Is there a banking regulatory authority? If so, please describe directly it or them and the reference	Is there an insurance regulatory authority? If so, please describe directly it or them and the reference	Is there a securities market regulatory authority? If so, please describe directly it and the reference	Is there a financial holding company? If so, please directly show references
112	Estonia	Europe	Bank of Estonia (https://www.eestipank.ee/en)	Eesti Pank (https://www.eestipank.ee/en/publication/varia/2013/review-estonian-financial-system-january-2013)	Ministry of Finance (https://www.eestipank.ee/en/publication/varia/2013/review-estonian-financial-system-january-2013)	Ministry of Finance (https://www.eestipank.ee/en/publication/varia/2013/review-estonian-financial-system-january-2013)	https://www.eestipank.ee/en/financial-holding-company
113	Finland	Europe	The Bank of Finland (https://www.suomenpankki.fi/en/)	Financial Supervisory Authority (https://uk-practicallaw-thomsonreuters-com.proxy.scd.u-psud.fr/w-007-3856?transitionType=Default&contextData=(sc.Default)&firstPage=true)	Financial Supervisory Authority (https://iclg.com/practice-areas/insurance-and-reinsurance-laws-and-regulations/finland)	Financial Supervisory Authority (https://www.finanssivalvonta.fi/en/capital-markets/stock-exchange-and-other-trading-venues/)	https://www.swfinstitute.org/profile/598cdaa50124e9fd2d05a7f5
114	France	Europe	La Banque de France (https://www.banque-france.fr/)	The European Central Bank/Prudential and Resolution Control Authority (ACPR)/The Minister of Economy and the Financial Markets Authority (AMF)/Banque de France (https://uk-practicallaw-thomsonreuters-com.proxy.scd.u-psud.fr/w-007-9978?transitionType=Default&contextData=(sc.Default))	Prudential and Resolution Control Authority (ACPR) (https://acpr.banque-france.fr/en/page-sommaire/insurance-supervision)	The Autorité des Marchés Financiers (AMF) (https://reglement-general.amf-france.org/reglement/en_US/RG-en-vigueur)	https://acpr.banque-france.fr/en/authorisation/banking-industry-procedures/licensing-authorisation-and-registration/financial-holding-company-and-combined-financial-holding-companies

(continued)

(continued)

Serial number	Member States of UN	Continent	Is there a central bank? If yes, please directly specify it and the reference	Is there a banking regulatory authority? If so, please describe directly it or them and the reference	Is there an insurance regulatory authority? If so, please describe directly it or them and the reference	Is there a securities market regulatory authority? If so, please describe directly it and the reference	Is there a financial holding company? If so, please directly show references
115	Germany	Europe	The Deutsche Bundesbank (https://www.bundesbank.de/en/tasks/central-bank-of-the-federal-republic-of-germany-626946)	The European Central Bank (ECB)/the Federal Financial Services Supervisory Authority/Deutsche Bundesbank (https://uk-practicallaw-thomsonreuters-com.proxy.scd.u-psud.fr/w-007-4084?transitionType=Default&contextData=(sc.Default)&firstPage=true)	Federal Financial Supervisory Authority/ the authorities of the Federal States (https://iclg.com/practice-areas/insurance-and-reinsurance-laws-and-regulations/germany)	Federal Financial Supervisory Authority (https://complyadvantage.com/knowledgebase/bafin-what-is-the-federal-financial-supervisory-authority/#:~:text=BaFin%20is%20Germany's%20financial%20regulator,Germany's%20financial%20markets%20and%20institutions.)	https://www.cftc.gov/sites/default/files/idc/groups/public/@otherif/documents/ifdocs/euexcncobankingact.pdf
116	Greece	Europe	The Bank of Greece (https://www.bankofgreece.gr/en/homepage)	The Bank of Greece (https://uk-practicallaw-thomsonreuters-com.proxy.scd.u-psud.fr/w-007-6441?transitionType=Default&contextData=(sc.Default)&firstPage=true)	The Bank of Greece (https://iclg.com/practice-areas/insurance-and-reinsurance-laws-and-regulations/greece)	The Hellenic Capital Market Commission (https://en.wikipedia.org/wiki/Hellenic_Capital_Market_Commission#:~:text=The%20HCMC%20is%20a%20Member,in%20Greece%2C%20including%20tender%20offers.)	https://uk-practicallaw-thomsonreuters-com.proxy.scd.u-psud.fr/w-007-6441?transitionType=Default&contextData=(sc.Default)

(continued)

(continued)

Serial number	Member States of UN	Continent	Is there a central bank? If yes, please directly specify it and the reference	Is there a banking regulatory authority? If so, please describe directly it or them and the reference	Is there an insurance regulatory authority? If so, please describe directly it or them and the reference	Is there a securities market regulatory authority? If so, please describe directly it and the reference	Is there a financial holding company? If so, please directly show references
117	Hungary	Europe	The Hungarian National Bank (https://www.mnb.hu/en)	The Hungarian National Bank (https://uk-practicallaw-thomsonreuters-com.proxy.scd.u-psud.fr/5-638-6395?transitionType=Default&contextData=(sc.Default)&firstPage=true#co_anchor_a952608)	The Hungarian National Bank (https://uk-practicallaw-thomsonreuters-com.proxy.scd.u-psud.fr/5-638-6395?transitionType=Default&contextData=(sc.Default)&firstPage=true#co_anchor_a952608)	The Central Bank of Hungary (https://gss.unicreditgroup.eu/sites/default/files/markets/profiles/Market%20Profile%20Hungary%20June%202018.pdf)	https://www.reuters.com/article/us-hungary-mkb-takarek/hungarys-mkb-and-mtb-in-merger-talks-as-local-banks-gain-sway-idUSKBN22R2TI
118	Ireland	Europe	Central Bank of Ireland (http://www.centralbank.ie/)	Central Bank of Ireland and European Central Bank (https://uk-practicallaw-thomsonreuters-com.proxy.scd.u-psud.fr/w-006-9529?transitionType=Default&contextData=(sc.Default)&firstPage=true)	Central Bank of Ireland (https://www.centralbank.ie/regulation/industry-market-sectors/insurance-reinsurance)	Central Bank of Ireland (https://www.centralbank.ie/regulation)	https://www.swfinstitute.org/profile/598cdaa50124e9fd2d05b4ef

(continued)

(continued)

Serial number	Member States of UN	Continent	Is there a central bank? If yes, please directly specify it and the reference	Is there a banking regulatory authority? If so, please describe directly it or them and the reference	Is there an insurance regulatory authority? If so, please describe directly it or them and the reference	Is there a securities market regulatory authority? If so, please describe directly it and the reference	Is there a financial holding company? If so, please directly show references
119	Monaco	Europe	1. the Monegasque banks have access to the French central bank's payment facilities (https://www.cmb.mc/en/financial-center/the-financial-center) 2. European Central Bank (https://www.ecb.europa.eu/euro/coins/html/mo.en.html)	The French Prudential Control and Resolution Authority (ACPR) (https://www.lexology.com/library/detail.aspx?g=110ba7ab-9594-4eed-90b8-653cc89540c9#:~:text=Credit%20institutions%20in%20Monaco%20are,reception%20and%20transmission%20of%20orders)	The French Prudential Control and Resolution Authority (ACPR) (https://delforgelaw.com/insurance-law-monaco/)	Commission for the Control of Financial Activities (CCAF) (http://www.ccaf.mc/en/the-ccaf-in-one-click/the-monegasque-financial)	Unknown
120	Italy	Europe	The Bank of Italy (https://www.bancaditalia.it/chi-siamo/?com.dotmarketing.htmlpage.language=1)	The Bank of Italy (https://www.bancaditalia.it/compiti/vigilanza/index.html?com.dotmarketing.htmlpage.language=1)	Italian Institute for the Supervision of Insurance (IVASS) (https://uk-practicallaw-thomsonreuters-com.proxy.scd.u-psud.fr/4-501-3463?transitionType=Default&contextData=(sc.Default)&firstPage=true)	The Italian Companies and Exchange Commission (CONSOB) (https://en.wikipedia.org/wiki/Commissione_Nazionale_per_le_Societ%C3%A0_e_la_Borsa)	https://www.bancaditalia.it/compiti/vigilanza/intermediari/index.html?com.dotmarketing.htmlpage.language=1

(continued)

(continued)

Serial number	Member States of UN	Continent	Is there a central bank? If yes, please directly specify it and the reference	Is there a banking regulatory authority? If so, please describe directly it or them and the reference	Is there an insurance regulatory authority? If so, please describe directly it or them and the reference	Is there a securities market regulatory authority? If so, please describe directly it and the reference	Is there a financial holding company? If so, please directly show references
121	Latvia	Europe	The Bank of Latvia (https://en.wikipedia.org/wiki/Bank_of_Latvia)	Financial and Capital Market Commission (https://www.fktk.lv/en/)	Financial and Capital Market Commission (https://www.fktk.lv/en/)	Financial and Capital Market Commission (https://www.fktk.lv/en/market/results?page=market&search=securities)	https://www.global-regulation.com/translation/latvia/7833823/financial-conglomerates-act.html
122	Liechtenstein	Europe	National Bank of Liechtenstein (https://en.wikipedia.org/wiki/National_Bank_of_Liechtenstein)	The Liechtenstein Financial Markets Authority (https://www.globallegalinsights.com/practice-areas/banking-and-finance-laws-and-regulations/liechtenstein#:~:text=Liechtenstein%20banks%20are%20supervised%20by,prudential%20supervision%20and%20consumer%20protection.)	The Liechtenstein Financial Markets Authority (https://www.fma-li.li/en/client-protection/safeguarding-client-protection-in-different-sectors/insurance-undertakings-insurance-intermediaries.html)	The Liechtenstein Financial Markets Authority (https://www.fma-li.li/en/supervision/securities-and-markets-division/securities-prospectuses.html)	https://www.fma-li.li/en/client-protection/safeguarding-client-protection-in-different-sectors/banks.html
123	Lithuania	Europe	Bank of Lithuania (https://www.lb.lt/en/)	Bank of Lithuania (https://www.lb.lt/en/supervision-of-financial-market-participants)	Bank of Lithuania (https://www.oecd.org/countries/lithuania/Lithuania-review-of-the-insurance-system-2018.pdf)	Bank of Lithuania (https://www.lb.lt/en/supervision-of-financial-market-participants)	https://e-seimas.lrs.lt/portal/legalAct/lt/TAD/996f5e80483811e68f45bcf65e0a17ee?jfwid=f4nne5s3y

(continued)

(continued)

Serial number	Member States of UN	Continent	Is there a central bank? If yes, please directly specify it and the reference	Is there a banking regulatory authority? If so, please describe directly it or them and the reference	Is there an insurance regulatory authority? If so, please describe directly it or them and the reference	Is there a securities market regulatory authority? If so, please describe directly it and the reference	Is there a financial holding company? If so, please directly show references
124	Luxembourg	Europe	Banque centrale du Luxembourg (http://www.bcl.lu/fr/index.html)	The Minister of Finance (https://uk-practicallaw-thomsonreuters-com.proxy.scd.u-psud.fr/w-007-9691?transitionType=Default&contextData=(sc.Default))	The Commissariat aux Assurances (https://uk-practicallaw-thomsonreuters-com.proxy.scd.u-psud.fr/0-555-3868?transitionType=Default&contextData=(sc.Default)&firstPage=true)	The Commission de Surveillance du Secteur Financier (https://www.cssf.lu/en/about-the-cssf/)	https://armonesicomo.com/news/220/scpari
125	Malta	Europe	The Central Bank of Malta (https://www.centralbankmalta.org/)	Malta Financial Services Authority (https://www.mfsa.mt/firms/regulated-firms/financial-institutions/regulation/banking-supervision/)	Malta Financial Services Authority (https://www.mfsa.mt/)	Malta Financial Services Authority (https://www.mfsa.mt/firms/regulation/securities-and-market/)	https://www.mfsa.mt/firms/legislation/malta-financial-services-authority/
126	Montenegro	Europe	Central Bank of Montenegro (https://www.cbcg.me/en)	Central Bank of Montenegro (https://www.imf.org/external/pubs/ft/scr/2016/cr16201.pdf)	Insurance Supervision Agency (https://www.cbcg.me/en/core-functions/financial-stability/financial-system-of-montenegro)	Capital Market Authority (https://www.cbcg.me/en/core-functions/financial-stability/financial-system-of-montenegro)	http://www.poreskauprava.gov.me/ResourceManager/FileDownload.aspx?rid=27640&rType=2&file=9%20X%20-%20NP%20Chapter%209.pdf

(continued)

(continued)

Serial number	Member States of UN	Continent	Is there a central bank? If yes, please directly specify it and the reference	Is there a banking regulatory authority? If so, please describe directly it or them and the reference	Is there an insurance regulatory authority? If so, please describe directly it or them and the reference	Is there a securities market regulatory authority? If so, please describe directly it and the reference	Is there a financial holding company? If so, please directly show references
127	Netherlands	Europe	De Nederlandsche Bank (https://www.dnb.nl/en/)	European Central Bank (ECB) Dutch Central Bank (De Nederlandsche Bank) (DNB) Dutch Authority for the Financial Markets (Autoriteit financiële markten) (https://uk-practicallaw-thomsonreuters-com.proxy.scd.u-psud.fr/w-007-9667?transitionType=Default&contextData=(sc.Default)&firstPage=true)	Netherlands Authority for the Financial Markets (https://www.afm.nl/en/over-afm)	Netherlands Authority for the Financial Markets (https://www.afm.nl/en/zoeken?q=securities)	https://www.fxempire.com/stocks/country/netherlands/industries/financial-conglomerates
128	North Macedonia	Europe	National Bank of the Republic of North Macedonia (https://en.wikipedia.org/wiki/National_Bank_of_North_Macedonia)	National Bank of the Republic of North Macedonia (http://www.nbrm.mk/bankarska_supervizija_i_rieghulativa-en.nspx)	Insurance Supervision Agency (ISA) (http://www.nbrm.mk/ostanati_institutsii_nadliezhni_za_rieghuliranjie_i_nadzor_na_finansiski_institutsii-en.nspx)	Securities and Exchange Commission of the Republic of North Macedonia (http://www.nbrm.mk/ostanati_institutsii_nadliezhni_za_rieghuliranjie_i_nadzor_na_finansiski_institutsii-en.nspx)	Unknown

(continued)

(continued)

Serial number	Member States of UN	Continent	Is there a central bank? If yes, please directly specify it and the reference	Is there a banking regulatory authority? If so, please describe directly it or them and the reference	Is there an insurance regulatory authority? If so, please describe directly it or them and the reference	Is there a securities market regulatory authority? If so, please describe directly it and the reference	Is there a financial holding company? If so, please directly show references
129	Norway	Europe	Norges Bank (https://www.norges-bank.no/en/)	The Financial Supervisory Authority of Norway (https://www.finanstilsynet.no/en/supervision/)	The Financial Supervisory Authority of Norway (https://www.finanstilsynet.no/en/supervision/)	The Financial Supervisory Authority of Norway (https://www.finanstilsynet.no/en/supervision/)	https://www.reuters.com/companies/NOFI.OL
130	Poland	Europe	Narodowy Bank Polski (https://en.wikipedia.org/wiki/National_Bank_of_Poland)	The Polish Financial Supervision Authority (PFSA) (https://en.wikipedia.org/wiki/Financial_Supervision_Authority_(Poland))	The Polish Financial Supervision Authority (PFSA) (https://en.wikipedia.org/wiki/Financial_Supervision_Authority_(Poland))	The Polish Securities and Exchange Commission (https://en.wikipedia.org/wiki/Securities_and_Exchange_Commission_(Poland)#:~:text=The%20Polish%20Securities%20and%20Exchange,the%20Polish%20Financial%20Supervision%20Authority)	https://esas-joint-committee.europa.eu/Publications/Guidelines/JC%202019%2072%20%28List%20of%20identified%20Financial%20Conglomerates%202019%29-%20Final%20.pdf
131	Portugal	Europe	Banco de Portugal (https://www.bportugal.pt/en)	Banco de Portugal (https://www.globallegalinsights.com/practice-areas/banking-and-finance-laws-and-regulations/portugal)	Autoridade de Supervisão de Seguros e Fundos de Pensões (ASF) (https://cms.law/en/int/expert-guides/cms-expert-guide-to-insurance/portugal)	Comissão do Mercado de Valores Mobiliários (https://www.cmvm.pt/en/The_CMVM/Overview/Pages/Who-We-Are.aspx)	https://www.swfinstitute.org/profile/598cdaa50124e9fd2d05b055

(continued)

(continued)

Serial number	Member States of UN	Continent	Is there a central bank? If yes, please directly specify it and the reference	Is there a banking regulatory authority? If so, please describe directly it or them and the reference	Is there an insurance regulatory authority? If so, please describe directly it or them and the reference	Is there a securities market regulatory authority? If so, please describe directly it and the reference	Is there a financial holding company? If so, please directly show references
132	Republic of Moldova	Europe	The National Bank of Moldova (https://en.wikipedia.org/wiki/National_Bank_of_Moldova#:~:text=The%20National%20Bank%20of%20Moldova,of%20the%20Republic%20of%20Moldova.)	The National Bank of Moldova (https://www.bnm.md/en/content/banking-regulation-and-supervision)	National Commission of Financial Market (NCFM) (https://gladei.md/docs/Moldova%20insurance%20guide%202019.pdf)	National Commission of Financial Market (NCFM) (http://old.cnpf.md/en/prez/)	https://www.bnm.md/en/content/regulation-requirements-regarding-members-governing-body-bank-financial-holding-company-or
133	Romania	Europe	The National Bank of Romania (https://www.bnr.ro/National-Bank-of-Romania-1144-Mobile.aspx)	The National Bank of Romania (https://www.bankersalmanac.com/addcon/infobank/bank-regulators.aspx)	The Romanian Financial Services Authority (https://asfromania.ro/en/supervision/insurance-market)	The Financial Supervisory Authority (https://asfromania.ro/en/about-asf/about-us)	https://www.lexmundi.com/Document.asp?DocID=2996

(continued)

(continued)

Serial number	Member States of UN	Continent	Is there a central bank? If yes. please directly specify it and the reference	Is there a banking regulatory authority? If so, please describe directly it or them and the reference	Is there an insurance regulatory authority? If so, please describe directly it or them and the reference	Is there a securities market regulatory authority? If so, please describe directly it and the reference	Is there a financial holding company? If so, please directly show references
134	Russian Federation	Europe	The Central Bank of Russian Federation (https://www.cbr.ru/eng/)	The Central Bank of Russian Federation (https://uk-practicallaw-thomsonreuters-com.proxy.scd.u-psud.fr/w-023-9296?transitionType=Default&contextData=(sc.Default))	The Central Bank of Russian Federation and the Ministry of Finance (https://uk-practicallaw-thomsonreuters-com.proxy.scd.u-psud.fr/8-523-9078?__lrTS=20200721230944237&transitionType=Default&contextData=(sc.Default)&firstPage=true)	The Federal Financial Markets Service (https://en.wikipedia.org/wiki/Federal_Financial_Markets_Service)	https://en.wikipedia.org/wiki/IFD_Kapital_Group
135	Serbia	Europe	National Bank of Serbia (https://www.nbs.rs/internet/english/)	National Bank of Serbia (https://www.nbs.rs/internet/english/50/index.html)	National Bank of Serbia (https://www.nbs.rs/internet/english/60/index.html)	The Securities Commission of the Republic of Serbia (http://www.sec.gov.rs/index.php/en/)	https://www.nbs.rs/internet/english/20/laws/law_banks.pdf

(continued)

(continued)

Serial number	Member States of UN	Continent	Is there a central bank? If yes, please directly specify it and the reference	Is there a banking regulatory authority? If so, please describe directly it or them and the reference	Is there an insurance regulatory authority? If so, please describe directly it or them and the reference	Is there a securities market regulatory authority? If so, please describe directly it and the reference	Is there a financial holding company? If so, please directly show references
136	Slovakia	Europe	National Bank of Slovakia (https://en.wikipedia.org/wiki/National_Bank_of_Slovakia)	National Bank of Slovakia (https://www.nbs.sk/en/financial-market-supervision1/supervision)	National Bank of Slovakia (https://www.nbs.sk/en/financial-market-supervision1/supervision)	National Bank of Slovakia (https://www.nbs.sk/en/financial-market-supervision1/supervision)	https://esas-joint-committee.europa.eu/Publications/Guidelines/JC%202016%2077%20%28List%20of%20identified%20Financial%20Conglomerates%202016%29.pdf
137	Slovenia	Europe	The Bank of Slovenia (https://en.wikipedia.org/wiki/Bank_of_Slovenia)	The Bank of Slovenia (https://www.bsi.si/en/financial-stability/banking-system-supervision)	Insurance Supervision Agency (https://www.a-zn.si/en/)	The Securities Market Agency (https://www.a-tvp.si/eng)	https://www.dnb.com/business-directory/company-profiles.financial_holding_sro.c9ab7745e1f98572bd134e40b7f372ce.html

(continued)

(continued)

Serial number	Member States of UN	Continent	Is there a central bank? If yes, please directly specify it and the reference	Is there a banking regulatory authority? If so, please describe directly it or them and the reference	Is there an insurance regulatory authority? If so, please describe directly it or them and the reference	Is there a securities market regulatory authority? If so, please describe directly it and the reference	Is there a financial holding company? If so, please directly show references
138	Spain	Europe	Bank of Spain (https://en.wikipedia.org/wiki/Bank_of_Spain)	Bank of Spain (https://www.bde.es/bde/en/areas/supervision/normativa/regulacion/)	The Spanish Central Administration (https://uk-practicallaw-thomsonreuters-com.proxy.scd.u-psud.fr/9-501-3408?transitionType=Default&contextData=(sc.Default)&firstPage=true)	The National Securities Market Commission (https://www.cnmv.es/portal/quees/Funciones/Funciones.aspx?lang=en)	https://uk.tradingview.com/markets/stocks-spain/sectorandindustry-industry/financial-conglomerates/
139	Sweden	Europe	Sveriges Riksbank (https://www.riksbank.se/en-gb/)	Swedish Financial Supervisory Authority (SFSA) (https://www.lexology.com/library/detail.aspx?g=5334b243-b4a5-4f00-92d7-8be8e92e00e1#:~:text=The%20primary%20authority%20is%20the%20Swedish%20Financial%20Supervisory%20Authority%20(SFSA).&text=The%20SFSA%20is%20responsible%20for,has%20disciplinary%20and%20enforcement%20powers.)	Swedish Financial Supervisory Authority (https://iclg.com/practice-areas/insurance-and-reinsurance-laws-and-regulations/sweden)	The Swedish Securities Council (http://www.aktiemarknadsnamnden.se/about-the-swedish-securities-council__10)	https://www.swfinstitute.org/profile/5cd636fc3a0a2078913e5a3f

(continued)

(continued)

Serial number	Member States of UN	Continent	Is there a central bank? If yes, please directly specify it and the reference	Is there a banking regulatory authority? If so, please describe directly it or them and the reference	Is there an insurance regulatory authority? If so, please describe directly it or them and the reference	Is there a securities market regulatory authority? If so, please describe directly it and the reference	Is there a financial holding company? If so, please directly show references
140	Switzerland	Europe	Swiss National Bank (https://www.snb.ch/en/)	Swiss Financial Market Supervisory Authority (https://www.swissbanking.org/en/topics/regulation/regulation)	Swiss Financial Market Supervisory Authority (https://finma.ch/en/finma/organisation/finma-s-divisions/insurance-division/)	Swiss Financial Market Supervisory Authority (https://www.finma.ch/en/supervision/banks-and-securities-firms/)	https://www.crunchbase.com/organization/swiss-financial-holding
141	Ukraine	Europe	National Bank of Ukraine (https://bank.gov.ua/en/)	National Bank of Ukraine (https://www.contactukraine.com/banking/major-banks-in-ukraine)	Antimonopoly Committee of Ukraine (https://cms.law/en/int/expert-guides/cms-expert-guide-to-insurance/ukraine)	National Securities and Stock Market Commission (https://en.wikipedia.org/wiki/National_Securities_and_Stock_Market_Commission_(Ukraine))	https://www.ebrd.com/work-with-us/projects/psd/ojsc-insurance-company-universalna.html
142	United Kingdom of Great Britain and Northern Ireland	Europe	Bank of England (https://en.wikipedia.org/wiki/Bank_of_England#:~:text=The%20Bank%20of%20England%20is,the%20world's%20eighth%2Doldest%20bank.)	Bank of England The Prudential Regulatory Authority The Financial Conduct Authority (https://uk-practicallaw-thomsonreuters-com.proxy.scd.u-psud.fr/w-008-0211?transitionType=Default&contextData=(sc.Default))	The Prudential Regulatory Authority The Financial Conduct Authority (https://uk-practicallaw-thomsonreuters-com.proxy.scd.u-psud.fr/0-501-2031?transitionType=Default&contextData=(sc.Default))	Financial Services Authority (https://uk-practicallaw-thomsonreuters-com.proxy.scd.u-psud.fr/8-518-3383?transitionType=Default&contextData=(sc.Default))	https://www.legislation.gov.uk/uksi/2014/3348/part/1/made

(continued)

(continued)

Serial number	Member States of UN	Continent	Is there a central bank? If yes, please directly specify it and the reference	Is there a banking regulatory authority? If so, please describe directly it or them and the reference	Is there an insurance regulatory authority? If so, please describe directly it or them and the reference	Is there a securities market regulatory authority? If so, please describe directly it and the reference	Is there a financial holding company? If so, please directly show reference
143	San Marino	Europe	The Central Bank of the Republic of San Marino (https://www.bcsm.sm/site/en/home.html)	The Central Bank of the Republic of San Marino (https://www.bcsm.sm/site/en/home/functions/statutary-functions/supervision.html)	The Central Bank of the Republic of San Marino (https://www.bcsm.sm/site/en/home/functions/statutary-functions/supervision.html)	No stock exchange (https://en.wikipedia.org/wiki/List_of_countries_without_a_stock_exchange)	Unknown
144	Bahamas	North America	Central Bank of The Bahamas (https://www.centralbankbahamas.com/)	Central Bank of The Bahamas (https://www.centralbankbahamas.com/legal_guidelines.php)	Insurance Commission of The Bahamas (https://insurancecommissionbahamas.com/)	The Securities Commission of The Bahamas (http://www.scb.gov.bs/who.html)	Unknown
145	Belize	North America	Central Bank of Belize (https://www.centralbank.org.bz/)	Central Bank of Belize (https://www.centralbank.org.bz/about-us/history)	The Office of Supervisor of Insurance & Private Pensions (https://osipp.gov.bz/)	International Financial Services Commission (https://en.wikipedia.org/wiki/International_Financial_Services_Commission_(Belize))	Unknown

(continued)

(continued)

Serial number	Member States of UN	Continent	Is there a central bank? If yes, please directly specify it and the reference	Is there a banking regulatory authority? If so, please describe directly it or them and the reference	Is there an insurance regulatory authority? If so, please describe directly it or them and the reference	Is there a securities market regulatory authority? If so, please describe directly it and the reference	Is there a financial holding company? If so, please directly show references
146	Cuba	North America	The Central Bank of Cuba (http://www.bc.gob.cu/)	Central Bank of Cuba (https://oncubanews.com/en/cuba/new-financial-regulations-in-cuba-monetary-policy-foreign-capital-and-microcredit/)	Ministry of Finance (https://irletter.com/international-insurance-supervisors-regulators-associations-central-banks/)	Habana Stock Exchange (https://books.google.fr/books?id=D3UjuAlARnkC&pg=PT239&lpg=PT239&dq=havana+securities+exchange+regulation&source=bl&ots=kjM4h4DdnU&sig=ACfU3U0nFaBCH3O559Od-eXH5liaPnwPgg&hl=fr&sa=X&ved=2ahUKEwjxk_fwnczqAhVwxoUKHRIHBc8Q6AEwAHoECAgQAQ#v=onepage&q=havana%20securities%20exchange%20regulation&f=false)	Unknown
147	Dominican Republic	North America	The Central Bank of the Dominican Republic (https://www.bancentral.gov.do/)	The Central Bank of the Dominican Republic (https://www.lexmundi.com/document.asp?docid=2980)	The Insurance Superintendence (http://www.lexmundi.com/Document.asp?DocID=1231)	The Securities Superintendency of the Dominican Republic (https://www.iosco.org/library/pubdocs/542/pdf/Securities%20Superintendency%20of%20the%20Dominican%20Republic.pdf)	Unknown

(continued)

(continued)

Serial number	Member States of UN	Continent	Is there a central bank? If yes, please directly specify it and the reference	Is there a banking regulatory authority? If so, please describe directly it or them and the reference	Is there an insurance regulatory authority? If so, please describe directly it or them and the reference	Is there a securities market regulatory authority? If so, please describe directly it and the reference	Is there a financial holding company? If so, please directly show references
148	Guatemala	North America	The Bank of Guatemala (https://en.wikipedia.org/wiki/Bank_of_Guatemala)	Superintendencia de Bancos de Guatemala (https://www.ifc.org/wps/wcm/connect/c99a7fd9-745d-4069-a3ef-a3e997cbb773/Guatemala+Market+Scoping+Report.pdf?MOD=AJPERES&CVID=mk1LmCK)	Superintendency of Banks of Guatemala (https://www.iflr.com/article/b1lv16kjfcjnyg/insurance-for-insurers)	The Securities and Merchandise Market Registry (https://practiceguides.chambers.com/practice-guides/fintech-2020/guatemala)	Unknown
149	Haiti	North America	Banque de la République d'Haïti (https://fr.wikipedia.org/wiki/Banque_de_la_R%C3%A9publique_d%27Ha%C3%AFti)	Banque de la République d'Haïti (http://cgbsnet.org/docs/profiles/profile_haiti.pdf)	The Ministre de l'Economie et des Finances (https://www.businesswire.com/news/home/20180312005939/en/Haiti-Insurance-Industry-Governance-Risk-Compliance-Report)	Haitian Stock Exchange (http://www.haitianstockexchange.com/hsm/)	Unknown
150	Honduras	North America	Central Bank of Honduras (https://www.bch.hn/eng/index.php)	The National Commission for Banks and Insurance Companies (https://www.centerforfinancialinclusion.org/client-protection-in-honduras)	The National Commission for Banks and Insurance Companies (https://www.centerforfinancialinclusion.org/client-protection-in-honduras)	The National Commission for Banks and Insurance Companies (https://www.centerforfinancialinclusion.org/client-protection-in-honduras)	Unknown

(continued)

(continued)

Serial number	Member States of UN	Continent	Is there a central bank? If yes, please directly specify it and the reference	Is there a banking regulatory authority? If so, please describe directly it or them and the reference	Is there an insurance regulatory authority? If so, please describe directly it or them and the reference	Is there a securities market regulatory authority? If so, please describe directly it and the reference	Is there a financial holding company? If so, please directly show references
151	Nicaragua	North America	Central Bank of Nicaragua (https://en.wikipedia.org/wiki/Central_Bank_of_Nicaragua)	Superintendencia de Bancos y de Otras Instituciones Financieras de Nicaragua (SIBOIF) (https://www.bnamericas.com/en/company-profile/superintendencia-de-bancos-y-de-otras-instituciones-financieras-de-nicaragua-siboif)	Superintendencia de Bancos y de Otras Instituciones Financieras de Nicaragua (SIBOIF) (https://www.worldservicesgroup.com/publications.asp?action=article&artid=4760)	Superintendencia de Bancos y de Otras Instituciones Financieras de Nicaragua (https://en.wikipedia.org/wiki/Bolsa_de_Valores_de_Nicaragua)	Unknown
152	Antigua and Barbuda	North America	Eastern Caribbean Central Bank (https://www.eccb-centralbank.org/p/antigua-and-barbuda)	Eastern Caribbean Central Bank (https://www.eccb-centralbank.org/p/antigua-and-barbuda)	The Financial Services Regulatory Commission (https://www.fsrc.gov.ag/)	The Eastern Caribbean Securities Regulatory Commission (http://laws.gov.ag/wp-content/uploads/2020/02/The-SECURITIES-Bill-2020.pdf)	http://legalaffairs.gov.ag/pdf/bills/International_Banking_Act_2016.pdf
153	Barbados	North America	The Central Bank of Barbados (http://www.centralbank.org.bb/)	The Central Bank of Barbados (http://www.centralbank.org.bb/financial-institutions)	Financial Services Commission (http://fsc.gov.bb/index.php/en/about-insurance)	Financial Services Commission (http://fsc.gov.bb/index.php/en/about-insurance)	http://www.centralbank.org.bb/bank-supervision/licensed-financial-institutions

(continued)

(continued)

Serial number	Member States of UN	Continent	Is there a central bank? If yes, please directly specify it and the reference	Is there a banking regulatory authority? If so, please describe directly it or them and the reference	Is there an insurance regulatory authority? If so, please describe directly it or them and the reference	Is there a securities market regulatory authority? If so, please describe directly it and the reference	Is there a financial holding company? If so, please directly show reference
154	Canada	North America	Bank of Canada (https://www.bankofcanada.ca/)	Minister of Finance of Canada (Finance Minister) Office of the Superintendent of Financial Institutions (OSFI) Bank of Canada Canada Deposit Insurance Corporation (CDIC) Financial Institutions Supervisory Committee (FISC) (https://uk-practicallaw-thomsonreuters-com.proxy.scd.u-psud.fr/w-007-6371?transitionType=Default&contextData=(sc.Default))	The Office of the Superintendent of Financial Institutions (OSFI) (https://uk-practicallaw-thomsonreuters-com.proxy.scd.u-psud.fr/2-501-7810?transitionType=Default&contextData=(sc.Default)&firstPage=true)	Canadian Securities Administrators (CSA) (https://en.wikipedia.org/wiki/Canadian_securities_regulation#:~:text=The%20securities%20regulator%20administers%20the,set%20of%20rules%20and%20regulations.&text=The%20provincial%20and%20territorial%20regulators,Canadian%20Securities%20Administrators%20(CSA).)	https://ca-practicallaw-thomsonreuters-com.proxy.scd.u-psud.fr/2-573-342[illegible]?transitionType=Default&contextData=(sc.Default)&firstPage=true&bhab=0&bhav=&bhsh=1080&bhsw=1920&bhqs=1

(continued)

(continued)

Serial number	Member States of UN	Continent	Is there a central bank? If yes, please directly specify it and the reference	Is there a banking regulatory authority? If so, please describe directly it or them and the reference	Is there an insurance regulatory authority? If so, please describe directly it or them and the reference	Is there a securities market regulatory authority? If so, please describe directly it and the reference	Is there a financial holding company? If so, please directly show references
155	Costa Rica	North America	The Central Bank of Costa Rica (https://www.bccr.fi.cr/SitePages/default.aspx)	The SUGEF (https://thecostaricanews.com/costa-rica-banking-laws-and-financial-sector/#:~:text=The%20Central%20Bank%20of%20Costa,and%20enforces%20Central%20Bank%20policies.)	The SUGEF (https://www.sugese.fi.cr/seccion-legal-framework/legal-framework)	Central Bank of Costa Rica Superintendencia General de Valores de Costa Rica National Stock Exchange (Costa Rica) Asamblea Legislativa (Costa Rica) José Rafael Brenes (https://www.centralamericadata.com/en/search?q1=content_en_le%3A%22Regulation+of+securities+market%22&q2=mattersInCountry_en_le%3A%22Costa+Rica%22)	https://books.google.fr/books?id=mjB7C_2RbWEC&pg=PA14&lpg=PA14&dq=Costa+Rica+financial+holding+company&source=bl&ots=Xd0fXtB4rx&sig=ACfU3U0yV5PwURs4-8im9BKK74DOaNyCcA&hl=fr&sa=X&ved=2ahUKEwiU35Ol-cvqAhUiAGMBHX_QD_cQ6AEwAnoECAQQAQ#v=onepage&q=Costa%20Rica%20financial%20holding%20company&f=false

(continued)

(continued)

Serial number	Member States of UN	Continent	Is there a central bank? If yes, please directly specify it and the reference	Is there a banking regulatory authority? If so, please describe directly it or them and the reference	Is there an insurance regulatory authority? If so, please describe directly it or them and the reference	Is there a securities market regulatory authority? If so, please describe directly it and the reference	Is there a financial holding company? If so, please directly show references
156	Dominica	North America	Eastern Caribbean Central Bank (https://www.eccb-centralbank.org/p/commonwealth-of-dominica)	Eastern Caribbean Central Bank (http://knowyourcountry.info/files/dominicaamlreportaug2014_-_Copy_2.pdf)	Financial Service Unit of the Commonwealth of Dominic (https://en.wikipedia.org/wiki/Financial_Service_Unit_of_the_Commonwealth_of_Dominica)	The Eastern Caribbean Securities Exchange (ECSE) (http://knowyourcountry.info/files/dominicaamlreportaug2014_-_Copy_2.pdf)	https://www.ecfh.com/
157	El Salvador	North America	The Central Reserve Bank of El Salvador (https://en.wikipedia.org/wiki/Central_Reserve_Bank_of_El_Salvador)	Financial System Superintendence (SSF) (https://www.bcr.gob.sv/eng/index.php?option=com_content&view=article&id=125&Itemid=313)	Superintendencia del Sistema Financiero (https://www.bnamericas.com/en/company-profile/superintendencia-del-sistema-financiero-ssf)	Securities Superintendence (https://www.bcr.gob.sv/eng/index.php?option=com_content&view=article&id=125&Itemid=313)	https://www.bnamericas.com/en/news/Agricola_to_Form_Financial_Holding
158	Grenada	North America	Eastern Caribbean Central Bank (https://www.eccb-centralbank.org/p/grenada)	Eastern Caribbean Central Bank (http://www.commonwealthofnations.org/sectors-grenada/business/banking_and_financial_services/)	Grenada Authority for the Regulation of Financial Institutions (GARFIN) (http://www.garfin.gd/index.php/regulated-sectors/insurance)	The Eastern Caribbean Securities Regulatory Commission (ECSRC) (https://www.ecsrc.com/cms/Cmspages/details/5/category/history)	https://www.questia.com/magazine/1G1-42175[illegible]/grenada-banks-stockholders-back-conversion-into-holding

(continued)

(continued)

Serial number	Member States of UN	Continent	Is there a central bank? If yes, please directly specify it and the reference	Is there a banking regulatory authority? If so, please describe directly it or them and the reference	Is there an insurance regulatory authority? If so, please describe directly it or them and the reference	Is there a securities market regulatory authority? If so, please describe directly it and the reference	Is there a financial holding company? If so, please directly show references
159	Jamaica	North America	Bank of Jamaica (https://en.wikipedia.org/wiki/Bank_of_Jamaica)	Bank of Jamaica (http://boj.org.jm/financial_sys/)	Financial Services Commission (http://www.fscjamaica.org/regulated-industries/)	Financial Services Commission (http://www.fscjamaica.org/about-the-fsc/content-1233.html)	http://boj.org.jm/uploads/news/proposal_for_drafting_instructions_for_bsa_fhc_licence_application_rules.pdf
160	Mexico	North America	Bank of Mexico (https://www.banxico.org.mx/indexen.html)	Comision Nacional Bancaria y de Valores (CNBV) (http://www.regulations-law.com/financial-regulation-mexico/#:~:text=Comision%20Nacional%20Bancaria%20y%20de,Banking%2C%20Financial%20and%20Securities%20institutions.)	The Comision Nacional de Seguros y Fianzas (CNSF) (https://content-next-westlaw-com.proxy.scd.u-psud.fr/2-501-3652?transitionType=Default&contextData=(sc.Default)&__lrTS=20200215213827362&firstPage=true&bhab=0&bhav=&bhqs=1)	National Banking and Securities Commission (CNBV) (https://globaledge.msu.edu/global-resources/resource/10699)	http://documents.worldbank.org/curated/en/621671508177153708/Mexico-2016-FSAP-Update-FSA-03232017.docx

(continued)

(continued)

Serial number	Member States of UN	Continent	Is there a central bank? If yes, please directly specify it and the reference	Is there a banking regulatory authority? If so, please describe directly it or them and the reference	Is there an insurance regulatory authority? If so, please describe directly it or them and the reference	Is there a securities market regulatory authority? If so, please describe directly it and the reference	Is there a financial holding company? If so, please directly show references
161	Panama	North America	None (https://en.wikipedia.org/wiki/National_Bank_of_Panama)	Superintendency of Banks of Panama (https://www.superbancos.gob.pa/en/advisory)	Superintendent of Insurance and Reinsurance (https://www.businesswire.com/news/home/20180308005606/en/Governance-Risk-Compliance-2018-Panamanian-Insurance-Industry#:~:text=The%20Panamanian%20insurance%20industry%20is,investment%20in%20the%20insurance%20industry.&text=Non%2Dadmitted%20insurers%20are%20not%20permitted%20in%20the%20industry.)	Panama's Securities Commission (https://www.imf.org/external/pubs/ft/scr/2007/cr0766.pdf)	https://www.superbancos.gob.pa/en/about-sbp/historical-review
162	Saint Kitts and Nevis	North America	Eastern Caribbean Central Bank (https://www.eccb-centralbank.org/p/saint-christopher-st-kitts-and-nevis)	Eastern Caribbean Central Bank (https://www.eccb-centralbank.org/p/legal-and-regulatory-framework)	Financial Services Regulatory Commission (https://www.fsrc.kn/)	The Eastern Caribbean Securities Regulatory Commission (https://www.ecsrc.com/website_management/faqCategories/list_faqs)	https://www.thestkittsnevisobserver.com/republic-financial-holdings-discusses-scotiabank-acquisition/

(continued)

(continued)

Serial number	Member States of UN	Continent	Is there a central bank? If yes, please directly specify it and the reference	Is there a banking regulatory authority? If so, please describe directly it or them and the reference	Is there an insurance regulatory authority? If so, please describe directly it or them and the reference	Is there a securities market regulatory authority? If so, please describe directly it and the reference	Is there a financial holding company? If so, please directly show references
163	Saint Lucia	North America	Eastern Caribbean Central Bank (https://www.eccb-centralbank.org/p/saint-lucia)	Eastern Caribbean Central Bank (https://www.eccb-centralbank.org/p/legal-and-regulatory-framework)	Financial Services Regulatory Authority (https://fsrastlucia.org/)	The Eastern Caribbean Securities Regulatory Commission (https://www.ecsrc.com/licenses_management/license_types/register_of_licensees)	https://www.ecfh.com/
164	Saint Vincent and the Grenadines	North America	Eastern Caribbean Central Bank (https://www.eccb-centralbank.org/p/saint-vincent-and-the-grenadines)	Eastern Caribbean Central Bank (EECB) (http://www.commonwealthofnations.org/sectors-st_vincent_and_the_grenadines/business/banking_and_financial_services/#)	Financial Services Authority (http://svgfsa.com/)	Capital Market Association of the Eastern Caribbean (https://en.wikipedia.org/wiki/Saint_Vincent_and_the_Grenadines_Securities_Exchange)	https://www.bosvg.com/about-us
165	Trinidad and Tobago	North America	Central Bank of Trinidad and Tobago (https://www.central-bank.org.tt/)	Central Bank of Trinidad and Tobago (https://www.central-bank.org.tt/core-functions/regulated-commercial-banks)	Central Bank of Trinidad and Tobago (https://www.central-bank.org.tt/core-functions/supervision/insurance-sector)	Trinidad and Tobago Securities and Exchange Commission (https://www.ttsec.org.tt/about-us/contact/)	https://www.central-bank.org.tt/core-functions/regulated-financial-holding-companies

(continued)

(continued)

Serial number	Member States of UN	Continent	Is there a central bank? If yes, please directly specify it and the reference	Is there a banking regulatory authority? If so, please describe directly it or them and the reference	Is there an insurance regulatory authority? If so, please describe directly it or them and the reference	Is there a securities market regulatory authority? If so, please describe directly it and the reference	Is there a financial holding company? If so, please directly show references
166	United States of America	North America	Federal Reserve System (https://en.wikipedia.org/wiki/Federal_Reserve)	Federal Deposit Insurance Corporation, the Federal Reserve Board, or the Office of the Comptroller of the Currency (https://en.wikipedia.org/wiki/Bank_regulation_in_the_United_States)	Federal Insurance Office (https://en.wikipedia.org/wiki/Insurance_in_the_United_States#Federal_regulation_of_insurance)	Securities and Exchange Commission (https://fr.wikipedia.org/wiki/Securities_and_Exchange_Commission)	https://www.federalreserve.gov/supervisionreg/fhc.htm
167	Kiribati	Oceania	None (http://www.commonwealthofnations.org/sectors-kiribati/business/banking_and_financial_services/)	Ministry of Finance and Economic Development (http://www.commonwealthofnations.org/sectors-kiribati/business/banking_and_financial_services/)	Ministry of Finance and Economic Development (http://www.mfed.gov.ki/our-work/kiribati-insurance-corporation-0) (http://www.commonwealthofnations.org/sectors-kiribati/business/insurance_and_reinsurance/)	Ministry of Finance & Economic Development (https://www.utoledo.edu/law/library/financialregulators/k.html)	Unknown
168	Marshall Islands	Oceania	None (https://www.imf.org/~/media/Files/Publications/CR/2018/cr18271.ashx)	The Office of the Banking Commission (http://www.rmibankingcomm.org/)	FSM INSURANCE BOARD (http://www.fsminsuranceboard.com/regulations.asp)	None (https://www.doingbusiness.org/content/dam/doingBusiness/country/m/marshall-islands/MHL.pdf)	Unknown

(continued)

(continued)

Serial number	Member States of UN	Continent	Is there a central bank? If yes, please directly specify it and the reference	Is there a banking regulatory authority? If so, please describe directly it or them and the reference	Is there an insurance regulatory authority? If so, please describe directly it or them and the reference	Is there a securities market regulatory authority? If so, please describe directly it and the reference	Is there a financial holding company? If so, please directly show references
169	Nauru	Oceania	None (https://www.imf.org/~/media/Files/Publications/CR/2017/cr1782.ashx)	Australian Prudential Regulatory Authority (APRA) (http://www.naurugov.nr/government-information-office/media-release/nauru-formalises-agreement-to-set-up-banking-agency-in-nauru.aspx)	The Ministry of Finance (http://www.naurugov.nr/government/departments/department-of-finance.aspx); there are no private insurance companies (http://www.commonwealthofnations.org/sectors-nauru/business/insurance_and_reinsurance/)	None (http://www.commonwealthofnations.org/sectors-nauru/business/major_corporations/)	Unknown
170	Palau	Oceania	None (https://www.britannica.com/place/Palau/Economy)	The Financial Institutions Commission (FIC) (https://www.ropfic.org/)	Division of Revenue and Taxation (http://www.fatf-gafi.org/media/fatf/documents/reports/mer-fsrb/APG-Mutual-Evaluation%20Report-Palau.pdf)	No securities dealers (http://www.fatf-gafi.org/media/fatf/documents/reports/mer-fsrb/APG-Mutual-Evaluation%20Report-Palau.pdf)	Unknown

(continued)

(continued)

Serial number	Member States of UN	Continent	Is there a central bank? If yes, please directly specify it and the reference	Is there a banking regulatory authority? If so, please describe directly it or them and the reference	Is there an insurance regulatory authority? If so, please describe directly it or them and the reference	Is there a securities market regulatory authority? If so, please describe directly it and the reference	Is there a financial holding company? If so, please directly show references
171	Papua New Guinea	Oceania	Bank of Papua New Guinea (https://www.bankpng.gov.pg/)	Bank of Papua New Guinea (https://www.imf.org/external/pubs/ft/scr/2011/cr11163.pdf)	Office of the Insurance Commissioner (https://oxfordbusinessgroup.com/overview/steady-hands-while-challenging-sector-has-lot-offer-strong-players#:~:text=The%20Insurance%20Act%20of%201995%20stipulates%20that%20all%20risks%20in,licensed%20insurer%20outside%20the%20country.)	The Securities Commission of Papua New Guinea (SCPNG) (https://www.ipa.gov.pg/business-registration-regulation-and-certification/securities-commission-png/)	Unknown
172	Solomon Islands	Oceania	The Central Bank of Solomon Islands (https://en.wikipedia.org/wiki/Central_Bank_of_Solomon_Islands)	The Central Bank of Solomon Islands (http://www.cbsi.com.sb/financial-stability/regulatory-framework-solomon-islands/)	The Central Bank of Solomon Islands (http://www.cbsi.com.sb/legislation/insurance-act/)	The Central Bank of Solomon Islands (http://www.parliament.gov.sb/files/committees/bills&legislationcommittee/2020/Payment%20Systems%20Bill%202020.pdf)	Unknown

(continued)

(continued)

Serial number	Member States of UN	Continent	Is there a central bank? If yes, please directly specify it and the reference	Is there a banking regulatory authority? If so, please describe directly it or them and the reference	Is there an insurance regulatory authority? If so, please describe directly it or them and the reference	Is there a securities market regulatory authority? If so, please describe directly it and the reference	Is there a financial holding company? If so, please directly show references
173	Australia	Oceania	The Reserve Bank of Australia (https://www.rba.gov.au/)	The Australian Prudential Regulation Authority; the Australian Securities and Investments Commission (https://www.lexology.com/library/detail.aspx?g=a261716c-5660-442a-b9d9-20045513ec06#:~:text=Australia%20has%20a%20twin%20peaks,market%20conduct%20and%20consumer%20protection.)	The Australian Prudential Regulation Authority; the Australian Securities and Investments Commission (https://www.insurancecouncil.com.au/for-consumers/a-regulated-industry#:~:text=The%20two%20key%20regulators%20are,for%20the%20general%20insurance%20industry.&text=Insurance%20companies%20must%20abide%20by%20various%20other%20laws%20and%20regulations.)	The Australian Securities and Investments Commission (ASIC) Australian Stock Exchange (https://uk-practicallaw-thomsonreuters-com.proxy.scd.u-psud.fr/9-636-6809?transitionType=Default&contextData=(sc.Default))	https://www.swfinstitute.org/profiles/financial-holding-company/australia-and-pacific

(continued)

(continued)

Serial number	Member States of UN	Continent	Is there a central bank? If yes, please directly specify it and the reference	Is there a banking regulatory authority? If so, please describe directly it or them and the reference	Is there an insurance regulatory authority? If so, please describe directly it or them and the reference	Is there a securities market regulatory authority? If so, please describe directly it and the reference	Is there a financial holding company? If so please directly show references
174	Fiji	Oceania	The Reserve Bank of Fiji (https://www.rbf.gov.fj/)	The Reserve Bank of Fiji (http://www.winne.com/fiji/to14.html#:~:text=The%20RBF%20is%20the%20supervisory,the%20insurance%20industry%20in%20Fiji.&text=In%20carrying%20out%20its%20role,and%20banking%20activities%20in%20Fiji.)	The Reserve Bank of Fiji (https://www.rbf.gov.fj/Left-Menu/Regulatory-Framework/Prudential-Standards-and-Guidelines/Insurance-Policy-and-Supervision)	The Capital Markets Development Authority (CMDA) (https://www.rbf.gov.fj/Left-Menu/Financial-Stability/Capital-Markets/Regulations---Compliance)	https://www.rbf.gov.fj/Left-Menu/Regulatory-Framework/Licensed-Institutions
175	Tonga	Oceania	National Reserve Bank of Tonga (https://mobile-global-apps-store.life/away.php)	National Reserve Bank of Tonga (http://www.reservebank.to/index.php/about/about-the-nrbt-others/regulatory-framework.html)	National Reserve Bank of Tonga (http://www.commonwealthofnations.org/sectors-tonga/business/insurance_and_reinsurance/)	National Reserve Bank of Tonga (http://www.reservebank.to/index.php/94-about-us/246-exchange-control-policy.html)	Unknown

(continued)

(continued)

Serial number	Member States of UN	Continent	Is there a central bank? If yes, please directly specify it and the reference	Is there a banking regulatory authority? If so, please describe directly it or them and the reference	Is there an insurance regulatory authority? If so, please describe directly it or them and the reference	Is there a securities market regulatory authority? If so, please describe directly it and the reference	Is there a financial holding company? If so, please directly show references
176	Micronesia (Federated States of)	Oceania	None (https://www.imf.org/~/media/Files/Publications/CR/2019/1FSMEA2019001.ashx)	FSM Banking Board (https://www.nationsencyclopedia.com/Asia-and-Oceania/Micronesia-Federated-States-of-BANKING-AND-SECURITIES.html#:~:text=Micronesia%2C%20Federated%20States%20of%20%2D%20Banking,branches%20in%20Pohnpei%20and%20Truk.)	FSM Insurance Board (http://www.fsminsuranceboard.com/#:~:text=As%20the%20sole%20insurance%20regulatory,international%20insurance%20standards%20for%20the)	No securities regulation (http://fsmlaw.org/fsm/code/indexcode2014.html)	http://www.fsmlaw.org/fsm/code/PDF/FSMCA2014Tit29.pdf
177	New Zealand	Oceania	Reserve Bank of New Zealand (https://www.rbnz.govt.nz/)	Reserve Bank of New Zealand (https://www.rbnz.govt.nz/regulation-and-supervision/banks)	Reserve Bank of New Zealand (https://www.rbnz.govt.nz/regulation-and-supervision/insurers/regulation)	The Financial Markets Authority (FMA) (https://www.fma.govt.nz/about-us/what-we-do/)	http://www.fhlnz.co.nz/contactUs/
178	Tuvalu	Oceania	National Bank of Tuvalu (https://en.wikipedia.org/wiki/National_Bank_of_Tuvalu)	The minister of finance and National Bank of Tuvalu (http://www.commonwealthofnations.org/sectors-tuvalu/business/banking_and_financial_services/#:~:text=The%20minister%20of%20finance%20regulates,of%20Tourism%2C%20Trade%20and%20Commerce.)	National Bank of Tuvalu (https://tuvalu-legislation.tv/cms/images/LEGISLATION/PRINCIPAL/2011/2011-0003/BankingCommissionAct_1.pdf)	National Bank of Tuvalu (https://tuvalu-legislation.tv/cms/images/LEGISLATION/PRINCIPAL/2011/2011-0003/BankingCommissionAct_1.pdf)	Unknown

(continued)

(continued)

Serial number	Member States of UN	Continent	Is there a central bank? If yes, please directly specify it and the reference	Is there a banking regulatory authority? If so, please describe directly it or them and the reference	Is there an insurance regulatory authority? If so, please describe directly it or them and the reference	Is there a securities market regulatory authority? If so, please describe directly it and the reference	Is there a financial holding company? If so, please directly show references
179	Samoa	Oceania	The Central Bank of Samoa (https://www.cbs.gov.ws/)	The Central Bank of Samoa (https://www.cbs.gov.ws/index.php/banking-system/supervison-and-regulation/)	The Central Bank of Samoa (https://www.cbs.gov.ws/index.php/banking-system/supervison-and-regulation/)	The Central Bank of Samoa (https://www.cbs.gov.ws/index.php/about-us/our-legislation/)	https://offshoreleaks.icij.org/nodes/1[illegible]0824
180	Vanuatu	Oceania	Reserve Bank of Vanuatu (https://en.wikipedia.org/wiki/Reserve_Bank_of_Vanuatu)	Reserve Bank of Vanuatu (https://www.rbv.gov.vu/index.php/en/financial-services/banking)	Vanuatu Financial Services Commission (https://www.captive.com/docs/default-source/showcase/advantagevanuatubooklet.pdf?sfvrsn=2)	Vanuatu Financial Services Commission (https://www.vfsc.vu/laws-regulations/)	Unknown
181	Bolivia (Plurinational State of)	South America	The Central Bank of Bolivia (https://en.wikipedia.org/wiki/Central_Bank_of_Bolivia)	The Financial System Supervisory Authority (ASFI) (https://myworld.finance/country_info/Bolivia/)	The Autoridad de Fiscalizacin y Control de Pensiones y Seguros (APS) (https://www.businesswire.com/news/home/20190222005155/en/Bolivia-Insurance-Industry-Governance-Risk-Compliance-Report)	The Financial System Supervisory Authority (ASFI) (https://myworld.finance/country_info/Bolivia/)	Unknown

(continued)

(continued)

Serial number	Member States of UN	Continent	Is there a central bank? If yes, please directly specify it and the reference	Is there a banking regulatory authority? If so, please describe directly it or them and the reference	Is there an insurance regulatory authority? If so, please describe directly it or them and the reference	Is there a securities market regulatory authority? If so, please describe directly it and the reference	Is there a financial holding company? If so, please directly show references
182	Ecuador	South America	Central Bank of Ecuador (https://www.bce.fin.ec/en/)	Central Bank of Ecuador (https://corporatefinanceinstitute.com/resources/careers/companies/top-banks-in-ecuador/)	The Banking and Insurance Supervisory Agency (https://www.hlinsurancelaw.com/2014/07/latin-america-new-insurance-legislation-in-equador/)	Quito Stock Exchange (https://www.pwc.ec/es/publicaciones/assets/pdf/doing-business-ecuador-06-com-protecao.pdf)	Unknown
183	Argentina	South America	The Central Bank of the Argentine (https://www.bcra.gob.ar/Varios/English_information.asp)	The Central Bank of the Argentine (https://books.google.fr/books?id=5QWtDwAAQBAJ&pg=PA197&lpg=PA197&dq=argentina+commercial+bank+regulatory+authority&source=bl&ots=8drAH5sJsa&sig=ACfU3U3PO8MDfRy31LWUL1mxe2tkdozPUw&hl=fr&sa=X&ved=2ahUKEwiljIK3ubXqAhUCDmMBHZ2VAf4Q6AEwBHoECAgQAQ)	The Argentine Superintendence of Insurance (https://uk-practicallaw-thomsonreuters-com.proxy.scd.u-psud.fr/2-518-2131?transitionType=Default&contextData=(sc.Default)&firstPage=true)	National Securities Commission (https://content-next-westlaw-com.proxy.scd.u-psud.fr/Document/I2ef12b231ed511e38578f7ccc38dcbee/View/FullText.html?contextData=(sc.Default)&transitionType=Default&firstPage=true&bhab=0&bhav=&bhqs=1)	financial services holding company (https://en.wikipedia.org/wiki/Grupo_Financiero_Galicia)

(continued)

(continued)

Serial number	Member States of UN	Continent	Is there a central bank? If yes, please directly specify it and the reference	Is there a banking regulatory authority? If so, please describe directly it or them and the reference	Is there an insurance regulatory authority? If so, please describe directly it or them and the reference	Is there a securities market regulatory authority? If so, please describe directly it and the reference	Is there a financial holding company? If so, please directly show references
184	Brazil	South America	Central Bank of Brazil (https://www.bcb.gov.br/en)	Central Bank of Brazil (https://www.lexology.com/library/detail.aspx?g=25d77bfb-15b6-4f86-b428-49db2a5821e9)	SUSEP (Superintendence of Private Insurance) and the CNSP (National Council of Private Insurance) (http://www.susep.gov.br/menuingles/about_bim)	Securities and Exchange Commission of Brazil (http://www.cvm.gov.br/subportal_ingles/index.html)	https://www.bnamericas.com/en/company-profile/ccb-brazil-financial-holding-investimentos-e-participa%C3%A7%C3%B5es-ccb-brazil-financial-holding-investimentos-e-participa%C3%A7%C3%B5es
185	Chile	South America	Central Bank of Chile (https://www.bcentral.cl/en/web/banco-central/home)	The Commission for the Financial Market (CMF) and the Central Bank of Chile (https://uk-practicallaw-thomsonreuters-com.proxy.scd.u-psud.fr/w-007-9128?transitionType=Default&contextData=(sc.Default)&firstPage=true)	The Commission for the Financial Market Commission (Comisin para el Mercado Financiero - CMF) (https://www.businesswire.com/news/home/20191018005361/en/Chile-Insurance-Industry-Governance-Risk-Compliance-Report)	The Commission for the Financial Market Commission (https://globaledge.msu.edu/global-resources/resource/10626#:~:text=The%20Supervision%20of%20Securities%20and,the%20Chilean%20financial%20services%20industry.)	https://www.swfinstitute.org/profile/598cdaa50124e9fd2d05adac

(continued)

(continued)

Serial number	Member States of UN	Continent	Is there a central bank? If yes, please directly specify it and the reference	Is there a banking regulatory authority? If so, please describe directly it or them and the reference	Is there an insurance regulatory authority? If so, please describe directly it or them and the reference	Is there a securities market regulatory authority? If so, please describe directly it and the reference	Is there a financial holding company? If so, please directly show references
186	Colombia	South America	The Bank of the Republic (https://www.banrep.gov.co/en)	The President and the Ministry of Finance (https://uk-practicallaw-thomsonreuters-com.proxy.scd.u-psud.fr/w-007-7982?transitionType=Default&contextData=(sc.Default)&firstPage=true)	Financial Superintendency of Colombia (https://en.superfinanciera.gov.co/jsp/Publicaciones/publicaciones/loadContenidoPublicacion/id/10015491/dPrint/1/c/00)	The Superintendencia Financiera de Colombia (SFC) (https://en.wikipedia.org/wiki/Superintendencia_Financiera_de_Colombia#:~:text=The%20Superintendencia%20Financiera%20de%20Colombia,and%20develop%20the%20securities%20market.)	https://www.iflr.com/article/b11mx9d05lpqt8/colombia-the-financial-conglomerates-law
187	Guyana	South America	Bank of Guyana (https://www.bankofguyana.org.gy/bog/)	Bank of Guyana (https://www.bankofguyana.org.gy/bog/legal-regulatory-framework/legislation)	Bank of Guyana (https://www.bankofguyana.org.gy/bog/legal-regulatory-framework/overview)	The Guyana Securities Council (GSC) (https://www.emintelligence.com/frontier-market/guyana-frontier-market-making-2.html#:~:text=The%20Guyana%20Securities%20Council%20(GSC)%2C%20a%20statutory%20body%20created,renamed%20the%20Guyana%20Securities%20Commission.)	https://rfhl.com/company-history/

(continued)

(continued)

Serial number	Member States of UN	Continent	Is there a central bank? If yes, please directly specify it and the reference	Is there a banking regulatory authority? If so, please describe directly it or them and the reference	Is there an insurance regulatory authority? If so, please describe directly it or them and the reference	Is there a securities market regulatory authority? If so, please describe directly it and the reference	Is there a financial holding company? If so, please directly show references
188	Paraguay	South America	Central Bank of Paraguay (https://en.wikipedia.org/wiki/Central_Bank_of_Paraguay)	Central Bank of Paraguay (https://corporatefinanceinstitute.com/resources/careers/companies/top-banks-in-paraguay/)	The Superintendent of Insurance (https://www.businesswire.com/news/home/20160105006031/en/Research-Markets-Governance-Risk-Compliance-Paraguays-Insurance)	National Exchange Commission Resolutions (https://www.cnv.gov.py/?page_id=2068&lang=en)	https://www.fmo.nl/news-detail/fd2a49ff-aC9a-4f00-a85c-612fcffdc19b/fmo-announces-first-equity-stake-in-paraguay
189	Peru	South America	The Central Reserve Bank of Peru (https://en.wikipedia.org/wiki/Central_Reserve_Bank_of_Peru)	Superintendencia de Banca, Seguros y AFP (https://corporatefinanceinstitute.com/resources/careers/companies/top-banks-in-peru/#:~:text=Formed%20in%201932%2C%20Superintendencia%20de,banks%20in%20Peru%20to%20positive.)	Superintendencia de Banca, Seguros y AFP SBS (https://insurancenewsnet.com/oarticle/peru-insurance-industry-governance-risk-and-compliance-report-2019-researchandmarkets-com#.XykieBNLhhE)	The Peruvian Securities and Exchange Commission (CONASEV) (https://www.smv.gob.pe/uploads/LMV_complete.pdf)	https://www.swfinstitute.org/profile/598cdaa50124e9fd2[illegible]05adce

(continued)

(continued)

Serial number	Member States of UN	Continent	Is there a central bank? If yes, please directly specify it and the reference	Is there a banking regulatory authority? If so, please describe directly it or them and the reference	Is there an insurance regulatory authority? If so, please describe directly it or them and the reference	Is there a securities market regulatory authority? If so, please describe directly it and the reference	Is there a financial holding company? If so, please directly show references
190	Venezuela, Bolivarian Republic of	South America	Central Bank of Venezuela (https://en.wikipedia.org/wiki/Central_Bank_of_Venezuela)	Central Bank of Venezuela (https://corporatefinanceinstitute.com/resources/careers/companies/banks-in-venezuela/#:~:text=Governmental%20organization%20Central%20Bank%20of,the%20country's%20central%20monetary%20authority.&text=Founded%20in%201939%2C%20BCV%20oversees,rate%20for%20the%20Venezuelan%20bol%C3%ADvar.)	Insurance Activity Superintendency (https://www.financierworldwide.com/insurance-regulatory-developments-in-venezuela#.Xy7TGhNLihc)	National Securities Superintendence (https://www.cfatf-gafic.org/index.php/documents/follow-up-reports-2/venezuela/135-venezuela-4th-follow-up-report/file)	Unknown
191	Suriname	South America	The Central Bank of Suriname (https://en.wikipedia.org/wiki/Central_Bank_of_Suriname)	The Central Bank of Suriname (https://www.cbvs.sr/en/about-cbvs/institutional-profile)	The Central Bank of Suriname (https://www.cbvs.sr/en/acts/426-laws-and-regulations-on-the-supervision-of-the-financial-system)	The Stock Exchange of Suriname (https://www.surinamestockexchange.com/nl)	https://www.republicbankanguilla.com/pdfs/RFHL-CORPORATE-PROFILE-2020.pdf
192	Uruguay	South America	Central Bank of the Uruguay (https://en.wikipedia.org/wiki/Central_Bank_of_Uruguay)	Central Bank of the Uruguay (https://www.bcu.gub.uy/Servicios-Financieros-SSF/Paginas/Acerca-de-los-Bancos.aspx)	Central Bank of the Uruguay (https://www.bcu.gub.uy/Ingles/Paginas/Insurance.aspx)	Central Bank of the Uruguay (https://www.bcu.gub.uy/Ingles/Paginas/Securities-Intermediaries.aspx)	https://www.imf.org/external/pubs/ft/scr/2013/cr13152.pdf

The manufacturer's authorised representative in the EU is Springer
Nature Customer Service Centre GmbH, Europaplatz 3, 69115 Heidelberg,
Germany. If you have any concerns regarding our products, please
contact ProductSafety@springernature.com

Printed and bound by CPI Group (UK) Ltd, Croydon, CR0 4YY
01/10/2026
02225956-0010